T0345183

Access Control, Security, and Trust
A Logical Approach

Published Titles

Jonathan Katz and Yehuda Lindell, Introduction to Modern Cryptography

Antoine Joux, Algorithmic Cryptanalysis

M. Jason Hinek, Cryptanalysis of RSA and Its Variants

Burton Rosenberg, Handbook of Financial Cryptography and Security

Shiu-Kai Chin and Susan Older, Access Control, Security, and Trust: A Logical Approach

Forthcoming Titles

Maria Isabel Vasco, Spyros Magliveras, and Rainer Steinwandt, Group Theoretic Cryptography

CHAPMAN & HALL/CRC
CRYPTOGRAPHY AND NETWORK SECURITY

Access Control, Security, and Trust

A Logical Approach

Shiu-Kai Chin

Syracuse University
Syracuse, New York, USA

Susan Older

Syracuse University
Syracuse, New York, USA

CRC Press
Taylor & Francis Group
Boca Raton London New York

CRC Press is an imprint of the
Taylor & Francis Group, an **informa** business

A CHAPMAN & HALL BOOK

About the cover: The cover image of a mother loon carrying her chick across the water depicts the interdependent nature of this book's main themes: access-control, security, and trust. Loons are fiercely protective of their offspring. In turn, the chicks often ride on their parents' backs, trusting them to provide both warmth and protection from predators.

Chapman & Hall/CRC
Taylor & Francis Group
6000 Broken Sound Parkway NW, Suite 300
Boca Raton, FL 33487-2742

© 2011 by Taylor and Francis Group, LLC
Chapman & Hall/CRC is an imprint of Taylor & Francis Group, an Informa business

No claim to original U.S. Government works

ISBN 13: 978-1-58488-862-8 (hbk)

Library of Congress Cataloging-in-Publication Data

Chin, Shiu-Kai.
  Access control, security, and trust : a logical approach / Shiu-Kai Chin, Susan Beth Older.
      p. cm. -- (Chapman & Hall/CRC cryptography and network security)
    Includes bibliographical references and index.
    ISBN 978-1-58488-862-8 (hardcover : alk. paper)
    1. Computers--Access control. 2. System design. I. Older, Susan Beth. II. Title. III. Series.

QA76.9.A25C446 2011
005.8--dc22   2010022619

Visit the Taylor & Francis Web site at
http://www.taylorandfrancis.com

and the CRC Press Web site at
http://www.crcpress.com

To Linda, Benjamin, Emily, and my mom for their love and support

To Garth, for his patience; and to Ryan, who couldn't wait for this book to be completed

Contents

List of Tables

List of Figures

Preface

Our intent in developing this textbook is to serve the needs of computer engineers and computer scientists who are responsible for designing, implementing, and verifying secure computer and information systems. Engineers who serve in the roles of designers and verifiers must be able to translate concepts and ideas into calculations and derivations as part of the design and verification process. For example, electrical-engineering students routinely learn how to specify, implement, and verify control and communications systems using Laplace and Fourier transforms. They can translate their concepts into networks of system transfer functions and use Laplace and Fourier transforms to analyze, predict, and verify the behavior of their designs. Computer-hardware designers rely on switching theory, discrete mathematics, and finite-state machines to specify, implement, and verify their designs. In an analogous fashion, our goal is to equip engineers with an access-control logic they can use to specify, implement, and verify their security designs.

Our focus is on access control and reference monitors. Controlling access to protected objects is central to any security requirement. Reference monitors are the means to protect objects of value in systems. Just as propositional logic and finite-state machines are used to define and explain computer hardware design and verification principles, we use a propositional modal logic to explain access-control principles. Our view is this: if you are the hardware designer and you are given the input values to your design, then you should be able to justify mathematically whether or not the value on any particular output is a 0 or a 1. Similarly, if you are the engineer who has security requirements to meet and you are given a policy and a request, you should be able to justify mathematically if your answer is a *yes* or a *no*.

To be explicit, the logic we present is meant to *inform* an implementation, not *be* the implementation. The logic is not a programming language, and we are not suggesting that access controllers should be implemented as theorem provers. Rather, we believe the logic is a useful tool for analyzing security designs and for making explicit the conditions upon which access-control decisions depend. Access controllers can be implemented as checklists that check and verify the relevant artifacts (e.g., certificates and credentials) against existing policies and trust assumptions. These checklists correspond to provably sound inference rules in the logic.

Another intent of our book is to fill a gap left by many books on computer and network security. Several are compendiums of computer security models and methods. They are highly mathematical and encyclopedic—and usually beyond the skills and interests of design engineers. Most do not have illustrative examples or exercises. While excellent references, the breadth and depth of mathematics are beyond what is needed by most engineers. In contrast, many other books are introductory in nature and are primarily descriptive. To make security concepts accessible to a wide audience, these books deliberately omit mathematical treatments of security. While informative, this approach does not equip engineers to do the derivations and calculations with the same degree of mathematical precision and accuracy expected of hardware and electrical engineers. The result is that security is often taught at the lowest levels of knowledge—recall and comprehension—as opposed to the higher knowledge levels expected of engineers: application, analysis, synthesis, and evaluation.

To fill this gap, we use a single access-control logic based on a simple propositional modal logic throughout this textbook. We introduce the basic logic early in the book and use it throughout to define and derive access-control principles and properties. Our focus is on reference monitors because they are the parts of a system that systems engineers must worry about specifying, designing, implementing, and verifying. Reference monitors in security play an analogous role to the role played by finite-state machines in computer hardware.

We developed much of the content of this book in our own courses at Syracuse University and in intense summer courses on access control for hundreds of Air Force Reserve Officer Training Corp (ROTC) cadets from over forty US universities. Our experience is that "practice makes perfect" and that our students benefited from having illustrations and exercises. Thus, we have included numerous examples to illustrate principles, as well as many exercises to serve as assessments of knowledge. We have annotated each exercise to indicate the level of knowledge it assesses, according to the following legend:

- The symbol ✎ denotes exercises at the *application* level of knowledge. These exercises typically ask the reader to apply particular knowledge or use particular techniques to solve a problem in a new context. Straightforward calculations fall into this category of exercises.

- The symbol ＼ denotes exercises at the *analysis* level of knowledge. These exercises generally require the reader to decompose a problem into its constituent parts in order to perform the necessary calculations or experiments necessary to solve the problem.

- The symbol ⚒ denotes exercises at the *synthesis* level of knowledge. These exercises typically require the reader to integrate various techniques or components to design, construct, or formulate an entirely new structure, pattern, or proof.

- The symbol ⚖ denotes exercises at the *evaluation* level of knowledge. These exercises require the reader to identify and use relevant criteria to assess and judge the suitability of a solution to a given problem.

Exercises at higher levels of knowledge are not necessarily harder than exercises at lower levels of knowledge. We recommend that readers try at least one exercise at each level of knowledge to get the most benefit.

We have taught both undergraduate and graduate students using this book. We recommend that all students learn what is in Part I (*Preliminaries*). This part covers the syntax and semantics of the access-control logic, basic access control concepts, and an introduction to confidentiality and integrity policies. Our experience with ROTC cadets is that undergraduates who have successfully mastered a sophomore discrete-mathematics course do master the syntax and semantics of the access-control logic. Undergraduates can skip the section on soundness in Chapter 3.

Part II (*Distributed Access Control*) and Part III (*Isolation and Sharing*) focus on access control in networks and access control in hardware, respectively. These parts are relatively independent of one another. For courses with an emphasis on networks, Part III may be omitted. For courses with an emphasis on hardware and virtual machines, Part II may be omitted. Most everything in these parts is well within the capabilities of undergraduate students who have mastered the preliminaries in Part I. Part III includes a primer that provides a brief review of sophomore-level courses on assembly language and computer architecture; our experience is that this primer is sufficient for those students with limited hardware backgrounds (e.g., many computer-science majors).

Part IV (*Access Policies*) is a treatment of confidentiality, integrity, and role-based access control in the access-control logic. Although it does make use of delegation (introduced in Part II), it is largely independent of Part III. Readers can pick and choose the policies of interest to them without reading this part's chapters in order.

Acknowledgments We are grateful for the support of numerous colleagues and students. Our first attempts at the graduate level took place in CIS/CSE 774: Principles of Distributed Access Control. Over the course of seven summers, we further refined our text at the undergraduate level with the cadets of the Advanced Course in Engineering (ACE) Cybersecurity Bootcamp at the Air Force Research Laboratory in Rome, New York, and on our own Syracuse University students in CIS/CSE 400. The outstanding tenacity of these students convinced us of the feasibility of teaching undergraduates a logical and rigorous approach to access control. Dr. Kamal Jabbour, Air Force Research Laboratory Senior Scientist for Information Assurance, was unwavering in his support of us and our methods in ACE.

Our book was typeset using LaTeX 2_ε. The clip art in our book comes from the Open Clip Art Library.

Finally, this book would not exist were it not for the encouragement and patience of our editor, Robert Stern, Executive Editor, Taylor & Francis Group.

Chapter 1

Access Control, Security, Trust, and Logic

This book is about access control, security, and trust. We wrote this book for people who specify, design, build, or certify computer and information systems that must be trustworthy and secure. Most every information system or computer has some security requirement. Common examples include computers handling sensitive information such as financial information, health records, or military secrets. If you are responsible for designing, building, testing, or certifying systems that have security concerns, then you are concerned with the following:

- who or what can access protected resources,

- how to protect the confidentiality, integrity, and availability of those resources,

- who or what is trusted or believed, and

- compelling reasons to conclude a system is worthy of trust.

For example, if you are responsible for the specification, design, or operation of computers holding bank accounts, you are very concerned about the following questions:

- Who can withdraw funds from a customer's bank account electronically?

- Who is allowed to alter the balance or available funds in a customer's account?

- Who has authority to grant account access?

- What evidence is there to substantiate that the computerized banking system is secure and operating correctly?

When we talk about access control, security, and trust in this book, we mean the following:

- *Access control* is concerned with the policies and mechanisms that permit or deny the use of a resource or capability.

- *Security* is concerned with the policy and mechanisms that protect the confidentiality, integrity, and availability of information, resources, or capabilities.

- *Trust* focuses on who or what is believed and under what circumstances.

If a system has appropriate policies, mechanisms, and trust assumptions for access control and security, and if these policies and mechanisms are logically consistent and correctly implemented, then we are more likely to willingly believe or depend on the system. That is, we are more likely to deem the system as *trustworthy* and less likely to fail. Systems fail for at least four reasons. They wear out; they are flawed; they are used in unintended ways; the operating or design assumptions are wrong. While this book does not deal with wear as a cause of failure, this book does address the remaining three causes.

Any engineer or computer scientist who has designed, certified, or worked with systems of any size or consequence knows that a key question is *how will we know?* They know that undetected design flaws or inappropriate assumptions that are built into deployed systems are potentially disastrous and life threatening. They know that flaws in deployed systems are orders of magnitude more costly to remedy when compared to corrections made in the design phase. They know that undetected flaws potentially destroy systems, destroy reputations, and destroy credibility, leading to failed missions, failed services, and failed corporations. In short, as systems become larger and more complex, it is increasingly difficult for designers and certifiers to get a good night's sleep.

Our purpose in writing this book is to help designers and certifiers sleep well at night. Our experience shows us that the system designers and certifiers who sleep best at night are those who combine their experience and intuition with mathematics and logic. Experience and intuition are powerful tools that inform the selection of a design approach. Mathematics and logic are unparalleled in providing assurances of correct coverage of all cases and instances, some of which might not have been imagined by designers or certifiers.

We follow the same approach used by civil, mechanical, and electrical engineers. Mathematics and logic properly used clarify the underlying principles and properties of systems. Systems with mathematical and logical descriptions are amenable to independent and automated verification and testing. The effects of system changes or consequences of altering assumptions are easier to deduce with logic than without.

Our experience shows us that flaws and misconceptions often exist *between* levels of abstraction in systems. For example, how will we know that a security policy related to information integrity is correctly implemented by hardware and software together? Requirement writers, software engineers, and hardware engineers might interpret the meaning of integrity differently leading to improper assumptions, flawed policies, flawed designs, and failed systems. Our approach to dealing with this observation is to use a logic that spans many levels of abstraction including hardware, software, and policy.

The logic used here describes policies and mechanisms at the hardware level, the network level, and the abstract level of certificates, jurisdiction of authority, delegations, confidentiality models, and integrity models. What you will find is that the logic and calculations (proofs) in the logic are straightforward. We use logic as a means to an end. It is a language for describing policies and mechanisms with the added benefit of having a semantics that allows us to do calculations. If requirements writers, software and hardware engineers, and system certifiers use the same language with a mathematical semantics, differences in interpretation and the effects of assumptions are sorted out rigorously. Thus, only two chapters are devoted to the logic itself. The remaining chapters are all about access control, security, and trust.

A key ability we intend for you to acquire is the ability to translate informal descriptions of system requirements and behavior into formal logic. Often, this translation is done by breaking down an informal system description into its conceptual parts by answering questions regarding what is being protected, what is being requested, who or what are the guards, and on what basis do the guards decide to grant or deny access requests.

We often rely on everyday situations as illustrations. The following example and the exercises that follow illustrate the types of common access-control decisions we encounter daily.

Example 1.1
Consider a movie theater. What is being protected, what is requested by patrons, who are the guards, and how do the guards make their decisions?

In a movie theater, what is being protected is the ability to see (and hear) the movies being shown. Patrons request access to see and hear the movie of their choice. There are typically two guards. The first guard is the box-office attendant, who handles requests for tickets: he grants tickets to patrons when there are available seats and when the patrons have paid. The second guard governs access into the theater itself: she checks to see if the movie patron has a valid ticket. The ticket symbolizes the capability of the ticket bearer to see the movie named on the ticket. ◊

✎ **Exercise 1.0.1** *Consider a public library. What exactly is being requested, what is being protected, and who are the guards? How do the guards make their access decisions?*

✎ **Exercise 1.0.2** *Consider a bank that offers online access to customer accounts. What exactly is being requested, what is being protected, and who or what are the guards? How do the guards make their access decisions?*

✎ **Exercise 1.0.3** *Recall the last time you took a commercial flight from an airport. Identify all of the guards you encountered, from the moment you stepped into the airport until you boarded your flight. From the perspective of each of these guards, what exactly were you requesting? How did the guards make their access decisions?*

1.1 Deconstructing Access-Control Decisions

A common adage among security pundits is that security must be built in from the beginning and not added on as an afterthought. However, engineers and system designers must wrestle with design details at the chip, board, software, middleware, and network levels while fighting changing requirements, specifications, deadlines, and resources. The challenge for engineers and designers is to quickly and accurately comprehend what is needed security-wise and to be able to routinely account for security specifications along with all the other functional and resource specifications and constraints.

Our goal in writing this book is to provide system creators and verifiers with a means to reason about the system's security requirements in a rigorous manner. Specifically, we hope to provide them with analogous mathematical tools to those that hardware engineers enjoy, as illustrated in the following example.

Example 1.2

Amanda is one of the lead hardware engineers on a project. At a critical design review, a reviewer Frank says "Show me how you've met the requirement to track all 221 cases." Amanda replies that there is an 8-bit register used to index each case. Frank then asks Amanda, "What exactly happens when the input x_2 is a 1 and input y_2 is a 0?" Amanda answers that x_2 and y_2 are inputs to a two-input *or-gate*, and she writes "$1 \lor 0 = 1$" to demonstrate the calculation. Later during the review, Frank challenges Amanda with the statement "I don't think your design works in this case!" Amanda calmly responds by putting up two formulas, one representing the specification and another representing her hardware implementation. Both look very different. She uses the laws of switching theory to show that both formulas have the same meaning. $\lozenge$

Breaking down the engineer's answers to the reviewer's questions and challenges, the following points emerge:

- Amanda **implies** that she has met the requirement to track all 221 cases of interest by appealing to the mathematical property that an 8-bit register can account for as many as $2^8 = 256$ cases. This approach also allows room for some requirements creep (i.e., the tendency for requirements to grow in size).

- Amanda is able to account precisely for the **consequences** of her design when asked what happens for a particular assignment of values to x_2 and y_2. A two-input or-gate has a precise meaning (in this case, the value of $x_2 \lor y_2$).

- When challenged to show that her implementation meets the specification, Amanda gives a formal representation of both and *uses the laws of switching theory (i.e., propositional logic) to prove* that both are the same. Her proof compels the reviewer to **conclude** that her design is correct.

One of our goals for this textbook is to give Amanda and other engineers the same kind of logical support that will enable them to answer questions about access control. The central concept we rely upon is that of the *reference monitor*. Reference monitors are the guards that protect resources such as file systems, memory, communications channels, and so on. Reference monitors play an analogous role in access control to the role played by finite-state machine controllers in hardware: they determine whether to grant access requests based on access-control policies. In this book, we will look at reference monitors and access-control decisions in a multitude of contexts, from the security guard at an airport who checks picture identification cards and airline tickets, to virtual-machine monitors and electronic requests made by users acting in particular roles.

As we will see many times over, access-control decisions are made within the context of (1) **information or evidence** in the form of statements, credentials, licenses, tickets, or certificates, (2) **trust assumptions** regarding proxy relationships or the jurisdiction of authorities, and (3) some **interpretation** of credentials and other statements. The following example and subsequent exercises highlight these aspects across a variety of common scenarios.

Example 1.3

Imagine you are a rental agent for a rental car company in the United States. You are directed by the company's policy to ask for a valid US driver's license from the renter. If the renter presents a current driver's license with their picture on it issued by a department of motor vehicles (DMV) office in one of the fifty states, the renter is allowed to rent a car (assuming he or she can pay for it). What is the thinking behind this policy?

1. A license that is free from physical or electronic tampering and has been issued by a state DMV is interpreted as evidence that the person named and pictured on the license is certified by that state as having the required skills to drive a car legally.

2. The recognition of the state's authority to certify drivers is indicated by the rental car company's policy to accept a valid US driver's license as evidence of being a legal driver.

3. There is a trust assumption that licenses free from physical or electronic tampering truly represent the states' DMV findings. In other words, the assumption is that licenses truly speak for the states' DMV.

If any one of the preceding things change, then the rental procedure will likely need to be changed too. For example, suppose it is discovered that, due to some security breach, tens of thousands of counterfeit licenses bearing the seal of the State of New York were issued. What changes would you make and why?

A plausible change is to require a customer presenting a New York State driver's license to undergo additional scrutiny, perhaps by consulting a New York State database of legal drivers and asking for additional picture ID. In this case, we would want to make sure that the New York database is trustworthy (i.e., accessible only from a secure site), and we would ask for an additional picture ID such as a US passport. ◊

Exercise 1.1.1   *Suppose that you are an online merchant who accepts credit cards over the Internet. What assumptions about evidence, authority, and trust are you making when you ask a customer over the Internet for their name, card number, expiration date, and the three- or four-digit security code on the back of the card?*

Exercise 1.1.2   *Suppose that you are the airport security guard that checks picture IDs and boarding passes before letting passengers into the security line that checks carry-on baggage and passengers. What assumptions about evidence, authority, and trust are you using when you ask a passenger for their ticket and picture ID?*

Exercise 1.1.3   *Suppose that you own a bar next to a college campus and that the legal drinking age is twenty-one. You can lose your liquor license if you serve alcohol to people under twenty-one. What do you ask your bartender to do before serving drinks? If you have someone guarding the door, what do you ask them to do? What assumptions are you making about evidence, authority, and trust?*

1.2   A Logical Approach to Access Control

The exercises at the end of the preceding section share an underlying structure, but their descriptions quickly become verbose and unwieldy: how would you convince a boss or critic in a project review that the system is making the correct access decision in a given situation? A calculus based only on natural language is at best cumbersome and at worst impossible to use. In this book, we present a formal logic that allows us to represent and reason about these scenarios concisely and symbolically.

The use of formal logic allows us to more easily detect patterns of correct or incorrect reasoning. The capability to recognize familiar patterns of reasoning, albeit in many different guises, is a good thing. The realization that situations that on the surface seem different are really the same helps tremendously by giving us insight and clarity, reducing the apparent complexity of problems. The access-control logic that we introduce in the next chapter will allow us to see succinctly the form or structure behind a policy, a set of trust assumptions, and the access decisions made by a reference monitor.

We shall also see that, in most cases, the actual proofs are quite easy, which is a good thing: few people like complicated proofs. The value of having an access-control logic is that it provides a means for describing situations *precisely* using formulas that have *precise meanings*. Second, recall the rationale for preliminary design reviews: it is important to account for assumptions when determining the likely adequacy of a proposed approach. Using an access-control logic with inference rules requires one to account for all necessary assumptions *explicitly* in order to reach the desired conclusions. Finally, having the basis for access-control decisions and reference monitors described formally in an access-control logic gives us the capacity to quickly determine how we are potentially affected or made vulnerable if certain assumptions change—this information can direct us into determining how to adapt to changing requirements or situations.

Throughout this textbook, we use this access-control logic in much the same way as hardware engineers use switching theory and propositional logic to specify, design, and verify hardware. Just as the laws of switching theory are used to calculate whether a signal is 0 or 1, we use the access-control logic to determine if an access-control request should be honored or not. To be explicit, the logic is a useful tool for analyzing security designs and for making explicit the conditions upon which access-control decisions depend. Although the logic can be used to *inform* an implementation, it is not a programming language, and we are not suggesting that access controllers be implemented as theorem provers. Instead, access controllers can be implemented as checklists that check and verify the relevant artifacts (e.g., certificates and credentials) against existing policies and trust assumptions; these checklists correspond to provably sound inference rules in the logic.

Two chapters (Chapter 2 and Chapter 3) are devoted to formally defining the syntax and semantics of the logic. The logic is straightforward and typical of the kinds of modal and temporal logics used by industry for hardware verification and model checking. The remainder of the book focuses on access control itself, from basic concepts (e.g., tickets, lists, authentication) to applications (e.g., virtual machines and network protocols) to models (e.g., role-based access control).

Part I

Preliminaries

Chapter 2

A Language for Access Control

In this chapter we introduce the core logic that relates *principals* to the statements they make. The term *principal* refers to any person, process, or agent that attempts to exercise an action on an object (i.e., assert its *rights*). The statements we care about include access requests (e.g., Alice states her desire to read a certain file), as well as statements of rights (e.g., the Department of Motor Vehicles states that Bob is authorized to drive a truck), authority, and jurisdiction (e.g., the Department of Motor Vehicles has the jurisdiction to authorize Bob to drive a truck), and even the association of keys with principals (e.g., a specific 128-bit encryption key is associated with Carol).

In subsequent chapters, we will express and reason about a variety of access-control concepts using this logic. The purpose of this chapter and the next is to provide a primer to the logic itself. There are three important components of any logic: the *syntax* ("what do the formulas look like?"), the *semantics* ("what do the formulas mean?"), and the *logical rules* ("how can I manipulate formulas to carry out my reasoning?"). We introduce the first two of these components in this chapter, leaving the inference rules for Chapter 3. However, we begin by reviewing important concepts and notation from discrete mathematics that we will use throughout this book, including sets, relations, and certain operations on them.

2.1 Sets and Relations

We assume a working knowledge of discrete mathematics and propositional logic, and thus we do not provide a detailed introduction to them. Instead, we briefly introduce the notation that we will be using, and we review some simple and common approaches for proving properties about sets and relations.

The exercises in this section can be used as a guide to determine whether you have the requisite knowledge of discrete mathematics and propositional logic. Also, the references at the end of this chapter contain several suggested texts to consult if you need a detailed introduction.

2.1.1　Notation

We use standard set notation. Set elements are contained within braces, as in $\{e_0, e_1, \ldots, e_n\}$. The *empty set* (i.e., the set that has no elements) is denoted as either $\{\}$ or $\emptyset$. Set *union* is denoted by $\cup$, set *intersection* is denoted by $\cap$, and set *difference* is denoted by $-$, as illustrated by the following simple examples:

$$\{1,2\} \cup \{1,3,4\} = \{1,2,3,4\}$$
$$\{1,2,3\} \cap \{2,3,4,5\} = \{2,3\}$$
$$\{2,3,4,5\} - \{1,4,5\} = \{2,3\}.$$

The order in which elements are listed in a set is unimportant. Thus, for example, $\{1,2\}$ and $\{2,1\}$ denote the same set.

We write $x \in S$ to indicate that x is an element of the set S; likewise, $x \notin S$ indicates that x is not an element of the set S.

A set S is a *subset* of T, written $S \subseteq T$, if every element of S is also an element of T. The *power set* of a set S, written $\mathcal{P}(S)$, is the set of all subsets of S. For example, the power set of $\{red, blue\}$ is

$$\mathcal{P}(\{red, blue\}) = \{\{\}, \{red\}, \{blue\}, \{red, blue\}\}.$$

Note that the empty set is a subset of every set (i.e., $\emptyset \subseteq S$ for all S), and every set S is a subset of itself (i.e., $S \subseteq S$). Thus, $\emptyset$ and S are always elements of $\mathcal{P}(S)$.

The *Cartesian product* of sets A and B (written $A \times B$) is the set of ordered pairs whose first component is drawn from A and whose second component is drawn from B:

$$A \times B = \{(a,b) \mid a \in A \text{ and } b \in B\}.$$

A *binary relation* is simply a set $R \subseteq A \times B$ of pairs whose first components are drawn from A and whose second components are drawn from B. We say that R is a *binary relation over (or on) A* when $R \subseteq A \times A$.

The *identity relation* on a set A is the relation $\mathrm{id}_A \subseteq A \times A$ defined by:

$$\mathrm{id}_A = \{(a,a) \mid a \in A\}.$$

The *composition* of relations $R_1 \subseteq A \times B$ and $R_2 \subseteq B \times C$ is the relation $R_1 \circ R_2 \subseteq A \times C$ defined as follows:

$$R_1 \circ R_2 = \{(x,z) \mid \text{there exists } y \text{ such that } ((x,y) \in R_1 \text{ and } (y,z) \in R_2)\}.$$

Finally, given a relation $R \subseteq A \times B$ and an element $a \in A$, we define $R(a)$ to be the *image of R under a*:

$$R(a) = \{b \in B \mid (a,b) \in R\}.$$

That is, $R(a)$ is the set of elements in B related to a by the relation R. For example, if S is the relation

$$S = \{(1,2), (2,3), (2,4), (3,5), (3,1), (4,1), (5,2)\},$$

then $S(2) = \{3,4\}$ and $S(3) = \{5,1\}$.

✎ **Exercise 2.1.1** *Let T and U be relations over the set $A = \{1,2,3,4\}$, as follows:*

$$T = \{(1,1),(2,1),(3,3),(4,4),(3,4)\}$$
$$U = \{(2,4),(1,3),(3,3),(3,2)\}.$$

Calculate the following sets:

a. $\mathcal{P}(\{x,y,z\})$

b. $U(3)$

c. $U(4)$

d. $T \cup U$

e. $T \cap U$

f. $T - U$

g. $U \circ T$

h. $T \circ U$

2.1.2 Approaches for Mathematical Proofs

Throughout this book, our examples and exercises include mathematical proofs involving sets, relations, and relationships among them. We highlight some common approaches for structuring these proofs.

Recall that a set S is a subset of T if every element of S is also an element of T. Thus, to prove that some set A is a subset of B, it suffices to demonstrate that any arbitrary element of A is necessarily also an element of B. The following simple example demonstrates this proof approach.

Example 2.1
Property: The subset relation is *transitive*: that is, if $A \subseteq B$ and $B \subseteq C$, then $A \subseteq C$.

Proof: Consider sets A, B, C such that $A \subseteq B$ and $B \subseteq C$, and consider an arbitrary element $x \in A$; we need to show that $x \in C$ as well.

Because $A \subseteq B$, we know that $x \in B$; because $B \subseteq C$, it follows that $x \in C$ as necessary.   ◇

Two sets A and B are equal (i.e., contain exactly the same elements) provided that each is a subset of the other. This fact forms the foundation for another standard proof approach: to prove that $A = B$, it suffices to demonstrate that $A \subseteq B$ and that $B \subseteq A$. The following example, which includes a useful property for subsequent sections, demonstrates this proof approach.

Example 2.2

Property: Suppose that R and T are arbitrary relations over a set A and that Y is a set; then the following equality holds:

$$\{x \mid (R \cup T)(x) \subseteq Y\} = \{x \mid R(x) \subseteq Y\} \cap \{x \mid T(x) \subseteq Y\}.$$

Proof: Consider arbitrary relations R, T and an arbitrary set Y. Our analysis involves two steps:

1. Consider an arbitrary element $a \in \{x \mid (R \cup T)(x) \subseteq Y\}$: thus $(R \cup T)(a) \subseteq Y$. By definition,

$$
\begin{aligned}
(R \cup T)(a) &= \{b \mid (a,b) \in R \cup T\} \\
&= \{b \mid (a,b) \in R\} \cup \{b \mid (a,b) \in T\} \\
&= R(a) \cup T(a).
\end{aligned}
$$

   Therefore, $R(a) \cup T(a) \subseteq Y$, and hence we also have that $R(a) \subseteq Y$ and $T(a) \subseteq Y$. It follows that $a \in \{x \mid R(x) \subseteq Y\}$ and $a \in \{x \mid T(x) \subseteq Y\}$, and therefore $a \in \{x \mid R(x) \subseteq Y\} \cap \{x \mid T(x) \subseteq Y\}$. Because a was an arbitrary element of $\{x \mid (R \cup T)(x) \subseteq Y\}$, we have shown that

$$\{x \mid (R \cup T)(x) \subseteq Y\} \subseteq \{x \mid R(x) \subseteq Y\} \cap \{x \mid T(x) \subseteq Y\}.$$

2. Consider an arbitrary element $a \in \{x \mid R(x) \subseteq Y\} \cap \{x \mid T(x) \subseteq Y\}$. It follows that $R(a) \subseteq Y$ and $T(a) \subseteq Y$, and hence $R(a) \cup T(a) \subseteq Y$. Because $R(a) \cup T(a) = (R \cup T)(a)$, we also have that $(R \cup T)(a) \subseteq Y$, and thus $a \in \{x \mid (R \cup T)(x) \subseteq Y\}$. Because a was an arbitrary element of $\{x \mid R(x) \subseteq Y\} \cap \{x \mid T(x) \subseteq Y\}$, we have shown that

$$\{x \mid R(x) \subseteq Y\} \cap \{x \mid T(x) \subseteq Y\} \subseteq \{x \mid (R \cup T)(x) \subseteq Y\}.$$

Having demonstrated that each set is a subset of the other, we have shown that

$$\{x \mid (R \cup T)(x) \subseteq Y\} = \{x \mid R(x) \subseteq Y\} \cap \{x \mid T(x) \subseteq Y\}. \qquad \Diamond$$

One often encounters statements that indicate a given property (say, *Property 1*) is true *if and only if* another property (say, *Property 2*) is true. Proving that an "if and only if" statement is true involves two steps: (1) demonstrating that, whenever *Property 1* holds, *Property 2* must also hold; and (2) demonstrating that, whenever *Property 2* holds, *Property 1* must also hold. The following example demonstrates this proof approach to prove a property that will be useful for calculations in subsequent sections.

Example 2.3

Property: Let A, X, and Y be sets such that X and Y are both subsets of A. Then $A \subseteq (A - X) \cup Y$ if and only if $X \subseteq Y$.

Proof: Our analysis involves two steps:

1. The "forward" direction: suppose $A \subseteq (A - X) \cup Y$, and consider any $x \in X$. Since $X \subseteq A$, $x \in A$, and thus $x \notin A - X$. Therefore, x must be an element of Y. Since x was arbitrary, $X \subseteq Y$.

2. The "reverse" direction: suppose $X \subseteq Y$, and consider any $a \in A$. If $a \in X$, then by the definition of subset, $a \in Y$, and hence $a \in (A - X) \cup Y$ as necessary; if, instead, $a \notin X$, then $a \in (A - X)$ and therefore $a \in (A - X) \cup Y$. Since a was arbitrary, $A \subseteq (A - X) \cup Y$.

Having shown that each property implies the other, we have demonstrated that $A \subseteq (A - X) \cup Y$ if and only if $X \subseteq Y$. $\Diamond$

The exercises that follow include properties that will be useful for exercises in subsequent sections.

Exercise 2.1.2 *Prove that, for all relations R, S, T, the following property holds:*

If $R \subseteq S$, then $R \circ T \subseteq S \circ T$.

Exercise 2.1.3 *Prove that, for all relations R, S, T, the following property holds:*

$$(R \cup S) \circ T = (R \circ T) \cup (S \circ T).$$

Exercise 2.1.4 *Prove that, for all sets A, B, C, the following property holds:*

$$((A - B) \cup C) \cap ((A - C) \cup B) = (B \cap C) \cup ((A - B) \cap (A - C)).$$

Exercise 2.1.5 *Prove that, for all relations R, S, sets X, and items u, the following property holds:*

$$(R \circ S)(u) \subseteq X \text{ if and only if } R(u) \subseteq \{y \mid S(y) \subseteq X\}.$$

2.2 Syntax

Our goal is to define a logic for expressing access-control policies and analyzing their ramifications. However, to do so, we must first identify the most primitive concepts that we wish to express.

The first step is to introduce the *syntax* of the logic: that is, we must specify what the formulas of the logic look like. To do so, we make use of *BNF (Backus-Naur Form) specifications*, which provide a way to state syntactic rules precisely and unambiguously. We explain how BNF specifications work through the following example, which describes the syntax for a simple language of arithmetic expressions:

$$\textbf{AExp} ::= \textbf{BinNumber}$$
$$\textbf{AExp} ::= (\ \textbf{AExp} + \textbf{AExp}\ )$$
$$\textbf{AExp} ::= (\ \textbf{AExp} * \textbf{AExp}\ )$$
$$\textbf{BinNumber} ::= \textbf{Bit}$$
$$\textbf{BinNumber} ::= \textbf{Bit BinNumber}$$
$$\textbf{Bit} ::= 0$$
$$\textbf{Bit} ::= 1$$

The items in boldface (e.g., **AExp** and **BinNumber**) are called *non-terminal symbols* and represent *syntactic categories* (i.e., collections of syntactic expressions). The symbols "(", ")", "+", "*","0", and "1" are called *terminal symbols* (or *terminals*) and correspond to actual symbols in the syntax. The notation " ::= " is meta-notation for specifying *production rules* for the syntax. In general, each line of form

$$\textbf{AExp} ::= \textit{right-hand-side}$$

provides a rule for creating new elements of **AExp** (and likewise for **BinNumber** and **Bit**). A *syntactic derivation* is a sequence of rewriting steps: each step uses one of the production rules to replace one occurrence of a nonterminal symbol. The syntactic derivation is complete when there are no more nonterminal symbols to replace.

The following two examples contain syntactic derivations that respectively demonstrate that 101 belongs to the syntactic category **BinNumber** and that $(11 * (1 + 10))$ belongs to the syntactic category **AExp**. Note that a given piece of syntax (such as 101) may have multiple derivations possible, corresponding to choosing different nonterminals to expand at a given step. The order in which nonterminal symbols are replaced is not important; what *is* important is that at least one syntactic derivation must exist for a given piece of syntax in order for it to be considered *well formed*.

Example 2.4
The following derivation demonstrates that 101 belongs to the syntactic category **BinNumber**:

$$\textbf{BinNumber} \rightsquigarrow \textbf{Bit BinNumber}$$
$$\rightsquigarrow 1\ \textbf{BinNumber}$$
$$\rightsquigarrow 1\ \textbf{Bit BinNumber}$$
$$\rightsquigarrow 1\ \textbf{Bit Bit}$$
$$\rightsquigarrow 10\ \textbf{Bit}$$
$$\rightsquigarrow 101 \qquad\qquad \Diamond$$

Example 2.5
The following derivation demonstrates that $(11 * (1 + 10))$ belongs to the syntactic category **AExp**:

$$
\begin{aligned}
\mathbf{AExp} &\rightsquigarrow (\ \mathbf{AExp} * \mathbf{AExp}) \\
&\rightsquigarrow (\ \mathbf{AExp} * (\ \mathbf{AExp} + \mathbf{AExp})) \\
&\rightsquigarrow (\ \mathbf{AExp} * (\ \mathbf{BinNumber} + \mathbf{AExp})) \\
&\rightsquigarrow (\ \mathbf{AExp} * (\ \mathbf{Bit} + \mathbf{AExp})) \\
&\rightsquigarrow (\ \mathbf{AExp} * (\ 1 + \mathbf{AExp})) \\
&\rightsquigarrow (\ \mathbf{AExp} * (\ 1 + \mathbf{BinNumber})) \\
&\rightsquigarrow (\ \mathbf{AExp} * (\ 1 + \mathbf{Bit}\ \mathbf{BinNumber})) \\
&\rightsquigarrow (\ \mathbf{AExp} * (\ 1 + 1\ \mathbf{Bit})) \\
&\rightsquigarrow (\ \mathbf{AExp} * (\ 1 + 10)) \\
&\rightsquigarrow (\ \mathbf{BinNumber} * (\ 1 + 10)) \\
&\rightsquigarrow (\ \mathbf{Bit}\ \mathbf{BinNumber}\ * (\ 1 + 10)) \\
&\rightsquigarrow (\ \mathbf{Bit}\ \mathbf{Bit}\ * (\ 1 + 10)) \\
&\rightsquigarrow (\ 1\ \mathbf{Bit}\ * (\ 1 + 10)) \\
&\rightsquigarrow (\ 11\ * (\ 1 + 10)) \qquad\qquad\qquad \Diamond
\end{aligned}
$$

Multiple production rules for the same syntactic category can be combined into a single rule by using the meta-symbol " / ", which separates possible alternatives. For example, the three production rules for the **AExp** syntactic category could instead be specified as follows:

$$\mathbf{AExp} \ ::= \ \mathbf{BinNumber} \ / \ (\ \mathbf{AExp} + \mathbf{AExp}\ ) \ / \ (\ \mathbf{AExp} * \mathbf{AExp}\ )$$

This production rule states that an element of the syntactic category **AExp** has either the form **BinNumber**, the form (**AExp** + **AExp**), or the form (**AExp** $*$ **AExp**).

2.2.1 Principal Expressions

Principals are the major actors in a system. They are the entities that make requests, and the class of principals includes (but is not limited to) people, processes, cryptographic keys, personal identification numbers (PINs), userid–password pairs, and so on.

In general, principals may be either *simple* or *compound*. A simple principal is an entity that cannot be decomposed further: individuals, cryptographic keys, and userid–password pairs are all simple principals. We define **PName** to be the collection of all simple principal names, which can be used to refer to any simple principal. For example, the following are all allowable principal names: *Alice*, *Bob*, the key K_{Alice}, the PIN 1234, and the userid–password pair $\langle \texttt{alice}, bAdPsWd! \rangle$.

Compound principals are abstract entities that connote a combination of principals: for example, "the President in conjunction with Congress" connotes an abstract principal comprising both the President and Congress. Intuitively, such a principal makes exactly those statements that are made by *both* the President and Congress. Similarly, "the reporter quoting her source" connotes an abstract principal that comprises both the reporter and her source. Intuitively, a statement made by such a principal represents a statement that the reporter is (rightly or wrongly) attributing to his source.

The set **Princ** of *all* principal expressions is given by the following BNF specification:

$$\textbf{Princ} ::= \textbf{PName} \;/\; \textbf{Princ \& Princ} \;/\; \textbf{Princ} \mid \textbf{Princ}$$

That is, a principal expression is either a simple name, an expression of form $P \& Q$ (where P and Q are both principal expressions), or an expression of form $P \mid Q$ (where, again, P and Q are both principal expressions).

The principal expression $P \& Q$ denotes the abstract principal "P in conjunction with Q," while $P \mid Q$ denotes the abstract principal "P quoting Q." Thus, the expression *President & Congress* denotes the abstract principal "the President together with *Congress*," and *Reporter | Source* denotes the abstract principal "the reporter quoting her source." In subsequent chapters, we will introduce a few more compound principal expressions to cover other important concepts, such as *delegation*. However, we shall see that those additional expressions are merely special cases of quoting and conjunctive principals.

Parentheses can be added to disambiguate compound principal expressions. For example, $(Sal \& Ted) \mid Uly$ denotes the conjunctive principal *Sal & Ted* quoting the principal *Uly*. In contrast, $Sal \& (Ted \mid Uly)$ denotes the principal *Sal* acting in concert with the compound principal *Ted | Uly*. The standard convention in such expressions is that & binds more tightly than |, so that (for example) $Sal \& Ted \mid Uly$ is equivalent to $(Sal \& Ted) \mid Uly$. However, in this book we shall always include the parentheses necessary to disambiguate principal expressions. Both & and | are associative operators, and hence it is unnecessary to include parentheses around principal expressions such as *Fritz & Hans & Leon* or *Terry | Kitty | Sandy*.

2.2.2   Access-Control Statements

Ultimately, we are concerned with being able to determine with precision and accuracy which access requests from which principals should be granted, and which should be denied. Thus, we need to be able to express our assumptions and our expectations, such as which authorities we trust, which principals should be granted access to which objects, and so on. Toward this end, we introduce a language of statements that will allow us to express these sorts of concepts.

The simplest statements are basic requests, such as "read file *foo*" or "modify file *bar*." We will represent such statements in our logic by *propositional variables*, in much the same way that statements such as "it is raining" can be represented in propositional logic.[1]

However, a simple request such as "read file *foo*" by itself is generally insufficient for determining whether or not to grant the request. At a minimum, we need some way of accounting for the *source* of the request. In our logic, we can associate requests (and other statements) with their source by statements of the form

$$P \text{ says } \varphi,$$

where *P* is a principal and φ is a specific statement. For example, if *rff* is a propositional variable representing the request "read file *foo*," then we can represent Deena's request to read the file *foo* by the statement

$$Deena \text{ says } rff.$$

The says operator can also ascribe non-request statements to particular principals. For example, we may wish to express that Rob believes (or has stated) that Deena is making a request to read file foo. We can express such a concept in the logic by the statement

$$Rob \text{ says } (Deena \text{ says } rff).$$

Access policies specify which principals are authorized to access particular objects. Such authorizations can be expressed in our logic by statements of the form

$$P \text{ controls } \varphi,$$

where *P* is a principal and φ is a specific statement. Thus, for example, we can express Deena's entitlement to read the file *foo* as the statement

$$Deena \text{ controls } rff.$$

Note that this statement is different from Deena's request to read the file. This statement merely says that *if* Deena says that it's a good idea to read file *foo* (i.e., if Deena makes the request), then it is indeed a good idea to read file *foo* (i.e., the request should be granted).

In any given situation, there are particular authorities who are deemed to have *jurisdiction* over particular statements: that is, we will unquestioningly believe certain statements that they make. For example, Anna's New York State driver's license in effect represents a statement from the New York State Department of Motor Vehicles (DMV) that vouches for Anna's ability to drive a car. Anyone who accepts the DMV's jurisdiction for making that statement will, upon seeing Anna's valid driving license, accept as truth that she is entitled to drive. Like authorizations, jurisdiction is represented in our logic by statements of the form

$$P \text{ controls } \varphi,$$

---

[1]Technically, propositions are statements that are interpreted to be either true or false, such as the proposition "it is raining." If we view an access request such as "read file *foo*" as shorthand for "it would be a good thing to let me read file *foo*," then we indeed have a legitimate proposition.

where P is a principal with jurisdiction over the statement φ.

Finally, we would like a way to be able to make statements about the relative trustedness of different principals, which we do through the use of the operator $\Rightarrow$ (pronounced "speaks for"). Intuitively, the statement

$$P \Rightarrow Q$$

describes a proxy relationship between the two principals P and Q such that any statement made by P can also be safely attributed to Q (i.e., acted upon as if Q had made it).

In addition to the sorts of statements mentioned above, we make use of the standard logical operators: negation ($\neg \varphi$), conjunction ($\varphi_1 \wedge \varphi_2$), disjunction ($\varphi_1 \vee \varphi_2$), implication ($\varphi_1 \supset \varphi_2$), and equivalence ($\varphi_1 \equiv \varphi_2$). Having provided an informal overview of our logic, we give a formal definition of our logic's syntax in the next subsection.

2.2.3 Well-Formed Formulas

We give the name **PropVar** to the collection of all propositional variables, and we typically use lowercase identifiers (such as p, q, r) to range over this set. We can construct more interesting statements from these simple propositional variables and from our set **Princ** of principal expressions. The set **Form** of all well-formed expressions (also known as *well-formed formulas*) in our language is given by the following BNF specification:

> **Form** ::= **PropVar** / $\neg$ **Form** / (**Form** $\vee$ **Form**) /
> (**Form** $\wedge$ **Form**) / (**Form** $\supset$ **Form**) / (**Form** $\equiv$ **Form**) /
> (**Princ** $\Rightarrow$ **Princ**) / (**Princ** says **Form**) / (**Princ** controls **Form**)

This BNF specification provides all of the information necessary to determine the structure of well-formed formulas in our access-control logic. The following are examples of well-formed formulas:

$$r$$
$$((\neg q \wedge r) \supset s)$$
$$(Jill \text{ says } (r \supset (p \vee q)))$$

Convention: Throughout this book, we will distinguish between principal names and propositional variables through capitalization. Specifically, we will use *capitalized* identifiers—such as *Josh* and *Reader*—for simple principal names. We will use *lowercase* identifiers—such as r, *write*, and *rff*—for propositional variables.

Example 2.6

The following syntactic derivation demonstrates that $(\textit{Jill} \text{ says } (r \supset (p \lor q)))$ is a well-formed formula:

$$
\begin{aligned}
\textbf{Form} &\rightsquigarrow (\textbf{Princ} \text{ says } \textbf{Form}) \\
&\rightsquigarrow (\textbf{PName} \text{ says } \textbf{Form}) \\
&\rightsquigarrow (\textit{Jill} \text{ says } \textbf{Form}) \\
&\rightsquigarrow (\textit{Jill} \text{ says } (\textbf{Form} \supset \textbf{Form})) \\
&\rightsquigarrow (\textit{Jill} \text{ says } (\textbf{PropVar} \supset \textbf{Form})) \\
&\rightsquigarrow (\textit{Jill} \text{ says } (r \supset \textbf{Form})) \\
&\rightsquigarrow (\textit{Jill} \text{ says } (r \supset (\textbf{Form} \lor \textbf{Form}))) \\
&\rightsquigarrow (\textit{Jill} \text{ says } (r \supset (\textbf{PropVar} \lor \textbf{Form}))) \\
&\rightsquigarrow (\textit{Jill} \text{ says } (r \supset (p \lor \textbf{Form}))) \\
&\rightsquigarrow (\textit{Jill} \text{ says } (r \supset (p \lor \textbf{PropVar}))) \\
&\rightsquigarrow (\textit{Jill} \text{ says } (r \supset (p \lor q))) \qquad\qquad \Diamond
\end{aligned}
$$

In contrast, the following examples are *not* well-formed formulas, for the reasons stated:

- *Orly* & *Mitch* is a principal expression, but not an access-control formula.

- $\neg Orly$, because *Orly* is a principal expression, not an access-control formula; the negation operator $\neg$ must precede an access-control formula.

- $(Orly \Rightarrow (p \land q))$, because $(p \land q)$ is not a principal expression: the speaks-for operator $\Rightarrow$ must appear between two principal expressions.

- $(Orly \text{ controls } Mitch)$, because *Mitch* is a principal expression, not an access-control formula; the controls operator requires its second argument to be an access-control formula.

The parentheses ensure that the grammar is completely unambiguous, but their excessive proliferation can make the language cumbersome to use. Thus, we typically omit the outermost parentheses, and we occasionally also omit additional parentheses according to standard conventions for operator precedence: $\neg$ binds most tightly, followed in order by $\land$, $\lor$, $\supset$, and $\equiv$. Thus, for example, the formula $p \supset q \land r$ is an abbreviation of $(p \supset (q \land r))$. Likewise, the formulas $((\neg q \land r) \supset s)$ and $(\textit{Jill} \text{ says } (r \supset (p \lor q)))$ can be abbreviated respectively as follows:

$$
\neg q \land r \supset s, \quad \textit{Jill} \text{ says } (r \supset p \lor q).
$$

When the same binary operator appears multiple times in a formula—for example, $p \supset q \supset r$—the parentheses associate from left to right: $(p \supset q) \supset r$. The operators says and controls bind even more tightly than $\land$, and thus have as small a scope as possible. For example, *Kent* says $r \lor p \supset q$ is equivalent to $(((\textit{Kent says } r) \lor p) \supset q)$, and similarly for controls. Because $\Rightarrow$ is an operator that relates only principal expressions (as opposed to logical formulas), its use is always unambiguous.

✎ **Exercise 2.2.1**   *Which of the following are well-formed formulas in the access-control logic? Support your answers by appealing to the BNF specification.*

    a. $((p \land \lnot q) \supset (\textit{Cal controls } r))$

    b. $((\textit{Gin} \Rightarrow r) \land q)$

    c. $(\textit{Mel} \mid \textit{Ned says } (r \supset t))$

    d. $(\lnot t \Rightarrow \textit{Sal})$

    e. $(\textit{Ulf controls } (\textit{Vic} \mid \textit{Wes} \Rightarrow \textit{Tor}))$

    f. $(\textit{Pat controls } (\textit{Quint controls } (\textit{Ryne says } s)))$

✎ **Exercise 2.2.2**   *Fully parenthesize each of the following formulas:*

    a. $p \supset \lnot q \lor r \supset s$

    b. $\lnot p \supset r \equiv q \lor r \supset t$

    c. $X \textit{ controls } t \lor s \supset Y \textit{ says } q \supset r$

    d. $\textit{Cy says } q \land \textit{Di controls } p \supset r$

    e. $\textit{Ike} \Rightarrow \textit{Jan} \land \textit{Kai \& Lee controls } q \land r$

2.3   Semantics

Although we provided an informal reading of the logical formulas in the previous section, we have not yet provided sufficient details to enable precise or rigorous use of the logic. In the next chapter, we introduce logical rules that we can use to reason about a variety of access-control situations. However, as with any logic, several important questions arise:

> *What statements are true in this logic, and how do we know? What does a given statement really mean? How do we know that the inference rules are trustworthy? Under what conditions can we add new inference rules and guarantee that the logic's trustworthiness is preserved?*

p	q	r	$p \wedge q$	$(p \wedge q) \supset r$
true	true	true	true	true
true	true	false	true	false
true	false	true	false	true
true	false	false	false	true
false	true	true	false	true
false	true	false	false	true
false	false	true	false	true
false	false	false	false	true

Table 2.1: Truth table for the propositional formula $(p \wedge q) \supset r$

The key to answering these questions for any logic is to have rigorous, mathematical semantics that define precisely what a given statement means. These formal semantics provide a basis by which one can independently assess the trustworthiness of a logical system. For example, in propositional logic, the formal meaning of a statement such as

$$(p \wedge q) \supset r$$

can be calculated using a truth table, as illustrated in Table 2.1. Each line in the truth table corresponds to a particular interpretation of the propositional variables (i.e., a mapping of variables to specific truth values). Truth tables calculate the meaning of larger formulas in a *syntax-directed* way, based on the meanings of their components: for example, the meaning of $(p \wedge q) \supset r$ for a given interpretation is calculated using the meanings of $p \wedge q$ and r, as well as a specific rule for the operator $\supset$. A propositional-logic formula is a *tautology*—and therefore safe to use as an axiom of the system—if it is true for *every* possible interpretation of the propositional variables.

These same core ideas apply to the semantics for our access-control logic. Because we must account for the interpretation of *principals* in addition to *propositional variables*, the semantics requires a little more structure than truth tables provide. We can find this additional structure in the form of *Kripke structures*.

2.3.1 Kripke Structures

Kripke structures are useful models for analyzing a variety of situations. They are commonly used to provide semantics for modal and temporal logics, providing a basis for automated model checking.

Definition 2.1 *A Kripke structure* $\mathcal{M}$ *is a three-tuple* $\langle W, I, J \rangle$*, where:*

- W *is a nonempty set, whose elements are called* worlds.

- $I : \textbf{\textit{PropVar}} \to \mathcal{P}(W)$ *is an* interpretation *function that maps each propositional variable to a set of worlds.*

- $J : \textbf{\textit{PName}} \rightarrow \mathcal{P}(W \times W)$ *is a function that maps each principal name to a relation on worlds (i.e., a subset of $W \times W$).* ■

Before we look at some examples of Kripke structures, a few comments about this definition are in order. First, the concept of *worlds* is an abstract one. In reality, W is simply a set: its contents (whatever they may be) are called worlds. In many situations, the notion of worlds corresponds to the notion of system states or to the concept of possible alternatives.

Second, the functions I and J provide meanings (or *interpretations*) for our propositional variables and simple principals. These meanings will form the basis for our semantics of arbitrary formulas in our logic. Intuitively, $I(p)$ is the set of worlds in which we consider p to be true. $J(A)$ is a relation that describes how the simple principal A views the relationships between worlds: each pair $(w, w') \in J(A)$ indicates that, when the current world is w, principal A believes it possible that the current world is w'.

For illustration purposes, we introduce some examples of Kripke structures. The first example provides some intuition as to what the interpretation functions I and J represent, illustrating how each relation $J(P)$ might reflect principal P's understanding of the universe.

Example 2.7
Consider the situation of three young children (*Flo*, *Gil*, and *Hal*), who are being looked after by an overprotective babysitter. This babysitter will let them go outside to play only if the weather is both sunny and sufficiently warm.

To keep things simple, let us imagine that there are only three possible situations: it is sunny and warm, it is sunny but cool, or it is not sunny. We can represent these possible alternatives with a set of three worlds: $W_0 = \{sw, sc, ns\}$.

We use the propositional variable g to represent the proposition "The children can go outside." The baby sitter's overprotectiveness can be represented by any interpretation function

$$I_0 : \textbf{PropVar} \rightarrow \mathcal{P}(\{sw, sc, ns\})$$

for which $I_0(g) = \{sw\}$. That is, the proposition g ("the children can go outside") is true only in the world sw (i.e., when the weather is both sunny and warm).

Now, the children themselves are standing by the window, trying to determine whether or not they'll be allowed to go outside. *Gil*, who is tall enough to see the outdoor thermometer, possesses perfect knowledge of the situation, as he will be able to determine whether it is both sunny and sufficiently warm. This perfect knowledge corresponds to a possible-worlds relation

$$J_0(Gil) = \{(sw, sw), (sc, sc), (ns, ns)\}.$$

Whatever the current situation is, *Gil* has the correct understanding of the situation. (Note that $J_0(Gil)$ is the identity relation id_{W_0} over the set W_0.)

In contrast, *Flo* is too short to see the outdoor thermometer, and thus she cannot distinguish between the "sunny and warm" and "sunny and cool" alternatives. This uncertainty corresponds to a possible-worlds relation

$$J_0(Flo) = \{(sw, sw), (sw, sc), (sc, sw), (sc, sc), (ns, ns)\}.$$

Thus, for example, if the current situation is "sunny and warm" (i.e., sw), *Flo* considers both "sunny and warm" and "sunny and cool" as legitimate possibilities. That is, $J_0(Flo)(sw) = \{sw, sc\}$.

Finally, *Hal* is too young to understand that it can be simultaneously sunny and cool: he believes that the presence of the sun automatically makes it warm outside. His confusion corresponds to a possible-worlds relation

$$J_0(Hal) = \{(sw, sw), (sc, sw), (ns, ns)\}.$$

Whenever the actual weather is sunny and cool, *Hal* believes it to be sunny and warm: $J_0(Hal)(sc) = \{sw\}$.

The tuple $\langle W_0, I_0, J_0 \rangle$ forms a Kripke structure. ◇

The next example introduces a Kripke structure that does not necessarily reflect any particular scenario or vignette. Rather, the Kripke structure is merely a three-tuple that contains a set and two functions that match the requirements of Definition 2.1.

Example 2.8
Let $W_1 = \{w_0, w_1, w_2\}$ be a set of worlds, and let $I_1 : \mathbf{PropVar} \to \mathcal{P}(W_1)$ be the interpretation function defined as follows[2]:

$$I_1(q) = \{w_0, w_2\},$$
$$I_1(r) = \{w_1\},$$
$$I_1(s) = \{w_1, w_2\}.$$

In addition, let $J_1 : \mathbf{PName} \to \mathcal{P}(W_1 \times W_1)$ be the function defined as follows[3]:

$$J_1(Alice) = \{(w_0, w_0), (w_1, w_1), (w_2, w_2)\},$$
$$J_1(Bob) = \{(w_0, w_0), (w_0, w_1), (w_1, w_2), (w_2, w_1)\}.$$

The three-tuple $\langle W_1, I_1, J_1 \rangle$ is a Kripke structure. Intuitively, proposition q is true in worlds w_0 and w_2, r is true in world w_1, and s is true in worlds w_1 and w_2. All other propositions are false in all worlds. ◇

---

[2] In this example and those that follow, we adopt the convention of specifying only those propositional variables that the interpretation function maps to nonempty sets of worlds. Thus, for any propositional variable p not explicitly mentioned, we assume that $I_1(p) = \emptyset$.

[3] We adopt a similar convention for principal-mapping functions J: for any principal name A for which $J(A)$ is not explicitly defined, we assume that $J(A) = \emptyset$.

	Next State	
Present State	*x = 0*	*x = 1*
A	*A*	*D*
B	*A*	*C*
C	*C*	*B*
D	*C*	*A*

Table 2.2: State-transition table for finite-state machine M

World	*p*	*q*	*r*	*s*
A	true	true	false	true
B	false	true	false	true
C	true	false	false	true
D	false	true	false	true

Table 2.3: Truth values of primitive propositions *p*, *q*, *r*, and *s* in each world

The next example illustrates how a Kripke structure might be used to represent a state machine.

Example 2.9
Consider the state-transition table for a finite-state machine M shown in Table 2.2. This machine has four states: A, B, C, and D. The column labeled "Present State" lists the possible *present states* of M. The two columns under the label "Next State" list the *next states* of M if the input x is either 0 or 1, respectively. For example, the second row of Table 2.2 describes M's behavior whenever it is currently in state B: if the input is x is 0, then the next state will be A; if x is 1, then the next state will be C.

We can construct a Kripke structure $\langle W_2, I_2, J_2 \rangle$ to model this machine by defining W_2 to be the set of M's states:

$$W_2 = \{A, B, C, D\}.$$

Now, suppose that there are four primitive propositions (p, q, r, s) associated with the state machine M, with their truth values in the various states given by Table 2.3. This table effectively specifies the interpretation function I_2 on these propositions, namely:

$$I_2(p) = \{A, C\},$$
$$I_2(q) = \{A, B, D\},$$
$$I_2(r) = \{\},$$
$$I_2(s) = \{A, B, C, D\}.$$

Finally, imagine that there is an observer *Obs* of the machine's execution. This observer has faulty knowledge of M's states: whenever M is in state C, *Obs* incorrectly believes M to be in state D. We'll assume that the observer *does* correctly know when M is in states A, B, or D.

This observer's state knowledge can be captured by the following relation:

$$J_2(Obs) = \{(A,A),(B,B),(C,D),(D,D)\}.$$

In the relation $J_2(Obs)$, the first element of each pair represents the present state of M, and the second element is the observed state of M. Thus the pair (C,D) reflects that, whenever M is in state C, *Obs* always believes the current state is D.

The tuple $\langle \{A,B,C,D\}, I_2, J_2 \rangle$ forms a Kripke structure. ◇

In the next example, we model the same state machine, but we consider the inputs (i.e., "x=0" or "x=1") as the "observers" of the state machine, and we use each "next state" as the perceived state by the particular observer. Although the set of worlds and the interpretation function do not change, the principal-mapping function does change.

Example 2.10
Let W_2 and I_2 be as defined in Example 2.9, and define J_3 as follows:

$$J_3(X_0) = \{(A,A),(B,A),(C,C),(D,C)\},$$
$$J_3(X_1) = \{(A,D),(B,C),(C,B),(D,A)\}.$$

The tuple $\langle \{A,B,C,D\}, I_2, J_3 \rangle$ forms a Kripke structure. ◇

Just as the interpretation function I of a Kripke structure provides the base interpretation for propositional variables, the function J provides a base interpretation for simple principal names. We extend J to work over arbitrary *principal expressions*, using set union and relational composition as follows:

$$J(P \,\&\, Q) = J(P) \cup J(Q),$$
$$J(P \mid Q) = J(P) \circ J(Q).$$

Example 2.11
Suppose that we have the following relations:

$$J(Andy) = \{(w_0,w_0),(w_0,w_2),(w_1,w_1),(w_2,w_1)\},$$
$$J(Stu) = \{(w_1,w_2)\},$$
$$J(Keri) = \{(w_0,w_2),(w_1,w_2),(w_2,w_2)\}.$$

Then $J(Keri \mid (Andy \,\&\, Stu))$ is calculated as follows:

$J(Keri \mid (Andy \,\&\, Stu))$
$$= J(Keri) \circ J(Andy \,\&\, Stu),$$
$$= J(Keri) \circ (J(Andy) \cup J(Stu)),$$
$$= J(Keri) \circ \{(w_0,w_0),(w_0,w_2),(w_1,w_1),(w_2,w_1),(w_1,w_2)\}$$
$$= \{(w_0,w_1),(w_1,w_1),(w_2,w_1)\}. \qquad ◇$$

✎ **Exercise 2.3.1**   *Recall the Kripke structure $\langle W_0, I_0, J_0 \rangle$ from Example 2.7, and further suppose that*

$$J_0(Ida) = \{(sw, sc), (sc, sw), (ns, sc), (ns, ns)\}.$$

Calculate the following relations:

    a. $J_0(Hal \,\&\, Gil)$

    b. $J_0(Gil \mid Hal)$

    c. $J_0(Flo \,\&\, Ida)$

    d. $J_0(Hal \mid Ida)$

    e. $J_0(Ida \mid Hal)$

    f. $J_0(Hal \,\&\, (Ida \mid Hal))$

    g. $J_0(Hal \mid (Ida \,\&\, Hal))$

2.3.2   Semantics of the Logic

The Kripke structures provide the foundation for a formal, precise, and rigorous interpretation of formulas in our logic. For each Kripke structure $\mathcal{M} = \langle W, I, J \rangle$, we can define what it means for formulas in our logic to be *satisfied* in the structure. We can also identify those worlds in W for which a given formula is said to be true.

To define the semantics, we introduce a family of *evaluation functions*. Each Kripke structure $\mathcal{M} = \langle W, I, J \rangle$ gives rise to an evaluation function $\mathcal{E}_{\mathcal{M}}$ that maps well-formed formulas in the logic to subsets of W. Intuitively, $\mathcal{E}_{\mathcal{M}}[\![\varphi]\!]$ is the set of worlds from the Kripke structure $\mathcal{M}$ for which the well-formed formula φ is considered true. We say that $\mathcal{M}$ *satisfies* φ (written $\mathcal{M} \models \varphi$) whenever φ is true in *all* of the worlds of $\mathcal{M}$: that is, when $\mathcal{E}_{\mathcal{M}}[\![\varphi]\!] = W$. It follows that a Kripke structure $\mathcal{M}$ *does not satisfy* φ (written $\mathcal{M} \not\models \varphi$) when there exists at least one $w \in W$ such that $w \notin \mathcal{E}_{\mathcal{M}}[\![\varphi]\!]$.

Each $\mathcal{E}_{\mathcal{M}}$ is defined inductively on the structure of well-formed formulas, making use of the interpretation functions I and J within the Kripke structure $\mathcal{M} = \langle W, I, J \rangle$. We discuss the individual cases separately, starting with the standard propositional operators and then moving on to the access-control specific cases. The full set of definitions is also summarized in Figure 2.1.

Standard Propositional Operators

The semantics for propositional variables and the standard logical connectives (e.g., negation, conjunction, implication) are very similar to the truth-table interpretations for standard propositional logic. The interpretation function I identifies those worlds in which the various propositional variables are true, while the semantics of the other operators are defined using standard set operations. We handle these cases in turn.

FIGURE 2.1 Semantics of core logic, for each $\mathcal{M} = \langle W, I, J \rangle$

$$\mathcal{E}_{\mathcal{M}}[\![p]\!] = I(p)$$
$$\mathcal{E}_{\mathcal{M}}[\![\neg\varphi]\!] = W - \mathcal{E}_{\mathcal{M}}[\![\varphi]\!]$$
$$\mathcal{E}_{\mathcal{M}}[\![\varphi_1 \wedge \varphi_2]\!] = \mathcal{E}_{\mathcal{M}}[\![\varphi_1]\!] \cap \mathcal{E}_{\mathcal{M}}[\![\varphi_2]\!]$$
$$\mathcal{E}_{\mathcal{M}}[\![\varphi_1 \vee \varphi_2]\!] = \mathcal{E}_{\mathcal{M}}[\![\varphi_1]\!] \cup \mathcal{E}_{\mathcal{M}}[\![\varphi_2]\!]$$
$$\mathcal{E}_{\mathcal{M}}[\![\varphi_1 \supset \varphi_2]\!] = (W - \mathcal{E}_{\mathcal{M}}[\![\varphi_1]\!]) \cup \mathcal{E}_{\mathcal{M}}[\![\varphi_2]\!]$$
$$\mathcal{E}_{\mathcal{M}}[\![\varphi_1 \equiv \varphi_2]\!] = \mathcal{E}_{\mathcal{M}}[\![\varphi_1 \supset \varphi_2]\!] \cap \mathcal{E}_{\mathcal{M}}[\![\varphi_2 \supset \varphi_1]\!]$$
$$\mathcal{E}_{\mathcal{M}}[\![P \Rightarrow Q]\!] = \begin{cases} W, & \text{if } J(Q) \subseteq J(P) \\ \emptyset, & \text{otherwise} \end{cases}$$
$$\mathcal{E}_{\mathcal{M}}[\![P \text{ says } \varphi]\!] = \{w \,|\, J(P)(w) \subseteq \mathcal{E}_{\mathcal{M}}[\![\varphi]\!]\}$$
$$\mathcal{E}_{\mathcal{M}}[\![P \text{ controls } \varphi]\!] = \mathcal{E}_{\mathcal{M}}[\![(P \text{ says } \varphi) \supset \varphi]\!]$$

Propositional Variables: The truth of a propositional variable p is determined by the interpretation function I: a variable p is considered true in world w precisely when $w \in I(p)$. Thus, for all propositional variables p,

$$\mathcal{E}_{\mathcal{M}}[\![p]\!] = I(p).$$

For example, if $\mathcal{M}_0$ is the Kripke structure $\langle W_0, I_0, J_0 \rangle$ from Example 2.7, $\mathcal{E}_{\mathcal{M}_0}[\![g]\!] = I_0(g) = \{sw\}$.

Negation: A formula with form $\neg\varphi$ is true in precisely those worlds in which φ is *not* true. Because (by definition) $\mathcal{E}_{\mathcal{M}}[\![\varphi]\!]$ is the set of worlds in which φ is true, we define

$$\mathcal{E}_{\mathcal{M}}[\![\neg\varphi]\!] = W - \mathcal{E}_{\mathcal{M}}[\![\varphi]\!].$$

Thus, returning to Example 2.7,

$$\mathcal{E}_{\mathcal{M}_0}[\![\neg g]\!] = W_0 - \mathcal{E}_{\mathcal{M}_0}[\![g]\!] = \{sw, sc, ns\} - \{sw\} = \{sc, ns\}.$$

Notice that $\mathcal{E}_{\mathcal{M}_0}[\![\neg g]\!]$ is the set of worlds in which the children are *not* allowed to go outside.

Conjunction: A conjunctive formula $\varphi_1 \wedge \varphi_2$ is considered true in those worlds for which *both* φ_1 and φ_2 are true: that is, $\varphi_1 \wedge \varphi_2$ is true in those worlds w for which $w \in \mathcal{E}_{\mathcal{M}}[\![\varphi_1]\!]$ *and* $w \in \mathcal{E}_{\mathcal{M}}[\![\varphi_2]\!]$. Thus, we can define $\mathcal{E}_{\mathcal{M}}[\![\varphi_1 \wedge \varphi_2]\!]$ in terms of set intersection:

$$\mathcal{E}_{\mathcal{M}}[\![\varphi_1 \wedge \varphi_2]\!] = \mathcal{E}_{\mathcal{M}}[\![\varphi_1]\!] \cap \mathcal{E}_{\mathcal{M}}[\![\varphi_2]\!].$$

Disjunction: Likewise, a disjunctive formula $\varphi_1 \vee \varphi_2$ is considered true in those worlds for which *at least one of* φ_1 and φ_2 is true: that is, $\varphi_1 \vee \varphi_2$ is true in those worlds w for which $w \in \mathcal{E}_{\mathcal{M}}[[\varphi_1]]$ *or* $w \in \mathcal{E}_{\mathcal{M}}[[\varphi_2]]$. Thus, we define $\mathcal{E}_{\mathcal{M}}[[\varphi_1 \vee \varphi_2]]$ in terms of set union:

$$\mathcal{E}_{\mathcal{M}}[[\varphi_1 \vee \varphi_2]] = \mathcal{E}_{\mathcal{M}}[[\varphi_1]] \cup \mathcal{E}_{\mathcal{M}}[[\varphi_2]].$$

Implication: An implication $\varphi_1 \supset \varphi_2$ is true in those worlds w for which either φ_2 is true (i.e., $w \in \mathcal{E}_{\mathcal{M}}[[\varphi_2]]$) or φ_1 is not true (i.e., $w \notin \mathcal{E}_{\mathcal{M}}[[\varphi_1]]$, and thus $w \in \mathcal{E}_{\mathcal{M}}[[\neg\varphi_1]]$). That is, $\varphi_1 \supset \varphi_2$ is true in those worlds in which, if φ_1 is true, then φ_2 is also true; if φ_1 is false, then φ_2's interpretation is immaterial. Thus, we define the semantics of implications as follows:

$$\mathcal{E}_{\mathcal{M}}[[\varphi_1 \supset \varphi_2]] = (W - \mathcal{E}_{\mathcal{M}}[[\varphi_1]]) \cup \mathcal{E}_{\mathcal{M}}[[\varphi_2]].$$

Equivalence: An equivalence $\varphi_1 \equiv \varphi_2$ is true in exactly those worlds w in which the implications $\varphi_1 \supset \varphi_2$ and $\varphi_2 \supset \varphi_1$ are *both* true. Thus, we define the semantics of implications as follows:

$$\mathcal{E}_{\mathcal{M}}[[\varphi_1 \equiv \varphi_2]] = \mathcal{E}_{\mathcal{M}}[[\varphi_1 \supset \varphi_2]] \cap \mathcal{E}_{\mathcal{M}}[[\varphi_2 \supset \varphi_1]].$$

Example 2.12
Let $\mathcal{M}_1$ be the Kripke structure $\langle W_1, I_1, J_1 \rangle$ from Example 2.8. The set $\mathcal{E}_{\mathcal{M}_1}[[q \supset (r \wedge s)]]$ of worlds in W_1 in which the formula $q \supset (r \wedge s)$ is true is calculated as follows:

$$\begin{aligned}
\mathcal{E}_{\mathcal{M}_1}[[q \supset (r \wedge s)]] &= (W_1 - \mathcal{E}_{\mathcal{M}_1}[[q]]) \cup \mathcal{E}_{\mathcal{M}_1}[[r \wedge s]] \\
&= (W_1 - I_1(q)) \cup (\mathcal{E}_{\mathcal{M}_1}[[r]] \cap \mathcal{E}_{\mathcal{M}_1}[[s]]) \\
&= (W_1 - \{w_0, w_2\}) \cup (I_1(r) \cap I_1(s)) \\
&= \{w_1\} \cup (\{w_1\} \cap \{w_1, w_2\}) \\
&= \{w_1\} \cup \{w_1\} \\
&= \{w_1\}.
\end{aligned}$$

$\Diamond$

In the following example, we evaluate the same formula as in the previous example, but with respect to a different Kripke structure.

Example 2.13
Let $\mathcal{M}_2$ be the Kripke structure $\langle W_2, I_2, J_2 \rangle$ from Example 2.9. The set $\mathcal{E}_{\mathcal{M}_2}[\![q \supset (r \wedge s)]\!]$ of worlds W_2 in which the formula $q \supset (r \wedge s)$ is true is calculated as follows:

$$
\begin{aligned}
\mathcal{E}_{\mathcal{M}_2}[\![q \supset (r \wedge s)]\!] &= (W_2 - \mathcal{E}_{\mathcal{M}_2}[\![q]\!]) \cup \mathcal{E}_{\mathcal{M}_2}[\![r \wedge s]\!] \\
&= (W_2 - I_2(q)) \cup (\mathcal{E}_{\mathcal{M}_2}[\![r]\!] \cap \mathcal{E}_{\mathcal{M}_2}[\![s]\!]) \\
&= (W_2 - \{A, B, D\}) \cup (I_2(r) \cap I_2(s)) \\
&= \{C\} \cup (\emptyset \cap \{A, B, C, D\}) \\
&= \{C\} \cup \emptyset \\
&= \{C\}. \qquad \qquad \qquad \Diamond
\end{aligned}
$$

Access-Control Operators

The access-control operators of the logic (e.g., says , controls , and $\Rightarrow$) have more interesting semantics.

Says: A formula P says φ is meant to denote a situation in which the principal P makes the statement φ. Intuitively, a principal should make statements that they *believe* to be true. What does it mean for a principal to believe a statement is true in a given world? The standard answer is that a principal P believes φ to be true in a specific world w if φ is true in all of the worlds w' that P *can conceive* the current world to be (i.e., all w' such that (w, w') is in $J(P)$). Of course, this set of *possible worlds* is simply the set $J(P)(w)$; φ is true in every world in $J(P)(w)$ if and only if $J(P)(w) \subseteq \mathcal{E}_{\mathcal{M}}[\![\varphi]\!]$. Therefore, we define

$$\mathcal{E}_{\mathcal{M}}[\![P \text{ says } \varphi]\!] = \{w \mid J(P)(w) \subseteq \mathcal{E}_{\mathcal{M}}[\![\varphi]\!]\}.$$

Controls: Formulas of the form P controls φ express a principal P's jurisdiction or authority regarding the statement φ. We interpret P controls φ as syntactic sugar for the statement $(P \text{ says } \varphi) \supset \varphi$, which captures the desired intuition: if the authority P says that φ is true, then φ is true. Thus, we give the meaning of P controls φ directly as the meaning of this rewriting:

$$\mathcal{E}_{\mathcal{M}}[\![P \text{ controls } \varphi]\!] = \mathcal{E}_{\mathcal{M}}[\![(P \text{ says } \varphi) \supset \varphi]\!].$$

Speaks For: To understand the semantics of formulas with form $P \Rightarrow Q$, recall the purpose of such formulas: we wish to express a proxy relationship between P and Q that will permit us to safely attribute P's statements to Q as well, independent of a particular world. That is, if $P \Rightarrow Q$, then it should be reasonable to interpret any statement from P as being a statement that Q would also make. In terms of the semantics, we have seen that a principal P making a statement φ in a world w means that $J(P)(w) \subseteq \mathcal{E}_{\mathcal{M}}[\![\varphi]\!]$. Thus, if we wish to associate *all* of P's statements to Q, then we need to know that $J(Q)(w) \subseteq J(P)(w)$ for all worlds w. If $J(Q) \subseteq J(P)$, then this relationship naturally holds. Therefore, we define

$$\mathcal{E}_{\mathcal{M}}[\![P \Rightarrow Q]\!] = \begin{cases} W, & \text{if } J(Q) \subseteq J(P) \\ \emptyset, & \text{otherwise.} \end{cases}$$

The following examples illustrate these semantic definitions.

Example 2.14
Recall $\mathcal{M}_0 = \langle W_0, I_0, J_0 \rangle$ from Example 2.7. The set of worlds in W_0 in which the formula *Hal* says g is true is given by $\mathcal{E}_{\mathcal{M}_0}[\![\textit{Hal} \text{ says } g]\!]$, which is calculated as follows:

$$\begin{aligned} \mathcal{E}_{\mathcal{M}_0}[\![\textit{Hal} \text{ says } g]\!] &= \{w \mid J_0(\textit{Hal})(w) \subseteq \mathcal{E}_{\mathcal{M}_0}[\![g]\!]\} \\ &= \{w \mid J_0(\textit{Hal})(w) \subseteq \{sw\}\} \\ &= \{sw, sc\}. \end{aligned}$$

This result captures *Hal*'s mistaken belief that, whenever it is sunny (i.e., when the current world is either *sw* or *sc*), the children will be able to go outside.

In contrast, recall that *Flo* is unable to distinguish the two worlds *sw* and *sc*. Specifically, the relation $J_0(\textit{Flo})$ has the following properties:

$$\begin{aligned} J_0(\textit{Flo})(sw) &= \{sw, sc\}, \\ J_0(\textit{Flo})(sc) &= \{sw, sc\}, \\ J_0(\textit{Flo})(ns) &= \{ns\}. \end{aligned}$$

Thus, the worlds in which *Flo* says g is true can be calculated as follows:

$$\begin{aligned} \mathcal{E}_{\mathcal{M}_0}[\![\textit{Flo} \text{ says } g]\!] &= \{w \mid J_0(\textit{Flo})(w) \subseteq \mathcal{E}_{\mathcal{M}_0}[\![g]\!]\} \\ &= \{w \mid J_0(\textit{Flo})(w) \subseteq \{sw\}\} \\ &= \emptyset. \end{aligned}$$

That is, there are no worlds in which *Flo* is convinced that the children will be able to go outside. $\Diamond$

Example 2.15
Recall $\mathcal{M}_1 = \langle W_1, I_1, J_1 \rangle$ from Examples 2.8 and Example 2.12. The set of worlds in W_1 in which the formula *Alice* says $(q \supset (r \wedge s))$ is true is given by $\mathcal{E}_{\mathcal{M}_1}[\![\textit{Alice} \text{ says } (q \supset (r \wedge s))]\!]$, calculated as follows:

$$\begin{aligned} \mathcal{E}_{\mathcal{M}_1}[\![\textit{Alice} \text{ says } (q \supset (r \wedge s))]\!] &= \{w \mid J_1(\textit{Alice})(w) \subseteq \mathcal{E}_{\mathcal{M}_1}[\![q \supset (r \wedge s)]\!]\} \\ &= \{w \mid J_1(\textit{Alice})(w) \subseteq \{w_1\}\} \\ &= \{w_1\}. \end{aligned}$$

This result is not surprising, because *Alice* had perfect knowledge of the separate worlds: thus, she believes $q \supset (r \wedge s)$ to be true in precisely those worlds in which it is true. $\Diamond$

Example 2.16
Consider the same Kripke structure $\mathcal{M}_1 = \langle W_1, I_1, J_1 \rangle$ as in the previous example, but now we investigate *Bob*'s view of the situation. Recall the following details about $J_1(Bob)$:

$$J_1(Bob)(w_0) = \{w_0, w_1\},$$
$$J_1(Bob)(w_1) = \{w_2\},$$
$$J_1(Bob)(w_2) = \{w_1\}.$$

The set of worlds in W_1 in which the formula *Bob* says $(q \supset (r \wedge s))$ is true is given by $\mathcal{E}_{\mathcal{M}_1}[\![Bob \text{ says } (q \supset (r \wedge s))]\!]$, which is calculated as follows:

$$
\begin{aligned}
\mathcal{E}_{\mathcal{M}_1}[\![Bob \text{ says } (q \supset (r \wedge s))]\!] &= \{w \mid J_1(Bob)(w) \subseteq \mathcal{E}_{\mathcal{M}_1}[\![q \supset (r \wedge s)]\!]\} \\
&= \{w \mid J_1(Bob)(w) \subseteq \{w_1\}\} \\
&= \{w_2\}. \hspace{3cm} \Diamond
\end{aligned}
$$

As remarked at the beginning of this section, a particular Kripke structure $\mathcal{M} = \langle W, I, J \rangle$ *satisfies* a formula φ, written $\mathcal{M} \models \varphi$, if and only if φ is true of every world in W (i.e., if $\mathcal{E}_{\mathcal{M}}[\![\varphi]\!] = W$). The following examples illustrate this concept.

Example 2.17
Recall the Kripke structure $\mathcal{M}_1 = \langle W_1, I_1, J_1 \rangle$ from Examples 2.8 and 2.12. $\mathcal{M}_1$ satisfies the formula $q \vee r$, but not the formula $q \supset (r \wedge s)$:

$$
\begin{aligned}
\mathcal{E}_{\mathcal{M}_1}[\![q \vee r]\!] &= \{w_0, w_1, w_2\} = W_1, \\
\mathcal{E}_{\mathcal{M}_1}[\![q \supset (r \wedge s)]\!] &= \{w_1\} \neq W_1.
\end{aligned}
$$

Thus, we write $\mathcal{M}_1 \models q \vee r$ and $\mathcal{M}_1 \not\models q \supset (r \wedge s)$. $\hspace{2cm} \Diamond$

Example 2.18
The same Kripke structure $\mathcal{M}_1 = \langle W_1, I_1, J_1 \rangle$ from Examples 2.8 and 2.12 also satisfies the formula *Alice* controls $(q \supset (r \wedge s))$, because:

$$
\begin{aligned}
\mathcal{E}_{\mathcal{M}_1}&[\![Alice \text{ controls } (q \supset (r \wedge s))]\!] \\
&= \mathcal{E}_{\mathcal{M}_1}[\![(Alice \text{ says } (q \supset (r \wedge s))) \supset (q \supset (r \wedge s))]\!] \\
&= (W_1 - \mathcal{E}_{\mathcal{M}_1}[\![Alice \text{ says } (q \supset (r \wedge s))]\!]) \cup \mathcal{E}_{\mathcal{M}_1}[\![q \supset (r \wedge s)]\!] \\
&= (W_1 - \{w_1\}) \cup \{w_1\} \\
&= W_1.
\end{aligned}
$$

Therefore, we can write $\mathcal{M}_1 \models Alice \text{ controls } (q \supset (r \wedge s))$. $\hspace{2cm} \Diamond$

The following exercises provide opportunities to use the Kripke semantics to calculate the meanings of access-control formulas, to identify structures that satisfy given formulas, and to prove useful properties about the semantics.

✎ **Exercise 2.3.2**   *Suppose $\mathcal{M}$ is the Kripke structure $\langle W, I, J \rangle$, where W, I, and J are defined as follows:*

$$W = \{w_0, w_1, w_2\}$$
$$I(s) = \{w_1, w_2\}$$
$$I(t) = \{w_2\}$$
$$J(Cy) = \{(w_1, w_0), (w_1, w_1), (w_2, w_0)\}$$
$$J(Di) = \{(w_0, w_1), (w_1, w_0), (w_2, w_2)\}.$$

For each of the following formulas, give the set of worlds in W for which the formula is true (i.e., calculate $\mathcal{E}_{\mathcal{M}}[\![\varphi]\!]$ for each formula φ).

a. $s \supset t$

b. $\neg(s \supset t)$

c. $Cy \text{ says } (s \supset t)$

d. $Cy \text{ says } \neg(s \supset t)$

e. $Di \text{ says } (s \supset t)$

f. $Di \text{ says } \neg(s \supset t)$

g. $(Cy \& Di) \text{ says } (s \supset t)$

h. $(Cy \& Di) \text{ says } \neg(s \supset t)$

i. $(Di \mid Cy) \text{ says } (s \supset t)$

j. $(Di \mid Cy) \text{ says } \neg(s \supset t)$

k. $Di \Rightarrow Cy$

l. $Cy \text{ says } (Di \Rightarrow Cy)$

m. $Di \text{ says } (Di \Rightarrow Cy)$

n. $Di \text{ says } (Di \& Cy \Rightarrow Cy)$

✎ **Exercise 2.3.3**   *Let $\mathcal{M}$ be the Kripke structure $\langle W, I, J \rangle$, where W, I, and J are defined as follows:*

- $W = \{t, u, v, x, y, z\}$

- $I : \textbf{PropVar} \rightarrow 2^W$ *given by:*

$$I(p) = \{x, y, z\}$$
$$I(q) = \{x, y, t\}$$
$$I(r) = \{y, t, u, z\}$$

- $J : \textbf{PName} \rightarrow 2^{W \times W}$ *given by:*

$$J(A) = \{(w, w) \mid w \in W\} \cup \{(x, y), (x, z), (z, t), (y, v), (v, y), (v, x)\}$$
$$J(B) = \{(x, w) \mid w \in W\} \cup \{(y, t), (z, t), (t, v)\}.$$

Calculate each of the following sets.

a. $\mathcal{E}_\mathcal{M}[\![(p \supset q) \supset r]\!]$

b. $\mathcal{E}_\mathcal{M}[\![A \text{ says } (p \supset r)]\!]$

c. $\mathcal{E}_\mathcal{M}[\![A \text{ says } (B \text{ says } q)]\!]$

d. $\mathcal{E}_\mathcal{M}[\![B \text{ says } (B \text{ says } q)]\!]$

e. $\mathcal{E}_\mathcal{M}[\![A \text{ controls } (B \text{ says } q)]\!]$

f. $\mathcal{E}_\mathcal{M}[\![A \text{ controls } (B \text{ controls } q)]\!]$

Exercise 2.3.4 *Let $\mathcal{M}$ be the Kripke structure $\langle W, I, J \rangle$, where*

$$W = \{n, r, c, d, rc, rd, cd, rcd\}$$
$$I(read) = \{r, rc, rd, rcd\}$$
$$I(copy) = \{c, rc, cd, rcd\}$$
$$I(del) = \{d, rd, cd, rcd\}$$

$$J(X) = \{(w, rcd) \mid w \in W\}$$
$$J(Y) = id_W$$
$$J(Z) = \{(w, n) \mid w \in W\}.$$

a. *Prove that $\mathcal{M} \models Y \text{ controls } (read \wedge copy)$.*

b. *Prove that $\mathcal{M} \not\models X \text{ controls } del$.*

Exercise 2.3.5 *Let $\mathcal{A} = \langle W_A, I_A, J_A \rangle$ and $\mathcal{B} = \langle W_B, I_B, J_B \rangle$ be the Kripke structures* *defined by:*

$$W_A = \{a_1, a_2, a_3\}$$
$$I_A(p) = \{a_3\}$$
$$I_A(q) = \{a_1, a_3\}$$
$$I_A(r) = \{a_1, a_2\}$$
$$J_A(Val) = \{(a_1, a_1), (a_1, a_2), (a_2, a_1), (a_3, a_2)\}$$
$$J_A(Wyn) = \{(a_1, a_3), (a_2, a_3), (a_3, a_2)\}.$$

$$W_B = \{b_1, b_2, b_3, b_4\}$$
$$I_B(p) = \{b_2, b_1\}$$
$$I_B(q) = \{b_3\}$$
$$I_B(r) = \{b_2, b_4, b_1\}$$
$$J_B(Val) = \{(b_1, b_2), (b_2, b_3), (b_2, b_4), (b_4, b_4)\}$$
$$J_B(Wyn) = \{(b_1, b_1), (b_2, b_1), (b_3, b_2), (b_3, b_4), (b_4, b_2)\}.$$

Which of the following statements are true? Support your answers with calculations using the evaluation functions $\mathcal{E}_{\mathcal{A}}[\![-]\!]$ and $\mathcal{E}_{\mathcal{B}}[\![-]\!]$.

a. $\mathcal{A} \models p \vee (q \supset r)$

b. $\mathcal{B} \models p \vee (q \supset r)$

c. $\mathcal{A} \models Val \Rightarrow Wyn$

d. $\mathcal{B} \models Val \Rightarrow Wyn$

e. $\mathcal{A} \models Val \mid Wyn$ says r

f. $\mathcal{B} \models Val \mid Wyn$ says r

g. $\mathcal{A} \models Wyn$ controls $(p \wedge r)$

h. $\mathcal{B} \models Wyn$ controls $(p \wedge r)$

Exercise 2.3.6   *For each of the following formulas φ, find Kripke structures $\mathcal{M}_x$ and $\mathcal{M}_y$ such that $\mathcal{M}_x \models \varphi$ and $\mathcal{M}_y \not\models \varphi$.*

a. *Ned says* $(p \equiv q)$

b. *Olaf controls q*

c. *Pam says* (*Rue controls r*)

d. *Sal controls* (*Tom* $\Rightarrow$ *Ugo*)

Exercise 2.3.7   *Prove that, for any Kripke structure* $\mathcal{M} = \langle W, I, J \rangle$, *principal P, and formulas* φ_1 *and* φ_2, *the following relationship holds:*

$$\mathcal{E}_{\mathcal{M}}\llbracket P \text{ says } (\varphi_1 \equiv \varphi_2) \rrbracket \cap \mathcal{E}_{\mathcal{M}}\llbracket P \text{ says } \varphi_1 \rrbracket \subseteq \mathcal{E}_{\mathcal{M}}\llbracket P \text{ says } \varphi_2 \rrbracket.$$

Exercise 2.3.8   *Prove that, for every Kripke structure* $\mathcal{M} = \langle W, I, J \rangle$, *principal P, and formulas* φ_1 *and* φ_2, *the following relationship holds:*

$$\mathcal{M} \models P \text{ says } (\varphi_1 \equiv \varphi_2) \supset (P \text{ says } \varphi_1 \supset P \text{ says } \varphi_2).$$

Hint: Exercise 2.3.7 is helpful here.

Exercise 2.3.9   *Prove that, for any Kripke structure* $\mathcal{M} = \langle W, I, J \rangle$ *and formulas* φ_1 *and* φ_2, $\mathcal{E}_{\mathcal{M}}\llbracket \varphi_1 \equiv \varphi_2 \rrbracket = W$ *if and only if* $\mathcal{E}_{\mathcal{M}}\llbracket \varphi_1 \rrbracket = \mathcal{E}_{\mathcal{M}}\llbracket \varphi_2 \rrbracket$. *That is, prove the following two statements:*

   a. If $\mathcal{E}_{\mathcal{M}}\llbracket \varphi_1 \equiv \varphi_2 \rrbracket = W$, *then* $\mathcal{E}_{\mathcal{M}}\llbracket \varphi_1 \rrbracket = \mathcal{E}_{\mathcal{M}}\llbracket \varphi_2 \rrbracket$.

   b. If $\mathcal{E}_{\mathcal{M}}\llbracket \varphi_1 \rrbracket = \mathcal{E}_{\mathcal{M}}\llbracket \varphi_2 \rrbracket$, *then* $\mathcal{E}_{\mathcal{M}}\llbracket \varphi_1 \equiv \varphi_2 \rrbracket = W$.

2.4   Summary

Providing and maintaining security—in both the physical and digital worlds—requires us to be able to determine whether or not any given decision to grant access to resources or services is correct. Unfortunately, natural language expressions have imprecise meanings. We need a way to unambiguously express the policies, trust assumptions, recognized authorities, and statements made by various principals and be able to justify the resulting access-control decisions.

In this chapter, we introduced a language that allows us to express our policies, trust assumptions, recognized authorities, and statements in a precise and unambiguous way. Expressions in this language are given precise, mathematical meanings through the use of Kripke structures. This Kripke semantics provides the initial basis for mathematically justifying access-control decisions: given a Kripke structure and an expression in the language, we can compute those worlds in which the expression is true. This semantics will allow us to introduce sound rules for justifying access-control decisions, as demonstrated in the next chapter.

The learning outcomes associated with this chapter appear in Figure 2.2.

2.5   Further Reading

For a detailed introduction to discrete mathematics and propositional logic, we direct the interested reader to some of the standard undergraduate textbooks on the

---

FIGURE 2.2 Learning outcomes for Chapter 2

After completing this chapter, you should be able to achieve the following learning outcomes at several levels of knowledge:

Application

- Determine whether or not a given collection of symbols constitutes a well-formed formula of the access-control logic.

- When given an informal statement in English, translate it into a well-formed formula of the access-control logic.

- When given a Kripke structure and a formula of the access-control logic, determine the set of worlds in which the formula is true.

Analysis

- When given a formula and a Kripke structure that satisfies it, prove that the Kripke structure satisfies it.

Synthesis

- When given a satisfiable formula, construct a Kripke structure that satisfies the formula.

- When given a refutable formula, construct a Kripke structure that refutes (i.e., fails to satisfy) the formula.

- When given a general property regarding Kripke structures, prove that the property holds.

Evaluation

- When given a Kripke structure and a formula, determine whether or not the Kripke structure satisfies the formula.

---

subject (Rosen, 2003; Ross and Wright, 2002).

The access-control logic presented here is based on the logic of Abadi, Lampson, and colleagues (Lampson et al., 1992; Abadi et al., 1993), which in turn was built on top of a standard modal logic. Modal logic is the logical study of necessity and possibility, and Hughes and Cresswell provide an excellent introduction to the field (Hughes and Cresswell, 1996).

Chapter 3

Reasoning about Access Control

In the previous chapter, we introduced a language for describing access-control scenarios. We presented the syntax for well-formed statements in the language (i.e., formulas). We also specified their semantics through the use of Kripke structures.

Although Kripke structures provide precise meanings for these statements, it is not practical to analyze access-control situations at such a low level. First of all, Kripke structures are cumbersome to use for even simple situations. Second, in any given situation, it is unclear which structures accurately capture the state of the universe. How could we possibly know which Kripke structure to use for any given analysis?

In this chapter, we introduce a collection of *inference rules* that will provide the basis for reasoning rigorously about access control. These rules describe a system for manipulating well-formed formulas as a way of calculating the consequences of various assumptions. A crucial property for these rules is that they must be *sound* with respect to the Kripke-structure semantics. That is, the rules should ensure that, in any situation where a given Kripke structure satisfies all of a rule's premises, the Kripke structure also satisfies the rule's consequent. Informally, soundness means that it is impossible to deduce a "false" statement from "true" ones. In this chapter, we demonstrate how to verify that the rules we introduce are sound.

3.1 Logical Rules

The logical rules are summarized in Figure 3.1. Each rule of the logic has the form

$$\frac{H_1 \quad \cdots \quad H_k}{C},$$

where the items written above the line (e.g., $H_1, \ldots H_k$) correspond to *hypotheses* (or *premises*) and the item below the line (e.g., C) corresponds to a *consequence* (or *conclusion*). A special case occurs when there are no hypotheses on the top of the rule (i.e., when $k = 0$): an inference rule with an "empty top" is called an *axiom*.

Informally, we often read such rules as "If all the assertions on the top are true, then the consequence below the line will also be true." More accurately, however, the logical rules describe a system for manipulating well-formed formulas of the logic. In fact, one can think of the logical rules as defining a game, in which a player writes

---

FIGURE 3.1 Logical rules for the access-control logic

Taut $\dfrac{}{\varphi}$ if φ is an instance of a prop-logic tautology

Modus Ponens $\dfrac{\varphi \quad \varphi \supset \varphi'}{\varphi'}$ *Says* $\dfrac{\varphi}{P \text{ says } \varphi}$

MP Says $\dfrac{}{(P \text{ says } (\varphi \supset \varphi')) \supset (P \text{ says } \varphi \supset P \text{ says } \varphi')}$

Speaks For $\dfrac{}{P \Rightarrow Q \supset (P \text{ says } \varphi \supset Q \text{ says } \varphi)}$

& Says $\dfrac{}{(P \,\&\, Q \text{ says } \varphi) \equiv ((P \text{ says } \varphi) \wedge (Q \text{ says } \varphi))}$

Quoting $\dfrac{}{(P \mid Q \text{ says } \varphi) \equiv (P \text{ says } Q \text{ says } \varphi)}$

Idempotency of $\Rightarrow$ $\dfrac{}{P \Rightarrow P}$

Transitivity of $\Rightarrow$ $\dfrac{P \Rightarrow Q \quad Q \Rightarrow R}{P \Rightarrow R}$ *Monotonicity of* $\Rightarrow$ $\dfrac{P \Rightarrow P' \quad Q \Rightarrow Q'}{P \mid Q \Rightarrow P' \mid Q'}$

Equivalence $\dfrac{\varphi_1 \equiv \varphi_2 \quad \psi[\varphi_1/q]}{\psi[\varphi_2/q]}$

$P \text{ controls } \varphi \;\overset{\text{def}}{=}\; (P \text{ says } \varphi) \supset \varphi$

FIGURE 3.2 Common propositional-logic tautologies

$p \vee \neg p$	$p \supset (q \supset (p \wedge q))$
$p \equiv (\neg\neg p)$	$(p \wedge q) \supset (p \supset q)$
$p \supset (q \vee p)$	$(p \wedge q) \supset (q \wedge p)$
$p \supset (q \supset p)$	$(p \equiv q) \supset (p \supset q)$
$(p \wedge q) \supset p$	$((p \vee q) \wedge \neg p) \supset q$
$\neg(\neg p \wedge p)$	$((p \supset q) \wedge (q \supset r)) \supset (p \supset r)$

(i.e., *derives*) various formulas on a piece of paper. Each rule states that, if all the premises of an inference rule have already been written down (derived), then the conclusion can also be written down (derived). Axioms can always be written down.

We return to this notion of derivations in Section 3.2, where we introduce *formal proofs*. For now, however, we discuss each of the logical rules in turn.

3.1.1 The *Taut* Rule

The simplest rule is the axiom *Taut*:

$$Taut \quad \frac{}{\varphi} \quad \text{if } \varphi \text{ is an instance of a prop-logic tautology}$$

This axiom states that any instance of a *tautology* from propositional logic can be introduced at any time as a derivable statement in the access-control logic. To understand what this rule means, first recall that a propositional-logic tautology is a formula that evaluates to *true* under *all* possible interpretations of its propositional variables. For example, the propositional formula $p \vee \neg p$ always evaluates to *true*, independent of whether the propositional variable p is assigned the value *true* or the value *false*. In contrast, the formula $p \supset \neg p$ is not a tautology, because it evaluates to *false* whenever p is assigned the value *true*. Although it does not constitute a complete listing, Figure 3.2 summarizes some common propositional-logic tautologies.

A formula φ is *an instance* of the formula ψ if there exist propositional variables $p_1, \ldots, p_k$ (for some $k \geq 0$) and modal formulas $\varphi_1, \ldots, \varphi_k$ such that φ is obtained by replacing each p_i in ψ by φ_i. For example, the formula

$$(Alice \text{ says } go) \vee ((sit \wedge read) \supset (Alice \text{ says } go))$$

is an instance of the formula $q \vee (r \supset q)$: it can be obtained by replacing every q by $(Alice \text{ says } go)$ and every r by $(sit \wedge read)$. In contrast, the formula

$$(Alice \text{ says } go) \vee ((sit \wedge read) \supset stay)$$

is *not* an instance of the formula $q \vee (r \supset q)$, because the two separate occurrences of q were not replaced by the same formula.

Thus, the *Taut* rule allows us to introduce (i.e., derive) any formula that can be obtained from a propositional-logic tautology by a uniform substitution as described above. For example, since $p \lor \neg p$ is a tautology, we can derive the following formula:

$$(\textit{Paul controls } (\textit{read} \land \textit{write})) \lor \neg(\textit{Paul controls } (\textit{read} \land \textit{write}))$$

3.1.2   The *Modus Ponens* Rule

Another common rule is *Modus Ponens*:

$$\textit{Modus Ponens} \quad \frac{\varphi \qquad \varphi \supset \varphi'}{\varphi'}$$

This rule states that, if both the implication $\varphi_1 \supset \varphi_2$ and the formula φ_1 have been previously introduced, then we can also introduce the formula φ_2.

For example, if we have previously derived the two formulas

$$(\textit{Bill says sell}) \supset \textit{buy} \qquad \text{and} \qquad \textit{Bill says sell},$$

then we can use the *Modus Ponens* rule to also derive *buy*.

3.1.3   The *Says* Rule

The *Says* rule is defined as follows:

$$\textit{Says} \quad \frac{\varphi}{P \text{ says } \varphi}$$

Informally, this rule states that any principal can make any statement (or safely be assumed to have made any statement) that has already been derived. Thus, for example, if we have previously derived $(\textit{read} \land \textit{copy})$, then we can derive *Cara* says $(\textit{read} \land \textit{copy})$.

3.1.4   The *MP Says* Rule

The *MP Says* axiom serves as a version of modus ponens for statements made by principals:

$$\textit{MP Says} \quad \frac{}{(P \text{ says } (\varphi \supset \varphi')) \supset (P \text{ says } \varphi \supset P \text{ says } \varphi')}$$

In effect, this rule allows us to distribute the says operator over implications. For example, this axiom allows us to derive the following formula:

$$(\textit{Graham says } (\textit{sit} \supset \textit{eat})) \supset ((\textit{Graham says } \textit{sit}) \supset (\textit{Graham says } \textit{eat})).$$

3.1.5 The *Speaks For* Rule

The *Speaks For* axiom is defined as follows:

$$\textit{Speaks For} \quad \overline{P \Rightarrow Q \supset (P \text{ says } \varphi \supset Q \text{ says } \varphi)}$$

In effect, this rule captures our intuition about the speaks-for relation. It states that, if P speaks for Q, then any statements P makes should also be attributable to Q. For example, this axiom allows us to derive the following statement:

$$\textit{Del} \Rightarrow \textit{Ed} \supset ((\textit{Del} \text{ says } \textit{buy}) \supset (\textit{Ed} \text{ says } \textit{buy})).$$

Were we to subsequently to derive the formula $\textit{Del} \Rightarrow \textit{Ed}$, the *Modus Ponens* rule would let us also derive the formula

$$(\textit{Del} \text{ says } \textit{buy}) \supset (\textit{Ed} \text{ says } \textit{buy}).$$

3.1.6 The *& Says* and *Quoting* Rules

There are two rules that relate statements made by compound principals to those made by simple principals. The first of these is the *& Says* rule:

$$\textit{\& Says} \quad \overline{(P \text{ \& } Q \text{ says } \varphi) \equiv ((P \text{ says } \varphi) \wedge (Q \text{ says } \varphi))}$$

This rule reflects the conjunctive nature of a principal $P\&Q$: the statements made by the compound principal $P\&Q$ (i.e., P in conjunction with Q) are precisely those statements that both P and Q are willing to make individually. For example, the *& Says* rule allows us to derive the following formula:

$$(\textit{Faith} \text{ \& } \textit{Gale} \text{ says } \textit{sing}) \equiv ((\textit{Faith} \text{ says } \textit{sing}) \wedge (\textit{Gale} \text{ says } \textit{sing})).$$

The second such rule is the *Quoting* rule:

$$\textit{Quoting} \quad \overline{(P \mid Q \text{ says } \varphi) \equiv (P \text{ says } Q \text{ says } \varphi)}$$

This rule captures the underlying intuition behind the compound principal $P \mid Q$: the statements made by $P \mid Q$ (i.e., P quoting Q) are precisely those statements that P claims Q has made. As an example, here is an instance of the *Quoting* rule:

$$(\textit{Iona} \mid \textit{Jürgen} \text{ says } \textit{vote for Kory}) \equiv (\textit{Iona} \text{ says } \textit{Jürgen} \text{ says } \textit{vote for Kory}).$$

3.1.7 Properties of $\Rightarrow$

There are three rules that relate to properties of the $\Rightarrow$ relation, namely idempotency, transitivity, and monotonicity. These rules are all quite simple, but they are useful for analyzing situations that involve chains of principals speaking for one another.

The *Idempotency of* $\Rightarrow$ rule states that every principal speaks for itself:

$$\text{Idempotency of} \Rightarrow \quad \frac{}{P \Rightarrow P}$$

Thus, for example, with this rule we can derive the following formula:

$$Wallace \Rightarrow Wallace.$$

Although this rule may seem both obvious and unnecessary, it can be useful in conjunction with monotonicity to reason about quoting principals, as illustrated later in this subsection.

The *Transitivity of* $\Rightarrow$ rule supports reasoning about chains of principals that represent one another:

$$\text{Transitivity of} \Rightarrow \quad \frac{P \Rightarrow Q \qquad Q \Rightarrow R}{P \Rightarrow R}$$

This rule states that, if one principal speaks for a second and the second also speaks for a third, then it is also safe to view the first principal as speaking for the third principal. For example, if we have previously derived the two formulas

$$Kanda \Rightarrow Theo, \qquad Theo \Rightarrow Vance,$$

then the *Transitivity of* $\Rightarrow$ rule allows us to also derive

$$Kanda \Rightarrow Vance.$$

Finally, the *Monotonicity of* $\Rightarrow$ rule states that quoting principals preserve the speaks-for relationship:

$$\text{Monotonicity of} \Rightarrow \quad \frac{P \Rightarrow P' \quad Q \Rightarrow Q'}{P \mid Q \Rightarrow P' \mid Q'}$$

As an example, suppose that we have already derived the following two formulas:

$$Lowell \Rightarrow Minnie, \qquad Norma \Rightarrow Orson.$$

The *Monotonicity of* $\Rightarrow$ rule allows us to also derive the formula

$$Lowell \mid Norma \Rightarrow Minnie \mid Orson.$$

To see the utility of idempotency, consider the case where we have already derived the formula *Penny* $\Rightarrow$ *Ronald*, and we would like to derive that

$$Penny \mid Sylvester \Rightarrow Ronald \mid Sylvester.$$

By first using idempotency to derive *Sylvester* $\Rightarrow$ *Sylvester*, we can use monotonicity to derive the desired formula.

3.1.8   The *Equivalence* Rule

The *Equivalence* rule allows one to replace subformulas in a formula with equivalent subformulas:

$$\text{Equivalence} \quad \frac{\varphi_1 \equiv \varphi_2 \qquad \psi[\varphi_1/q]}{\psi[\varphi_2/q]}$$

To understand this rule, one must first understand the meta-notation $\psi[\varphi/q]$, which denotes the result of replacing every occurrence of the propositional variable q within the formula ψ by the formula φ. For example,

$$(t \supset (P \text{ says } (r \wedge t)))[Q \text{ says } s/t]$$

is simply the formula

$$(Q \text{ says } s) \supset (P \text{ says } (r \wedge Q \text{ says } s)).$$

Thus, the equivalence rule states that, if formulas φ_1 and φ_2 are equivalent, then every occurrence of φ_1 in a formula $\psi[\varphi_1/q]$ can be replaced by φ_2, resulting in the formula $\psi[\varphi_2/q]$. For example, suppose that we have already derived the following two formulas:

$$s \wedge t \equiv \textit{Tom} \text{ says } r, \qquad \textit{Arnie} \mid \textit{May} \text{ controls } (s \wedge t).$$

Because the latter formula is equivalent to $(\textit{Arnie} \mid \textit{May} \text{ controls } p)[(s \wedge t)/p]$, the *Equivalence* rule allows us to derive the formula

$$\textit{Arnie} \mid \textit{May} \text{ controls } (\textit{Tom} \text{ says } r).$$

In fact, by choosing ψ and the propositional variable q judiciously, one can also use the *Equivalence* rule to replace only some of the occurrences of φ_1 with φ_2. As an example, suppose that we have previously derived the following two formulas:

$$(t \supset r) \equiv P \text{ says } w, \qquad ((R \text{ says } (t \supset r)) \wedge (t \supset r)) \supset (T \mid R \text{ controls } (t \supset r)).$$

The latter formula can be obtained by any of the following substitutions (among others):

$$(((R \text{ says } (t \supset r)) \wedge q) \supset (T \mid R \text{ controls } (t \supset r)))[t \supset r/q]$$
$$(((R \text{ says } (t \supset r)) \wedge q) \supset (T \mid R \text{ controls } q))[t \supset r/q]$$
$$(((R \text{ says } q) \wedge q) \supset (T \mid R \text{ controls } q))[t \supset r/q].$$

Consequently, the *Equivalence* rule would allow us to derive *any* of the following formulas:

$$(((R \text{ says } (t \supset r)) \wedge q) \supset (T \mid R \text{ controls } (t \supset r)))[P \text{ says } w/q]$$
$$(((R \text{ says } (t \supset r)) \wedge q) \supset (T \mid R \text{ controls } q))[P \text{ says } w/q]$$
$$(((R \text{ says } q) \wedge q) \supset (T \mid R \text{ controls } q))[P \text{ says } w/q].$$

✎ **Exercise 3.1.1**   *Calculate the results of each of the following substitutions.*

  a. $((t \supset r) \vee (P \text{ says } r))[Q \text{ controls } t / r]$

  b. $w \supset P \text{ says } t[P \mid Q \text{ says } r / w]$

  c. $((s \wedge (Q \text{ says } s)) \supset Q \text{ says } p)[P \text{ says } q / s]$

  d. $((s \wedge (Q \text{ says } t)) \supset Q \text{ says } p)[P \text{ says } q / s]$

✎ **Exercise 3.1.2**   *For each pair of formulas* (φ, φ') *given below, give formulas* $\psi, \varphi_1, \varphi_2$ *such that* $\psi[\varphi_1/q]$ *is* φ *and* $\psi[\varphi_2/q]$ *is* φ'. *The formula* ψ *should represent as much shared structure as possible between* φ *and* φ', *allowing* φ_1 *and* φ_2 *to be as simple as possible.*

  a. $\varphi = (P \,\&\, Q \text{ says } (s \supset t)) \supset t$
     $\varphi' = (P \mid Q \text{ says } w) \supset t$

  b. $\varphi = (Q \text{ controls } (P \text{ controls } t)) \wedge (P \mid Q \text{ says } t)$
     $\varphi' = (Q \text{ controls } (P \text{ controls } t)) \wedge ((P \text{ controls } (Q \text{ controls } t)) \supset t)$

  c. $\varphi = ((R \text{ says } s) \wedge (Q \text{ says } R \text{ says } s)) \supset (Q \text{ controls } (R \text{ says } s))$
     $\varphi' = ((R \text{ says } s) \wedge (Q \text{ says } R \text{ says } t)) \supset (Q \text{ controls } (R \text{ says } t))$

  d. $\varphi = ((R \text{ says } s) \wedge (Q \text{ says } R \text{ says } s)) \supset (Q \text{ controls } (R \text{ says } s))$
     $\varphi' = ((T \text{ controls } w) \wedge (Q \text{ says } T \text{ controls } w)) \supset (Q \text{ controls } (T \text{ controls } w))$

3.1.9   The *Controls* Definition

Finally, the following definition[1] governs the use of controls in our logic:

$$P \text{ controls } \varphi \stackrel{\text{def}}{=} (P \text{ says } \varphi) \supset \varphi$$

This definition states that a formula of the form P controls φ is *syntactic sugar* for the longer expression $(P \text{ says } \varphi) \supset \varphi$. That is, controls doesn't give our logic any additional expressiveness, but it provides a useful way to make more explicit what will turn out to be a common idiom. This definition means that, any time we see an expression of form P controls φ, we can replace it by $(P \text{ says } \varphi) \supset \varphi$, and vice versa. This definition matches the semantics we defined for our logic in Section 2.3.2: we defined the meaning of P controls φ to be the meaning of $(P \text{ says } \varphi) \supset \varphi$.

As an example of the use of this definition, we can replace any occurrence of the formula *Lily* controls *read*—even within the context of a larger formula—by the

---

[1]Note that $\stackrel{\text{def}}{=}$ is meta-notation, rather than a part of the logic's syntax. The net effect, however, of this definition is the same as if we introduced an axiom stating P controls $\varphi \equiv ((P \text{ says } \varphi) \supset \varphi)$, in that either side of the definition may safely be replaced by the other in any formula.

FIGURE 3.3 A simple formal proof

1. *Al* says $(r \supset s)$	Assumption
2. *r*	Assumption
3. $(Al$ says $(r \supset s)) \supset (Al$ says $r \supset Al$ says $s)$	MP Says
4. *Al* says $r \supset Al$ says s	1,3 Modus Ponens
5. *Al* says *r*	2 Says
6. *Al* says *s*	4,5 Modus Ponens

FIGURE 3.4 A formal proof of the *Controls* rule

1. *P* controls φ	Assumption
2. *P* says φ	Assumption
3. $(P$ says $\varphi) \supset \varphi$	1 Def^n controls
4. φ	2,3 Modus Ponens

formula $(Lily$ says $read) \supset read$, and vice versa. Thus, for example, the *Controls* definition allows us to replace the formula

$$Manny \text{ says } (Lily \text{ controls } read)$$

by the formula

$$Manny \text{ says } ((Lily \text{ says } read) \supset read).$$

3.2   Formal Proofs and Theorems

A *formal proof* is a sequence of statements of the logic, where each statement is either an assumption or a statement that can be derived by applying one of the inference rules (or definitions) to previous statements in that sequence. It is customary to sequentially number each of these statements, and to label them either with "Assumption" or with the statement numbers and inference-rule name by which it was deduced. In this book, we will always place all assumptions at the beginning of the proof, so that it is quick and easy to determine the premises upon which a conclusion depends.

For example, Figure 3.3 presents a simple formal proof. In this case, only the first two statements in the proof are assumptions; every other statement is either an instance of axiom (e.g., Step 3) or a consequence of applying one of the inference rules. As another simple example, Figure 3.4 demonstrates how the definition of the controls operator can be used in a formal proof.

Every formal proof represents a *theorem*, which is really just a derived inference rule. Specifically, if the only assumptions of the formal proof are statements

$H_1, \ldots H_k$, and if the final statement of the proof is C, then the proof corresponds to a derived inference rule with the following form:

$$\frac{H_1 \quad \cdots \quad H_k}{C}.$$

Thus, the formal proofs in Figure 3.3 and Figure 3.4 correspond respectively to the following two derived theorems[2]:

$$\frac{Al \text{ says } (r \supset s) \quad r}{Al \text{ says } s} \qquad \frac{P \text{ controls } \varphi \quad P \text{ says } \varphi}{\varphi}.$$

These theorems can now be used as additional inference rules in any future proof, without affecting that proof's validity. We shall find the latter derived rule very useful in subsequent chapters, and hence we give it a specific name (*Controls*). In fact, there are several derived rules—some from propositional logic and others related to access control—that we will find convenient to have in our arsenal. For easy reference, we summarize those rules (along with *Controls*) in Figure 3.5, leaving most of their proofs as exercises for the reader. However, Figure 3.6 gives a proof for the *Conjunction* rule, which also demonstrates the general form for many of the other proofs.

✎ **Exercise 3.2.1**   *Give a formal proof of the Hypothetical Syllogism derived rule from Figure 3.5.*

✎ **Exercise 3.2.2**   *Technically speaking, the Equivalence rule given in Figure 3.1 permits replacements in only direction: having deduced $\varphi_1 \equiv \varphi_2$, one can replace occurrences of φ_1 in a formula by φ_2, but not vice versa.*

   Give a formal proof of the following derived rule which permits replacements in the opposite direction[3]:

$$\frac{\varphi_1 \equiv \varphi_2 \quad \psi[\varphi_2/q]}{\psi[\varphi_1/q]}.$$

✎ **Exercise 3.2.3**   *Give a formal proof for the* Derived Speaks For *rule given in Figure 3.5.*

✎ **Exercise 3.2.4**   *Give a formal proof for the* Derived Controls *rule given in Figure 3.5.*

✎ **Exercise 3.2.5**   *Give a formal proof for the* Says Simplification *derived rules given in Figure 3.5.*

✎ **Exercise 3.2.6**   *Give a formal proof for the following derivable inference rule:*

---

[2]Technically, the proof of Figure 3.4 is a *proof schema* that represents a *theorem schema*, in that P and φ are *meta-variables* that range over (respectively) all possible principal expressions and formulas. Thus, it provides a recipe for any particular instances of P and φ. In this book, we shall blur the distinction between proofs and proof schemas, as well as theorems and theorem schemas.

[3]Henceforth in this book, we shall not distinguish between these two versions of *Equivalence*.

FIGURE 3.5 Some useful derived rules

$$\text{Conjunction} \quad \frac{\varphi_1 \qquad \varphi_2}{\varphi_1 \wedge \varphi_2}$$

$$\text{Simplification (1)} \quad \frac{\varphi_1 \wedge \varphi_2}{\varphi_1} \qquad\qquad \text{Simplification (2)} \quad \frac{\varphi_1 \wedge \varphi_2}{\varphi_2}$$

$$\text{Disjunction (1)} \quad \frac{\varphi_1}{\varphi_1 \vee \varphi_2} \qquad\qquad \text{Disjunction (2)} \quad \frac{\varphi_2}{\varphi_1 \vee \varphi_2}$$

$$\text{Modus Tollens} \quad \frac{\varphi_1 \supset \varphi_2 \qquad \neg\varphi_2}{\neg\varphi_1} \qquad\qquad \text{Double negation} \quad \frac{\neg\neg\varphi}{\varphi}$$

$$\text{Disjunctive Syllogism} \quad \frac{\varphi_1 \vee \varphi_2 \qquad \neg\varphi_1}{\varphi_2} \qquad\qquad \text{Hypothetical Syllogism} \quad \frac{\varphi_1 \supset \varphi_2 \qquad \varphi_2 \supset \varphi_3}{\varphi_1 \supset \varphi_3}$$

$$\text{Controls} \quad \frac{P \text{ controls } \varphi \quad P \text{ says } \varphi}{\varphi}$$

$$\text{Derived Speaks For} \quad \frac{P \Rightarrow Q \quad P \text{ says } \varphi}{Q \text{ says } \varphi} \qquad\qquad \text{Derived Controls} \quad \frac{P \Rightarrow Q \quad Q \text{ controls } \varphi}{P \text{ controls } \varphi}$$

$$\text{Says Simplification (1)} \quad \frac{P \text{ says } (\varphi_1 \wedge \varphi_2)}{P \text{ says } \varphi_1} \qquad\qquad \text{Says Simplification (2)} \quad \frac{P \text{ says } (\varphi_1 \wedge \varphi_2)}{P \text{ says } \varphi_2}$$

FIGURE 3.6 A formal proof of *Conjunction*

1. φ_1		Assumption
2. φ_2		Assumption
3. $\varphi_1 \supset (\varphi_2 \supset (\varphi_1 \wedge \varphi_2))$		Taut
4. $\varphi_2 \supset (\varphi_1 \wedge \varphi_2)$		1,3 Modus Ponens
5. $\varphi_1 \wedge \varphi_2$		2,4 Modus Ponens

$$\frac{P \text{ says } \varphi_1 \quad P \Rightarrow Q}{Q \text{ says } (\varphi_2 \supset \varphi_1)}.$$

✎ **Exercise 3.2.7**   *Give a formal proof for the following derivable inference rule:*

$$\frac{P \text{ says } (Q \text{ controls } \varphi) \quad P \mid Q \text{ says } \varphi}{P \text{ says } \varphi}.$$

✎ **Exercise 3.2.8**   *Give a formal proof for the following derivable inference rule:*

$$\frac{(P \mid Q) \text{ controls } \varphi \quad R \Rightarrow Q \quad P \text{ says } R \text{ says } \varphi}{\varphi}.$$

3.3   Soundness of Logical Rules

The rules presented in Section 3.1 are merely rules for manipulating formulas. Up to this point, we have no reason to believe in their *logical consistency*, which makes using them a risky prospect. To show that the inference rules are consistent, we must first use the Kripke-structure semantics to prove their *soundness*.

Specifically, an inference rule

$$\frac{H_1 \quad \cdots \quad H_k}{C}$$

is *sound* with respect to the Kripke semantics provided that, whenever a Kripke structure $\mathcal{M}$ satisfies all of the rule's hypotheses (i.e., $H_1, \ldots H_k$), it also satisfies the rule's consequent. It follows that an inference rule is *not sound* if there exists even just a single Kripke structure $\mathcal{M} = \langle W, I, J \rangle$ such that, for each H_i, $\mathcal{M} \models H_i$ and yet $\mathcal{M} \not\models C$.

We now use the Kripke semantics given in Figure 2.1 to prove the soundness of the inference rules *Taut*, *Modus Ponens*, and *Says*; we also provide a proof sketch for the soundness of *Equivalence*. The proofs of soundness for the remaining rules are left as exercises for the reader.

Example 3.1 (Soundness of Taut)

Let φ be an instance of a propositional-logic tautology ψ. We need to show that, for every Kripke structure $\mathcal{M} = \langle W, I, J \rangle$, φ is true in every world in W (i.e., $\mathcal{E}_{\mathcal{M}}[\![\varphi]\!] = W$).

Let $\mathcal{M}_a = \langle W_a, I_a, J_a \rangle$ be an arbitrary Kripke structure. Because φ is an instance of ψ, there exist propositional variables $p_1, \ldots, p_k$ and modal formulas $\varphi_1, \ldots, \varphi_k$ such that φ is obtained from ψ by replacing each p_i by φ_i. Without loss of generality, we assume that the variables $p_1, \ldots, p_k$ do not appear in φ.

We now construct a new model $\mathcal{M}' = \langle W_a, I', J_a \rangle$, where I' is defined as follows: for each p_i $(1 \le i \le k)$, $I'(p_i) = \mathcal{E}_{\mathcal{M}_a}[\![\varphi_i]\!]$; for all other propositional variables q, $I'(q) = I(q)$. Thus, for each $1 \le i \le k$,

$$\mathcal{E}_{\mathcal{M}'}[\![p_i]\!] = \mathcal{E}_{\mathcal{M}_a}[\![\varphi_i]\!];$$

likewise, for all other propositional variables q,

$$\mathcal{E}_{\mathcal{M}'}[\![q]\!] = \mathcal{E}_{\mathcal{M}_a}[\![q]\!].$$

From these facts, it is straightforward to show by induction on the structure of ψ that

$$\mathcal{E}_{\mathcal{M}'}[\![\psi]\!] = \mathcal{E}_{\mathcal{M}_a}[\![\varphi]\!].$$

Because ψ is a propositional-logic tautology, ψ is true in all worlds, independent of the interpretation of its propositional variables. Therefore, $\mathcal{E}_{\mathcal{M}'}[\![\psi]\!] = W_a$, and thus $\mathcal{E}_{\mathcal{M}_a}[\![\varphi]\!] = W_a$ as well.

Because $\mathcal{M}_a$ was arbitrary, we have shown that the *Taut* rule is sound. $\Diamond$

Example 3.2 (Soundness of Modus Ponens)

To prove that the *Modus Ponens* inference rule is sound, we must prove the following, for all formulas φ and φ', and for all Kripke structures $\mathcal{M} = \langle W, I, J \rangle$:

If $\mathcal{M} \models \varphi$ and $\mathcal{M} \models \varphi \supset \varphi'$, then $\mathcal{M} \models \varphi'$.

That is, we need to show that, whenever $\mathcal{E}_{\mathcal{M}}[\![\varphi]\!] = W$ and $\mathcal{E}_{\mathcal{M}}[\![\varphi \supset \varphi']\!] = W$, it is also the case that $\mathcal{E}_{\mathcal{M}}[\![\varphi']\!] = W$.

Therefore, we consider an arbitrary model $\mathcal{M}_a = \langle W_a, I_a, J_a \rangle$ for which $\mathcal{E}_{\mathcal{M}_a}[\![\varphi]\!] = W_a$ and $\mathcal{E}_{\mathcal{M}_a}[\![\varphi \supset \varphi']\!] = W_a$, and we will show that $\mathcal{E}_{\mathcal{M}_a}[\![\varphi']\!] = W_a$ necessarily follows. Working straight from the definition of the evaluation functions $\mathcal{E}_{\mathcal{M}}[\![-]\!]$ given in Figure 2.1, we see that

$$\begin{aligned} \mathcal{E}_{\mathcal{M}_a}[\![\varphi \supset \varphi']\!] &= (W_a - \mathcal{E}_{\mathcal{M}_a}[\![\varphi]\!]) \cup \mathcal{E}_{\mathcal{M}_a}[\![\varphi']\!] \\ &= (W_a - W_a) \cup \mathcal{E}_{\mathcal{M}_a}[\![\varphi']\!] \\ &= \mathcal{E}_{\mathcal{M}_a}[\![\varphi']\!]. \end{aligned}$$

Thus, $\mathcal{E}_{\mathcal{M}_a}[\![\varphi']\!] = \mathcal{E}_{\mathcal{M}_a}[\![\varphi \supset \varphi']\!] = W_a$. Because $\mathcal{M}_a$ was arbitrary, we have shown that the *Modus Ponens* rule is sound. $\Diamond$

Example 3.3 (Soundness of Says)

To prove that the inference rule *Says* is sound, we must prove the following, for all Kripke structures $\mathcal{M} = \langle W, I, J \rangle$:

If $\mathcal{M} \models \varphi$, then (for all principals P) $\mathcal{M} \models P$ says φ.

That is, we need to show that whenever $\mathcal{E}_{\mathcal{M}}[\![\varphi]\!] = W$, it is also the case that (for every principal P) $\mathcal{E}_{\mathcal{M}}[\![P \text{ says } \varphi]\!] = W$.

As before, we start by considering an arbitrary Kripke structure $\mathcal{M}_a = \langle W_a, I_a, J_a \rangle$ that satisfies the formula φ (i.e., for which $\mathcal{E}_{\mathcal{M}_a}[\![\varphi]\!] = W_a$). We also let Q be an arbitrary principal. From the semantic definitions of Figure 2.1, we see that

$$\mathcal{E}_{\mathcal{M}_a}[\![Q \text{ says } \varphi]\!] = \{w \mid J_a(Q)(w) \subseteq \mathcal{E}_{\mathcal{M}_a}[\![\varphi]\!]\} = \{w \mid J_a(Q)(w) \subseteq W_a\}.$$

Because $J_a(Q)$ is by definition a subset of $W_a \times W_a$, every $w' \in W_a$ satisfies the constraint that $J_a(Q)(w') \subseteq W_a$, and thus $\mathcal{E}_{\mathcal{M}_a}[\![Q \text{ says } \varphi]\!] = W_a$. Because both Q and $\mathcal{M}_a$ were arbitrary, we have shown that the *Says* inference rule is sound.   ◇

Example 3.4 (Soundness of Equivalence)

To prove that the inference rule *Equivalence* is sound, we must prove the following, for all formulas $\varphi_1, \varphi_2, \psi$, propositional variables q, and Kripke structures $\mathcal{M} = \langle W, I, J \rangle$:

If $\mathcal{M} \models \varphi_1 \equiv \varphi_2$ and $\mathcal{M} \models \psi[\varphi_1/q]$, then $\mathcal{M} \models \psi[\varphi_2/q]$.

That is, we need to show that whenever $\mathcal{E}_{\mathcal{M}}[\![\varphi_1 \equiv \varphi_2]\!] = W$ and $\mathcal{E}_{\mathcal{M}}[\![\psi[\varphi_1/q]]\!] = W$, it is also the case that $\mathcal{E}_{\mathcal{M}}[\![\psi[\varphi_2/q]]\!] = W$.

The proof proceeds by a straightforward induction on the structure of ψ, using the fact from Exercise 2.3.9 that $\mathcal{E}_{\mathcal{M}}[\![\varphi_1]\!] = \mathcal{E}_{\mathcal{M}}[\![\varphi_2]\!]$ whenever $\mathcal{E}_{\mathcal{M}}[\![\varphi_1 \equiv \varphi_2]\!] = W$.   ◇

Exercise 3.3.1   *Prove the soundness of the Speaks For inference rule.*

Exercise 3.3.2   *Prove the soundness of the & Says inference rule. (Hint: Exercise 2.3.9 is useful here.)*

Exercise 3.3.3   *Prove the soundness of the Quoting inference rule. (Hint: Exercise 2.3.9 is useful here.)*

Exercise 3.3.4   *Prove the soundness of the Transitivity of $\Rightarrow$ inference rule.*

Exercise 3.3.5   *Prove the soundness of the Monotonicity of $\Rightarrow$ inference rule.*

Exercise 3.3.6   *Consider the following formula, which intuitively states that every principal has the jurisdiction to select its own proxies:*

$$(P \text{ says } (Q \Rightarrow P)) \supset (Q \Rightarrow P).$$

Prove that this formula would not make for a sound axiom. That is, find a particular Kripke structure $\mathcal{M} = \langle W, I, J \rangle$ such that

$$\mathcal{M} \not\models (P \text{ says } (Q \Rightarrow P)) \supset (Q \Rightarrow P).$$

Exercise 3.3.7 *Consider the following formula, which intuitively states that* controls *distributes over conjunction:*

$$(P \text{ controls } (\varphi_1 \wedge \varphi_2)) \equiv ((P \text{ controls } \varphi_1) \wedge (P \text{ controls } \varphi_2)).$$

Prove that this formula would not make for a sound axiom. That is, find particular formulas φ_1, φ_2 *and a particular Kripke structure* $\mathcal{M} = \langle W, I, J \rangle$ *such that*

$$\mathcal{M} \not\models (P \text{ controls } (\varphi_1 \wedge \varphi_2)) \equiv ((P \text{ controls } \varphi_1) \wedge (P \text{ controls } \varphi_2)).$$

Exercise 3.3.8 *Consider the following plausible inference rule:*

$$\frac{P \, \& \, Q \text{ controls } \varphi \qquad P \text{ says } \varphi}{Q \text{ controls } \varphi}.$$

Determine whether or not this rule is sound, *and justify your answer:*

- *If you determine that the rule is sound, prove its soundness.*

- *If you determine that the rule is not sound, give (and explain) a particular Kripke structure, principals P and Q, and formula* φ *that demonstrate the lack of soundness.*

Exercise 3.3.9 *Consider the following plausible inference rule:*

$$\frac{P \Rightarrow R \quad R \Rightarrow Q}{R \text{ says } \varphi \equiv P \, \& \, Q \text{ says } \varphi}.$$

Determine whether or not this rule is sound, *and justify your answer:*

- *If you determine that the rule is sound, prove its soundness.*

- *If you determine that the rule is not sound, give (and explain) a particular Kripke structure, principals P, Q, R and formula* φ *that demonstrate the lack of soundness.*

Exercise 3.3.10 *Consider the following plausible inference rule:*

$$\frac{P \Rightarrow Q \qquad Q \Rightarrow P}{P \text{ says } \varphi \equiv Q \text{ says } \varphi}.$$

Determine whether or not this rule is sound, *and justify your answer:*

- *If you determine that the rule is sound, prove its soundness.*

- *If you determine that the rule is not sound, give (and explain) a particular Kripke structure, principals P, Q, R and formula* φ *that demonstrate the lack of soundness.*

Exercise 3.3.11　*Consider the following plausible inference rule:*

$$\frac{P \text{ controls } (\varphi_1 \wedge \varphi_2)}{P \text{ controls } \varphi_1}.$$

Determine whether or not this rule is sound, *and justify your answer:*

- *If you determine that the rule is sound, prove its soundness.*

- *If you determine that the rule is not sound, give (and explain) a particular Kripke structure, principals P, Q, R and formula φ that demonstrate the lack of soundness.*

3.4　Summary

As seen in the previous chapter, Kripke structures provide precise meanings for the statements of the access-control logic. However, reasoning at the level of Kripke structures is extremely cumbersome. Furthermore, it is not always possible to know which Kripke structures accurately represent a particular situation.

To avoid the necessity of reasoning about particular structures, we introduced a collection of inference rules that are *sound*. The Kripke-structure semantics provide the basis for guaranteeing this soundness. The benefits of reasoning with sound inference rules include the convenience they provide as well as the guarantee they provide: any situation that satisfies the initial assumptions is guaranteed to satisfy the deduced consequences. We therefore have a basis for answering the question "Should this access-control request be granted?", as well as an explicit accounting for all assumptions on which the analysis depends.

The learning outcomes associated with this chapter appear in Figure 3.7.

3.5　Further Reading

The inference rules of the access-control logic are based on the semantics presented in the previous chapter. Our semantics is similar to the logic of Abadi, Lampson, and colleagues (Lampson et al., 1992; Abadi et al., 1993). The notion of soundness based on Kripke models is part of standard modal logic. The reader can consult Hughes and Cresswell (Hughes and Cresswell, 1996) for more on this subject.

FIGURE 3.7 Learning outcomes for Chapter 3

After completing this chapter, you should be able to achieve the following learning outcomes at several levels of knowledge:

Analysis

- When given a set of assumptions and a goal that logically follows from those assumptions, you should be able to give a formal proof of that goal.

Synthesis

- When given a sound axiom or inference rule for the access-control logic, you should be able to prove its soundness in the underlying Kripke model.

- When given a potential inference rule for the access-control logic that is *not sound*, you should be able to construct a Kripke structure that demonstrates its lack of soundness.

Evaluation

- When given a theory, inference rules, and a proof, you should be able to judge if the proof is correct.

- When given a proposed inference rule, you should be able to judge whether or not it is sound.

Chapter 4

Basic Concepts

In the preceding two chapters, we introduced a modal logic that we will use throughout this book to describe and reason about various aspects of access control. This access-control logic and its collection of inference rules provide a rigorous and formal basis for answering the question "Should this request be granted?"

In learning any language for the first time, it's important to start using the language to describe objects and concepts of interest to us. We begin this chapter by introducing the concept of a reference monitor, which provides a context for the remainder of this chapter. We then develop the fundamental access-control concepts of tickets, capabilities, and access-control lists. We also discuss various authentication mechanisms and how they relate to access control. Throughout this chapter, there are numerous examples to illustrate how the access-control logic is used.

4.1 Reference Monitors

Access control is about guarding objects, assets, resources, services, communications, files, databases, information, or people. In everyday life, physical locks of various forms guard against unauthorized access to all sorts of resources, ranging from house doors and high-school lockers to automobile ignitions and safety-deposit boxes. In other situations, a person or machine may require us to provide an artifact (e.g., subway token or bus pass) to gain access to particular resources. For example, we need a boarding pass to get on a bus, train, or airplane. We need to have a ticket before we can get in to see a movie. If we are invited to a formal dinner such as a wedding reception, there may be a guest list and name cards at each seat in the banquet hall.

In computer and information systems, the guards are called *reference monitors*, and they protect resources such as memory, files, databases, programs, and communication channels. Figure 4.1 provides an abstract view of how a reference monitor fits into a system. Initially, a principal—either a person, machine, or process—makes a request to the reference monitor to perform some operation on a protected object. Principals that make requests are often referred to as *subjects*, and the right to perform an operation on an object is typically called an *access right* or *privilege*. The reference monitor's decision regarding whether or not to grant the request depends on

FIGURE 4.1 Abstract view of reference monitors

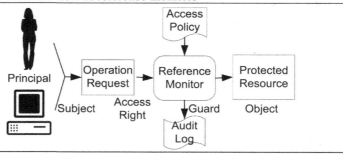

several factors: what is being asked for, potentially the identity and other attributes of the subject making the request, and finally the access policy. When a decision is made, it is recorded in an audit log where a record of all the access requests and decisions are kept.

All reference monitors must satisfy three essential properties:

1. *Completeness:* The reference monitor cannot be bypassed.

   Completeness means that there is no way to access a protected resource without coming under the scrutiny of the guard or reference monitor. Physically, completeness means that there is no "hole in the fence." In information systems, completeness means that all paths to a state in which access is granted go through an access controller.

2. *Isolation:* The reference monitor is tamper proof.

   Isolation is primarily satisfied by physical protection mechanisms. For example, machines on which sensitive information is stored must be housed in locked and guarded machine rooms where access to the machine rooms is constantly watched.

3. *Verifiable:* The reference monitor is correctly implemented.

   The property of being verified correct means that we must have fully and precisely specified what the reference monitor is supposed to do.

Conceptually, the desired access-control behavior of a system can be easily represented by *an access-control matrix*, as introduced by Lampson (Lampson, 1971). The rows of an access-control matrix M are labeled by possible subjects (i.e., principals), while the columns are labeled by the protected objects. Each entry $M_{s,o}$ in the matrix indicates the access rights that subject s possesses with respect to the object o. As an example, Table 4.1 contains a simple access-control matrix for a system involving three subjects (with identifiers alice, bob, carol) and four protected objects (files numbered 1 through 4). According to this table, the principal alice has the rights to read $file_1$, to read or write $file_2$, and to execute $file_4$; alice has no

	file$_1$	file$_2$	file$_3$	file$_4$
`alice`	read	read, write		execute
`bob`		read	execute	
`carol`	read, write		execute	execute

Table 4.1: Example of an access-control matrix

access rights for *file$_3$*. In contrast, `bob` has no access rights for *file$_1$* or *file$_4$*, but can read *file$_2$* and execute *file$_3$*.

When assigning rights to principals, it is wise to follow the *principle of least privilege* (Saltzer and Schroeder, 1975): principals should be assigned only the rights necessary for completing their tasks and no more.

Access-control matrices provide a very simple and straightforward way to describe systems, particularly those that have relatively small numbers of subjects and objects. However, they alone are insufficient for reasoning about access control in more complex systems that involve large numbers of subjects and objects or that permit proxies and delegation. In particular, they do not address issues related to how subjects are authenticated or the trust assumptions that underlie the authentication process.

The purpose of the access-control logic is to bridge this gap, to help us to deduce and to specify what a reference monitor's behavior should be for any given policy and request. From a logical point of view, a reference monitor decides whether or not to approve an access request based on the inference rules of the access-control logic and within the context of an access policy and trust assumptions.

As we have already seen, we can use the logic to describe a subject's request to access a particular object as follows:

Subject says ⟨*access right, object*⟩.

To grant the request, the reference monitor must be able to determine that the access policy authorizes the subject to perform the requested operation. In terms of the logic, this determination amounts to using the inference rules of the logic to derive the atomic proposition

⟨*access right, object*⟩

from assumptions about the given policy and any additional trust assumptions that are relevant to the situation.

Policy statements state who or what has jurisdiction over certain statements, as well as who or what is authorized with certain rights. These statements usually take the form

P controls φ,

where *P* is the authority and φ is the statement over which *P* has jurisdiction.

Trust assumptions are usually assumptions about proxies or symbols of authority, such as the queen's seal, a principal's public key, or tickets issued by an airline.

These statements usually have the form

$$P \Rightarrow Q,$$

where P is the recognized proxy for principal Q. As we will see in the subsequent sections, these statements express explicitly the reference monitor's reliance on the unforgeability of certificates and credentials.

A *certificate* is a signed statement made by a recognized authority, such as a birth certificate (signed perhaps by a town's health department) or a driver's license (signed by a state department of motor vehicles). A *credential* is a certificate that asserts a particular principal's authorization to perform some action; for example, a driver's license asserts a given driver's authorization to drive a certain class of vehicle.

The next section develops the specifics of requests, policy statements, and trust assumptions within the context of tickets and access-control lists. Subsequent sections introduce the notions of certificates and credentials, particularly as they apply to both identity-based and group-based authentication.

4.2   Access-Control Mechanisms: Tickets and Lists

As we have already seen, reference monitors guard those objects deemed necessary to protect. There are two common protection schemes employed by reference monitors: one is based on *tickets* (or *capabilities*), while the other depends on *access-control lists*.

Tickets signify a *capability* to access a resource. For example, a ticket to a movie theater grants the holder of a theater ticket access to a seat in a particular theater at a particular time. Tickets are presumed to be unforgeable—only the appropriate controlling authorities are able to issue tickets. In ticket-oriented protection schemes, principals possess tickets for the resources or objects to which they have access. Principals gain access to protected resources or objects by presenting the appropriate ticket to the reference monitors protecting those resources.

In list-oriented protection schemes, an *access-control list* has the names of principals who are allowed to access the resource being protected. An example application of access-control lists is a restaurant where patrons are seated at dining tables only if they have a reservation. The access-control list itself must also be protected: that is, only certain principals are recognized to have the authority to adjust whose names appear on the access-control list.

In this section, we formalize the concepts of tickets and access-control lists using the access-control logic.

4.2.1   Tickets

Tickets are a common means to control access to protected objects. For example, when airline passengers prepare to board an airplane, the gate agents check each passenger's ticket or boarding pass to see if the person presenting the ticket is authorized to board the airplane. The gate agents are the reference monitors guarding access to the airplane's doors. The boarding pass signifies the capability to access a particular flight. Ideally, it is an unforgeable document issued by the airline (i.e., the controlling authority) granting permission to board a particular airplane at a particular time.

In general, ticket-oriented access control requires the following four components, which we express as statements in the logic:

1. The access policy:

$$authority \text{ controls } (subject \text{ controls } \langle access\ right,\ object \rangle)$$

The policy statement asserts that the controlling authority has jurisdiction over which subjects can exercise an access right on an object.

2. The ticket:

$$ticket \text{ says } (subject \text{ controls } \langle access\ right,\ object \rangle)$$

A ticket is a credential stating that the subject has the right to access a particular object.

3. Additional trust assumption:

$$ticket \Rightarrow authority$$

This assumption states that tickets are tokens of authority issued by the controlling authority. As such, it is imperative that these tokens or tickets be unforgeable.

4. The access request:

$$subject \text{ says } \langle access\ right,\ object \rangle$$

The access request occurs when the subject actually presents the ticket. For example, an airline passenger presenting a ticket is requesting to sit at her assigned seat on the designated flight. Of course, a subject may request access without actually presenting a ticket, but the reference monitor should not grant access in that case. For example, a person in the air terminal who tries to board an airplane without presenting a valid ticket should not be allowed to do so.

Together, these four components provide sufficient information for the reference monitor to determine that the requested action $\langle access\ right,\ object \rangle$ should be permitted. If we generalize the atomic proposition $\langle access\ right,\ object \rangle$ to an arbitrary

FIGURE 4.2 Formal proof of the Ticket Rule

1. *subject* says φ	Access request
2. *authority* controls (*subject* controls φ)	Access policy
3. *ticket* ⇒ *authority*	Trust assumption
4. *ticket* says (*subject* controls φ)	Ticket
5. *authority* says (*subject* controls φ)	3, 4 speaks for
6. *subject* controls φ	2, 5 controls
7. φ	6, 1 controls

statement φ, we can derive the following useful inference rule:

$$Ticket \; \frac{subject \text{ says } \varphi \quad authority \text{ controls } (subject \text{ controls } \varphi)}{\varphi} \quad \frac{ticket \Rightarrow authority \quad ticket \text{ says } (subject \text{ controls } \varphi)}{}.$$

The formal proof of this rule appears in Figure 4.2. The next example illustrates how the Ticket Rule applies to the airline-ticket scenario.

Example 4.1
Suppose Tina has an airplane ticket assigning her to seat 25D on Smooth Air Flight #1. When her row is called, she presents her ticket to the gate agents for flight #1, and she is granted access.

The following analysis justifies the decision by the gate agents to let Tina board the airplane:

1. Tina says ⟨seat 25D, flight #1⟩	Tina's request
2. Smooth Air controls (Tina controls ⟨seat 25D, flight #1⟩)	Access policy
3. ticket ⇒ Smooth Air	Trust assumption
4. ticket says (Tina controls ⟨seat 25D, flight #1⟩)	Tina's ticket
5. ⟨seat 25D, flight #1⟩	1, 2, 3, 4 ticket rule

Line 1 represents Tina's request to board flight #1 and sit in seat 25D, which happens when Tina walks up to the gate agent and presents her ticket. Line 2 indicates that the gate agent recognizes Smooth Air's authority over which subjects can access flight #1. Line 3 states that tickets represent the authority of Smooth Air; that is, the gate agent assumes that Smooth Air will issue tickets only to people who should be passengers on flight #1. Implicit in this line is that the gate agent recognizes the ticket as being a valid ticket issued by Smooth Air. For example, if Tina were to present a piece of notebook paper that has her name and a seat assignment scribbled on it, the gate agent would not accept that paper as representing the authority of Smooth Air.

Line 4 describes what the ticket says, namely that Tina is assigned to seat 25D on flight #1. Line 5—which is obtained from the previous lines through the Ticket Rule—demonstrates that the gate agent's decision to allow Tina to board flight #1 is justified, given the previous conditions.   ◊

In the preceding example, the boarding pass really is a ticket in the technical sense: the gate agent checks only the validity of the boarding pass and does not confirm Tina's identity. Most likely, anyone who handed Tina's valid boarding pass to the gate agent would be allowed on the plane, regardless of their actual identity.

✎ **Exercise 4.2.1** *Suppose a theater ticket is sold by the box office to a patron to see* Gone with the Wind *in Theater 5 at 7:30 p.m. Using the access-control logic, describe the patron's request, the access-control policy of the theater, the trust assumptions, and movie ticket. Based on your descriptions, formally justify admitting the patron to see the movie.*

4.2.2 Lists

Another widely used access-control mechanism is a *list* of principals with their access rights to protected objects. These lists are known as *access-control lists* (ACLs).

In access-control list schemes, reference monitors possess the list of authorized users and their privileges. Principals identify themselves and make their requests to access the protected resources. The reference monitor compares the request to the access-control list: if there is a match, then access is granted. Unlike ticket-oriented access control, principals do not possess a credential that says they have a right to access a protected resource.

ACLs are a very common protection mechanism. For example, if a scientist wants to visit a secure government or commercial facility, she must call ahead to ensure that the guards at the gates of the facility have her name on a visitor's list. When she arrives at the gate, she identifies herself to the guard, who checks her identity and looks to see if she is on the guest list. If her name is on the list, then she is allowed into the facility. A more benign but common example is a wedding or formal party where a greeter (acting as the reference monitor) checks off guest names on a guest list.

In general, protection schemes involving access-control lists require the following components:

1. Access policy:

$$\textit{authority} \ \textsf{controls} \ (\textit{subject} \ \textsf{controls} \ \langle \textit{access right, object} \rangle)$$

The guard or reference monitor recognizes the jurisdiction of some controlling authority to decide who is allowed what access to the protected object.

2. Access-control list:

$$\textit{ACL} \ \textsf{says} \left\{ \begin{array}{l} \textit{subject}_1 \ \textsf{controls} \ \langle \textit{access right}_1, \textit{object}_1 \rangle \wedge \\ \textit{subject}_2 \ \textsf{controls} \ \langle \textit{access right}_2, \textit{object}_2 \rangle \wedge \\ \cdots \wedge \\ \textit{subject}_n \ \textsf{controls} \ \langle \textit{access right}_n, \textit{object}_n \rangle \end{array} \right.$$

An ACL is essentially a listing of subjects and their access rights.

3. Trust assumption:

$$ACL \Rightarrow authority$$

This assumption states that the ACL *always* reflects the wishes of the authority. As is the case with tickets, it is imperative that the ACL's integrity be assured.

4. Access request:

$$subject \text{ says } \langle access\ right,\ object \rangle$$

The request occurs when the subject presents herself to the guard (who can establish her identity, as necessary) and makes the request.

With the exception of the form of the access-control list, these components are the same as those for tickets. Authorities determine who has access, and trust assumptions are needed to interpret statements from authority. It is within this context that subjects' requests are considered.

The only difference is in the statements directly associated with the ticket and with the access-control list. A ticket associates a specific subject with a specific authorization:

$$ticket \text{ says } (subject_i \text{ controls } \varphi_i)$$

In contrast, an access-control list associates many subjects with many authorizations, having the following general form:

$$ACL \text{ says } \begin{cases} subject_1 \text{ controls } \varphi_1\ \wedge \\ \cdots \\ subject_i \text{ controls } \varphi_i\ \wedge \\ \cdots \end{cases}$$

However, it is possible to extract from an access-control list the relevant authorization, using the *Says Simplification* rules introduced in Exercise 3.2.5:

$$\frac{P \text{ says } (\varphi_1 \wedge \varphi_2)}{P \text{ says } \varphi_1} \qquad \frac{P \text{ says } (\varphi_1 \wedge \varphi_2)}{P \text{ says } \varphi_2}$$

Using a combination of these two rules, we can extract (for any i)

$$ACL \text{ says } (subject_i \text{ controls } \varphi_i)$$

from the access-control list description.

It is therefore possible to use the *Ticket Rule* to also reason about access-control lists. The following example is an illustration.

Example 4.2

Suppose Erika is invited to a dinner meeting where delicate negotiations are to be held. Because of the sensitive nature of the talks, the meeting is being held in a private dining room. At the door of the dining room is a maître d' with a guest list of all the attendees. The guest list, which was authorized by the restaurant's manager, has three names: Erika, Darnell, and Gina.

To gain entry to the dining room, Erika identifies herself to the maître d' and he lets her in. For simplicity, we will assume that the maître d' recognizes Erika, Darnell, and Gina by sight, so that no further identification is needed. (We will consider more realistic and complicated situations later in this chapter.). The following analysis justifies the decision of the maître d' to let Erika into the private dining room:

1. Erika says ⟨enter, dining room⟩	Erika's request
2. Manager controls (Erika controls ⟨enter, dining room⟩)	Access policy
3. ACL ⇒ Manager	Trust assumption
4. ACL says $\begin{cases} \text{Erika controls ⟨enter, dining room⟩} \land \\ \text{Darnell controls ⟨enter, dining room⟩} \land \\ \text{Gina controls ⟨enter, dining room⟩} \end{cases}$	Guest List
5. ACL says (Erika controls ⟨enter, dining room⟩)	4 simplify says
6. ⟨enter, dining room⟩	1, 2, 3, 5 ticket rule

Line 1 represents Erika's spoken request to be let into the private dining room. Line 2 reflects the restaurant's policy that the manager in charge has authority over who can enter the private dining room. Line 3 represents the maître d's belief that the guest list is authorized by the manager and accurately reflects the manager's wishes. Line 4 describes the guest list—a list of subjects who can exercise entry rights to the private dining room. Line 5 is obtained by repeated application of the *Simplify Says* inference rule to Line 4, and Line 6 is obtained by the Ticket Rule.   ◇

When expressing ACLs in the logic, it is important to remember that the two formulas

$$(P \text{ controls } \varphi_1) \land (P \text{ controls } \varphi_2)$$

and

$$P \text{ controls } (\varphi_1 \land \varphi_2)$$

are *not* equivalent (see Exercise 3.3.7). In the former case, P is trusted on *each* of φ_1 and φ_2; P's request to perform *either* should be granted. In the latter case, however, P is trusted on the *conjunction* of φ_1 and φ_2: P must request *both* in order for either to be granted. For this reason, an ACL will often contain many separate clauses for the same principal, detailing all of the individual access rights that principal has.

Similarly, the two formulas

$$(P \text{ controls } \varphi) \land (Q \text{ controls } \varphi)$$

and

$$P \And Q \text{ controls } \varphi$$

are not equivalent. The first formula states that both *P* and *Q* are *individually* authorized for φ. In contrast, the second formula states that both *P* and *Q* must request φ for access to be granted. For instance, in Example 4.2, Erika, Darnell, and Gina are each authorized to enter the private dining room, and each may enter the room without the others. Suppose instead that the ACL were defined in the following way:

$$\text{ACL says } \textit{Erika \& Darnell \& Gina} \text{ controls } \langle \text{enter, dining room} \rangle .$$

This case would correspond to restaurants that seat parties only after everyone has arrived: Erika, Darnell, and Gina could enter the dining room only if all three make the request to do so.

Exercise 4.2.2   *In operating systems with discretionary access control, a user can specify who else can read, write, or execute her files. Suppose Carter creates a program* foo, *and he wants Dan to be able to execute* foo *but neither read* foo *nor write to it. Also, Carter wishes to grant read, write, and execute privileges to Jan. Assume that Dan and Jan have userids* dan *and* jan, *respectively. Formalize the above description and formally justify why Jan's request to execute* foo *should be granted.*

Exercise 4.2.3   *Prove that the formulas*

$$P \& Q \text{ controls } \varphi, \qquad (P \text{ controls } \varphi) \land (Q \text{ controls } \varphi)$$

are not equivalent. That is, find a particular formula φ *and a particular Kripke structure* $\mathcal{M} = \langle W, I, J \rangle$ *such that*

$$\mathcal{M} \not\models (P \& Q \text{ controls } \varphi) \equiv ((P \text{ controls } \varphi) \land (Q \text{ controls } \varphi)).$$

4.2.3   Logical and Pragmatic Implications

We have looked in detail at ticket-oriented and list-oriented mechanisms for controlling access to protected objects. As we have seen, tickets and lists differ in the following two ways:

1. Tickets are typically possessed—or easily accessible—by principals wishing to access a protected object. In contrast, ACLs are possessed by reference monitors.

2. Typically, when tickets are used, the reference monitor does not need to identify the principal making the request. Instead, the principal possessing the ticket needs only give it to the reference monitor to exercise the rights corresponding to the ticket. In contrast, a reference monitor using an ACL must somehow determine the identity of the principal requesting access to determine what rights, if any, the principal has.

Despite these differences, tickets and ACLs share similar logical meanings and logical contexts:

1. Logically speaking, tickets and ACLs make statements of the same form:

$$ticket \text{ says } (subject \text{ controls } \varphi)$$
$$ACL \text{ says } (subject \text{ controls } \varphi)$$

   In the case of tickets, the *subject* may simply be *Bearer*, in that anyone bearing or possessing the ticket has the corresponding access right. In the case of ACLs, specific principals are generally identified.

2. Both tickets and ACLs are used in the context of policies that specify which authority has jurisdiction over access decisions. These policies regarding jurisdiction are expressed in the logic as follows:

$$authority \text{ controls } (subject \text{ controls } \varphi)$$

3. Both tickets and ACLs are the mechanisms for controlling access and thus must be protected from fraud. As a result, both must faithfully represent the desires of the authorities they represent. Statements regarding this faithful representation of the authority are expressed in the logic as follows:

$$ticket \Rightarrow authority$$
$$ACL \Rightarrow authority$$

From a logical standpoint, it is no accident that reference monitors depend upon the same inference rules to deduce whether an access request should be granted. Although ticket-based access may appear on the surface to be very different from list-based access, the information conveyed by tickets and lists is the same, as is the larger context of policy statements and trust assumptions.

There is an important pragmatic consideration regarding the use of the derived *Ticket Rule* in our examples. Recall that the ticket rule is as follows:

$$
\text{Ticket Rule} \quad \frac{subject \text{ says } \varphi \quad authority \text{ controls } (subject \text{ controls } \varphi)}{\varphi} \\
\frac{ticket \Rightarrow authority \quad ticket \text{ says } (subject \text{ controls } \varphi)}{\varphi}
$$

From an implementation standpoint, an engineer designing a reference monitor *will not* implement a general purpose inference engine or theorem prover based on the inference rules of the access-control logic. Instead, what he or she will build amounts to a mechanization of a derived inference rule specific to his or her situation.

In particular, many reference monitors are essentially implemented as *checklists*. They determine whether the various necessary tickets and certificates are present; if so, access is granted. Such approaches can be justified by derived inference rules where the elements on the checklist are the *premises* and the desired action on an object is the *conclusion*. Furthermore, there is usually a specific *context* within which the reference monitor operates. These contexts will sometimes provide *implicit* premises, rather than *explicit* checklist items.

For example, suppose that Margaret is an engineer building a reference monitor for a copy machine. The intention is that, if a person has a ticket—perhaps a card he inserts into the copy machine—then he can make copies. In the actual implementation, Margaret's chief concern is to develop a way to check the validity of an inserted copy card; if it is valid, then a copy operation should be performed whenever the copy button is pressed. The verified validity of the copy card amounts to a statement of the form

$$card \text{ says } (bearer \text{ controls } copy),$$

while each press of the copy button amounts to the following statement:

$$bearer \text{ says } copy.$$

The *Ticket* rule allows Margaret to justify her design formally, but only by explicitly stating the implicit assumptions about what card validity means. Specifically, the analysis requires her to acknowledge an authority that governs who can make copies and that the copy card must speak for that authority:

$$auth \text{ controls } (bearer \text{ controls } copy), \quad card \Rightarrow auth.$$

The value of such an analysis is that potentially implicit assumptions are made explicit. If there are future changes to the operating context (e.g., the card-making equipment is stolen or compromised), then it is easier to determine whether or not systems need to be reconfigured or even redesigned.

4.3 Authentication

Authentication is the task of identifying a subject who is making a request. More abstractly, authentication is the task of associating one principal (e.g., the process requesting access to a guarded resource or the face and person requesting access to a guarded facility) with another principal (e.g., an individual or group included on an ACL).

In this section we take a detailed look at several authentication scenarios and describe them in the access-control logic.

4.3.1 Two-Factor Authentication

Authentication is generally based on one or more kinds of information or *factors*:

- Type 1: something you *know*, such as a PIN, or password.

- Type 2: something you *have*, such as card, key, or token.

- Type 3: something you *are*, such as your fingerprint, face, or voice.

Authentication can be performed using one or more items of information drawn from each factor. *Two-factor authentication* uses information drawn from two of the preceding types. An example of two-factor authentication based on information drawn from types 1 and 2 is identifying a principal based on a personal identification number PIN (type 1) and a badge or certificate (type 2).

Many badges have the principal's name and the PIN associated with the principal in protected form on the badge. A typical security badge might have a person's name, face, and security clearance on the front of the badge, and have the name, security clearance, and PIN stored in encrypted form accessible by a magnetic card reader. Most cards have both physical and electronic security. Physical security measures include the way the card was manufactured: the person's picture is part of the plastic, there is a stamp or signature written over visible information such as security clearances and names, and so on. Electronic security can include encryption and signing of electronic information such as names, PINs, and security clearances. If a smart card is used, key information will be wiped out if physical tampering is attempted.

For an older picture ID with a magnetic stripe that contains a protected PIN, we can express the two-factor authentication as follows:

$$\text{authority says } ((\text{face}_{subject} \ \& \ \text{PIN}_{subject}) \Rightarrow \text{subject}).$$

We recognize that the above formula is exactly the form of a certificate (i.e., a signed statement) issued by an authority: the certificate in this case associates a particular face and PIN with a particular subject or principal. The ID badge is used by the reference monitor as a certificate. Again, it is crucial that badges and other certificates be impossible—or at least very difficult—to counterfeit.

Figure 4.3 contains an analysis of two-factor authentication based on certificates. Line 1 represents the subject using $factor_1$ and $factor_2$ to make a request φ. Line 2 is the access policy that states that $authority_1$ is in charge of who has access. Line 3 corresponds to an access-control list entry stating that *subject* has access right φ. Line 4 state that $authority_2$ has jurisdiction over certificates identifying principals using $factor_1$ and $factor_2$. Line 5 is the information contained in the certificate or badge possessed by the *subject*. Lines 6 through 9 are derived using the inference rules of the access-control logic.

The two-factor proof of Figure 4.3 corresponds to the following derived inference rule:

Two Factor Auth
$$\frac{\begin{array}{c}(factor_1 \ \& \ factor_2) \text{ says } \varphi \\ authority_1 \text{ controls } (subject \text{ controls } \varphi) \\ authority_1 \text{ says } (subject \text{ controls } \varphi) \\ authority_2 \text{ controls } ((factor_1 \ \& \ factor_2) \Rightarrow subject) \\ authority_2 \text{ says } ((factor_1 \ \& \ factor_2) \Rightarrow subject)\end{array}}{\varphi}.$$

The following example demonstrates the use of this derived rule for reasoning about access based on two-factor authentication.

FIGURE 4.3 Template for two-factor authentication

1. $(factor_1 \ \& \ factor_2)$ says φ	Access request
2. $authority_1$ controls (subject controls φ)	Access policy
3. $authority_1$ says (subject controls φ)	ACL entry
4. $authority_2$ controls $((factor_1 \ \& \ factor_2) \Rightarrow subject)$	Jurisdiction
5. $authority_2$ says $((factor_1 \ \& \ factor_2) \Rightarrow subject)$	Certificate
6. $(factor_1 \ \& \ factor_2) \Rightarrow subject$	4, 5 Controls
7. subject says φ	6, 1 Says
8. subject controls φ	2, 3 Controls
9. φ	8, 7 Controls

Example 4.3

Omar works for a military research lab. The security office has issued Omar a badge ($badge_{Omar}$) and personal identification number (PIN_{Omar}). The doors to the lab are protected by card readers with keypads. To enter the lab, Omar must swipe his badge in the card reader and then punch in his PIN. If Omar uses his card and punches in his PIN, then the reference monitor controlling the door is able to identify him, look him up on an electronic access-control list, and determine that he is an employee in good standing and should be admitted.

This description corresponds to two-factor authentication. Omar must know his PIN (a type-1 factor) and then he must possess a badge (a type-2 factor). The combination of the two are used to identify Omar to the electronic reference monitor that guards the lab doors.

As is the case with many badges, the magnetic stripe on Omar's card contains protected information, such as a badge identifier and Omar's PIN. The card reader on the doors can identify both the badge identifier and protected PIN.

The following proof justifies letting Omar enter the lab when he presents his badge and PIN.

1. $(badge_{Omar} \ \& \ PIN_{Omar})$ says $\langle enter, lab \rangle$	Access request
2. security office controls (Omar controls $\langle enter, lab \rangle$)	Access policy
3. security office says (Omar controls $\langle enter, lab \rangle$)	ACL entry
4. security office controls $((badge_{Omar} \ \& \ PIN_{Omar}) \Rightarrow Omar)$	Jurisdiction
5. security office says $((badge_{Omar} \ \& \ PIN_{Omar}) \Rightarrow Omar)$	Info in badge
6. $\langle enter, lab \rangle$	Two Factor ACL

The preceding scenario is largely analogous to the use of bank cards and PINs by automated teller machines. The important difference is that withdrawals also depend on conditions related to the account balances.

4.3.2   Using Credentials from Other Authorities

So far we have described access scenarios that depend on credentials issued by the same authority responsible for the protected resource. In many situations, however, this need not be the case. For example, airlines routinely use state-issued driver's licenses with pictures and federally issued passports to identify passengers. Guards at airports use a combination of government-issued documents with pictures (such as passports and licenses) coupled with airline boarding passes.

The informal justification that allows such credentials to be used is based on trust in the process by which these credentials are issued. For example, government-issued picture IDs are accepted based on the assumption that it is hard to dupe the government into issuing a fake picture ID. That is, the government's registration process for issuing picture IDs is deemed to be sufficiently robust. Likewise, airline tickets are accepted as credentials because airlines have strong economic interests to control who can get on their airplanes: it is consequently difficult to defraud an airline and obtain a ticket without paying for it (either with money or frequent-flyer miles).

A typical goal when making access-control decisions based on other credentials is two-fold: first, determine whether the subject making the request is who they say they are, and then determine whether they have access rights to some other object that is meaningful and relevant to you.

A template for this type of situation appears in Figure 4.4. Lines 1 through 9 are the initial assumptions. Line 1 describes a subject with a face, voice, fingerprint, or userid and password, making a request φ_1. Lines 2 and 3 are the recognition of the jurisdiction of authority A_1 regarding φ_1 and the stated access policy. Note that the policy expressed in line 3 differs in form from previous examples: it states that, if the subject has access to the object corresponding to φ_2, then the subject also has access to the object corresponding to φ_1. For example, if Penny has permission to board an airplane leaving from a given airport, then Penny has permission to enter that airport. Lines 4 through 6 relate to recognizing the jurisdiction of authority A_2 on associating a factor with a subject (factor $\Rightarrow$ subject), the credential itself, and its assumed integrity. Similarly lines 7 through 9 relate to recognizing the jurisdiction of A_3 to control φ_2 and the integrity of the certificate authorizing *subject* to control φ_2.

The proof in Figure 4.4 yields the following derived inference rule:

$$ID \& Ticket \quad \frac{\begin{array}{c} \text{factor says } \varphi_1 \\ A_1 \text{ controls } ((\text{subject controls } \varphi_2) \supset \text{subject controls } \varphi_1) \\ A_1 \text{ says } ((\text{subject controls } \varphi_2) \supset \text{subject controls } \varphi_1) \\ A_2 \text{ controls } (\text{factor} \Rightarrow \text{subject}) \\ \text{certificate says } (\text{factor} \Rightarrow \text{subject}) \\ \text{certificate} \Rightarrow A_2 \\ A_3 \text{ controls } (\text{subject controls } \varphi_2) \\ \text{ticket says } (\text{subject controls } \varphi_2) \\ \text{ticket} \Rightarrow A_3 \end{array}}{\varphi_1}.$$

To be explicit, this template illustrates one particular way that credentials from multiple authorities might fit together as part of an access-control scheme. Not all

FIGURE 4.4 Template for using credentials from multiple authorities

1. factor says φ_1	Request
2. A_1 controls $((\text{subject controls } \varphi_2) \supset \text{subject controls } \varphi_1)$	Jurisdiction
3. A_1 says $((\text{subject controls } \varphi_2) \supset \text{subject controls } \varphi_1)$	Access policy
4. A_2 controls $(\text{factor} \Rightarrow \text{subject})$	Jurisdiction
5. certificate says $(\text{factor} \Rightarrow \text{subject})$	ID card
6. certificate $\Rightarrow A_2$	Trust assumption
7. A_3 controls $(\text{subject controls } \varphi_2)$	Jurisdiction
8. ticket says $(\text{subject controls } \varphi_2)$	Ticket
9. ticket $\Rightarrow A_3$	Trust assumption
10. subject controls $\varphi_2 \supset$ subject controls φ_1	2, 3 Controls
11. A_2 says $(\text{factor} \Rightarrow \text{subject})$	6, 5 Derived speaks for
12. factor $\Rightarrow$ subject	4, 11 Controls
13. subject says φ_1	12, 1 Derived speaks for
14. A_3 says $(\text{subject controls } \varphi_2)$	9, 8 Speaks for
15. subject controls φ_2	7, 14 Controls
16. subject controls φ_1	15, 10 Modus ponens
17. φ_1	16, 13 Controls

situations will necessarily fit into this specific template. The following example applies the *ID & Ticket* rule to a common situation that does fit this template: the task of controlling access to an airport terminal where only ticketed passengers with DMV-issued driver's licenses can enter.

Example 4.4

Penny is a ticketed passenger on flight #1. To gain entry to the airport terminal, she must show a state-issued picture ID along with her boarding pass. When she reaches airport security, she presents her driver's license. She also presents her boarding pass for flight #1. The following formalization justifies why Penny is allowed to enter the airport terminal:

1. Face says $\langle$enter, airport$\rangle$	Request
2. Security controls $((\text{Penny controls } \langle 25D, \text{flight } \#1\rangle) \supset$ Penny controls $\langle$enter, airport$\rangle)$	Jurisdiction
3. Security says $((\text{Penny controls } \langle 25D, \text{flight } \#1\rangle) \supset$ Penny controls $\langle$enter, airport$\rangle)$	Access policy
4. DMV controls $(\text{Face} \Rightarrow \text{Penny})$	Jurisdiction
5. license says $(\text{Face} \Rightarrow \text{Penny})$	ID card
6. license $\Rightarrow$ DMV	Trust assumption
7. Airline controls $(\text{Penny controls } \langle 25D, \text{flight } \#1\rangle)$	Jurisdiction
8. ticket says $(\text{Penny controls } \langle 25D, \text{flight } \#1\rangle)$	Ticket
9. ticket $\Rightarrow$ Airline	Trust assumption
10. $\langle$enter, airport$\rangle$	1,2,3,4,5,6,7,8,9 ID & Ticket Rule

Line 1 is the request as interpreted by airport security: a specific face is making a request to enter the airport terminal. Line 2 corresponds to the security guard at the airport recognizing the authority of airport security to make policy. Line 3 is the actual policy stating that, if the person presenting the ticket is really Penny (i.e., her face matches the face on the driver's license), then Penny can enter the airport. Lines 4 through 6 correspond to the guard recognizing the authority of the state DMV, seeing Penny's driver's license with her picture on it, and accepting the license as authentically issued by the DMV. Lines 7 through 9 have a similar interpretation with respect to the airline and Penny's airplane ticket. ◇

Exercise 4.3.1   *Meg keeps a safe-deposit box (box #1205) at her local bank, in which she stores important documents. She can access those documents by visiting the bank, getting the safe-deposit box, and then opening it with her bank-issued keycard ($card_M$) and PIN (PIN_M).*

At the bank, access to safe-deposit boxes is governed as follows:

- *As a strategy to prevent theft, safe-deposit boxes can be removed from the vault only through the cooperation of the Vault Officer and the Teller Supervisor. Specifically, the Vault Officer and the Teller Supervisor must simultaneously insert special keys (key_{VO} and key_{TS}, respectively) and enter the specific box's number.*

- *Once removed from the vault, the safe-deposit box is brought to the account holder (in this case, Meg), who may open the box by inserting her keycard and entering the correct PIN number.*

Let $\langle release, \#1205 \rangle$ and $\langle open, \#1205 \rangle$ be (respectively) the operations of releasing box 1205 from the vault and of opening box 1205. Use expressions in the access-control logic to answer the following questions regarding the certifications, credentials, and access-control policies needed for the bank's safe-deposit system.

- a. *What are the specific access requests that are placed to release box 1205 from the vault and to open box 1205?*

- b. *What are the ACL (access-control list) entries that govern the vault's release and Meg's opening of box 1205?*

- c. *What are the additional certificates, recognition of authority, and trust assumptions that are necessary for determining whether to grant release or open requests for box 1205?*

- d. *Suppose that Meg's safe-deposit box is brought to her, and that her keycard is valid. Using the relevant assumptions from Parts (1), (2), and (3) above, give a formal proof that the request $\langle open, \#1205 \rangle$ will be granted.*

Exercise 4.3.2   *Suppose you are the chief operating officer of a rental car company. One of your primary objectives is to make sure you rent cars only to qualified drivers.*

a. *Informally describe your method for assessing whether a domestic customer is qualified to rent a car, what evidence you will use, how you will check the authenticity of the evidence, and who you trust in the process.*

b. *Formally describe your method using the access-control logic.*

c. *Most domestic rental car companies rent cars to international customers but require additional credentials. Describe your process for establishing the qualifications of international customers.*

d. *Formally describe your method using the access-control logic.*

4.3.3   Groups

In many situations, access control is *group based*, rather than *individual based*. That is, access-control decisions may be based on whether the requester belongs to a specific group, rather than on the specific identity of the individual. As a common example, access to the teacher's lounge in a high school is typically granted to all members of the faculty.

In reality, groups are simply another sort of principal, and group-based access policies are defined in the same way as identity-based policies. For example, the following statement expresses the access policy for the high-school teacher's lounge:

$$Faculty \text{ controls } \langle enter, lounge \rangle.$$

Group membership can be expressed using the speaks-for relationship, as in the following statement:

$$Leslie \Rightarrow Faculty.$$

Using the *Derived Controls* rule, it is straightforward to deduce that any request from Leslie to enter the teacher's lounge should be granted.

Many everyday documents are certificates that assert group membership of one kind or another. Alec's United States passport is a certificate issued by the U.S. State Department that asserts that Alec is a U.S. citizen:

$$US\ State\ Department \text{ says } Alec \Rightarrow US\ Citizen.$$

Miranda's student identification card, issued by New State University (NSU) when she first enrolled, is a certificate stating that she is an NSU student:

$$NSU \text{ says } Miranda \Rightarrow NSU\ Student.$$

Exercise 4.3.3   *Oliver has recently become a Premium member of the frequent-flyer club of Fly-By-Night Airlines. The membership package he received from Fly-By-Night included a membership card with his name and frequent-flyer number printed on it. As a Premium member, Oliver is eligible to enter the Fly-By-Night lounges at participating airports. On his next trip, Oliver decides to use this benefit: he* heads to the Fly-By-Night lounge and presents his membership card and a photo identification (his driver's license) to the staffer who is guarding the door.

Formally describe the access-policy of the lounge, Oliver's request to enter, and any other necessary trust assumptions required for Oliver to be granted access to the lounge. Based on these descriptions, formally justify letting Oliver into the Fly-By-Night lounge.

Exercise 4.3.4 *Sam is a citizen and resident of the United States, returning home after visiting Canada. She arrives at the US border with her passport in hand.*

    a. *The act of driving her car to the border agent's station can be interpreted as a request to enter the United States. Express this request in the access-control logic.*

    b. *Sam's passport can be interpreted as a certificate (i.e., a signed statement) from the U.S. State Department that associates Sam's face with her name. It also identifies Sam as belonging to the group of U.S. citizens.*

    Formalize Sam's passport as an expression in the access-control logic.

    c. *The standard policy is that US citizens with proof of citizenship may enter the country, provided the border agent deems them not to be a threat (i.e., the border agent may exercise discretion).*

    Formalize this policy in the access-control logic.

    d. *Suppose that the border agent deems Sam not to be a threat.*

    Identify any other necessary assumptions (expressed as formulas in the access-control logic) about certificates, jurisdiction, et cetera to justify letting Sam enter the United States.

    e. *Using only those expressions given in the previous parts of the question, give a formal proof justifying Sam's entry into the United States.*

4.4 Summary

Our goal is to be able to justify an answer to the question "Should this access-control request be granted?" Answering this question correctly relies on sorting through the maze of tickets, certificates, credentials, access-control lists, and various means of authentication. This analysis further depends upon the authorities that are recognized and the extent of their jurisdiction.

In this chapter, we demonstrated how to describe the mechanisms (e.g., tickets, ACLs, certificates) and the broader context (e.g., recognized authorities and jurisdictions) in our access-control logic. We also demonstrated several derived rules that support reasoning about access requests. In the process, we developed templates for

FIGURE 4.5 Learning outcomes for Chapter 4
After completing this chapter, you should be able to achieve the following learning outcomes at several levels of knowledge:

Application

- Express requests, access-control policies, credentials, and notions of jurisdiction in the access-control logic.
- Express tickets, access-control lists, authentication factors, and group membership in the access-control logic.

Synthesis

- When given a scenario that involves tickets, lists, and individual or group-based authentication, formalize the scenario, identify all necessary trust assumptions, and formally justify the granting of a request.

---

analyzing a wide variety of access-control scenarios. These templates demonstrate the utility of derived rules that can be reused in a variety of situations. They also illustrate how the language can be used to describe new mechanisms and concepts.

The learning outcomes associated with this chapter appear in Figure 4.5.

4.5   Further Reading

For classic papers on access control and protection, we suggest Butler Lampson's "Protection" (Lampson, 1971) and Saltzer and Schroeder's "The Protection of Information in Computer Systems" (Saltzer and Schroeder, 1975). In addition, Matt Bishop's textbook *Computer Security: Art and Science* (Bishop, 2003) provides a compendium of access-control models and devotes a chapter to authentication.

Chapter 5

Security Policies

In Chapter 4, we focused on security *mechanisms*, which provide the *means* to enforce security policies. We now turn to security policies themselves, which define what is allowed and what is prohibited.

Typically, policies specify the permissible actions that *subjects* can perform on *objects*. Subjects are active entities: they include the users, system processes, and services that perform actions, such as sending messages, reading and writing files, and so on. Subjects correspond to the principals of our access-control logic. Objects are the passive entities acted upon, such as databases, files, etc. Subjects and objects are mutually exclusive, but both are protected by access-control policies.

There are three aspects of security policies: *confidentiality, integrity, and availability*. Confidentiality addresses who may see what; integrity addresses who may modify what; and availability addresses the required levels of service. In this chapter, we give high-level definitions of each, with the understanding that more precise definitions of each depend upon the specific system and the context in which it is used.

Security policies are classified in several ways. One way to classify policies is based on whether they are *discretionary* or *mandatory*. A second way is to classify policies based on their use context: *military* or *commercial*. A third way is to describe policies based on which aspect of security is addressed: confidentiality, integrity, or availability. We introduce these different classifications in this chapter, providing examples of each.

5.1   Confidentiality, Integrity, and Availability

The three core aspects of security policies are confidentiality, integrity, and availability (collectively known as the C-I-A triad).

Confidentiality   Confidentiality boils down to the inaccessibility of information or resources. For example, consider Lara's grade in her Writing 101 course. The confidentiality (or privacy) rules for the university's computer system might state that only Lara, the university Registrar, and Lara's Writing 101 instructor can read Lara's Writing 101 grade. As a consequence, the university's computer systems are not authorized to release Lara's Writing 101 grade to her parents. *Secrecy* is an aspect of confidentiality: it defines who may know or possess information. For example, the general leading an army is permitted to know the date of when the army will attack, whereas the general's cook is not permitted to know this date.

Integrity   *Integrity* refers to the *accuracy* and *credibility* of information. Integrity is a more subtle property than confidentiality. In the case of confidentiality, either the information is compromised (leaked) or not. However, integrity has multiple aspects. One aspect is content related: are the data correct and uncorrupted? The other aspect is origin related: who or what is the source of the data?

For example, consider bonds issued by corporations. Bonds are used to raise money with the promise to lenders that they will be repaid with interest. The simplest aspect of a bond is the interest rate. Its accuracy is easily verified. The vastly more difficult aspect is evaluating how credible the promise of repayment is. To deal with credibility and integrity, we often rely on a rating or grading system. Bonds are rated as AAA, AA, A, BBB, BB, B, CCC, CC, and C, where AAA is the highest (and presumably most risk free), C is the lowest (the highest likelihood of default), and anything with a BB rating or lower is considered junk.

Mechanisms that support integrity fall into two classes: *detection* and *prevention*. Detection mechanisms look for corruption or alteration of data. For example, parity checking coupled with parity bits is used to detect the corruption of values stored in computer memory. In contrast, prevention mechanisms deny unauthorized attempts to change data. For example, students are not granted write access to their college transcripts.

Lack of corruption alone is insufficient to guarantee integrity, because integrity also includes *trust*. For example, suppose that Trish receives a message to install a specific program on her machine, and the message arrives intact and without any corruption in its transmission. Trish's actions depend on whether she *trusts* the originator of the message. If the originator is a system administrator who has authority over her computer, then Trish will likely comply and install the program. On the other hand, if the request is from an unknown or untrusted source, then she most likely will not comply.

Assumptions about who or what is trusted affect the integrity and security of a system directly. When these assumptions are implicit and unstated, a system may become vulnerable as the result of changing circumstances. As seen throughout this book, trust assumptions and statements of authority and jurisdiction are crucial to virtually every analysis.

Availability   A system is available if it can be used with some minimum level of performance or quality of service. For example, a personal computer system might be considered to be available if all requests to access files on the local hard drives are satisfied within one second.

When resources or systems are unavailable or perform beneath expected levels of service, it is difficult to judge whether the system is suffering from a so-called *denial of service attack* or from routine use. As an example, consider a highway that is often jammed during rush hour. When a driver encounters bumper-to-bumper traffic, she typically might conclude that its cause is rush-hour traffic. On the other hand, she might come to a very different conclusion if she read about a planned protest by local farmers who intended to drive at the legal minimum speed in all lanes of the highway that day. The key difference is the intent behind accessing or using a resource. In the case of rush-hour traffic, the intent of most highway users is to get to work. In the case of protesters, it is to deny, frustrate, or degrade the quality of service to other highway users in order to draw attention to the issues of concern to them. Assessing whether or not a denial of service attack is occurring can be difficult, because determining intent from observable behavior is difficult.

5.2   Discretionary Security Policies

Discretionary policies are *dynamic* (i.e., they can be changed), and they are typically under user control. In particular, *discretionary access control* (DAC) policies are policies where users control access to protected objects over which they have jurisdiction. Often, DAC policies are based on *identity*, providing examples of *identity-based access control* (IBAC).

In the access-control logic, IBAC policies are recognizable by *controls* statements that relate access rights (such as $\langle operation, object \rangle$) to a subject's identity:

$$Subject \text{ controls } \langle operation, object \rangle.$$

Such statements reflect the identity-based portion of an access-control policy. Furthermore, in the case of DAC policies, there is some principal (typically the owner of the object) who specifies the policy, resulting in a statement of the following form:

$$Principal \text{ says } (Subject \text{ controls } \langle operation, object \rangle).$$

The discretionary nature of the policy—that is, that a given principal has the authority to set such policies—can be expressed as follows:

$$Principal \text{ controls } (Subject \text{ controls } \langle operation, object \rangle).$$

The expected behavior or response to subjects' access requests can be expressed as theorems or derived inference rules. Expressing behavior as theorems in the form of derived inference rules enables our expectations to be checked for validity.

For example, given the above identity-based statements, we can express our expectations of behavior as a derivable inference rule of the following form:

$$\frac{\begin{array}{c} Principal \text{ says } (Subject \text{ controls } \langle operation, object \rangle) \\ Principal \text{ controls } (Subject \text{ controls } \langle operation, object \rangle) \\ Subject \text{ says } \langle operation, object \rangle \end{array}}{\langle operation, object \rangle}.$$

	foo
April	read
Bill	read, write
Carla	execute

Table 5.1: Access-control matrix for *foo* under Susan's control

Of course, depending on the actual situation, the inference rules may be more complicated and include various conditions. The following example is typical of discretionary access-control policies.

Example 5.1

Suppose Susan creates a program *foo*. Susan is allowed to specify that April can read *foo*, Bill can read and write (modify) *foo*, and Carla can execute *foo*. The access-control matrix for *foo* is shown in Table 5.1.

In the access-control logic, we represent the table as follows:

$$Susan \text{ says } (April \text{ controls } \langle read, foo \rangle) \wedge$$
$$Susan \text{ says } (Bill \text{ controls } \langle read, foo \rangle) \wedge$$
$$Susan \text{ says } (Bill \text{ controls } \langle write, foo \rangle) \wedge$$
$$Susan \text{ says } (Carla \text{ controls } \langle execute, foo \rangle).$$

This statement reflects the access policy on *foo*, as dictated by Susan.

We represent Susan's discretion or authority to dictate access to *foo* as follows:

$$Susan \text{ controls } (April \text{ controls } \langle read, foo \rangle) \wedge$$
$$Susan \text{ controls } (Bill \text{ controls } \langle read, foo \rangle) \wedge$$
$$Susan \text{ controls } (Bill \text{ controls } \langle write, foo \rangle) \wedge$$
$$Susan \text{ controls } (Carla \text{ controls } \langle execute, foo \rangle).$$

Both statements, taken together, describe the discretionary access-control policy for the file *foo*.

The behavior of the system that controls access to *foo* can be described by theorems or derived inference rules. For example, given the above discretionary access-control policy statements, we can derive the response to the request

$$Carla \text{ says } \langle execute, foo \rangle.$$

In particular, the response to Carla's request is given by the following derivable inference rule:

$$\frac{Susan \text{ says } (Carla \text{ controls } \langle execute, foo \rangle) \quad Susan \text{ controls } (Carla \text{ controls } \langle execute, foo \rangle) \quad Carla \text{ says } \langle execute, foo \rangle}{\langle execute, foo \rangle}. \qquad \Diamond$$

✎ **Exercise 5.2.1** *Consider the following access-control matrix for subjects $S_1 \cdots S_3$ and objects $O_1 \cdots O_4$ (the owner of each object appears in parentheses):*

Subject	$O_1(S_1)$	$O_2(S_2)$	$O_3(S_3)$	$O_4(S_4)$
S_1	read, write	read	read	read
S_2	read	read, write	read	read
S_3	read	read	read, write	read, write

Use the access-control logic to formulate the access-control rules for each object.

🔨 **Exercise 5.2.2** *Sunita and her husband Anand are organizing their files on their home computer system, which is shared with their son Samuel. Sunita is a distinguished author who is working on her next book, and she keeps her draft on the family's home computer system in the file* bookDraft. *Sunita routinely relies on Anand and Samuel to read her draft. She keeps a running list of their comments in the files* AnandsComments *and* SamuelsComments, *which Anand and Samuel use to record their reactions to her draft.*

It is important to Sunita that she be the only one who can make changes to the book draft. She wants to allow Anand and Samuel to read the draft and each other's comments, but it is important to her that Anand's and Samuel's comments be separate from one another.

Devise answers to the following questions.

a. *Create access-control matrices for the files* bookDraft, AnandsComments, *and* SamuelsComments. *Explain how your access-control matrices satisfy Sunita's concerns.*

b. *Write the policy statements for each file in the access-control logic.*

c. *Describe in words what happens when given each of the following requests:*

$$\text{Anand says } \langle write, \texttt{AnandsComments} \rangle,$$
$$\text{Anand says } \langle write, \texttt{SamuelsComments} \rangle,$$
$$\text{Samuel says } \langle read, \texttt{AnandsComments} \rangle.$$

For each request that is granted, give the derivable inference rule that justifies granting access.

d. *Prove that your inference rules are valid.*

5.3 Mandatory Security Policies

Mandatory security policies are policies that apply to everyone and everything all the time: they are static and cannot be changed, and individuals have no discretion

FIGURE 5.1 Conceptual diagram of a virtual machine and monitor

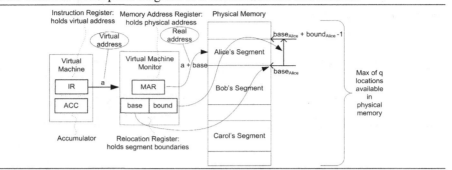

or control over them. *Mandatory access control* (MAC) policies in computers are typically implemented by the operating system or by the hardware. For resources protected by a MAC policy, neither the owner nor the requester can influence the access-control decision. Unlike DAC policies, MAC policies typically do not name specific subjects or principals in policy statements. The rules for access usually depend on considerations other than identity.

As an important example of a MAC policy, let us consider the rules for accessing physical memory in support of virtual memory for virtual machines. We study virtual machines in detail in Chapter 10. For now, it suffices to know that virtual machines provide self-contained operating environments that provide users the illusion of working on a single-user system. To maintain this illusion successfully, the operating environment must separate and isolate individual virtual machines from one another, so that no virtual machine can interfere with the operation of another virtual machine. Consequently, all virtual-machine attempts to access the host operating system or hardware must be monitored and checked by a reference monitor called the *virtual machine monitor*.

Figure 5.1 contains a simple conceptualization of a virtual machine and its relationship with physical memory and the virtual machine monitor (VMM). The virtual machine has two registers:

1. The instruction register (IR) holds the current instruction being executed by the virtual machine.

2. The accumulator register (ACC) holds intermediate values of computations.

Physical memory has q locations, with the addresses ranging from 0 through $q - 1$. The virtual machine monitor regulates virtual-machine access to physical memory.

As mentioned previously, the virtual machine provides to users the illusion that they are operating in a single-user environment. For this reason, user programs use *logical* (or *virtual*) addresses, which must then be translated into *physical* addresses. For example, a program might contain an instruction to *load the accumulator register ACC with the contents of virtual address* A (LDA @A). To execute LDA @A, the virtual machine loads the instruction into the instruction register IR and requests access to the virtual address A. The virtual machine monitor must determine whether the request would cause a security violation. Whether or not a security violation exists depends on the relationship between virtual and real memory addresses.

Conceptually, the VMM is implemented as part of a memory management unit (MMU). The VMM's job is twofold: (1) to isolate user programs from one another, and (2) to provide an execution environment for each virtual machine. Isolation is accomplished by partitioning physical memory into *segments*, where each segment corresponds to the virtual-memory space available to its corresponding user. The execution environment is provided by associating with each virtual machine VM the physical location of the VM's memory segment. Thus, Alice's VM has one segment, and Bob's VM has another separate segment. Alice's and Bob's programs may both execute the instruction LDA @A, but the VMM can distinguish the two address references because Alice and Bob use different memory segments.

The physical location of a memory segment depends on two parameters: the *base* and the *bound*. The *base* value is the segment's starting address in physical memory. The *bound* value gives the segment's size. These two values are stored in the *relocation register* RR, as shown in Figure 5.1.

If there are no security violations (a situation we discuss shortly), then the physical address associated with the virtual address A can be calculated relative to the *base* value for the current segment:

$$\text{PHYSICAL ADDRESS} = base + \text{A}.$$

If a user's program accesses virtual address A and there are no security violations, then the physical address $base + \text{A}$ is stored in the MMU's memory address register (MAR).

There are two possible security violations that may occur. The first occurs when the limit of physical memory (i.e., q) is exceeded:

$$base + \text{A} \geq q.$$

The second occurs when the boundary of the individual VM's segment is exceeded:

$$\text{A} \geq bound.$$

If either of these violations occur, then the instruction is *trapped*: user control over the virtual machine is terminated, and control is passed on to a trusted supervisory control program that can assess the situation and determine what to do next.

The following example illustrates the basic ideas of virtual memory, how MAC policies are formally described, and how the behavior of virtual machine monitors can be described as derived inference rules. We will discuss virtual machines and virtual machine monitors in fuller detail in Chapter 10.

Example 5.2
Consider the virtual machine environment illustrated in Figure 5.1, with three distinct memory segments.

Suppose that the current instruction being executed by the virtual machine VM is LDA @A (i.e., load the contents of virtual address A into ACC). We can formalize this situation by the formula

$$IR \text{ says } \langle \text{LDA @A} \rangle,$$

where $\langle \text{LDA @A} \rangle$ is interpreted as "*it would be a good idea to execute* LDA @A." The virtual machine—via the instruction register IR—requests that VMM permit the execution of LDA @A.

The virtual machine monitor provides an execution environment for virtual machines in general, and for VM in this specific case. Because the execution environment is determined by the values *base* and *bound* in the relocation register RR, we can describe it by the statement

$$RR \text{ says } \langle (base, bound) \rangle,$$

where $\langle (base, bound) \rangle$ is interpreted as "*the pair (base,bound) describes the current active memory segment.*"

A primary distinction between mandatory and discretionary policies is that mandatory policies are enforced by the operating system or hardware, whereas users are in control in discretionary policies. In the case of enforcing mandatory access control for physical memory, the memory management unit MMU has the authority and responsibility for enforcing the MAC policy. This MAC policy imposes conditions on the states of the VM and VMM registers and on the size of physical memory, as stated by the following two formulas:

$$IR \text{ says } \langle \text{LDA @A} \rangle \supset (RR \text{ says } \langle (base, bound) \rangle \supset (((base + \text{A} \geq q) \lor (\text{A} \geq bound)) \supset \langle trap \rangle)),$$
$$IR \text{ says } \langle \text{LDA @A} \rangle \supset (RR \text{ says } \langle (base, bound) \rangle \supset ((base + \text{A} < q) \supset ((\text{A} < bound) \supset \langle \text{LDA @A} \rangle))).$$

The first formula expresses the conditions under which an address violation occurs and is trapped. The second formula states that, when there is no address violation, the instruction LDA @A is executed. In both formulas, the relevant states of VM and VMM are expressed by the values in IR and RR.

The behavior of the MMU is expressed through derived inference rules. The following rule, which is provable using the inference rules of the access-control logic, describes when the instruction LDA @A should be trapped:

LDA @A *trap*
$$\frac{\begin{array}{c} IR \text{ says } \langle \text{LDA @A} \rangle \supset \\ (RR \text{ says } \langle (base, bound) \rangle \supset (((base + \text{A} \geq q) \lor (\text{A} \geq bound)) \supset \langle trap \rangle)) \\ IR \text{ says } \langle \text{LDA @A} \rangle \\ RR \text{ says } \langle (base, bound) \rangle \\ (\text{A} + base \geq q) \lor (\text{A} \geq bound) \end{array}}{\langle trap \rangle}$$

The inference rule describing when LDA @A is approved for execution and the proof of its validity are left as exercises for the reader.   ◊

Exercise 5.3.1 *Recall the* LDA @ A *instruction illustrated in Figure 5.1. Devise and prove valid an inference rule that describes when* LDA @ A *is approved for execution.*

Exercise 5.3.2 *The instruction* STO @ A *takes the contents of the accumulator ACC and stores it in virtual address* A. *Devise and prove valid inference rules that describe when* STO @ A *is trapped and when* STO @ A *is executed.*

5.4   Military Security Policies

Military security policies are focused on controlling the disclosure of information (i.e., providing confidentiality). These policies regulate the flow of information by describing who is allowed to know what. Information is *classified* or *labeled* using security levels, where the security classification levels are ordered. Principals are assigned a *security clearance level* using the same classification levels. Reference monitors can then control the flow of information by limiting access based on these classification levels.

For example, the classic classification scheme involves the following four classification levels, in increasing order: UNCLASSIFIED, CONFIDENTIAL, SECRET, and TOP SECRET. To read a file that has been classified at the SECRET level, one must possess an appropriate clearance level (SECRET or TOP SECRET) *and* have an appropriate need to know.

To express and reason about military security policies, we must augment our logic to support security classification levels. Fortunately, these modifications are very straightforward, as we shall see.

5.4.1   Extending the Logic with Security Levels

As we have seen in previous chapters, a logic has three important components: the syntax (i.e., how formulas are written), the semantics (i.e., what the formulas mean), and the logical rules (i.e., how the formulas are manipulated). In augmenting our logic to support security levels, we address each of these components in turn.

Syntax   The first step is to introduce syntax for describing and comparing security levels. We define **SecLabel** to be the collection of *simple security labels*, which are used as names for the various security levels associated with a military access policy; possible elements of this set include TS, S, C, and UC, among others.

In addition to these specific security labels, we will often want to refer abstractly to the security level assigned to a particular principal P. For this reason, we define the larger set **SecLevel** of *all* possible security-level expressions:

$$\textbf{SecLevel} ::= \textbf{SecLabel} \;/\; \mathsf{slev}(\textbf{PName})$$

That is, a security-level expression is either a simple security label or an expression of the form $\mathsf{slev}(A)$, where A is a simple principal name.[1] Informally, $\mathsf{slev}(A)$ refers to the security level of principal A.

Finally, we extend our definition of well-formed formulas to support comparisons of security levels:

$$\textbf{Form} ::= \textbf{SecLevel} \leq_s \textbf{SecLevel} \,/\, \textbf{SecLevel} =_s \textbf{SecLevel}$$

Informally, the formula $C \leq_s \mathsf{slev}(Kate)$ states that Kate's security level is greater than or equal to the security level C. Similarly, the formula $\mathsf{slev}(Barry) =_s \mathsf{slev}(Joe)$ states that Barry and Joe have been assigned the same security level.

Semantics Providing formal and precise meanings for the newly added syntax requires us to first extend our Kripke structures with additional components that describe security classification levels. Specifically, we introduce extended Kripke structures of the form

$$\mathcal{M} = \langle W, I, J, K, L, \preceq \rangle,$$

where:

- W, I, and J are defined as in Definition 2.1.

- K is a non-empty set, which serves as the universe of *security levels*.

- $L : (\textbf{SecLabel} \cup \textbf{PName}) \rightarrow K$ is a function that maps each security label and each simple principal name to a security level.

  L is extended to work over arbitrary security-level expressions, as follows:

  $$L(\mathsf{slev}(A)) = L(A),$$

  for every simple principal name A.

- $\preceq \subseteq K \times K$ is a partial order on K: that is, $\preceq$ is *reflexive* (for all $k \in K$, $k \preceq k$), *transitive* (for all $k_1, k_2, k_3 \in K$, if $k_1 \preceq k_2$ and $k_2 \preceq k_3$, then $k_1 \preceq k_3$), and *anti-symmetric* (for all $k_1, k_2, k_3 \in K$, if $k_1 \preceq k_2$ and $k_2 \preceq k_1$, then $k_1 = k_2$).

Using these extended Kripke structures, we define the semantics for our new well-formed expressions as follows:

$$\mathcal{E}_{\mathcal{M}}[\![\ell_1 \leq_s \ell_2]\!] = \begin{cases} W, & \text{if } L(\ell_1) \preceq L(\ell_2) \\ \emptyset, & \text{otherwise} \end{cases}$$

$$\mathcal{E}_{\mathcal{M}}[\![\ell_1 =_s \ell_2]\!] = \mathcal{E}_{\mathcal{M}}[\![\ell_1 \leq_s \ell_2]\!] \cap \mathcal{E}_{\mathcal{M}}[\![\ell_2 \leq_s \ell_1]\!].$$

As these definitions suggest, the expression $\ell_1 =_s \ell_2$ is simply syntactic sugar for $(\ell_1 \leq_s \ell_2) \wedge (\ell_2 \leq_s \ell_1)$.

---

[1] This syntax precludes security-level expressions such as $\mathsf{slev}(P \,\&\, Q)$ or $\mathsf{slev}(P \mid Q)$, because there is no standard technique for associating security classification labels with compound principals.

FIGURE 5.2 Inference rules for relating security levels

$$\ell_1 =_s \ell_2 \overset{\text{def}}{=} (\ell_1 \leq_s \ell_2) \wedge (\ell_2 \leq_s \ell_1)$$

Reflexivity of $\leq_s$ $\quad \overline{\ell \leq_s \ell}$

Transitivity of $\leq_s$ $\quad \dfrac{\ell_1 \leq_s \ell_2 \qquad \ell_2 \leq_s \ell_3}{\ell_1 \leq_s \ell_3}$

FIGURE 5.3 Proof of $\leq_s$ Subst

1. $\mathsf{slev}(P) =_s \ell_1$	Assumption
2. $\mathsf{slev}(Q) =_s \ell_2$	Assumption
3. $\ell_1 \leq_s \ell_2$	Assumption
4. $(\mathsf{slev}(P) \leq_s \ell_1) \wedge (\ell_1 \leq_s \mathsf{slev}(P))$	1, Defn $=_s$
5. $(\mathsf{slev}(Q) \leq_s \ell_2) \wedge (\ell_2 \leq_s \mathsf{slev}(Q))$	2, Defn $=_s$
6. $\mathsf{slev}(P) \leq_s \ell_1$	4, Simplification
7. $\mathsf{slev}(P) \leq_s \ell_2$	6, 3 Transitivity of $\leq_s$
8. $\ell_2 \leq_s \mathsf{slev}(Q)$	5, Simplification
9. $\mathsf{slev}(P) \leq_s \mathsf{slev}(Q)$	7,8 Transitivity of $\leq_s$

Logical Rules The last task is to introduce logical rules that support using security levels to reason about access requests. Specifically, the definition and two sound inference rules in Figure 5.2 reflect that $\leq_s$ is a partial order. The antisymmetry of $\leq_s$ emerges directly from the definition of $\ell_1 =_s \ell_2$.

The following useful rule ($\leq_s$ Subst) is derivable, as shown by the proof in Figure 5.3:

$$\leq_s \text{ Subst} \quad \frac{\mathsf{slev}(P) =_s \ell_1 \quad \mathsf{slev}(Q) =_s \ell_s \quad \ell_1 \leq_s \ell_2}{\mathsf{slev}(P) \leq_s \mathsf{slev}(Q)}.$$

5.4.2 Expressing Military Security Policies

With these extensions to the logic in hand, we can now formulate a simple military security policy for managing information flow. There are two parts: (1) the *simple security condition*, which describes the conditions under which read access can be granted; and (2) the **-property*, which states when it is permissible to grant someone write access. Our presentation is based on the *Bell–La Padula* model (Bell and La Padula, 1973; Bell and La Padula, 1975). We provide a simplified discussion here, leaving the full details to Chapter 13.

Definition 5.1 *The **simple security condition** mandates that principal P can read object O if and only if:*

    1. P's security level is at least as high as O's (i.e., $\mathsf{slev}(O) \leq_s \mathsf{slev}(P)$), and

    2. P has discretionary read access to O (i.e., P controls $\langle read, O \rangle$). ■

The simple security condition reflects the thinking that people or processes should have read access to information at their security level or below, *provided* that they need to know. The first component ($\mathsf{slev}(O) \leq_s \mathsf{slev}(P)$) indicates that P can read O only if P's security level is at least as high as O's. The second component requires P to have discretionary read access to O, reflecting P's need to know (i.e., some controlling authority has granted P read access to O). The purpose of the simple security condition is to prevent a principal from reading information at a higher classification level than the principal possesses.

    Unauthorized reading of files, however, is not the only way that information might improperly flow from a higher classification level to a lower one. It is also necessary to prevent the "write-down" of information, whereby information from a file at one classification level is then written to a file with a lower classification level. The standard write policy that prevents such situations is known as the **-property (pronounced "star property")*.

Definition 5.2 *The *-property mandates that principal P can write to object O if and only if:*

    1. O's security level is at least as high as P's (i.e., $\mathsf{slev}(P) \leq_s \mathsf{slev}(O)$), and

    2. P has discretionary write access to O (i.e., P controls $\langle write, O \rangle$). ■

Restricting write access to files at or above a principal's clearance level means that information cannot flow downwards (i.e., to lower classification levels) through the writing of files. Taken together, the simple security condition and the *-property define the desired behavior of systems with a simple military security policy.

    It is straightforward to formalize the behavior mandated by the simple security condition and the *-property. Both the simple security condition and the *-property have two parts: (1) a mandatory access-control condition μ, and (2) a discretionary statement φ. Thus, each can be expressed by a statement of the form $\mu \supset \varphi$.

    In the case of the simple security condition, the mandatory access-control condition is

$$\mathsf{slev}(O) \leq_s \mathsf{slev}(P),$$

which mandates that the security level of object O must be no higher than the security level of subject P. The corresponding discretionary access statement to grant P read access to O is

$$P \text{ controls } \langle read, O \rangle.$$

Thus, we can specify the simple security condition for subject P and object O as follows:

$$(\mathsf{slev}(O) \leq_s \mathsf{slev}(P)) \supset (P \text{ controls } \langle read, O \rangle).$$

In such statements, P discretionary read access to O is conditioned upon P having sufficient clearance with respect to O.

Special note: It is important to realize that the simple security property really mandates *two* properties of a system. The first property states that it is permissible to grant read access to any principal who has both a sufficiently high security level and discretionary read access. It is this property that is expressed by a policy statement

$$(\mathsf{slev}(O) \leq_s \mathsf{slev}(P)) \supset (P \text{ controls } \langle read, O \rangle).$$

The second property asserts that read access should be granted *only* to those principals who have both a sufficiently high security level and discretionary read access. In other words, any principal who is able to obtain read access has sufficient clearance and is authorized, without exception. This second-property is in actuality a meta-property, in that one would have to inspect every consequence of the collection of rules governing access. It is impossible to express such a property in the logic itself.

A similar situation holds with respect to the *-property.

In the same manner, we can express the *-property as follows:

$$(\mathsf{slev}(P) \leq_s \mathsf{slev}(O)) \supset (P \text{ controls } \langle write, O \rangle).$$

That is, P's discretionary write access to O is contingent upon O having a sufficiently high security level (i.e., at least as high as P's).

The intended behavior described by both the simple security condition and the *-property can be captured by the following *Conditional Controls* derived inference rule:

$$\textit{Conditional Controls} \quad \frac{\begin{array}{c} \mu \supset P \text{ controls } \varphi \\ \mu \\ P \text{ says } \varphi \end{array}}{\varphi}.$$

In this rule, the statement $\mu \supset P$ controls φ is a military security policy statement corresponding to either the simple security condition or the *-property: μ is the mandatory access-control policy condition with respect to the subject's and object's security levels, and P controls φ is the discretionary access-control policy. The statement P says φ reflects the actual access request from P, where φ is the action being requested by P.

When writing military security policies for which we wish the simple security condition and the *-property to hold, it is important to follow the form of the *read* and *write* access-control statements presented earlier. Specifically, *all* read authorizations

Document	Classification
threat scenario	TS
status report	TS
requirements	S
design	S
artist renderings	C
press releases	UC

Table 5.2: Classification level of documents

on object O by subject P corresponding to the simple security condition should have the form:

$$(\text{ slev}(O) \leq_s \text{ slev}(P)) \supset (P \text{ controls } \langle read, O \rangle).$$

Similarly, all write authorizations on object O by subject P corresponding to the *-property should have the form:

$$(\text{ slev}(P) \leq_s \text{ slev}(O)) \supset (P \text{ controls } \langle write, O \rangle).$$

In some cases, it may seem simpler to adopt shortcuts, but they can produce unintended results when circumstances change. For example, suppose that Alice is assumed to have the highest security level, which in this case is TOP SECRET. Under the simple security condition, she has read access to all files to which she also has discretionary read access. One might be tempted to take a shortcut and simply state *Alice* controls $\langle read, O \rangle$. When Alice makes a read request—*Alice* says $\langle read, O \rangle$—the *Controls* inference rule allows one to conclude that Alice should be allowed to read O. However, now suppose that Alice's security clearance is later downgraded below TOP SECRET, and that O's security level is TOP SECRET. Because the access policy for Alice reading O does not mention her clearance level, she would still be granted read permission, in direct violation of the simple security condition.

5.4.3   Military Security Policies: An Extended Example

As an extended example, consider the following scenario involving the (fictional) defense contractor *DefenseSystemsRUs*:

> *DefenseSystemsRUs* has defense contracts across several branches of the military. In particular, they have separate contracts with both the Air Force and the Navy to develop air superiority fighters. The Air Force-funded project is called the FX-1, while the Navy-funded project is called the FX-2.
>
> The Defense Department wishes to order only one aircraft, and will select either the FX-1 or FX-2 to serve the needs of both the Air Force and Navy. To ensure a fair competition, the Defense Department has mandated that *DefenseSystemsRUs* have two totally independent design

Function	Clearance	FX-1	FX-2
Team Leader	TS	Amy	Arlen
Engineer	S	Biao	Burt
Artist	C	Sonja	Suresh
Public Relations	UC	Jude	Jodi

Table 5.3: FX-1 and FX-2 project personnel, functions, and clearances

teams, each working closely with the military branch that is funding the team.

As part of the FX-1 and FX-2 contracts, each design team has to work with several documents at various security classification levels. All the documents are stored in *DefenseSystemsRUs* computers. Thus, a security policy is required to control information flow within and between design teams. The policy relies on the four standard military classification levels, linearly ordered as follows (in increasing order): UNCLASSIFIED, CONFIDENTIAL, SECRET, and TOP SECRET.

Table 5.2 lists each document and its classification level. The *threat scenario* is considered TOP SECRET to prevent adversary nations from developing technologies to defeat the FX-1 or FX-2 before they are developed and deployed. The *requirements* document is at the SECRET level to guide design engineers at the SECRET level. Both the *threat scenario* and *requirements* documents are issued by the Department of Defense and cannot be changed by anyone in *DefenseSystemsRUs*. The artist renderings of the FX-1 and FX-2 are CONFIDENTIAL. Press releases are UNCLASSIFIED. Weekly status reports, which go to the government, are TOP SECRET.

The FX-1 and FX-2 teams are organized as shown in Table 5.3. Each team has a *team leader*. Team leaders hold TOP SECRET clearance and are able to read all reports related to their projects. As team leaders, they can write the weekly status reports. They cannot alter the threat scenario or requirements document, as both come from the Defense Department.

Engineers are at the SECRET level. They have read access to the *requirements* and *design* documents. They can modify the *design* documents, but not the *requirements* document.

Artists are at the CONFIDENTIAL level. They can create artist renderings of their aircraft.

Finally, public relations staff are at the UNCLASSIFIED level. They author press releases, which are available to the public.

Given the above scenario, we devise two access-control matrices, one for each project team, with the understanding that members of each team have no access rights to documents written by the other team. These matrices are shown in Tables 5.4 and 5.5. The threat scenario is accessible to both FX-1 and FX-2 team

FX-1 Document	Amy (TS)	Biao (S)	Sonja (C)	Jude (UC)
threat scenario (TS)	read			
status report (TS)	read, write	write	write	write
requirements (S)	read	read		
design (S)	read	read,write		
artist renderings (C)	read	read	read, write	
press releases (UC)	read	read	read	read, write

Table 5.4: FX-1 access matrix

FX-2 Document	Arlen (TS)	Burt (S)	Suresh (C)	Jodi (UC)
threat scenario (TS)	read			
status report (TS)	read, write	write	write	write
requirements (S)	read	read		
design (S)	read	read,write		
artist renderings (C)	read	read	read, write	
press releases (UC)	read	read	read	read, write

Table 5.5: FX-2 access matrix

leaders; the requirements document is accessible to the team leaders and engineers of both projects.

The access-control matrices adhere to the simple military security properties specified by the simple security condition and the *-property. Access to files is based on a need to know. For example, while there would be no violation of information flow policies if Jude in Public Relations were allowed to write to the FX-1 design documents, there is no compelling need to grant her write access.

Formal description: We translate the preceding informal descriptions into the access-control logic. Doing so provides us with a precise description of the scenario and enables us to do a rigorous analysis of behavior.

The first task is to identify the security labels for this application (e.g., UC, C, S, TS) and to specify the ordering among them. We can express the ordering as a series of statements in the logic, as follows:

$$UC \leq_s C, \qquad C \leq_s S, \qquad S \leq_s C.$$

Note that (for example) $UC \leq_s S$ can be deduced using the transitivity rule for $\leq_s$.

The second task is to state in the logic the assignment of security levels to principals and objects, as specified in Tables 5.2 and 5.3. We include here the statements related to the FX-1 project (those for the FX-2 project are similar):

$$\text{slev}(threatScenario) =_s \text{TS} \qquad \text{slev}(Amy) =_s \text{TS}$$
$$\text{slev}(status_{FX1}) =_s \text{TS} \qquad \text{slev}(Biao) =_s \text{S}$$
$$\text{slev}(reqs) =_s \text{S} \qquad \text{slev}(Sonja) =_s \text{C}$$
$$\text{slev}(design_{FX1}) =_s \text{S} \qquad \text{slev}(Jude) =_s \text{UC}$$
$$\text{slev}(artistRend_{FX1}) =_s \text{C}$$
$$\text{slev}(pressRel_{FX1}) =_s \text{UC}$$

In our simplified analysis, we just accept these statements as assumptions of the form $\text{slev}(status_{FX1}) =_s \text{TS}$ and $\text{slev}(Amy) =_s \text{TS}$. More detailed descriptions would include the source and jurisdiction of these statements: for example, a *security officer SO* might have the authority and responsibility to certify the security levels of people and documents. This would be described in the usual way as *SO* says ($\text{slev}(status_{FX1}) =_s \text{TS}$) and *SO* controls ($\text{slev}(status_{FX1}) =_s \text{TS}$). To keep things simple for this example, we will just assume these levels as stated.

Finally, at the object level of the access-control logic, we consider the access-control matrices in Tables 5.4 and 5.5. As we did with setting security levels, we take the access-control statements as assumptions. More detailed descriptions would include the source of these statements and the authority of the sources. For simplicity, we assume the content of these statements is appropriate and has the backing of those in authority. We can translate Table 5.4 into statements on who can access *FX-1 status reports* as follows (access to other documents can be similarly described):

$$\text{slev}(status_{FX1}) \leq_s \text{slev}(Amy) \supset (Amy \text{ controls } \langle read, status_{FX1} \rangle)$$
$$\text{slev}(Amy) \leq_s \text{slev}(status_{FX1}) \supset (Amy \text{ controls } \langle write, status_{FX1} \rangle)$$
$$\text{slev}(Biao) \leq_s \text{slev}(status_{FX1}) \supset (Biao \text{ controls } \langle write, status_{FX1} \rangle)$$
$$\text{slev}(Sonja) \leq_s \text{slev}(status_{FX1}) \supset (Sonja \text{ controls } \langle write, status_{FX1} \rangle)$$
$$\text{slev}(Jude) \leq_s \text{slev}(status_{FX1}) \supset (Jude \text{ controls } \langle write, status_{FX1} \rangle).$$

The *-property says that any FX-1 team member can submit their portion of the FX-1 status report. The simple security condition says that only Amy—as the team leader with a TOP SECRET clearance—can read the report.

If the read-access and write-access statements in the access-control matrices are translated into formulas following the pattern for military security policies, then the simplified security condition and the *-property describe the behavior of the system. For example, if Jude wishes to write her status report, the following derived inference rule describes what happens:

FIGURE 5.4 Proof justifying Jude's access to status report

1.	$\mathsf{slev}(Jude) \leq_s \mathsf{slev}(status_{FX1}) \supset (Jude \text{ controls } \langle write, status_{FX1} \rangle)$	Assumption
2.	$\mathsf{slev}(Jude) =_s \text{UC}$	Assumption
3.	$\mathsf{slev}(status_{FX1}) =_s \text{TS}$	Assumption
4.	$\text{UC} \leq_s \text{TS}$	Assumption
5.	$Jude \text{ says } \langle write, status_{FX1} \rangle$	Assumption
6.	$\mathsf{slev}(Jude) \leq_s \mathsf{slev}(status_{FX1})$	2, 3, 4 $\leq_s$ Subst
7.	$\langle write, status_{FX1} \rangle$	1, 6, 5 Cond'l Controls

---

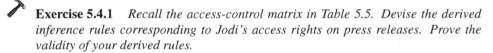

$$\frac{\begin{array}{c} \mathsf{slev}(Jude) \leq_s \mathsf{slev}(status_{FX1}) \supset (Jude \text{ controls } \langle write, status_{FX1} \rangle) \\ \mathsf{slev}(Jude) =_s \text{UC} \\ \mathsf{slev}(status_{FX1}) =_s \text{TS} \\ \text{UC} \leq_s \text{TS} \\ Jude \text{ says } \langle write, status_{FX1} \rangle \end{array}}{\langle write, status_{FX1} \rangle}.$$

The above rule has as its first hypothesis the write-access policy statement corresponding to the *-property: Jude can write to $status_{FX1}$ so long as the security level of $status_{FX1}$ is the same or is higher than Jude's security level. The next two hypotheses are Jude's and $status_{FX1}$'s security levels. The last hypothesis is Jude's write request.

Figure 5.4 contains a proof justifying that Jude be allowed to write the FX-1 status report.

Exercise 5.4.1 *Recall the access-control matrix in Table 5.5. Devise the derived inference rules corresponding to Jodi's access rights on press releases. Prove the validity of your derived rules.*

Exercise 5.4.2 *Recall the access-control matrix in Table 5.4. Suppose that artists renderings are now unclassified. Is the Bell–La Padula model still satisfied? If not, suggest a change in Table 5.4 that restores compliance with the Bell–La Padula model.*

5.5   Commercial Policies

Commercial policies are primarily concerned with *integrity*, namely the level of quality and trustworthiness. Businesses fail if the quality or trustworthiness of their products or services fail to live up to consumer expectations. For example, consider what happens to a restaurant that serves tainted food to its customers.

Commercial integrity policies use labels in many of the same ways that military security policies use labels. Integrity labels often reflect a grading of quality or trustworthiness levels. For example, a grading scheme we encounter in daily life is the grading of gasoline based on its octane level. The gasoline we pump into our cars is usually one of three grades: REGULAR, MID-GRADE, or PREMIUM. From the consumer standpoint, higher gasoline grades are more expensive. From the petroleum refinery's standpoint, higher gasoline grades require more refinement and are more costly to produce. The public expects gasoline grades and labels to match and feels defrauded when they do not.

Another grading scheme we encounter in daily life is level of customer service. For example, banking customers with balances of $200,000 or more in their accounts might qualify for PREMIUM customer service. Customers with lesser balances qualify for STANDARD customer service. It may be that STANDARD service includes 24-hour automated support and 24-hour phone support. PREMIUM support might include everything that STANDARD support has, plus the assignment of a personal banker available during working hours during the work week. Because higher levels of customer support are more costly to companies and meeting customer expectations is crucial to stay in business, well-run businesses establish and enforce service (integrity) policies to meet customer expectations while controlling costs.

In this section we introduce basic policies aimed at preserving integrity.

5.5.1 Extending the Logic with Integrity Levels

As we did for security labels, we extend our logic to incorporate integrity labels and a means to compare them. A variety of integrity labels are possible, and they are partially ordered. The formalization is nearly identical to that for security labels: the only difference is in our intention to distinguish integrity levels from security levels, so as to permit analyses that involve both (as in Chapter 13).

Syntax   We define **IntLabel** to be the collection of *simple integrity labels*, and we define **IntLevel** to be the set of *all* possible integrity-level expressions:

$$\textbf{IntLevel} ::= \textbf{IntLabel} \;/\; \mathsf{ilev}(\textbf{PName})$$

Informally, $\mathsf{ilev}(A)$ refers to the integrity—i.e., quality or trustworthiness—level of principal A.

We then extend our definition of well-formed formulas to support comparisons of security levels:

$$\textbf{Form} ::= \textbf{IntLevel} \leq_i \textbf{IntLevel} \;/\; \textbf{IntLevel} =_i \textbf{IntLevel}$$

The symbol $\leq_i$ denotes a partial ordering on integrity levels, in the same way that $\leq_s$ denotes a partial ordering on security levels. In particular, $\leq_i$ is reflexive, transitive, and antisymmetric.

FIGURE 5.5 Inference rules for relating integrity levels

$$\ell_1 =_i \ell_2 \overset{\text{def}}{=} (\ell_1 \leq_i \ell_2) \wedge (\ell_2 \leq_i \ell_1)$$

$$\textit{Reflexivity of} \leq_i \quad \overline{\ell \leq_i \ell}$$

$$\textit{Transitivity of} \leq_i \quad \frac{\ell_1 \leq_i \ell_2 \qquad \ell_2 \leq_i \ell_3}{\ell_1 \leq_i \ell_3}$$

Semantics   The semantics of integrity levels is added to the logic by extending Kripke structures in precisely the same way we did for security levels. Specifically, we introduce extended Kripke structures of the form

$$\mathcal{M} = \langle W, I, J, K, L, \preceq \rangle,$$

where:

- W, I, and J are defined as in Definition 2.1.

- K is a non-empty set, which serves as the universe of *integrity levels*.

- $L : (\textbf{IntLabel} \cup \textbf{PName}) \rightarrow K$ is a function that maps each integrity label and each simple principal name to a integrity level.

  L can be extended to work over arbitrary security-level expressions, as follows:

  $$L(\text{ ilev}(A)) = L(A),$$

  for every simple principal name A.

- $\preceq \subseteq K \times K$ is a partial order on K: that is, $\preceq$ is *reflexive* (for all $k \in K$, $k \preceq k$), *transitive* (for all $k_1, k_2, k_3 \in K$, if $k_1 \preceq k_2$ and $k_2 \preceq k_3$, then $k_1 \preceq k_3$), and *anti-symmetric* (for all $k_1, k_2, k_3 \in K$, if $k_1 \preceq k_2$ and $k_2 \preceq k_1$, then $k_1 = k_2$).

Using these extended Kripke structures, we define the semantics for our new well-formed expressions as follows:

$$\mathcal{E}_{\mathcal{M}}[\![\ell_1 \leq_i \ell_2]\!] = \begin{cases} W, & \text{if } L(\ell_1) \preceq L(\ell_2) \\ \emptyset, & \text{otherwise} \end{cases}$$

$$\mathcal{E}_{\mathcal{M}}[\![\ell_1 =_i \ell_2]\!] = \mathcal{E}_{\mathcal{M}}[\![\ell_1 \leq_i \ell_2]\!] \cap \mathcal{E}_{\mathcal{M}}[\![\ell_2 \leq_i \ell_1]\!].$$

As these definitions suggest, the expression $\ell_1 =_i \ell_2$ is simply syntactic sugar for $(\ell_1 \leq_i \ell_2) \wedge (\ell_2 \leq_i \ell_1)$. Given the semantics of integrity levels, it is straightforward to prove the soundness of the inference rules in Figure 5.5, which show that $\leq_i$ is a partial order.

Just as in the case of security levels, the following derived rule $\leq_i$ *Subst* holds true for integrity levels:

$$\leq_i Subst \quad \frac{\mathsf{ilev}(P) =_s \ell_1 \quad \mathsf{ilev}(Q) =_i \ell_i \quad \ell_1 \leq_i \ell_2}{\mathsf{ilev}(P) \leq_i \mathsf{ilev}(Q)}.$$

5.5.2 Protecting Integrity

The major concern of integrity policies is protecting the system and its resources from *damage, misappropriation, or corruption.* In the case of petroleum refineries, integrity policies might ensure that REGULAR, MID-GRADE, and PREMIUM grades have at least 87, 91, and 93 octane, respectively. In the case of banking services, service policies might guarantee that big depositors have immediate (e.g., less than one-minute wait times) access to a human banker during business hours while regular customers have access to human bankers only after having used automated support.

Some of the earliest work on integrity in computer systems was done in the 1970's by Biba. Although this work appeared prior to the threat of worms and viruses, the definitions and principles that informed the integrity policies then are still relevant now. Biba defined computer system integrity as follows (Biba, 1975):

> The concern of computer system integrity is thus the guarantee that a subsystem will perform as it was intended to perform by its creator. We assume that a subsystem has been initially certified (by some system external agency) to perform properly. We then wish to insure that the subsystem cannot be corrupted to perform in a manner contrary to its certification. The integrity problem is the formulation of access control policies and mechanisms that provide a subsystem with the isolation necessary for protection from subversion. Based on an initial assumption of proper behavior (according to some system external standard), we are primarily concerned with protection from intentionally malicious attack: unprivileged, intentionally malicious modification.

Subjects and objects have the same function in both integrity and confidentiality policies: subjects are active in that they make requests, whereas objects are passive and do not make requests.

We consider three kinds of access:

1. *Observation:* the viewing of information by a subject. The act of viewing also embodies the notion of *execution* or changing the state of the observing subject as a result of the observation. For example, program execution by a subject is accomplished by a subject observing (fetching) a program from an object.

2. *Modification:* a change in the object that is discernible by observation.

3. *Invocation:* a request for service by one subject of another. This is a form of modification, because the state of the invoked subject is changed by the request for service, if the request is accepted.

FIGURE 5.6 Subjects, objects, domains, and access

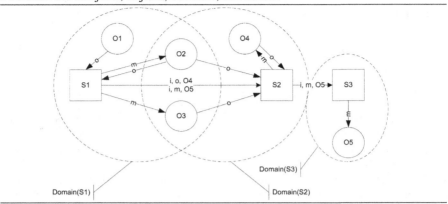

Each subject has an associated *domain*, which defines the objects and kind of access the subject has. The domain of a subject may overlap or be completely separate from the domain of any other subject.

Figure 5.6 shows three subjects S_1, S_2, and S_3, each with its own domain (access to objects). Subjects are represented by squares, objects by circles, and the kind of access allowed by labeled arcs connecting subjects and objects. The domains of S_1 and S_2 overlap; the domains of S_1 and S_3 do not.

For example, S_1's domain gives it access to three objects: O_1, O_2, and O_3. S_1 is able to observe objects O_1 and O_2, and is able to modify objects O_2 and O_3. Figure 5.6 also show the invocation rights of subjects. S_2 is able to invoke S_3 to modify O_5 and S_1 can invoke S_2 to observe O_4 and modify O_5.

In the next section, we introduce Biba's strict integrity property (Biba, 1975), which protects the integrity of both subjects and objects. It does so by ensuring that subjects observe or read only from objects of equal or greater integrity and that objects are modified only by subjects of equal or greater integrity.

5.5.3 Strict Integrity

The objective of strict integrity is to *preserve* the integrity of objects and subjects, which means that no access *degrades* the integrity of any object or subject. Informally, preserving integrity requires meeting the following conditions:

1. If there is a path by which the contents of O_1 can migrate to O_{n+1}, then the contents of O_{n+1} must not be degraded by the contents of O_1. Thus, the integrity of O_1 must be at least as high as that of O_{n+1}:

$$\mathsf{ilev}(O_{n+1}) \leq_i \mathsf{ilev}(O_1).$$

2. If subject S can observe object O, then S must not be degraded by the contents

of O. Thus, the integrity of O must be at least as high as that of S:

$$\mathsf{ilev}(S) \leq_i \mathsf{ilev}(O).$$

3. Degradation cannot occur due to a subject with greater integrity following the directions (invocations) of a subject with lesser integrity (e.g., a user telling the system administrator to turn off all anti-virus software).

The first two conditions deal with *direct* access, which we discuss in the rest of this chapter. The third condition deals with *indirect* access through invocation, which we defer until Chapter 13.

To formalize strict integrity, we must first introduce the notion of a transfer path.

Definition 5.3 *A transfer path is a sequence of objects $O_1, O_2, \cdots, O_{n+1}$ and subjects $S_1, S_2, \cdots, S_n$ such that:*

S_1 *can observe/take* O_1
S_1 *can modify/put* O_2
S_2 *can observe/take* O_2
S_2 *can modify/put* O_3
$\cdots$
S_n *can observe/take* O_n
S_n *can modify/put* O_{n+1}. ∎

A transfer path allows one or more subjects to collectively transfer or copy the contents of one object to another. The following example demonstrates both the concept of a transfer path and its expression in the logic.

Example 5.3
Suppose that the subject S_1 has the authority to observe object O_1 directly and to modify object O_2 directly. Representing the direct observation and modification of an object O by the primitive propositions $\langle o, O \rangle$ and $\langle m, O \rangle$, respectively, we can represent these two authorizations as follows:

$$S_1 \text{ controls } \langle o, O_1 \rangle,$$
$$S_1 \text{ controls } \langle m, O_2 \rangle.$$

Given S_1's authority, there is a transfer path (via S_1) from O_1 to O_2. Similarly, if subject S_2 has the authority to observe O_2 and modify O_3, then there is a transfer path from O_2 to O_3. Combining the transfer paths for S_1 and S_2 results in a transfer path from O_1 to O_3. ◇

Strict integrity mandates that no subject or object along a transfer path can ever possibly become degraded. That is, for any possible operation along a transfer path, the contents of a destination must never be contaminated with the contents of a source

FIGURE 5.7 Preparation of vegetarian and non-vegetarian meals

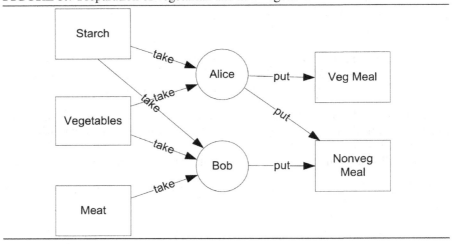

with a lower level of integrity. Thus, under strict integrity, if we wish to grant subject S the authority to *observe* an object O, we must first ensure that O's integrity level is at least as high as S's. In contrast, if we wish to grant S the authority to *modify* O, we must first ensure that S's integrity level is at least as high as O's.

Consequently, we can express strict integrity policies for direct observations and direct modifications as follows:

$$(\text{ilev}(S) \leq_i \text{ilev}(O)) \supset (S \text{ controls } \langle o, O \rangle),$$
$$(\text{ilev}(O) \leq_i \text{ilev}(S)) \supset (S \text{ controls } \langle m, O \rangle).$$

If the strict integrity conditions are violated, then access requests should be trapped:

$$\neg(\text{ilev}(S) \leq_i \text{ilev}(O)) \supset (S \text{ says } \langle o, O \rangle) \supset \langle trap \rangle,$$
$$\neg(\text{ilev}(O) \leq_i \text{ilev}(S)) \supset (S \text{ says } \langle m, O \rangle) \supset \langle trap \rangle.$$

5.5.4   An Extended Example of a Strict Integrity Policy

As a simple example of the application of strict integrity, consider the preparation of vegetarian and non-vegetarian meals. For the purpose of this example, we assume that the preparation of vegetarian meals requires following certain rules and procedures beyond the preparation of non-vegetarian meals. In other words, we assume that people cooking vegetarian meals require additional training beyond the training to cook non-vegetarian meals.

For the purposes of this example, we have two subjects (Alice and Bob) and five objects (starch, vegetables, meat, veg meal, and non-veg meal). Alice is a vegetarian cook, and Bob is a non-vegetarian cook. As a vegetarian cook, Alice takes from starch and vegetables to prepare items for veg meals. She can also provide veg dishes

Subject	Starch	Vegetables	Meat	Veg Meal	Non-veg meal
Alice	take	take	-	put	put
Bob	take	take	take	-	put

Table 5.6: Access matrix for vegetarian and non-vegetarian meals

Subject or Object	Integrity Level
Alice	V
Bob	NV
Starch	V
Vegetables	V
Meat	NV
Veg Meal	V
Non-veg Meal	NV

Table 5.7: Integrity levels for subjects and objects

for non-veg meals. In contrast, Bob (as a non-vegetarian cook) may draw upon all possible ingredients. Because his level of training does not qualify him to prepare certified vegetarian meals, however, he can only prepare items for non-veg meals.

Figure 5.7 shows Alice's and Bob's various capabilities, resulting in the following transfer paths:

- Starch and vegetables can be put into a veg meal through Alice.

- Starch and vegetables can be put into a non-veg meal through either Alice or Bob.

- Meat can be put into a non-veg meal through Bob.

The information in this figure corresponds to the access matrix in Table 5.6. However, the access matrix alone fails to capture the underlying certifications and rules that assure the integrity of vegetarian meals.

While we could implement the access matrix in Table 5.6, we would fail to capture the underlying certifications and rules that assure the integrity of vegetarian meals. To capture these aspects, we introduce two integrity levels (V and NV, with $NV \leq_i V$) and assign them to the subjects and objects as in Table 5.7.

FIGURE 5.8 Partial access diagram for gasoline

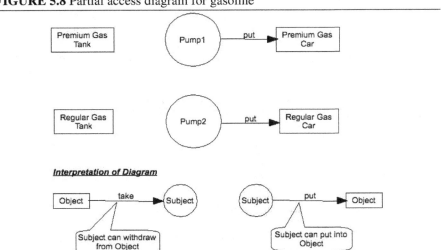

The resulting strict-integrity policy for Alice and Bob can be expressed as follows:

$$\text{ilev}(Alice) \leq_i \text{ilev}(Starch) \supset Alice \text{ controls } \langle take, Starch \rangle$$
$$\text{ilev}(Alice) \leq_i \text{ilev}(Vegetables) \supset Alice \text{ controls } \langle take, Vegetables \rangle$$
$$\text{ilev}(veg\ meal) \leq_i \text{ilev}(Alice) \supset Alice \text{ controls } \langle put, veg\ meal \rangle$$
$$\text{ilev}(non\text{-}veg\ meal) \leq_i \text{ilev}(Alice) \supset Alice \text{ controls } \langle put, non\text{-}veg\ meal \rangle$$
$$\text{ilev}(Bob) \leq_i \text{ilev}(Starch) \supset Bob \text{ controls } \langle take, Starch \rangle$$
$$\text{ilev}(Bob) \leq_i \text{ilev}(Vegetables) \supset Bob \text{ controls } \langle take, Vegetables \rangle$$
$$\text{ilev}(Bob) \leq_i \text{ilev}(Meat) \supset Bob \text{ controls } \langle take, Meat \rangle$$
$$\text{ilev}(non\text{-}veg\ meal) \leq_i \text{ilev}(Bob) \supset Bob \text{ controls } \langle put, non\text{-}veg\ meal \rangle.$$

Exercise 5.5.1   *Consider the following scenario. There are two grades of gasoline: P for premium gasoline and R for regular gasoline. There are also two pumps (Pump1 and Pump2) and two cars: one car (RGC) uses regular gasoline and the other car (PGC) requires premium gasoline.*

Assume that the typical relation on gasoline grades holds: premium gasoline is higher quality than regular gasoline. You may also assume that cars specified as taking a particular grade of gasoline can safely take that grade of gasoline or higher.

   a. *Provide the additional arrows (along with their proper labels) necessary for Figure 5.8 to satisfy the following:*

   (a) *Biba's strict integrity policy, and*

   (b) *Fuel requirements on cars.*

b. *Based on your completed diagram, for each pump below, give their domains:*

Pump1 =

Pump2 =

c. *Using P for* Premium *grade and R for regular grade, fill out the level assignments for the subject and objects in the following table:*

Subjects and Objects	Integrity Level
Premium Gas Tank PGT	
Regular Gas Tank RGT	
Pump1	
Pump2	
Premium Gas Car PGC	
Regular Gas Car RGC	

d. *Fill in the access-control matrix:*

Subject	PGT	RGT	PGC	RGC
Pump1				
Pump2				

e. *Express as a formula in the access-control logic the policy that states that Pump1 can* put *into* PGC.

f. *Propose a derived inference rule that states that Pump1 can* put *gasoline into* PGC. *Give a formal proof of the derived rule.*

Exercise 5.5.2 *A* cleanroom *is a room with a strictly maintained environment to control the level of contaminants—such as dust particles or microbes—that can contaminate manufacturing processes. Cleanrooms are classified according to the number and size of particles per volume of air.*

The International Standards Organization standard ISO 14644-1 rates the cleanliness of cleanrooms based on the log base 10 of the number of particles $0.1\mu m$ or larger permitted per cubic meter of air. Based on ISO 14644-1, an ISO Class 5 cleanroom has at most $10^5 = 100,000$ particles per m^3 of air. The ordering of cleanliness levels is

$$\cdots < class\ 6 < class\ 5 < class\ 4 < \cdots.$$

The cleanliness of cleanrooms is maintained by a combination of (1) special air handlers and filters to control the flow of air between cleanrooms and (2) airlocks using air showers to clean people to match the level of cleanliness of the cleanroom they are entering. As to be expected, higher levels of cleanliness require longer times in airlocks.

Suppose we have a semiconductor or biotechnology assembly line that starts in a class 4 *cleanroom and ends in a* class 6 *cleanroom. People and parts enter the cleanrooms as follows:*

- *People* enter *cleanrooms from* airlocks, *and*

- *People in cleanrooms* take *parts from* bins.

The access-control rules on people entering cleanrooms from airlocks *and people in* cleanrooms taking parts from bins *must satisfy the following integrity concerns:*

- Parts must be protected from contamination *or else the final product is contaminated or corrupted. These parts are rated* class 4, class 5, *and* class 6.

- *The* cleanrooms must be protected from contamination *from both parts and people.*

The following are the integrity levels for cleanrooms, bins, and airlocks.

$$ilev(Room_A) = ilev(Bin_A) = ilev(Airlock_A) = class\ 4$$
$$ilev(Room_B) = ilev(Bin_B) = ilev(Airlock_B) = class\ 5$$
$$ilev(Room_C) = ilev(Bin_C) = ilev(Airlock_C) = class\ 6$$

a. *We describe in the access-control logic people in* $Room_i$ taking *parts from* Bin_j *as follows:*

$$Room_i\ says\ \langle take, Bin_j \rangle.$$

(a) *Fill in the access-control matrix showing which rooms are allowed to* take *parts from which bins.*

Objects

Subjects	Bin_A	Bin_B	Bin_C
$Room_A$			
$Room_B$			
$Room_C$			

(b) *Based on the preceding access-control matrix, formulate in the access-control logic the integrity policy that states when* $Room_i$ *is allowed to* take *parts from* Bin_j, *for* $i, j = A, B, C$.

b. *We describe in the access-control logic people in* $Airlock_i$ *entering* $Room_j$ *as follows:*

$$Airlock_i\ says\ \langle enter, Room_j \rangle.$$

(a) *Fill in the access-control matrix showing which airlocks are allowed to* enter *which rooms.*

Objects

Subjects	Room$_A$	Room$_B$	Room$_C$
Airlock$_A$			
Airlock$_B$			
Airlock$_C$			

(b) *Based on the preceding access-control matrix, formulate in the access-control logic the integrity policy that states when Airlock$_i$ is allowed to enter Room$_j$, for $i, j = A, B, C$.*

5.6   Summary

Security policies state what is allowed and what is not. We examined security policies from several standpoints: mandatory policies, discretionary policies, confidentiality policies, and integrity policies. Mandatory policies apply to all subjects and objects. Discretionary policies typically are set by owners of objects.

We introduced Bell–La Padula simple security condition and *-property, as well as Biba's strict integrity property. We also augmented the access-control logic to support reasoning about policies that depends on security and integrity labels.

The learning outcomes associated with this chapter appear in Figure 5.9.

5.7   Further Reading

The original work by the pioneers of secure computing are well worth reading. Saltzer and Schroeder's classis paper "The Protection of Information in Computer Systems" (Saltzer and Schroeder, 1975) provides an excellent overview of memory protection for isolation and sharing. Bell and La Padula's confidentiality models are published as technical reports (Bell and La Padula, 1973) and (Bell and La Padula, 1975). Biba's original work on integrity also appears as a technical report (Biba, 1975). These are available electronically and should be read by serious students of security.

FIGURE 5.9 Learning outcomes for Chapter 5

After completing this chapter, you should be able to achieve the following learning outcomes at several levels of knowledge:

Comprehension

- When given an access-control matrix, interpret which requests are permitted and which are not.

Application

- When given an informal description, use the Bell–La Padula simple security condition and the *-property as guides for developing confidentiality levels and access rules.

- When given an informal description, use the Biba strict integrity model for developing integrity levels and access rules.

Synthesis

- When given an informal mandatory and discretionary access-control policy that is required to meet the simple security condition, *-property, and strict integrity, formalize access rules for subject and objects meeting the requirements.

- When given specific integrity or security levels and a partial ordering of those levels, devise an appropriate Kripke model supporting the semantics of $\leq_i$ and $\leq_s$.

Evaluation

- When given formal access-control rules, security levels, integrity levels, and trust assumptions, derive if an access request should be granted.

Part II

Distributed Access Control

Chapter 6

Digital Authentication

To make reasoned access-control decisions in a digital world, we need to explore in more depth how statements are signed and authenticated digitally. The basis for digital signatures rests on cryptographic keys and cryptographic hash functions in general, and on public-key cryptography in particular. Digital authentication using public-key infrastructure (PKI) is well suited for authentication in distributed environments such as the Internet.

In this chapter, we describe the details of digital authentication using the access-control calculus. Unlike traditional explanations, we do not go into the algorithmic details of any particular encryption or hash function. Rather, we describe the relationship between public and private keys, encryption and decryption, keys and principals, and certificates.

6.1   Public-Key Cryptography

At the core of public-key cryptography are two cryptographic keys: one is *public* and is openly shared (much like a telephone number or email address), and the other is *private* and must be known *only* by a single principal. In theory, the principal who possesses the private key is the only principal who can decrypt messages that were encrypted using the corresponding public key. This property is used to ensure *privacy*: that is, only a principal with the correct private key can read a message. Similarly, messages encrypted using a private key can be universally decrypted by anyone who possesses the corresponding (and publicly disclosed) public key. This property is used for *authenticity*: that is, one can establish the identity of the author of a message.

The public key K and private key K^{-1} together form a *key pair* (K, K^{-1}), and each key can undo the actions of the other. That is, if *encrypt* and *decrypt* are particular encryption and decryption functions, then the following properties must hold for all messages m:

$$decrypt(K^{-1}, encrypt(K, m)) = m,$$
$$decrypt(K, encrypt(K^{-1}, m)) = m.$$

In addition, the public and private keys are typically distinct (i.e., $K^{-1} \neq K$). Conse-

FIGURE 6.1 Process for using public-key encryption for privacy

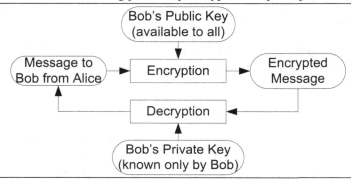

quently, public-key cryptography is often referred to synonymously as *asymmetric-key cryptography*. In the case of public-key algorithms such as RSA (Rivest et al., 1978), the same algorithm serves both to encrypt and decrypt messages.

There are two additional properties about encryption and decryption that are important if a cryptosystem is to be useful:

1. It should be computationally infeasible to read an encrypted message without knowing the correct decryption key.

   That is, given an encrypted message $encrypt(K_e, m)$, it should be computationally infeasible to determine m without knowing the reciprocal key K_d. (Note that K_e may be either a public or private key; K_d is the other half of the key pair.)

2. It should be computationally infeasible to successfully forge an encryption without knowing the encryption key K_e.

   That is, given a message m but without knowing K_e, it should be computationally infeasible to compute an x such that $decrypt(K_d, x) = m$.

These properties of public-key cryptography support privacy in the following way. If Alice wishes to send a message to Bob that only Bob can read, she encrypts the message with Bob's *public key K_{Bob}*. Thus, Alice sends to Bob the following:

$$encrypt(K_{Bob}, \text{message}).$$

The idea here is that the resulting cipher text should be decipherable only with knowledge of Bob's *private key K_{Bob}^{-1}*. Upon receipt, Bob uses his private key to decrypt the message:

$$decrypt(K_{Bob}^{-1}, encrypt(K_{Bob}, \text{message})).$$

Figure 6.1 illustrates schematically how Alice and Bob use Bob's keys to ensure privacy of the message sent to Bob.

The use of public-key cryptography is not limited solely to achieving privacy. More often, it is used to authenticate messages, such as website-connection requests,

FIGURE 6.2 Process for using private-key encryption for authenticity

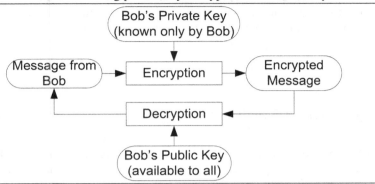

public-key certificates, and so on. For example, suppose that Bob wishes to communicate a message to the world in such a way that anyone can deduce that Bob authored the message. Such a situation might arise if Bob needs to establish his authorship of an article or book for intellectual-property protection. In this case, Bob can encrypt his book using his *private key* (which is known only by him):

$$encrypt(K_{Bob}^{-1}, book).$$

Anyone who cares to read Bob's book can read it using Bob's freely available *public key* to decrypt his encrypted file:

$$decrypt(K_{Bob}, encrypt(K_{Bob}^{-1}, book)).$$

The idea here is that *only* Bob could have created the original encrypted file, because only Bob knows the key K_{Bob}^{-1} used to create it. This sort of use of public-key cryptography for authenticity is illustrated in Figure 6.2.

One can combine these two approaches to achieve a combination of privacy and authenticity. For example, suppose that Alice wants to send a message that only Bob can read, while providing Bob assurance that the message is coming from her. To achieve this goal, Alice employs the following three-step process:

1. Alice encrypts her message m with her *private key*:

$$encrypt(K_{Alice}^{-1}, m).$$

   This step will allow Bob to deduce that Alice authored the message m, because Bob can retrieve m using Alice's *public key*.

2. Alice encrypts the result from step one with Bob's *public key*, resulting in the following:

$$encrypt(K_{Bob}, encrypt(K_{Alice}^{-1}, m)).$$

   This step provides Alice with assurance that only Bob can read her message, because only Bob's private key will be able to decrypt this cipher text.

3. Alice informs Bob in plain text that she is the author of the cipher text from step two. This hint tells Bob to look up Alice's public key so that he can decipher the message in such a way as to be assured that Alice was the author.

6.2   Efficiency Mechanisms

In theory, the approaches described in the previous section are sufficient to handle the needs of privacy and authenticity. In practice, however, the approaches described for authenticity are rarely used, because public-key algorithms are relatively slow and costly to use. In addition, the repeated use of a given key-pair on large amounts of text can expose the keys and make them vulnerable to cryptographic analysis and discovery. To address these pragmatic concerns, two additional steps can be taken: (1) we can use a *cryptographic hashing* algorithm, and (2) we can use a *session* or *data-encryption key* (DEK). We describe these steps—and their use in creating and verifying digital signatures—in this section.

6.2.1   Cryptographic Hash Functions

Hash functions are commonly used in computing as a way to map large data spaces to more compact spaces, substituting uniqueness for efficiency. A very simple example of a hash function is a word-level *parity check*: all 32-bit words with an even number of 1 bits are mapped to the bit 0, while all those with an odd number of 1 bits are mapped to the bit 1. In this case, a data space with 2^{32} elements is mapped to a data space of 2 elements, at the cost of uniqueness: 2^{16} values are hashed to the bit 0, and 2^{16} values are hashed to the bit 1.

Cryptographic hash functions are hash functions with an additional property: given any particular hash value, it must be *computationally infeasible* to determine an input that, when hashed, produces the given value. This property is known as the *one-way property* of cryptographic hashes: while hash values can be computed easily from a given input, it is computationally infeasible to do the reverse (i.e., compute an input that produces a particular hash value). Thus, for example, the parity check clearly fails the one-way property (and hence would not make for a cryptographic hash function), because it is trivial to find 32-bit words with parity 1.

The one-way property of cryptographic hashes makes it possible for fixed-length cryptographic hash values to simulate unique identifiers for messages of arbitrary length. For example, suppose Ellen wants to send a file to Todd that is several megabytes in length, and she wants Todd to be able to determine whether the file he receives has arrived unchanged and uncorrupted. To accomplish this goal, Ellen sends a *cryptographic hash* of the file—also known as the *cryptographic checksum*—along with the file itself:

$$(\textit{file}, \textit{cryptographic checksum}).$$

When Todd receives the file and the cryptographic checksum, he applies the hash algorithm to the received file and compares the value he computed with the checksum sent by Ellen. If they both match, then Todd concludes that the file he received is intact and free of any tampering or corruption.

6.2.2 Data-Encryption Keys

When privacy is also a concern for a large file, the sender may elect to also employ a *symmetric-key* encryption algorithm—such as the Advanced Encryption Standard (AES) (National Institute of Standards and Technology, 2001)—to create a one-time data-encryption key K_{dek}. Symmetric-key encryption algorithms use the same key for both encryption and decryption (i.e., $K_{dek} = K_{dek}^{-1}$). In addition, symmetric-key encryption algorithms are three orders of magnitude faster than typical public-key algorithms, because of the underlying operations they employ (i.e., exclusive-or and bit substitutions as opposed to modulo-n exponentiation).

If Ellen chooses this approach, she first creates a key K_{dek}; she then encrypts the file with K_{dek}, computes the cryptographic checksum of the file, and encrypts K_{dek} with Todd's public key K_{Todd}. Ellen sends these three items to Todd:

$$encrypt(K_{Todd}, K_{dek}), \qquad hash(file), \qquad encrypt(K_{dek}, file).$$

When Todd receives these three items, he first retrieves the data-encryption key K_{dek} by using his private key:

$$decrypt(K_{Todd}^{-1}, encrypt(K_{Todd}, K_{dek})) = K_{dek}.$$

He then uses the data-encryption key to retrieve the file:

$$decrypt(K_{dek}, encrypt(K_{dek}, file)) = file.$$

Finally, he checks the integrity of the retrieved file by determining whether it hashes to the cryptographic checksum that Ellen sent.

Unfortunately, however, this scheme is subject to fraud, because none of the sent items directly tie Ellen to the message that Todd receives. As a result, a third party could send their own message (along with its cryptographic checksum) to Todd, alleging that the message is from Ellen. Todd has no way of determining the truth of such a claim. We can address this problem by introducing digital signatures in the next subsection.

6.2.3 Digital Signatures

We can fix the potential fraud problem by one addition: Ellen creates a *digital signature* by encrypting the cryptographic checksum with her *private key*. Figure 6.3 illustrates a process for creating digital signatures that supports both integrity and authorship:

1. The message or file is hashed by a one-way function. The resulting fixed-length hash value identifies the contents of the message.

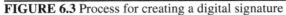

FIGURE 6.3 Process for creating a digital signature

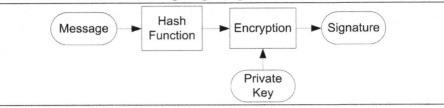

FIGURE 6.4 Process for verifying a digital signature

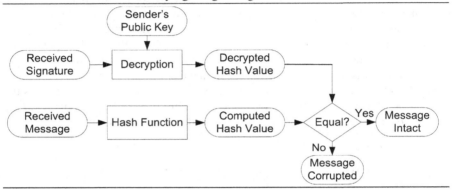

2. The hash value is then encrypted using the *private* key of the sender. The encrypted hash value identifies the sender, because the hash value can be retrieved only by using the sender's public key. Note that, because the hash value is much smaller than the message itself, this approach is much more efficient than the process described in Section 6.1.

Unlike human signatures, which remain relatively unchanged over time, digital signatures change depending on the contents of what is being signed.

Figure 6.4 illustrates the process of verifying a digital signature. The process simply compares the following two values: (1) the hash value obtained by decrypting the received signature using the sender's public key, and (2) the hash value obtained by hashing the contents of the received message. If the values match, then the received message is considered to be both intact and from the public key's owner.

6.3   Reasoning about Cryptographic Communications

In the previous two sections, we have seen how cryptography can be used to provide assurances of privacy and authenticity in distributed digital systems. In this

FIGURE 6.5 Simple analysis of digital signatures

1. K_{Ellen} says m Received message with signature verified using K_{Ellen}
2. $K_{Ellen} \Rightarrow Ellen$ Ellen's public key
3. $Ellen$ says m 2, 1 Derived speaks for

section, we see how the access-control logic can be used to express and reason about cryptographic communications.

As an example, suppose that Ellen uses the methods described in Section 6.2 to send Todd a digitally signed message. For this first case, let us imagine that Ellen sends the message itself in the clear (i.e., in plaintext with no encryption), but she digitally signs it. Thus, she sends to Todd the following combination of items:

$$m, \quad encrypt(K_{Ellen}^{-1}, hash(m)).$$

That is, she sends the message m, along with the encrypted hash (i.e., cryptographic checksum) of m.

When Todd receives the message, he applies the signature-verification protocol of Figure 6.4. If this process is successful, then Todd has evidence that Ellen's public key K_{Ellen} has been used to verify that the message m arrived intact and uncorrupted. This fact can be expressed in the access-control logic by recognizing m as a statement made by K_{Ellen}:

$$K_{Ellen} \text{ says } m.$$

If Todd believes that K_{Ellen} is Ellen's public key—perhaps he looked her key up in a public directory, or perhaps Ellen gave it to him sometime in the past—then he is willing to associate statements made (i.e., integrity-checked) by that key with Ellen. Thus, the belief that Ellen's public key is K_{Ellen} can be expressed in the logic as the following statement:

$$K_{Ellen} \Rightarrow Ellen.$$

Based on these two factors, Todd can deduce that Ellen originally sent the message m. In terms of the logic, this analysis uses the *Derived Speaks For* rule, as shown in the proof of Figure 6.5.

Having examined the simpler case, now let us consider the case where Ellen sends Todd a digitally signed message, using a data-encryption key K_{dek} to encrypt the message. Recall that Todd receives three items, along with a hint that Ellen is the sender:

$$encrypt(K_{Todd}, K_{dek}), \quad encrypt(K_{dek}, m), \quad encrypt(K_{Ellen}^{-1}, hash(m)).$$

Todd must decrypt the first component of this package to obtain the key K_{dek}, which he can then use to retrieve the message m. He then verifies Ellen's digital signature by computing the cryptographic hash of m and comparing it with the checksum that Ellen sent.

If this process is successful, then Todd once again used Ellen's public key to verify that the message m he received was indeed the one initially signed by Ellen. As we saw earlier, this situation can be expressed simply as follows:

$$K_{Ellen} \text{ says } m.$$

Although the signature-verification process itself may be more involved in this situation, it plays the same role in Todd's interpretation of the received message. From Todd's perspective, the important aspect is deducing that the message was initially signed by Ellen using the key K_{Ellen}^{-1}, which presumably only she possesses. Although he initially had to decrypt other components of the message using the keys K_{Todd}^{-1} and K_{dek}, those operations alone do not associate the message m to Ellen.

These two examples provide a general framework for expressing digitally signed and verified statements in our logic. Whenever a digitally signed message m has been verified using the key K_P in a process such as the one shown in Figure 6.4, we represent the message as

$$K_P \text{ says } m.$$

We can express the belief that the key K_P is associated with the principal P as follows:

$$K_P \Rightarrow P.$$

Finally, the *Derived Speaks For* rule allows us to conclude that m originated from the principal P:

$$P \text{ says } m.$$

The important aspect about this abstraction is that it moves beyond the details about signature verification and focuses our attention on who said what.

6.4   Certificates, Certificate Authorities, and Trust

In the examples of the previous section, Todd's reasoning depended crucially upon his assumption that K_{Ellen} was Ellen's key:

$$K_{Ellen} \Rightarrow Ellen.$$

What we have not directly addressed is how Todd—or anyone else, for that matter— would come to believe that K_{Ellen} is Ellen's public key.

In most cases, such a belief originates from a *public-key certificate*, which is issued by an alleged authority called a *certificate authority* (or *CA*, for short). A public-key certificate is a digitally signed statement that associates a given public key with a given principal. A certificate that associates the public key K_P with principal P can be expressed in the logic as

$$K_{CA} \text{ says } (K_P \Rightarrow P),$$

where K_{CA} is the public key of the issuing certificate authority.

Although digital certificates such as these provide necessary information, they alone are insufficient to establish why Todd would believe that $K_{Ellen} \Rightarrow Ellen$. Rather, such beliefs also depend on recognition of the certificate authority and their jurisdiction. For example, suppose that Cora issues a certificate signed with her private key K_{Cora}^{-1}:

$$K_{Cora} \text{ says } (K_{Ellen} \Rightarrow Ellen).$$

Furthermore, suppose that Todd believes that K_{Cora} is Cora's public key:

$$K_{Cora} \Rightarrow Cora.$$

From these two pieces of information, Todd is able to conclude the following:

$$Cora \text{ says } (K_{Ellen} \Rightarrow Ellen).$$

At this point, Todd has a decision to make: does he trust in Cora's integrity, authority, and accuracy when Cora says that $K_{Ellen} \Rightarrow Ellen$? That is, Todd must determine whether or not he is willing to make the following assumption regarding Cora's trustworthiness and jurisdiction:

$$Cora \text{ controls } (K_{Ellen} \Rightarrow Ellen).$$

As this example demonstrates, belief in a public key generally depends upon both a public-key certificate and trust in the certificate authority that issued the certificate. A formal analysis of such a situation typically has the following general form:

1. $K_{ca} \Rightarrow$ Certificate Authority — Trust assumption
2. K_{ca} says $K_P \Rightarrow P$ — Certificate
3. Certificate Authority controls $(K_P \Rightarrow P)$ — Jurisdiction
4. Certificate Authority says $K_P \Rightarrow P$ — 1, 2 Derived speaks for
5. $K_P \Rightarrow P$ — 3, 4 Controls

This proof demonstrates a common pattern that we will observe in many derivations regarding digitally signed statements. In fact, it gives rise to a useful derived rule, which we will see again in future chapters:

Certificate Verification
$$\frac{K_{ca} \Rightarrow \textit{Certificate Authority} \qquad K_{ca} \text{ says } (K_P \Rightarrow P) \qquad \textit{Certificate Authority} \text{ controls } (K_P \Rightarrow P)}{K_P \Rightarrow P}$$

However, the proof also demonstrates a key aspect of public-key infrastructures, which is that they ultimately depend upon trust in *some* public key. In the preceding proof, we rely on the trust assumption $K_{ca} \Rightarrow$ Certificate Authority to deduce that K_P is P's public key. If we were unwilling to make that assumption blindly, then we would require a public-key certificate for the Certificate Authority, which in turn would be signed by yet another CA. Ultimately, the process of evaluating cryptographically signed statements hinges upon the existence of some initial or *root* key that is trusted (i.e., not derived from another signed certificate). This key typically belongs to some top-level root certificate authority and is used to read other key certificates. The following example demonstrates the role of the trusted root key.

Example 6.1

Sally purchases a new computer from a reputable company with the operating system and applications such as web browsers already installed. Upon setting up her computer, Sally types the web address of her favorite Internet bookstore (Good-Books.com) into her web browser. She connects with the bookstore's web site and logs onto her account, which is handled by a secure portion of the web site that relies on a private and public key pair $(K^{-1}_{GoodBooks}, K_{GoodBooks})$. Because she is a careful computer user, she verifies that she has connected to the real GoodBooks.com site by having her web browser authenticate the identity of the site. Her browser reports the following:

> *The identity of this web site has been verified by TrueSignatures, Inc., a certificate authority you trust for this purpose.*

Using her browser, she looks at the public-key certificate of GoodBooks.com and sees that it is signed by TrueSignatures, Inc. She then makes her selections, places her order, enters her credit-card information, and then leaves the site.

We formalize Sally's thinking using the access-control logic as shown below:

1. $K_{TrueSignatures} \Rightarrow TrueSignatures$	Trust assumption
2. $K_{TrueSignatures}$ says $K_{GoodBooks} \Rightarrow$ GoodBooks	Public key certificate
3. $TrueSignatures$ controls $K_{GoodBooks} \Rightarrow$ GoodBooks	Jurisdiction
4. TrueSignatures says $K_{GoodBooks} \Rightarrow$ GoodBooks	1, 2 speaks for
5. $K_{GoodBooks} \Rightarrow$ GoodBooks	3, 4 controls

The preceding example provides a useful basis for exploring the basis of trust assumptions regarding root certificate authorities. Specifically, it is natural to ask whether the trust assumption

$$K_{TrueSignatures} \Rightarrow TrueSignatures$$

is appropriate and (if so) why. In Sally's case, the assumption seems warranted, because she is just an ordinary consumer who bought a computer with software from a reputable firm. Because she is not a high-value target, it is extremely unlikely that Sally is the target of an elaborate fraud scheme to plant a fraudulent key in place of the authentic $K_{TrueSignatures}$ in her computer. The company that sold her the computer is reputable and has safeguards against such fraud (e.g., they use legitimate copies of operating systems and application software). It is therefore reasonable for her to trust that the root certification authority's key $K_{TrueSignatures}$ is installed correctly on her machine.

FIGURE 6.6 Network of certificate authorities

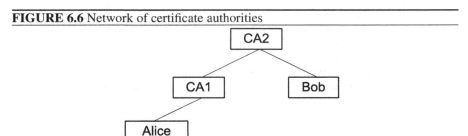

On the other hand, suppose that Sally were a military planner using the computer in a secure military complex. In this case, ruling out an elaborate fraud is not a good basis for trusting in a root-level certification authority. Instead, the corresponding trust assumption of the root certification authority would likely be based on a much more secure process in which a military security officer oversaw the installation of the root key.

Given the different needs of different entities, it is not unusual to have to account for several certificate authorities. In fact, multiple certificate authorities are common when two or more organizations collaborate. In such situations, one certificate authority will vouch for the public key of another certification authority by issuing a public-key certificate for the other authority. Principals who recognize the jurisdiction of the first authority can use that knowledge to rely upon or trust the public key of the second certificate authority. We illustrate this idea in the following example.

Example 6.2

Suppose that Alice wishes to find out Bob's public key, either to send him a message or to verify messages digitally signed by him. Let us also assume that Alice recognizes and trusts the authority of her certificate authority *CA1* and that she believes that $K_{CA1} \Rightarrow$ CA1. Figure 6.6 shows the network of certificate authorities: *CA2* is the certificate authority for both *CA1* and for Bob.

Because Alice knows the public key of *CA1*, she is able to verify and willing to believe the public-key certificate for *CA2* signed by *CA1*. Such a certificate is sometimes called a *reverse certificate*, because the signer is certifying a key for an entity higher up in the hierarchy. Once Alice deduces that $K_{CA2} \Rightarrow$ CA2, she is able to verify and willing to believe the public-key certificate for *Bob* signed by *CA2*. This certificate—in which the signer is certifying a key for an entity lower in the hierarchy—is sometimes called a *forward certificate*.

The following proof shows the trust assumptions made by Alice, as well as the authorities she chooses to recognize:

1. $K_{CA1} \Rightarrow CA1$ trust assumption
2. K_{CA1} says $(K_{CA2} \Rightarrow CA2)$ Key Certificate
3. K_{CA2} says $(K_{Bob} \Rightarrow Bob)$ Key Certificate
4. CA1 controls $(K_{CA2} \Rightarrow CA2)$ Jurisdiction
5. CA2 controls $(K_{Bob} \Rightarrow Bob)$ Jurisdiction
6. CA1 says $(K_{CA2} \Rightarrow CA2)$ 1,2 Derived Speaks For
7. $K_{CA2} \Rightarrow CA2$ 4,6 Controls
8. CA2 says $(K_{Bob} \Rightarrow Bob)$ 7, 3 Derived Speaks For
9. $K_{Bob} \Rightarrow Bob$ 5,8 Controls

The first line is Alice's belief that she knows the public key of *CA1*. Lines two and three are the public-key certificates for *CA2* (signed by *CA1*) and *Bob* (signed by *CA2*). Lines four and five represent Alice's trust in *CA1*'s reliability regarding certifying that K_{CA2} is *CA2*'s key, and in *CA2*'s authority to say truthfully that K_{Bob} is Bob's public key. Lines six through nine are the steps necessary for Alice to deduce that K_{Bob} is indeed Bob's public key.   ◊

Exercise 6.4.1   *Suppose Toni sends Blake a message in the clear that is digitally signed as follows:*

$$(\text{`You're hired!''}, encrypt(K_{Toni}^{-1}, hash(\text{You're hired!''})))$$

The above message is sent over an open channel, such as the Internet. Laura intercepts the message and retransmits it to Blake with one crucial change: "You're hired!" is changed to "You're fired!". Because she wants Blake to think that the message came from Toni, she reuses Toni's digital signature from the message she intercepted.

What happens when Blake receives the message? Is he able to detect the forgery or not?

Exercise 6.4.2   *Use the* Certificate Verification *rule to give an alternate proof for the situation in Example 6.2.*

Exercise 6.4.3   *This question relates to an online-purchase transaction, in which Zoey logs into a previously established account with her userid-password combination. She then attempts to purchase an airline ticket, using her credit card. In what follows, you should interpret CC_Z as a principal representing a specific credit-card number/account.*

   a. Give English translations for each of the following statements, using notions such as authority *(or* jurisdiction*),* signatures, sessions, *and* access requests.

     (a) PwdServer controls $(\langle zoey, pwd \rangle \Rightarrow Zoey)$

     (b) Visa controls $((Zoey \mid CC_Z)$ controls buyticket$)$

     (c) $K_P \Rightarrow PwdServer$

(d) $K_V \Rightarrow Visa$

(e) $(\langle \text{zoey}, pwd \rangle \mid CC_Z)$ says *buyticket*

(f) K_P says $(\langle \text{zoey}, pwd \rangle \Rightarrow Zoey)$

(g) K_V says $((Zoey \mid CC_Z)$ controls *buyticket*$)$

   b. Give a formal proof that buyticket can be deduced from the seven assumptions listed above.

Exercise 6.4.4 *Dana has registered her public key K_D with the certificate authority CA, whose public key is K_{CA}. She wishes to send a message m to Earl, who does not know Dana and does not recognize the authority of CA. Fortunately, Dana knows Earl's good friend Finn, who does recognize CA's authority.*

Furthermore, both Earl and Finn work at Gaggle and have registered their public keys (K_E and K_F, respectively) with the company's certificate authority; the public key for Gaggle's certificate authority is K_G. (Note that both Earl and Finn have access to Gaggle certificates, but they have never exchanged their public keys with one another before.)

Dana signs her message using her private key, and sends it to Finn. She asks Finn to forward it to Earl, which Finn does as follows:

- *Finn uses his private key to sign Dana's signed message, and sends the result to Earl.*

- *Finn also gets a copy of Dana's public-key certificate, and signs and sends that to Earl.*

- *Finn signs a message that indicates what CA's public key is, and sends that to Earl.*

- *Finally, Finn signs and sends to Earl a message stating his confidence in CA's jurisdiction over Dana's public key.*

a. Express in the access-control logic the four items that Finn sends to Earl.

b. Identify the additional certificates, recognitions of authority, and any other trust assumptions that Earl requires in order to deduce that the message m truly came from Dana. You should express each of these items in the access-control logic.

c. Give a formal proof that m can be deduced from your answers to parts (a) and (b).

d. In your opinion, which if any of the assumptions from part (b) are the most suspect? Explain your answer.

Exercise 6.4.5   *Two high-tech companies—NanoTech and PicoWare—are collaborating on a joint project called* ILLUMINA. *The project's repository and web page are housed at* PicoWare's *facilities .*

When the two companies initiated this project, they established a special certificate authority (CA) that both companies would trust with respect to high-level company keys for the purposes of this project *only.* *The public-private key pairs for the various entities are as follows:*

$$(K_{CA}, K_{CA}^{-1})$$ *CA's key pair, trusted by both companies*
$$(K_N, K_N^{-1})$$ *NanoTech's key pair, with K_N registered with CA*
$$(K_P, K_P^{-1})$$ *PicoWare's key pair, with K_P registered with CA*

This setup allows both NanoTech *and* PicoWare *to maintain their existing company key infrastructures, and neither company has to blindly trust the other's infrastructure. Specifically:*

- *NanoTech's public key has been installed on all machines at* NanoTech; *therefore* NanoTech *machines do not need to fetch* NanoTech's *certificate from CA.*

- *Likewise,* PicoWare's *public key has been installed on all machines at* PicoWare; *therefore* PicoWare *machines do not need to fetch* PicoWare's *certificate from CA.*

- *Neither company's public key has been installed on any of the other company's machines. Therefore, certificates from CA are necessary for any secure cross-company communication.*

- *Each company certifies its own internal keys: the keys for all* NanoTech *employees and* NanoTech *machines are certified by* NanoTech, *and the keys for all* PicoWare *employees and* PicoWare *machines are certified by* PicoWare.

(a) *The access-control policy for the* ILLUMINA *project web page grants* **both** *read access ($\langle read, iwp \rangle$) and write access ($\langle write, iwp \rangle$) to all members of the* ILLUMINA *project. Express this access-control policy as an expression in the access-control logic.*

(b) *Stan—a* NanoTech *employee—has been issued the key pair (K_S, K_S^{-1}). Express Stan's public-key certificate as an expression in the access-control logic.*

(c) *Stan has been assigned to the* ILLUMINA *project team, and the group database at* PicoWare *has been updated to reflect this group membership. If ever requested, the group-database server (GDS) can digitally sign a statement that attests to Stan's group membership; the group-database server's key pair is (K_{GDS}, K_{GDS}^{-1}).*

Express such a certificate as an expression in the access-control logic.

*Stan logs into his **NanoTech** office computer, using his **NanoTech**-issued smart card. He then tries to establish an SSL connection to the* ILLUMINA WEB PAGE *at **PicoWare**. To authenticate the SSL connection, Stan's smart card uses his private key to cryptographically sign a response to a challenge from the **PicoWare** server. The SSL connection is secured with a session key K_{ssl}. From the point of view of the web server at **PicoWare**, the result of successfully establishing this SSL connection is the following trust assumption:*

$$K_{ssl} \Rightarrow K_S \qquad (*)$$

(d) **PicoWare**'s *web server receives (via SSL) Stan's request to read the* ILLU-MINA *web page. Express this request as an expression in the access-control logic.*

(e) *What are the additional certificates, recognition of authority, and trust assumptions regarding keys that are necessary for the **PicoWare** web server to determine that the read request should be granted?*

(f) *Give a formal proof that justifies granting the request. Your only assumptions should be your answers to (a) through (e), plus the trust assumption (∗).*

Exercise 6.4.6 *Some access-control decisions are made based on* attributes *(properties such as one's age or the amount of money in your checking account) rather than* identity. *For example, consider what happens when you use a fare card like the Metro card in Washington, D.C.'s Metro system:*

- *From the standpoint of the rider, there are two resources to be accessed: the train at the starting destination and the exit to the street at the ending destination.*

- *The Metro card is a certificate issued by the individual Metro stations and possessed by the rider. Note, however, that while the* physical card *may be the same before entering and after leaving the Metro station, it is **not** the same certificate:*

    - *The information on the Metro card (particularly the amount of money left on the card) must be updated.*

    - *The authorities that sign or vouch for the amount on the card are different: the turnstile used at the beginning of a rider's trip is different from the turnstile used at the end of the trip. Distinguishing the separate turnstiles (more accurately, the different stations) permits one to charge different amounts for different trips: the exit turnstile can always determine where the trip originated and how much to deduct from the card.*

To see how this works, consider a rider who wishes to travel from Station A to Station B, which is a trip that costs $1. Let's assume that the rider's most recent exit was at Station C, with a balance of $5 on the card.

- *The rider inserts the Metro card into the turnstile at Station A. This card is (ultimately) interpreted as:*

$$\text{Station } C \text{ says } (balance{=}\$5 \wedge exit{=} \text{ Station } C).$$

  Because the balance is greater than \$0, access to the train is granted; the card is returned to the rider saying (in effect):

$$\text{Station } A \text{ says } (balance{=}\$5 \wedge entry{=} \text{ Station } A).$$

- *The rider boards the train and travels to Station B.*

- *The rider inserts his or her Metro card into the turnstile at Station B. Because the balance is sufficient to cover the cost of the trip, the turnstile returns the Metro card with an updated balance of \$4.*

Assume that the turnstiles at the three stations (A, B, and C) form a private network called MetroNet. There is a single certification authority CA that issues public/private key pairs and certifies membership in MetroNet. The relevant keys are as follows:

$$
\begin{array}{ll}
(K_{CA}, K_{CA}^{-1}) & \text{CA's key pair} \\
(K_A, K_A^{-1}) & \text{Station A's key pair} \\
(K_B, K_B^{-1}) & \text{Station B's key pair} \\
(K_C, K_C^{-1}) & \text{Station C's key pair}
\end{array}
$$

Digital signatures (based on the public and private keys distributed by the CA) are used to provide protection against fraudulent cards. Thus, the fare cards are actually digitally signed certificates.

Use expressions in the access-control logic to answer the following questions regarding the certifications, credentials, and access-control policies needed for a rider to travel from Station A to Station B. Treat attributes such as "balance=\$5," "balance > \$0," and "exit= Station C" as simple propositions. Use $\langle enter,A \rangle$ and $\langle exit,B \rangle$ to denote entering at Station A and leaving at Station B, respectively.

- a. *What are the necessary certificates, recognition of authority, and trust assumptions about keys for a turnstile at Station B to recognize Station A as belonging to MetroNet?*

- b. *What are the necessary certificates, recognition of authority, and trust assumptions about keys for a turnstile at Station B to interpret an arbitrary fare card signed by Station A?*

- c. *What is the access policy of turnstiles at Station A that guard entry to trains?*

- d. *Assuming that a turnstile at Station A grants entry access to a rider, what certificate is given back to the rider as he or she passes through the turnstile?*

- e. *Assuming that a turnstile at Station B allows a rider to exit, what certificate is given back to the rider as he or she passes through the turnstile?*

6.5 Symmetric-Key Cryptography

As mentioned earlier in this chapter, an alternative to public-key cryptography is *shared-key* cryptography, also known as *symmetric-key cryptography* because the same key is used for both encryption and decryption. If *encrypt* and *decrypt* are particular symmetric-key encryption and decryption functions, then the following property must hold for all messages m and keys K:

$$decrypt(K, encrypt(K, m)) = m.$$

Symmetric-key encryption algorithms—such as the Advanced Encryption Standard (AES) (National Institute of Standards and Technology, 2001)—provide a significant advantage over public-key algorithms in terms of efficiency. They are typically three orders of magnitude faster than public-key algorithms, because of the underlying operations they employ (i.e., exclusive-or and bit substitutions as opposed to modulo-n exponentiation). For this reason, it is often preferable to encrypt large messages or files using symmetric-key cryptography.

However, shared-key cryptography also has disadvantages that arise from its use of a single key. The first problem is one of planning: Alice can send a secure message to Bob *only* if they have previously agreed upon a specific key to use. Such an arrangement should happen via out-of-band communication, such as during a face-to-face meeting or some other reasonably secure means. In contrast, Alice can send a secure message to Bob via public-key cryptography even if they have never communicated before, as long as they have both published their public keys.

Another problem with shared-key cryptography is one of scale: each principal must maintain a separate key for every other principal with whom he or she wishes to communicate. Thus, a collection of n principals would require on the order of n^2 keys to support all possible two-way conversations; public-key cryptography would require only $2n$ keys (i.e., public and private keys for each principal).

Finally, shared-key cryptography does not support the separation of privacy and authenticity concerns. For example, suppose that Alice wishes to publish a message (i.e., allow it to be read by anyone) in a way that provides evidence of her authorship. We have already seen how to accomplish this goal using public-key cryptography. However, symmetric-key cryptography does not support this goal directly: anyone who has knowledge of the key to decrypt the message could forge a new message or even claim to be the original author.

These disadvantages can be somewhat mitigated through the use of *relays* to simulate a public-key infrastructure. We demonstrate how later in Examples 6.4 and 6.5, but we must first address one additional pragmatic difference between public-key and shared-key cryptography. A sender using public-key cryptography can tell the recipient the relevant key to use. For example, if Alice sends a digitally signed message to Bob, she can also send along her public key for his convenience. Likewise, if she sends a secret message to Bob using his public key, she can notify him which public key she used; that information is useless to anyone who does not know Bob's private key.

If Alice instead uses shared-key cryptography, then she obviously cannot directly indicate which key Bob should use to decrypt the message. However, she can accomplish the same goal by sending along a *key identifier* (or *key hint*) that will be meaningful only to Bob. A key identifier might be as simple as an index into a table of keys that is kept on Bob's machine. Alternatively, Bob may have a master key that he uses to encrypt all his other keys: the key identifier for a shared key K may be the result of encrypting K with that master key. The point here is that, when Alice and Bob set up their shared key, they must also have exchanged their individual key identifiers associated with that key. However, neither needs to know *how* the other selects their key identifiers. The following example demonstrates the use of key identifiers.

Example 6.3

Both Richard and Janet use master keys (K_R and K_J, respectively) to encrypt all their important keys. They have recently set up a shared key K_S that will allow them to communicate with one another securely. At that time, they also exchanged key identifiers:

- Richard keeps a table of encrypted keys on his computer, and he likes to use the indices of this table as his key identifiers. Richard adds the encrypted shared key (i.e., $encrypt(K_R, K_S)$) to this table, and gives the corresponding index (e.g., 213) to Janet as the key identifier to use for this key.

- Janet prefers to use encrypted keys themselves as key identifiers. She therefore encrypts the shared key with her master key and gives the result to Richard as *her* key identifier for the key: $encrypt(K_J, K_S)$.

When Janet sends a secure message to Richard using the shared key K_S, she also sends him his key identifier (i.e., 213) for the key. Richard is able to look up the appropriate entry in his table (i.e., $encrypt(K_R, K_S)$), decrypt it with his master key K_R to obtain K_S, and then use K_S to decrypt Janet's message.

Similarly, when Richard sends a secure message to Janet using the shared key K_S, he also includes her key identifier (i.e., $encrypt(K_J, K_S)$). Janet knows to decrypt this hint with her master key K_J to obtain the key necessary to decrypt Richard's message. ◇

As the preceding example shows, two principals may have very different key identifiers for the same shared key. What is important is that each knows the other's key identifier for the shared key, so that they can always clearly communicate which key is being used. (In fact, two principals may share multiple keys, using each for a different purpose. The use of key identifiers allows them to indicate which is relevant for the given communication.)

We adopt the notational convention[1] of using principals' names or initials as superscripts on keys to denote a given principal's key hint for a specific key. For example, we use K_S^R and K_S^J to denote Richard's and Janet's key hints for the shared key K_S. We can then associate the key hints with the statements that they make (i.e., with the messages encrypted by the keys they hint at). Thus, if Janet sends Richard the message m encrypted with the shared key K_s, we can express Richard's interpretation as follows:

$$K_S^R \text{ says } m.$$

If Richard trusts Janet to keep the shared key K_S private, then he should be willing to associate messages encrypted by K_S with Janet. That is, he should be willing to view the key hint K_S^R (and the key it represents) as a proxy for Janet:

$$K_S^R \Rightarrow Janet.$$

The following series of examples, inspired by a discussion in (Lampson et al., 1992), demonstrates how a symmetric-key system can mimic a public-key infrastructure by judicious use of key identifiers. The approach hinges on the use of *relays*, trusted agents that serve as encryption/decryption intermediaries. Just as any principal can register a public-key with a certificate authority in a PKI, the relay system requires that any principal Q be able to register with a special trusted agent. Furthermore, the trusted agent must know the relay's master key, which the relay uses for creating its key identifiers (similar to Janet's method for key identifiers in Example 6.3).

Example 6.4
Quinton wishes to use symmetric encryption to send a message that Shelby can read and verify as being from Quinton. Although Shelby and Quinton do not share a key, they have both previously established secret-key channels with the trusted relay R by registering with a trusted agent TA. When Quinton registered, TA created and sent back to Quinton two items:

1. A secret key K_q to be shared between Quinton and the relay R

2. R's key identifier $K_q^R = encrypt(K_m, K_q)$ for this key, which TA creates by encrypting the new key K_q with R's master key K_m

TA also publishes a *secret-key certificate* for Quinton that contains two components (we introduce the notation $\langle\langle m_1, m_2, \ldots, m_k \rangle\rangle$ to denote the concatenation of the k items m_1 through m_k):

$$encrypt(K_{ta}, \langle\langle K_q^Q, K_q^R, Quinton \rangle\rangle), \quad K_{ta}^R.$$

---

[1]For convenience, we often blur the distinction between keys and key identifiers when using the logic, such as in the network case studies of Chapter 8. The important point of this discussion is that key hints can be used both in practice and in the logic to shroud secret keys.

The first item associates the pair (K_q^Q, K_q^R) of key identifiers with Quinton; this item is signed by *TA* using the key K_{ta} that it shares with the relay. The second item is the relay's key hint for the shared key K_{ta}, so that anyone who wishes to read the certificate can direct the relay which key to use for decryption. Unlike a public-key certificate, the shared-key certificate is not readable by just anybody: only a principal that knows the secret key K_{ta} (such as *TA* and the relay) can read it.

Quinton encrypts his message m with the key K_q, sending both the encrypted message and the key hint K_q^R to Shelby:

$$encrypt(K_q, m), \quad K_q^R.$$

Shelby cannot decrypt the message directly, because she does not know the shared key that K_q^R identifies. However, because Shelby also registered with *TA*, she shares a secret key K_s with the relay and knows the relay's key hint K_s^R for that key. She therefore forwards these items on to the relay R, along with the key-identifier pair (K_s^S, K_s^R). In effect, Shelby is requesting a decryption of the encryption message and telling the relay how to return the answer. (Shelby can also forward on Quinton's shared-key certificate for decryption, if she wishes to authenticate the message. We leave this possibility for Example 6.5.)

The relay applies its master key K_m to the key hint K_q^R to obtain the key K_q:

$$decrypt(K_m, K_q^R) = decrypt(K_m, encrypt(K_m, K_q)) = K_q.$$

With this key, the relay can decrypt the message $encrypt(K_q, m)$ to obtain the original message m:

$$decrypt(K_q, encrypt(K_q, m)) = m.$$

The relay then repackages this message for Shelby by encrypting m with the shared key $K_s = decrypt(K_m, K_s^R)$, sending back the newly encrypted version as well as the key hint K_s^S:

$$encrypt(K_s, m), \quad K_s^S.$$

Upon receiving this package, Shelby uses the key hint K_s^S to identify the correct key (K_s) to use to decrypt the message:

$$decrypt(K_s, encrypt(K_s, m)) = m.$$

As a result of this process, Shelby interprets this message as follows:

$$K_s^S \text{ says } K_q^R \text{ says } m.$$

That is, the key identifier K_s^S is claiming that the key hint K_q^R was used to send the message m. If Shelby trusts the relay to keep the key K_s secret (i.e., if she believes that $K_s^S \Rightarrow R$) and to accurately translate messages (i.e., R controls K_q^R says m), then she will deduce that m was the original intended message she received (i.e., K_q^R says m).   ◇

The previous example demonstrated how secret-key cryptography can be used to exchange messages between principals who have not previously established a shared secret key. However, the example as it stands does not address authentication concerns: neither the relay nor Shelby are able to associate the key identifier K_q^R with Quinton at the end of the process described. To do so, they must also make use of Quinton's secret-key certificate as demonstrated in the next example.

Example 6.5

By the end of Example 6.4, Shelby had deduced that K_q^R says m. If she wishes to authenticate Quinton as the message's author (i.e., to associate the key hint K_q^R with Quinton), then she forwards Quinton's secret-key certificate to the relay along with her key-hint pair (K_s^S, K_s^R). As with the original message, the relay can decrypt the certificate, which can be expressed in the logic as follows:

$$K_{ta}^R \text{ says } ((K_q^Q, K_q^R) \Rightarrow Quinton).$$

That is, the key hint K_{ta}^R claims that the key-hint pair (K_q^Q, K_q^R) is associated with Quinton. If the relay trusts that the key hint K_{ta}^R (i.e., the key K_{ta}) represents TA and that TA has jurisdiction over which keys represent which principals, then it will be able to associate the key hint K_q^R with *Quinton*.

At this point, the relay must create for Shelby a new certificate that associates the key hint K_q^R with Quinton. The relay sends the following items to Shelby:

$$encrypt(K_s, \langle\langle K_q^R, Quinton \rangle\rangle), \quad K_s^S.$$

As before, Shelby can decrypt the message to interpret the certificate as follows:

$$K_s^S \text{ says } (K_q^R \Rightarrow Quinton). \qquad\qquad \Diamond$$

As a final twist on this scenario, suppose that Shelby wishes to exchange a series of messages with Quinton. She may wish to set up an authenticated channel between herself and Quinton, so that they can exchange messages directly without having to use the relay for continual translations. As the following example demonstrates, Shelby can enlist the relay's help to set up such a channel.

Example 6.6

To set up an authenticated channel with Quinton, Shelby proceeds in the same way as at the beginning of Example 6.5. She forwards Quinton's secret-key certificate to the relay along with her key-hint pair (K_s^S, K_s^R). The relay decrypts this certificate and interprets it as before:

$$K_{ta}^R \text{ says } ((K_q^Q, K_q^R) \Rightarrow Quinton).$$

The relay now creates a new channel for direct communication between Quinton and Shelby. Specifically, the relay creates a new key K and creates key identifiers for Quinton and Shelby by encrypting it with their individual keys:

$$K^Q = encrypt(K_q, K), \qquad K^S = encrypt(K_s, K).$$

The relay then creates a new certificate for Shelby that associates this new key-hint pair (K^Q, K^S) with Quinton:

$$encrypt(K_s, \langle\langle K^Q, K^S, Quinton \rangle\rangle), \quad K_s^S.$$

Shelby can interpret this certificate as follows:

$$K_s^S \text{ says } ((K^Q, K^S) \Rightarrow Quinton).$$

(If Quinton wishes to also authenticate Shelby, then the relay will need to obtain Shelby's original secret-key certificate and then generate a new one for Quinton to use in a similar fashion.) ◊

Exercise 6.5.1 *Consider the certificate that Shelby receives at the end of Example 6.5.*

    a. *What additional trust assumptions must Shelby make in order to identify Quinton as the sender of the original message from Example 6.4?*

    b. *Another possible interpretation in the logic of that certificate is as follows:*

$$K_s^S \text{ says } (K_s^S \mid K_q^R \Rightarrow Quinton).$$

    Given this interpretation, what additional trust assumptions must Shelby make in order to identify Quinton as the sender of the original message from Example 6.4?

    c. *Briefly describe the advantages and disadvantages of the two interpretations, and identify the situations where each might be more appropriate.*

Exercise 6.5.2 *What additional trust assumptions must Shelby make to associate the new key K (or its associated key-hint pair) with Quinton in Example 6.6?*

Exercise 6.5.3 *Suppose that two-way authentication is necessary in Example 6.6 (i.e., Quinton also wishes to authenticate Shelby).*

    a. *What messages need to be sent between Quinton and the relay?*

    b. *Express in the access-control logic how these messages are interpreted, along with the trust assumptions necessary for the protocol to succeed.*

6.6   Summary

We have already seen that authentication—that is, identifying the originator of a request—is critical to sound access control. In the digital world, authentication is made more difficult by the physical absence of the requesting principal: a request arrives as a sequence of bits, with only hints of its origin.

In this chapter, we saw how public-key infrastructures support digital authentication through the use of public and private keys, digital signatures, public-key certificates, and certificate authorities. A PKI supports integrity, privacy, and authentication by providing the means to associate specific keys—and, subsequently, specific statements—with specific principals. We explored how to express and reason about the fundamental concepts of PKI in the access-control logic. We also discussed the main differences between symmetric and asymmetric cryptography.

The learning outcomes associated with this chapter appear in Figure 6.7.

6.7   Further Reading

The *Handbook of Applied Cryptography* (Menezes et al., 1997) is a very mathematical and authoritative reference for cryptographic algorithms, hash algorithms, digital signatures, and cryptographic protocols. William Stallings' book *Cryptography and Network Security Principles and Practices* (Stallings, 2003) is a less comprehensive but more accessible reference.

FIGURE 6.7 Learning outcomes for Chapter 6

After completing this chapter, you should be able to achieve the following learning outcomes at several levels of knowledge:

Comprehension

- Describe the characteristics of private-key and secret-key cryptographic systems.
- Describe basic principles of trust topologies and networks of certification authorities.

Application

- When given protocol descriptions and trust hierarchies, you should be able to use the access-control logic to describe the protocol and trust relationships.
- When given a trust topology, you should be able to determine the necessary certificates for establishing trust in a key.

Analysis

- When given a set of certificates, you should be able to formally derive whether a key is associated with a particular principal.

Synthesis

- When given a description of a trust topology, you should be able to create a formal description of the certificates and trust relationships for the certification authorities.

Chapter 7

Delegation

Central to the study of distributed access control is the notion of *delegation*. A fundamental property of distributed systems is their *lack of locality*: the originators of requests, the principals that vouch for various forms of identity and authorizations, and the reference monitors that guard resources are generally not in the same location. Furthermore, requests are typically made by delegates, in many cases processes operating on behalf of people. Likewise, credentials are signed not by human hands but with digital signatures. A critical question naturally arises: how do we evaluate access requests made by principals acting on behalf of others?

In this chapter, we explore how to reason about delegation and evaluate such requests. We extend the access-control logic to formalize delegation, identifying some important properties along the way.

7.1 Simple Delegations

The simplest of delegations arises when one principal simply passes on a request from another principal. This situation occurs frequently in distributed systems, such as when a computer or software application communicates a request on behalf of a user. We can express such delegations in the access-control logic by quoting, as demonstrated in the following simple example.

Example 7.1
Linda is running late at work. She, her daughter Emily, and her husband have dinner reservations that evening for 7 p.m. Linda calls home and her daughter answers the phone. Linda says, "Emily, I'm running late at work. Would you ask Dad to call the restaurant to change our dinner reservations to 7:30 p.m.?" After hanging up the phone, Emily tells her father, "Dad, Mom just called to say she's running late at work. She wants you to call the restaurant to change the dinner reservations to 7:30." Dutifully, Emily's father picks up the phone, calls the restaurant, and changes their dinner reservation to 7:30 p.m. ◇

The above situation happens countless times in various forms every day. We can systematically analyze the structure of the above example from an access-control perspective. Consider the following sequence of questions and answers.

- *Who is making the request and on whose behalf is the request being made?*

  Emily is making the request on behalf of her mother. Emily is quoting Linda by passing on Linda's request to her father.

- *To whom is the request made?*

  Emily's father.

- *What is the request?*

  Change the dinner reservation to 7:30 p.m.

- *How do we represent Linda's request relayed by Emily?*

  The compound principal *Emily | Linda* represents Emily quoting Linda. The actual request is represented by the atomic proposition

  $$\langle Change\ to\ 7{:}30\ p.m.,\ dinner\ reservation \rangle.$$

  Putting everything together, the request is represented as follows:

  $$Emily \mid Linda\ \text{says}\ \langle Change\ to\ 7{:}30\ p.m.,\ dinner\ reservation \rangle$$

- *Emily's father acted as if he believed Emily was correctly relaying Linda's request. How is this belief represented?*

  Emily's father's trust in what Emily tells him essentially means that, if Emily says Linda says "change the dinner reservation to 7:30 p.m.," then he concludes Linda has indeed said "change the dinner reservation to 7:30 p.m." Emily's father's trust in her word is represented as:

  $$(Emily \mid Linda\ \text{says}\ \langle Change\ to\ 7{:}30\ p.m.,\ dinner\ reservation \rangle) \supset$$
  $$Linda\ \text{says}\ \langle Change\ to\ 7{:}30\ p.m.,\ dinner\ reservation \rangle.$$

- *Emily's father changed the reservation once he heard what he interpreted to be Linda's request. What is the basis for this decision?*

  Emily's father acted as if Linda had jurisdiction over changing the time of their dinner reservation. This belief is represented as follows:

  $$Linda\ \text{controls}\ \langle Change\ to\ 7{:}30\ p.m.,\ dinner\ reservation \rangle.$$

- *Given the above, is Emily's father's decision to change the dinner reservation justified?*

  Yes, and we can prove it using the inference rules of our access-control logic.

Situations like the previous example occur often in many forms. Formally capturing the logic behind this kind of situation enables us to reason about delegations. In the next section we formalize the notion of delegation illustrated in the above example, develop derived inference rules, and prove some important delegation properties.

7.2 Delegation and Its Properties

Delegation is used frequently in networks of all kinds—human, computer, and organization—where requests, authorities, and decisions are in different locations. The idea is that, in many situations, one principal must make a request on behalf of another principal. For example, an investor cannot directly sell her own stocks but must instead rely on her stockbroker to do so. Similarly, when a banking customer attempts to pay his bills online, the associated requests arrive not directly from him but from his web browser acting on his behalf.

When a principal P makes a request on behalf of principal Q *and* we believe as a result of P's statement that Q is making the request, then we say that P is Q's *delegate (or representative)* on that statement. To represent such situations in our logic, we extend the BNF specification of our logic with the following production rule:

$$\textbf{Form} ::= (\textbf{Princ reps Princ on } \varphi)$$

The reps operator has the same binding precedence as says and controls. Hence, for example, the formula *Jane* reps *Paul* on $\langle buy \rangle \wedge \langle sell \rangle$ is equivalent to

$$(\textit{Jane} \text{ reps } \textit{Paul} \text{ on } \langle buy \rangle) \wedge \langle sell \rangle.$$

As with the controls operator in Chapter 2, the reps operator is simply syntactic sugar for an implication:

$$P \text{ reps } Q \text{ on } \varphi \stackrel{\text{def}}{=} (P \mid Q \text{ says } \varphi) \supset Q \text{ says } \varphi.$$

Using this definition, it is easy to prove the following equivalence:

$$P \text{ reps } Q \text{ on } \varphi \equiv P \text{ controls } (Q \text{ says } \varphi).$$

Essentially, if we believe that P is Q's representative on the statement φ, then we trust P when she says that Q said φ.

There are three crucial properties of the delegation relationship that the formal definition of delegation must capture:

1. A recognized delegate should in fact have the authority to act on behalf of the principals they represent. That is, if a given policy allows principals to delegate to others and recognizes that Barb is Holly's delegate, then Barb should be able to act on Holly's behalf.

2. Delegates generally should not be able to restrict the scope of their duties as a principal's representative. For example, suppose that Garth delegates to Mary the task of withdrawing $500 from his checking account and depositing it to his savings account. Mary should not be able to withdraw the funds without also depositing them; to do so would be a violation of her responsibilities, not to mention theft.

3. The delegation relationship generally is not transitive: a delegate should not be able to pass on his responsibilities to someone else.

The first property—that recognized delegates should be able to act on behalf of the principals they represent—is reflected by the *Reps* rule:

$$\textit{Reps} \quad \frac{Q \text{ controls } \varphi \quad P \text{ reps } Q \text{ on } \varphi \quad P \mid Q \text{ says } \varphi}{\varphi}$$

This rule states that if Q is authorized to perform φ, P is recognized as Q's delegate on φ, and P requests φ on Q's behalf, then the request for φ should be granted. This rule can be derived from the definition of P reps Q on φ and our other inference rules, and thus the rule is sound itself.

The second and third properties both state things that should **not** happen. For that reason, it is necessary to verify that our definition of delegation **prohibits** the reduction or passing on of delegation duties. The following two rules, which would allow the undesired behavior, can easily be shown to be unsound with respect to the Kripke semantics:

$$\textit{Unsound Rule!} \quad \frac{P \text{ reps } Q \text{ on } (\varphi_1 \wedge \varphi_2)}{P \text{ reps } Q \text{ on } \varphi_1},$$

$$\textit{Unsound Rule!} \quad \frac{P \text{ reps } Q \text{ on } \varphi \quad Q \text{ reps } R \text{ on } \varphi}{P \text{ reps } R \text{ on } \varphi}.$$

The first rule—if sound—would allow a delegate to restrict the scope of his duties. The second rule—if sound—would allow a delegate to pass on her responsibilities to someone else.

Figure 7.1 contains the formal definition of delegation, along with some useful logical rules for delegation. Each of these rules can be derived from existing inference rules; the derivations themselves are left as exercises.

The following example illustrates how delegation can be used to represent common proxy situations, such as proxies at shareholder meetings. It also illustrates how principals can adjust the scope of delegation to meet their different needs.

Example 7.2

MagnaProfit Incorporated is a publicly traded company that produces accounting software. At this year's upcoming shareholder's meeting, there are three primary issues to be voted upon:

1. MagnaProfit wishes to make a change to their employee stock-purchase program (ESPP), which needs to be approved by a majority of shareholders.

2. MagnaProfit has selected Kim to fill a vacancy on the company's board of directors, a selection that must be ratified by a majority of shareholders.

3. A shareholder has proposed a revision to the selection procedure for MagnaProfit's board of directors; the change will happen only if supported by a majority of shareholders.

FIGURE 7.1 Logical rules for delegation

$$P \text{ reps } Q \text{ on } \varphi \overset{\text{def}}{=} P \mid Q \text{ says } \varphi \supset Q \text{ says } \varphi$$

$$Reps \quad \frac{Q \text{ controls } \varphi \quad P \text{ reps } Q \text{ on } \varphi \quad P \mid Q \text{ says } \varphi}{\varphi}$$

$$Rep\ Controls \quad \frac{}{A \text{ reps } B \text{ on } \varphi \equiv (A \text{ controls } (B \text{ says } \varphi))}$$

$$Rep\ Says \quad \frac{A \text{ reps } B \text{ on } \varphi \quad A \mid B \text{ says } \varphi}{B \text{ says } \varphi}$$

These votes all require a majority of *all shareholders* to approve them, regardless of which shareholders actually attend the meeting. Realizing that many shareholders cannot attend the meeting, MagnaProfit sent a proxy statement to each shareholder, which included a ballot as well as a designated default proxy (Janet). Shareholders may select a different proxy if they prefer. Shareholders can use the ballot to specify precisely how the proxy must vote on their behalf. If a shareholder fails to specify how the proxy should vote for a particular ballot issue, then the proxy may vote however he or she pleases.

Aaron and Ruth are both shareholders in MagnaProfit who are unable to attend the meeting. Aaron is in favor of all three proposals, and he is willing to accept Janet as his proxy. He therefore records his desired votes, signs the form, and mails it back to MagnaProfit. In effect, his signed form can be interpreted as follows:

Aaron says (*Janet* reps *Aaron* on ($\langle yes, ESPP \rangle \wedge \langle yes, Kim \rangle \wedge \langle yes, revise \rangle$)).

In this case, Janet must vote yes on *all three* proposals; she does not have the authority to cast other votes on Aaron's behalf.

In contrast, Ruth prefers to have her cousin Lou represent her at the meeting. Ruth is also in favor of both the stock-purchase plan and of Kim as a director, but she is undecided on the remaining issue. Because she believes that discussion at the meeting should be brought to bear on her vote, she decides to let Lou decide her vote on the shareholder proposal. She therefore records her two votes, leaves the third issue unmarked, designates Lou as her proxy, and mails the form back. Her signed form can be interpreted as follows:

Ruth says (*Lou* reps *Ruth* on ($\langle yes, ESPP \rangle \wedge \langle yes, Kim \rangle \wedge \langle yes, revise \rangle$)

$\wedge$ *Lou* reps *Ruth* on ($\langle yes, ESPP \rangle \wedge \langle yes, Kim \rangle \wedge \langle no, revise \rangle$)).

In this case, Lou must vote *yes* on the first two issues. However, Lou has the authority to cast either a *yes* or *no* vote on the proposal to revise the director-selection procedure.   ◇

It is important to note that the definition of *P* reps *Q* on φ and its properties describe a particular kind of delegation, in which delegation deals only with statements φ made by *Q*. In the following example, we analyze a situation that is often informally thought of as delegation but that does not correspond to our definition.

Example 7.3

Consider the following scenario:

> Beth is a director of a not-for-profit organization that is running a raffle as part of a fund-raising event. Beth reaches into a basket of names and draws Tanya's name. Tanya is not present to receive her prize, but she is still entitled to it. Dawn approaches Beth after the drawing and says that she is Tanya's friend and work colleague and that she will take Tanya's prize to her. Beth, for whatever reason, takes Dawn at her word and gives Tanya's prize to Dawn, with the expectation that Dawn will get the prize to Tanya.

Here, Dawn is acting on Tanya's behalf but *not* as her delegate; in fact, Tanya is currently unaware that Dawn is acting on her behalf. Instead, Dawn has asked to convey Tanya's prize to Tanya, in effect making the following statement to Beth:

> *"Give me Tanya's prize, and if you give me Tanya's prize I will give the prize to Tanya."*

From Beth's perspective, the request from Dawn corresponds to the following logical statement:

$$Dawn \text{ says } (\langle Give\ Dawn, prize \rangle \wedge (\langle Give\ Dawn, prize \rangle \supset \langle Give\ Tanya, prize \rangle)).$$

It is straightforward to see that Dawn's request does not match the form of a delegate acting on Tanya's behalf. Therefore, Dawn is *not* Tanya's delegate, even though she is doing a favor for her.

If Beth trusts Dawn, then this trust can be represented as follows:

$$Dawn \text{ controls } (\langle Give\ Dawn, prize \rangle \wedge (\langle Give\ Dawn, prize \rangle \supset \langle Give\ Tanya, prize \rangle)).$$

The *Controls* inference rule allows Beth to conclude

$$\langle Give\ Dawn, prize \rangle \wedge (\langle Give\ Dawn, prize \rangle \supset \langle Give\ Tanya, prize \rangle),$$

and the *Simplification* and *Modus Ponens* rules further allow her to conclude

$$\langle Give\ Tanya, prize \rangle.$$

That is, because Beth trusts Dawn, she concludes that she should give Tanya's prize to Dawn and that, by so doing, Tanya will receive her prize.   ◇

The previous example demonstrated an informal notion of delegation that did not match our definition. However, the same scenario does involve a delegation that *does* match our definition: Tanya serves as Beth's delegate to deliver the prize to Tanya. The following example highlights the relevant analysis.

Example 7.4
Recall the scenario from Exercise 7.3:

> Tanya won a prize in Beth's raffle, but was not present at the raffle draw-ing and did not know she won. Thus, Tanya was not able to pick up her prize herself. Tanya's friend and colleague Dawn was there and offered to take Tanya's prize to Tanya, which Beth accepted. Beth asks Dawn to take the prize to Tanya and give it to her, which Dawn does.

Here, Beth through Dawn is asking Tanya to accept the prize that she won at the raf-fle. From Tanya's perspective, the request she receives from Dawn can be expressed as follows:

$$Dawn \mid Beth \text{ says } \langle accept, \text{ } raffle \text{ } prize \rangle.$$

In this case, we can see that Dawn is Beth's delegate. Beth through Dawn is asking Tanya to accept the prize. If Tanya trusts Dawn about the raffle prize and also regards Beth as being in charge of the raffle, then she in effect believes the following two statements:

$$Dawn \text{ reps } Beth \text{ on } \langle accept, \text{ } raffle \text{ } prize \rangle,$$
$$Beth \text{ controls } \langle accept, \text{ } raffle \text{ } prize \rangle.$$

The *Reps Rule* allows Tanya to conclude that she should accept the prize:

$$\langle accept, \text{ } raffle \text{ } prize \rangle. \hspace{4cm} \Diamond$$

Exercise 7.2.1 *Using the formal definition of delegation and the* Reps *Rule, provide a formal analysis of Example 7.1.*

Exercise 7.2.2 *Give a formal proof of the* Reps *inference rule from Figure 7.1.*

Exercise 7.2.3 *Give a formal proof of the* Rep Controls *rule from Figure 7.1.*

Exercise 7.2.4 *Give a formal proof of the* Rep Says *rule from Figure 7.1.*

Exercise 7.2.5 *Suppose Naresh and Sunita are both professors in the Department of Electrical and Computer Engineering. Sunita will be away at a conference during the department faculty meeting when votes for department chair will be cast. Sunita wishes to cast her vote for Maja, and she trusts Naresh to be her proxy. Because it's an official vote, she writes on a piece of paper:*

FIGURE 7.2 Grace's health-care proxy

> ### **Health-Care Proxy**
>
> 1. I, Grace, hereby appoint Norm as my health care agent to make decisions on whether or not to resuscitate me in the event I am unable to make my own health care decisions.
>
> 2. Grace's signature.
>
> 3. Witness: I, Kirstin's signature, witnessed Grace sign this proxy of her own free will in my presence.

Naresh is my proxy. I authorize him to cast my vote for Maja as department chair.

Sunita turns the paper into George prior to the meeting. George is the faculty chair who will count the votes at the department meeting.

At the faculty meeting, the vote is called. Naresh casts his vote and then he says, "As Sunita's proxy I am casting her vote for Maja as department chair." George, who is tabulating the votes, notes Naresh's vote and then puts down one vote for Maja cast by Sunita.

Represent Naresh's casting of one vote for Maja by Sunita. What must the department policies be regarding proxy votes? Give the inference rule that corresponds to accepting Sunita's vote by proxy and prove that it is sound.

Exercise 7.2.6   *Consider Grace's health-care proxy as shown in Figure 7.2. Her proxy authorizes Norm to be her delegate in the event she is unable to make her own health care decisions. Her proxy is witnessed by Kirstin.*

In a tragic turn of events, Grace is involved in a car accident that leaves her in a coma. Grace is taken to the hospital where she is cared for by Dan, her physician. Norm tells Dan that Grace is not to be resuscitated. Dan, after reading Grace's health-care proxy, writes "Do Not Resuscitate" on Grace's chart.

Answer the following questions:

   a. Represent Grace's health-care proxy in the access-control logic.

   b. Express the hospital's policy regarding delegation and the rights of patients not to be resuscitated in the event they are unable to communicate for themselves.

   c. Represent Dan's decision not to resuscitate Grace as an inference rule.

   d. Formally derive and prove Dan's inference rule.

Exercise 7.2.7   *Demonstrate the unsoundness of the following inference rule:*

$$\text{Unsound Rule!}\quad \frac{P \text{ reps } Q \text{ on } (\varphi_1 \land \varphi_2)}{P \text{ reps } Q \text{ on } \varphi_1}.$$

Exercise 7.2.8 *Demonstrate the unsoundness of the following inference rule:*

$$\text{Unsound Rule!}\quad \frac{B \text{ controls } \varphi_1 \quad A \text{ reps } B \text{ on } (\varphi_1 \land \varphi_2) \quad A|B \text{ says } \varphi_1}{\varphi_1}.$$

Exercise 7.2.9 *Demonstrate the unsoundness of the following inference rule:*

$$\text{Unsound Rule!}\quad \frac{P \text{ reps } Q \text{ on } \varphi \quad Q \text{ reps } R \text{ on } \varphi}{P \text{ reps } R \text{ on } \varphi}.$$

7.3 A Delegation Example: Simple Checking

Delegation is so commonplace that we often do not even recognize its relevance to a given system. If we are responsible for designing or constructing a system that uses delegation, however, then we are well served if we understand precisely how delegation is being used, as well as the assurances that must be in place.

For example, the use of paper checks as payment instruments relies on notions of delegation, although most check writers never think about that in the course of conducting their daily business. In this section, we highlight the role of delegation in the use of paper checks in a simple consumer scenario; we expand on this treatment in Chapter 8.

For this example, we consider a situation where Alice wishes to purchase goods from Bob, her local grocer. For simplicity, we assume that Alice and Bob are both depositors of the same bank.[1] Alice wishes to pay Bob, but she does not have sufficient cash on hand (or she chooses not to use it). Instead, she writes a check to Bob, which is in fact an order to the bank to debit the given amount from her account and to pay it to Bob. Alice hands the check to Bob, as shown in Figure 7.3. Because Bob wishes to be paid, he heads to the bank, endorses Alice's check by signing the back of it, and presents the check to the teller for payment.

Suppose that we are in charge of designing the operation of the bank used by Alice and Bob. Our objective is to come up with a concept of operations that supports the use of checks written and cashed by bank customers. We would like to know that these operations are justified—that is, the operations should be logically sound with respect to bank policies set by relevant authorities. Accomplishing this goal requires three steps, which we follow:

1. Give a formal definition in the access-control logic of checks and endorsed checks.

---

[1]We address the more complicated situation where Alice and Bob are depositors of different banks in Chapter 8.

FIGURE 7.3 Simple checking

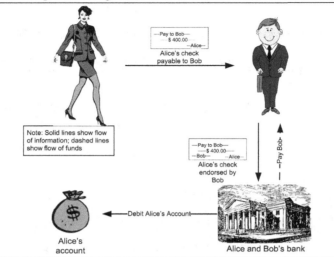

Note: Solid lines show flow of information; dashed lines show flow of funds

Pay to Bob—
$ 400.00
—Alice—
Alice's check
payable to Bob

Pay to Bob—
$ 400.00—
—Bob—   —Alice—
Alice's check
endorsed by
Bob

—Pay Bob—

—Debit Alice's Account—

Alice's
account

Alice and Bob's bank

2. Formally describe the bank policies regarding checks.

3. Describe the bank's operating rules with respect to checks as inference rules, which we prove to be sound by deriving them using our existing inference rules.

7.3.1   Formal Definitions of Checks

A *check* is a signed order from a principal (known as the *payer*) upon a bank to draw upon the payer's deposit of funds to pay a certain amount of money to another principal (known as the *payee*). If P is the payer and Q is the payee, we can represent a check written by P to Q as follows:

$$Signature_P \text{ says } (\langle pay \text{ amt}, Q \rangle \wedge \langle debit \text{ amt}, acct_P \rangle).$$

Here, $Signature_P$ is the signature of P, and hence we must also be able to associate the given signature with the payer. That is, we must be willing to believe that $Signature_P \Rightarrow P$.

A check is *endorsed* when the payee signs the check—typically on the back side of the check—issued to him or her. If P is the payer and Q is the payee, we can represent a check written by P and endorsed by Q as follows:

$$Signature_Q \mid Signature_P \text{ says } (\langle pay \text{ amt}, Q \rangle \wedge \langle debit \text{ amt}, acct_P \rangle).$$

Again, we must be willing to associate the given signatures with the relevant individuals:

$$Signature_P \Rightarrow P \quad Signature_Q \Rightarrow Q.$$

Note that the form of the endorsed check is the same as a delegation-based request: the payee (or his signature) is claiming that the payee (or her signature) wants her account to be debited. However, the delegation relationship between the payer and the payee exists only if the bank accepts checks as legal payment instruments.

7.3.2 Bank Policies on Checks

In our example, Alice and Bob use the same bank, and thus there is a single controlling authority (i.e., the bank owner). The bank's policies must allow the use of checks, which means that it must recognize Alice's right to write checks to Bob (i.e., Alice's right to designate Bob as her representative for withdrawing funds from her account). Taken together, the following pair of statements says that the bank allows payer P to write checks to Q (i.e., the bank recognizes Q as P's delegate on such matters):

> *Bank Owner* controls
>
> $(Q \text{ reps } P \text{ on } (\langle pay \text{ amt}, Q \rangle \wedge \langle debit \text{ amt}, acct_P \rangle))$,
>
> *Bank Owner* says
>
> $(Q \text{ reps } P \text{ on } (\langle pay \text{ amt}, Q \rangle \wedge \langle debit \text{ amt}, acct_P \rangle))$.

Note that the first statement refers to the bank owner's jurisdiction on the matter; the second statement indicates the actual bank policy. Using the *Controls* rule, it is straightforward to deduce the following single policy statement:

> $Q \text{ reps } P \text{ on } (\langle pay \text{ amt}, Q \rangle \wedge \langle debit \text{ amt}, acct_P \rangle)$.

At first glance, these statements may appear too strong: the bank recognizes *any possible payee* Q as a representative for the payer P. However, recognizing Q as P's delegate is insufficient for allowing Q to withdraw money from P's account. Instead, Q must be able to present the check with P's signature on it, which emphasizes the importance of being able to associate *Signature$_P$* with P herself. We return to this point in the next subsection.

Furthermore, the bank must have policies that state the conditions under which Bob should be paid from Alice's account. In particular, the bank will want to verify that P has enough funds in her account ($acct_P$) to cover the check she has written. This policy along with the bank's authority to set this policy can be represented by the following two statements:

> *Bank Owner* controls
>
> $((\langle \text{amt } covered, acct_P \rangle \supset P \text{ controls } (\langle pay \text{ amt}, Q \rangle \wedge \langle debit \text{ amt}, acct_P \rangle))$,
>
> *Bank Owner* says
>
> $((\langle \text{amt } covered, acct_P \rangle \supset P \text{ controls } (\langle pay \text{ amt}, Q \rangle \wedge \langle debit \text{ amt}, acct_P \rangle))$.

Again, the *Controls* rule allows us to derive the bank's policy that permits cashing the check, provided that P has sufficient funds in her account:

> $\langle \text{amt } covered, acct_P \rangle \supset P \text{ controls } (\langle pay \text{ amt}, Q \rangle \wedge \langle debit \text{ amt}, acct_P \rangle)$.

7.3.3   Operating Rules for Checks

The bank has specific procedures—that is, a concept of operations—for handling checks, designed to minimize processing costs (both time and money) and the likelihood of fraud. In particular, the bank allows a payment to be made (and the payment amount debited from the specified account) only if the following conditions are met:

1. A check is received with a payer's signature $Signature_P$ and endorsed with a payee's signature $Signature_Q$:

$$Signature_Q \mid Signature_P \text{ says } (\langle pay \text{ amt}, Q \rangle \wedge \langle debit \text{ amt}, acct_P \rangle).$$

2. The signatures on the check correspond to the payer and payee:

$$Signature_P \Rightarrow P, \qquad Signature_Q \Rightarrow Q.$$

3. There are enough funds in the account to cover the amount of the check:

$$\langle \text{amt } covered, acct_P \rangle.$$

4. The policy allows that, if there are sufficient funds in the account, then P can authorize payment to Q and debit the payment from her account:

$$\langle \text{amt } covered, acct_P \rangle \supset P \text{ controls } (\langle pay \text{ amt}, Q \rangle \wedge \langle debit \text{ amt}, acct_P \rangle).$$

5. The policy allows Q to be P's delegate:

$$Q \text{ reps } P \text{ on } (\langle pay \text{ amt}, Q \rangle \wedge \langle debit \text{ amt}, acct_P \rangle).$$

This concept of operations can be captured by the following derivable (and therefore sound) inference rule:

$$
\text{Simple Checking} \quad \frac{
\begin{array}{c}
Signature_Q \mid Signature_P \text{ says } (\langle pay \text{ amt}, Q \rangle \wedge \langle debit \text{ amt}, acct_P \rangle) \\
Signature_Q \Rightarrow Q \quad Signature_P \Rightarrow P \quad \langle \text{amt } covered, acct_P \rangle \\
\langle \text{amt } covered, acct_P \rangle \supset P \text{ controls } (\langle pay \text{ amt}, Q \rangle \wedge \langle debit \text{ amt}, acct_P \rangle) \\
Q \text{ reps } P \text{ on } (\langle pay \text{ amt}, Q \rangle \wedge \langle debit \text{ amt}, acct_P \rangle)
\end{array}
}{
\langle pay \text{ amt}, Q \rangle \wedge \langle debit \text{ amt}, acct_P \rangle
}.
$$

The proof of this rule is left as an exercise for the reader.

This extended example illustrates the point we made at the beginning of this section: an understanding of delegation can illuminate how existing systems work and the assumptions or assurances upon which they depend. In the simple-checking system, the delegates are the check payees. The analysis depends upon the delegation instruments—that is, the checks that must be integrity checked—and the statements that specify which authorities have jurisdiction over which statements. For a systems designer, each of these items—such as the integrity checking or jurisdiction statements—represents an assumption of fact. It is essential that we always ask ourselves, "Are these assumptions reasonable?" These assumptions reflect the potential risks to the system. If we deem them unreasonable, then our burden is to identify assumptions that we consider reasonable and redo the analysis.

Exercise 7.3.1   *Give a formal proof of the* Simple Checking *Rule.*

Exercise 7.3.2   *Consider the concept of operations of simple checking as presented in this section. What are the risks in simple checking as presented?*

Exercise 7.3.3   *This question concerns a university library and their policies that allow students and faculty to check out books.*

Let us adopt the notation ⟨checkout book, P⟩ *to denote a request to check out* book *on person P's account. Thus, for example,*

$$⟨\text{check out Animal Farm}, \textit{George}⟩$$

represents a request to check out the book Animal Farm *on George's account. Answer the following questions:*

   a. *Toby decides to check out the book* How Not to Write, *using his own library account. What is the specific request—expressed as a statement in the access-control logic—that Toby makes when he brings the book to the check-out counter? (Assume that the librarian recognizes Toby.)*

   b. *Toby's account is in good standing, and thus he is authorized to check out this book. Express this authorization as a statement in the logic.*

   c. *Sidney is a faculty member who wishes to have Toby (her graduate assistant) check out books on her behalf. The library requires her to sign a proxy form that states her willingness to be held responsible for all books that Toby checks out on her behalf. This form, which amounts to a* delegation certificate, *is kept on file at the library.*

   Express both this proxy form and Sidney's authority to sign it as statements in the logic. (Note: In theory, this proxy form applies to all *books in the library. For this exercise, it suffices to consider the specific book* Proving Refutations.)

   d. *Toby heads to the library to check out* Proving Refutations *on Sidney's behalf. What is the specific request—expressed as a statement in the access-control logic—that Toby makes when he brings the book to the check-out counter? (Assume again that the librarian recognizes Toby.)*

   e. *Sidney's account is in good standing. What is the library's policy (expressed as a statement in the logic) that governs Toby's request to check out* Proving Refutations *for Sidney?*

Exercise 7.3.4   *In recent years, Utopia College has spent a lot of money and effort in developing its computer infrastructure to support administrative operations in an integrative fashion across the college. Specifically, they have adopted a public-key infrastructure, and provided all students and staff with personal key pairs. All public keys in the college are certified by the IT department (ITD), with one exception: ITD's public key (K_I) is stored on all official campus servers.*

The annual housing lottery for students occurs online, and is scheduled for next week. Unfortunately, Vera will be participating in a workshop at that time, and so she wishes to have her friend Henry select a room on her behalf. There are two separate stages to this process:

Stage One   *In advance of the lottery, Vera and Henry must each fill out and sign (using their private keys) an electronic form requesting that Henry be authorized as Vera's room-selection proxy.*

The Office of Residential Life (ORL) approves only those requests that are signed by both individuals (i.e., the delegator and the delegate). If the request is approved, then ORL sends to Henry a proxy certificate, signed with ORL's private key, stating that Henry is authorized to make room selections on Vera's behalf.

Stage Two   *When the lottery begins and it is Vera's turn to select a room, Henry sends the following two items to the Lottery server:*

- *The proxy certificate obtained from ORL in Stage 1*

- *His selection (on Vera's behalf), signed with his private key*

Let K_V, K_H, and K_O be the public keys of Vera, Henry, and ORL, respectively. Let $\langle proxy, Henry, Vera \rangle$ denote the request "please assign Henry as Vera's proxy," and let $\langle select, 422 \rangle$ denote the request "Select Room 422." Thus, for example, the two electronic proxy-request forms sent in Stage 1 can be interpreted as follows:

$$K_V \text{ says } \langle proxy, Henry, Vera \rangle,$$
$$K_H \text{ says } \langle proxy, Henry, Vera \rangle.$$

Answer the following questions regarding the certifications, credentials, and access-control policies needed for the housing lottery. All answers should be given as expressions (or formal proofs, where requested) in the access-control logic.

- a. *ORL will grant the Stage 1 request only if $\langle proxy, Henry, Vera \rangle$ can be deduced. What recognition of authority/jurisdiction is implicit in ORL's requirement that both proxy participants sign the form?*

- b. *What additional certificates, recognition of authority, and trust assumptions regarding keys are necessary for the ORL to determine that the proxy request should be granted in Stage 1? Provide a formal justification for granting the request.*

- c. *Assuming that ORL grants the proxy request, what is the specific proxy certificate sent to Henry at the end of Stage 1?*

- d. *In Stage 2, Henry presents a room-selection request to the Housing Lottery server. What is the specific form of this room-selection request?*

e. *What additional certificates, recognition of authority, and trust assumptions regarding keys are necessary for the Housing Lottery system to determine that the room-selection request should be granted? Provide a formal justification for granting the request.*

7.4 Summary

Delegation is an essential aspect of distributed systems, but it also complicates the task of making access-control decisions. Under what circumstances should we act upon a statement made by a purported delegate?

In this chapter, we examined that question and demonstrated how to describe and reason about delegation in our access-control logic. We identified the role of jurisdiction in such decisions, as well as two important properties of delegation: nonreduction of responsibilities and nontransitivity of delegation.

The learning outcomes associated with this chapter appear in Figure 7.4.

7.5 Further Reading

The notion of delegation introduced in this chapter is statement-based: the scope of a delegate's responsibility is explicitly limited by detailing the statements that the delegate is authorized to make. In contrast, the work of Abadi, Lampson, and colleagues (Lampson et al., 1992; Abadi et al., 1993) uses a principal-based notion of delegation that relies on a virtual delegation server. In this setting, the scope of a delegate's responsibility is limited only by the access policy enforced by the reference monitor.

FIGURE 7.4 Learning outcomes for Chapter 7

After completing this chapter, you should be able to achieve the following learning
outcomes at several levels of knowledge:

Comprehension

- Describe the important properties of delegation relationships.

Application

- When given a particular delegation relationship, you should be able to
  use the access-control logic to describe that relationship.

Analysis

- When given a scenario involving delegation, you should be able to perform a formal analysis of it using the access-control logic.

Synthesis

- When given a scenario involving delegation, you should be able to express in the logic the primary principals (i.e., the originators of statements), their proxies, and the statements over which the proxies have
  jurisdiction.

Evaluation

- Given a formal analysis of a scenario involving delegation, you should
  be able to assess the possible risks associated with the analysis.

Chapter 8

Networks: Case Studies

The concepts of digital authentication and delegation—developed in the previous two chapters—are essential for analyzing networks, both public (such as the world wide web) and private (such as those used by financial institutions). With networks, the tasks of authenticating principals and authorizing access requests are made more difficult by the lack of locality among the policy makers (i.e., authorities), the access controllers (i.e., reference monitors), and the originators of requests.

Network operations are usually described in terms of protocols, which are sets of syntactic and semantic rules for exchanging information. These protocols are typically implemented by a series of requests and responses that produce a desired result, such as establishing a secure communications channel by exchanging cryptographic keys or transferring money from one person or account to another. In this chapter, we demonstrate how to describe such protocols as collections of derived inference rules using our access-control logic. The inference rules correspond to the operating rules used by the decision makers within the various protocols. Capturing the underlying logic of a protocol in this way makes explicit the context in which the protocol operates, revealing the inherent trust assumptions, jurisdiction of authority, certifications, and delegations upon which it depends.

We apply this approach to develop three different network case studies:

1. SSL and TLS, which support authentication across the web;

2. Kerberos, a widely used authentication and delegation protocol for distributed systems; and

3. ACH, a backbone of financial networks.

Taken together, these case studies illustrate how a formalization of a protocol can help to explicate its concept of operations (CONOPS).

8.1 SSL and TLS: Authentication across the Web

For web-based transactions, the primary security concerns are authentication, integrity, and privacy. These concerns are addressed by protocols such as SSL (Secure Sockets Layer) (Freier et al., 1996) and TLS (Transport Layer Security) (Dierks and Rescorla, 2006).

Both SSL and TLS rely on two protocols: a handshake protocol and a record protocol. The handshake protocol, which we examine in Subsection 8.1.1, is used to establish a communications channel between a client and a server. This channel may or may not require the client and the server to authenticate each other. The purpose of the handshake protocol is to establish a cryptographic key to secure the session.

The record protocol—which we describe in Subsection 8.1.2—is used to fragment, compress, provide for integrity checking, and encrypt application data transmitted on the web. The record protocol relies on the cryptographic keys and secrets shared between the client and server during the handshake protocol. The record protocol relies on key certificates for authentication, *nonces* (i.e., values created for a particular run of the protocol to guarantee freshness and to prevent replay attacks), and cryptographic hash functions for generating keys and secrets.

Although the SSL and TLS protocols are very similar, they differ in several areas, including their available cipher suites and how they compute message authentication codes and shared secrets. At the level of detail we are considering here, however, these differences are not significant. As a result, we will not distinguish between SSL and TLS in the discussion that follows.

8.1.1   Handshake Protocol

The handshake protocol used in SSL and TLS is the starting point for establishing secure communications. The handshake protocol does the following:

- Establishes agreement between the client and the server on cryptographic algorithms.

- Exchanges certificates between the client and the server allowing each to authenticate the other.

- Exchanges cryptographic parameters that enable the client and the server to create the same master secret.

Figure 8.1 contains a diagram of the handshake protocol, which is read from the top down. Messages and information—represented by arrows—are exchanged between the *client* and *server*. The direction of each arrow indicates the flow of the message; the arrows are annotated by the information sent or the type of message. The solid arrows represent messages that must appear as part of the SSL or TLS protocols. The dotted arrows represent messages that are optional, depending upon whether or not the client and/or server are to be authenticated.

8.1.1.1   Client and Server Hello Messages

To initiate a session, the client sends a *client hello* message to the server unencrypted and in the clear. This message, which initiates a negotiation between the client and server, contains the client's preferences: the version of the TLS/SSL protocol the client wishes to use (ideally, the most recent version that the client supports), a random number $random_C$ generated by the client, a list of the *cipher suites* that the

FIGURE 8.1 Handshake protocol: Establishing associations among principals and keys

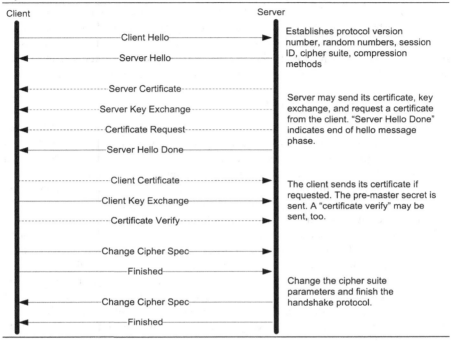

Client   Server

Client Hello → Establishes protocol version number, random numbers, session ID, cipher suite, compression methods
Server Hello ←

Server Certificate ← Server may send its certificate, key exchange, and request a certificate from the client. "Server Hello Done" indicates end of hello message phase.
Server Key Exchange ←
Certificate Request ←
Server Hello Done ←

Client Certificate → The client sends its certificate if requested. The pre-master secret is sent. A "certificate verify" may be sent, too.
Client Key Exchange →
Certificate Verify →

Change Cipher Spec →
Finished → Change the cipher suite parameters and finish the handshake protocol.
Change Cipher Spec ←
Finished ←

client supports, and a list of compression methods (if any) that the client supports. Each cipher suite contains three components related to how the client and server will exchange information:

1. The key-exchange method, which defines how the client and server will agree upon the shared secret key for the session (e.g., using Diffie-Hellman or Rivest-Shamir-Adelman (RSA)) and what sort of digital signatures to use (if any) during the key exchange

2. The symmetric crypto-algorithm to use for data transfer, such as stream ciphers, cipher-block-chaining ciphers, or no encryption at all

3. The message-digest function (mdf) to use —such as MD5 (Message Digest 5) or SHA1 (Secure Hash Algorithm)—to create *message authentication codes (MACs)* for integrity checking

The server responds by sending to the client a *server hello* message, also unencrypted in the clear. The *server hello* message contains the result of the negotiation: the version of TLS/SSL to be used, which is the most recent version that both the client and server can accommodate; a random number $random_S$ generated by the server; the session identifier corresponding to this connection; the cipher suite selected by the server, which must be one of those initially supplied by the client; and the compression method (if any) selected from the list supplied by the client.

None of the parameters exchanged in the client or server hello messages (e.g., protocol version number, random numbers, session ID, cipher suite, compression method) has any interpretation within the calculus. Rather, these items establish the computational infrastructure for messages, privacy, and integrity checking.

8.1.1.2 Server Authentication

After the *client hello* and *server hello* messages are exchanged, both the client and server will use the same cryptographic algorithms and compression method for the connection indexed by the session identifier. At this point, the client and server can authenticate themselves, if required, using certificates for RSA or Diffie-Hellman public keys. In particular, the server must authenticate itself whenever the key-exchange method agreed upon requires digital signatures.

If the server must authenticate itself, then it sends a *server certificate* message as indicated in Figure 8.1. This message contains a list of certificates, with the server's RSA or Diffie-Hellman key certificate at the head; the remaining certificates (if any) correspond to a chain of certificate authorities, each certifying the certificate directly preceding it. Thus, for example, the second certificate in the list belongs to the server's certificate authority, while the third certificate belongs to the authority that certified the server's certificate authority. As we have seen before, the server's certificate is a statement digitally signed by the server's certificate authority CA_S, whose public key is K_{CA_S}:

$$K_{CA_S} \text{ says } (K_S \Rightarrow Server).$$

If the client directly recognizes both the public key and the jurisdiction of CA_S regarding public-key certificates, then the client in effect accepts the following two statements:

$$K_{CA_S} \Rightarrow CA_S, \qquad CA_S \text{ controls } (K_S \Rightarrow Server).$$

In such a case, the client can conclude that K_S is truly the server's key:

$$K_S \Rightarrow Server.$$

This analysis corresponds to the *Certificate Verification* rule introduced in Chapter 6:

$$\text{Certificate Verification} \quad \frac{K_{ca} \Rightarrow Certificate\ Authority \qquad K_{ca} \text{ says } (K_P \Rightarrow P) \qquad Certificate\ Authority \text{ controls } (K_P \Rightarrow P)}{K_P \Rightarrow P}.$$

In those cases where the client does not recognize the authority of CA_S, the additional certificates in the certificate chain may provide the necessary support, as previously described in Example 6.2.

In some cases, the server's key K_S might be certified only for signing but not for encryption. In such situations, the server must also send a *server key exchange* message, which conveys either a signed RSA public key that will be used to encrypt the pre-master secret or signed Diffie-Hellman parameters that can be used to compute the pre-master secret. In effect, the server creates a temporary public key K_t to be used by the client, and the *server key exchange* message corresponds to the following statement:

$$K_S \text{ says } \langle use, K_t \rangle.$$

Because the server signs the RSA public key or the Diffie-Hellman parameters, the client has everything it needs to conclude that it in fact is communicating with the server. It can now associate with the server any messages sent using the public key K_S or temporary public key K_t. The remainder of the handshake protocol deals with the (optional) authentication of the client.

8.1.1.3   Client Authentication

When the cipher suite dictates, the server sends the client a *certificate request* message, which contains a list of the types of certificates requested (in descending order of preference) and a list of the distinguished names of acceptable certificate authorities. If no names are specified, then the client may send any certificate that matches the types of certificates specified by the server.

At this point, the server sends a mandatory *server hello done* message to indicate that it is done sending messages to support the key exchange and the client can proceed with its part to support the key exchange.

If the server requested a client certificate, the client sends a *client certificate* message with a suitable certificate, signed by the client's certificate authority CA_C:

$$K_{CA_C} \text{ says } (K_C \Rightarrow client).$$

If the server recognizes both the public key and jurisdiction of CA_C, then the server must accept the following two statements:

$$K_{CA_C} \Rightarrow CA_C, \qquad CA_C \text{ controls } (K_C \Rightarrow client).$$

It is straightforward for the server to then conclude that

$$K_C \Rightarrow client.$$

On the other hand, if the server does not request a client certificate, then the server will possess no cryptographic key to authenticate the identity of the client. The client in this case is *anonymous*.

8.1.1.4   Key Exchange

The next message is the mandatory *client key exchange* message. The client generates a random *pre-master secret* (typically 48 bits long), encrypts it with the public key (either from the server's certificate or the temporary key supplied in the key exchange message), and sends it on to the server.

At this point, both the client and the server can compute the *master secret* and the necessary keys for data encryption and message authentication. The *master secret* is computed by applying the message-digest function *mdf* specified in the *server hello* message to the *pre-master secret, random$_C$*, and *random$_S$*:

$$master\ secret = mdf(pre\text{-}master\ secret, random_C, random_S).$$

The *master secret* is used to create the *key block*, which contains all the cryptographic keys necessary for encryption and for computing message authentication codes. The key block is also computed using the message-digest function:

$$key\ block = mdf(master\ secret, random_C, random_S).$$

The key block contains all of the various keys required by the cipher specification; each key can be extracted from a specified portion of the key block. Specifically,

$$(client\ write\ MAC\ secret,\ server\ write\ MAC\ secret,\ client\ write\ key,\ server\ write\ key)$$

$$=$$

$$key\ block.$$

If the server requested a client certificate, then the client must also send a *certificate verify* message, which contains the digitally signed hash of all previous handshake messages sent or received. This message provides assurance to the server that it in fact has been communicating with the principal authenticated by the client's certificate.

At this point, both the client and the server possess the shared secret key K used to compute MACs and the write key K_W used to encrypt fragments if desired. The client associates the shared secret MAC key with the server:

$$K \Rightarrow Server.$$

Likewise, the server associates the shared secret MAC key with the client, who may or may not be authenticated:

$$K \Rightarrow \begin{cases} anonymous_{session\ ID}, & \text{if the client is not authenticated} \\ Authenticated\ Client, & \text{if the client is authenticated.} \end{cases}$$

Note that, in the case where clients are not authenticated (which is the case for many business to consumer connections), the server can still identify which anonymous client it is dealing with by the session identifier *session ID*.

At this point, the client sends a *change cipher spec* message to indicate that subsequent records will be sent using the newly negotiated cipher-suite parameters and keys. The client then also sends a *finished* message.

The handshake protocol ends when the server also sends a *change cipher spec* message followed by a *finished* message.

FIGURE 8.2 Record protocol: Payload construction

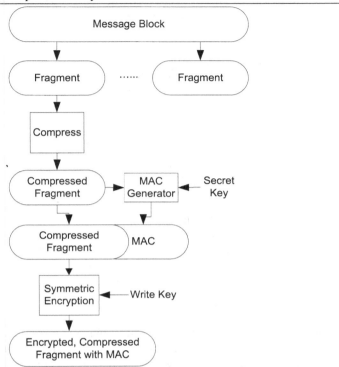

8.1.2 Record Protocol

After the completion of the Handshake Protocol, the client and server can exchange data relevant to the transaction (e.g., credit-card numbers or mailing addresses) using the Record Protocol. Figure 8.2 contains a flowchart of the record protocol used by SSL and TLS. Application data are divided into fragments of 2^{14} bytes or less, and then each fragment is compressed according to the agreed upon compression method. The message authentication code (MAC) for a compressed message fragment M is obtained by applying the agreed-upon message-digest function *mdf* as follows:

$$MAC = mdf(K, M, iopad, seq\_num),$$

where K is the shared secret key, *iopad* is a sequence of padding bits, and *seq_num* is the sequence number corresponding to the particular fragment being sent.

Figure 8.3 contains a diagram showing how payloads are integrity checked. To see how it works, suppose that Alice sends Bob a message using the record protocol, and Bob wants to check the integrity of a message fragment he receives. He first decrypts the message using the write key K_W obtained through the handshake protocol. The

FIGURE 8.3 Record protocol: Payload integrity checking

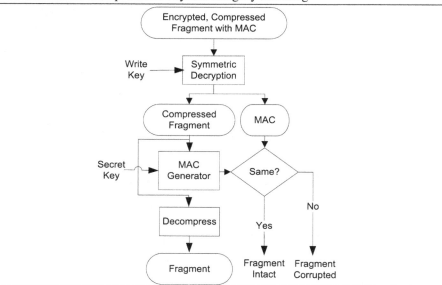

result has two components: the compressed fragment and the attached MAC. Bob uses the shared secret key K_W and the message-digest function *mdf* to compute a new message authentication code, which he compares with the attached MAC. If the two message authentication codes match, then Bob concludes that (because *mdf* is a one-way function) the sender of the message must have possessed the shared secret key K along with the correct sequence number. That is, Bob concludes that

$$K \text{ says } M.$$

Due to the handshake protocol, Bob associates the shared key K with Alice, and hence he concludes that the message originated with Alice:

$$Alice \text{ says } M.$$

Exercise 8.1.1 *Suppose that the server's key K_S is certified only for signing, and hence the server sends a key exchange message as explained in the text to convey a signed public key K_t. Formalize and prove the derived rule that captures the analysis that allows the client to associate K_t with the server.*

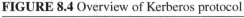

FIGURE 8.4 Overview of Kerberos protocol

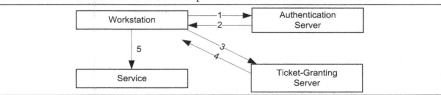

8.2 Kerberos: Authentication for Distributed Systems

Kerberos (Neuman et al., 2005) is an industry-standard protocol that supports both authentication and delegation on open networks. At the core of Kerberos lie two special services—the *authentication server (AS)* and the *ticket-granting server (TGS)*. Conceptually, these two services are distinct, but they are typically implemented on the same machine and collectively referred to as the *Key Distribution Center (KDC)*. The KDC has access to an authentication database that stores the individual Kerberos encryption keys for all users and services in the system. For this reason, the KDC should be in a physically secure location, as compromise of the authentication database would compromise the security of the entire system. Both services provide *tickets* to access other services: the AS provides *ticket-granting tickets (TGTs)* for accessing the TGS, while the TGS offers service-specific tickets for other services (such as a file system or print server).

For example, consider a user who, throughout the day at work, needs to access the (non-local) file system to obtain various files and also needs to print those files on a network printer. Both the file system and the printer need to authenticate the user to determine whether or not to provide access to the requested service. For reasons of both security and practicality, it is undesirable to require the user to repeatedly type in her password or rescan her smartcard each time she needs to access one of the services. Kerberos provides for *single signon*, whereby the user authenticates herself once and then receives an unforgeable token—called a *ticket-grating ticket*—that she can subsequently pass along to services to authenticate herself for a specified period of time (e.g., eight hours).

This example provides a backdrop to our explanation of the Kerberos protocol. We begin with simplest sort of case (i.e., not involving delegation), and then discuss how the protocol also supports proxies. Figure 8.4 illustrates the sequence of messages that comprise the Kerberos protocol. We examine these messages in turn.

8.2.1 Initial Authentication Requests

To understand how Kerberos works, let us consider what happens when Ursula arrives at work in the morning. Having fetched her coffee, Ursula sits down at her computer and types her userid (`ursa`) and password to log into the workstation. The

Kerberos client on her workstation uses a one-way function to calculate her secret (symmetric) encryption key K_u, which is the same key that the KDC associates with `ursa` in its authentication database. The client also saves this encryption key in the workstation's credentials cache. (The credentials cache should be emptied when the user logs out of the workstation, to prevent unauthorized use or replay of this key or other credentials.)

At this point, the Kerberos client sends *in the clear* an authentication request to the AS, which contains the following information: the user's name (`ursa`), the name of the service for which a ticket is being requested (i.e., the ticket-granting service TGS), and a random nonce n_u, which can be used to match requests with responses and also to detect possible replay attacks. This request may also contain additional information for the requested ticket-granting ticket (TGT), such as whether it should be *proxiable* or *forwardable*; for now, we ignore those possibilities, but we shall return to them later. This request corresponds to arrow 1 of Figure 8.4.

When the AS receives this request, it looks up the name `ursa` in its authentication database to verify that `ursa` is a registered user and to obtain Ursula's secret Kerberos key K_u. The AS also generates a *session key* $K_{u,tgs}$ to be used between the workstation's Kerberos client and the TGS. The AS then sends two encrypted items back to the Kerberos client, as represented by arrow 2 in Figure 8.4. The first uses Ursula's secret key K_u to encrypt both the newly generated session key and the client's original nonce (recall that the notation $\langle\langle m_1, m_2, \dots, m_k \rangle\rangle$ denotes the concatenation of the k items m_1 through m_k):

$$encrypt(K_u, \langle\langle K_{u,tgs}, n_u \rangle\rangle).$$

The second item is the ticket-granting ticket (TGT), which is encrypted with the secret Kerberos key that the authentication database associates with the TGS (K_{tgs}):

$$encrypt(K_{tgs}, \langle\langle K_{u,tgs}, \texttt{ursa}, add_u, \textit{ticket-validity period} \rangle\rangle).$$

The TGT contains the newly generated session key, the userid `ursa`, the network addresses that are allowed to use this ticket (in our case, only Ursula's workstation address add_u), and the period of time for which the TGT is valid (a system-specific value, which may be minutes or hours). Notice that, because the original request was sent in the clear, the AS has no way to verify that the request really arrived from a client representing `ursa` and not from an impostor. Rather, the AS constructs a response that should be useful only to a client working on her behalf (i.e., with knowledge of the secret key K_u), as described next.

Upon receiving these two items from the AS, Ursula's Kerberos client uses the shared secret key K_u to recover the original nonce (which associates the AS response with the initial client response) and the session key to use with the TGS:

$$K_u \text{ says } \langle \textit{use session key}, K_{u,tgs} \rangle.$$

The client associates the shared secret key K_u with the AS and also trusts the AS with respect to the assignment of session keys to use with the TGS:

$$K_u \Rightarrow AS,$$

$$AS \text{ controls } \langle use\ session\ key, K_{u,tgs} \rangle.$$

The client stores both the session key and the TGT for future use in requesting specific network services, as described in the next subsection. The client's decision to accept and store the session key corresponds to an instance of an application of the following derived rule:

$$\text{Session Key} \quad \frac{\begin{array}{c} Authority \text{ controls } \langle use\ session\ key, K_{session} \rangle \\ K \text{ says } \langle use\ session\ key, K_{session} \rangle \\ K \Rightarrow Authority \end{array}}{\langle use\ session\ key, K_{session} \rangle}.$$

In fact, this derived rule could be generalized significantly by replacing the action $\langle use\ session\ key, K_{session} \rangle$ with a generic statement φ, and in fact we have indirectly used such a generic rule multiple times throughout this book. However, stating the explicit rule in this context-specific way allows us to explicitly capture the operating behavior of the Kerberos client.

8.2.2 Requests for Service-Specific Tickets

A little later that morning, Ursula wants to make some changes to the file book.tex. When she selects the file to open, her Kerberos client must obtain a ticket for the appropriate file server. To do so, the Kerberos client sends to the TGS a request for a file-server ticket. This request contains the following components, many of which we have seen before: the user name ursa, the name of the requested service (in this case, the file server FS), a (new) random nonce n_w, the TGT previously received and stored, and an *authenticator* for the TGT. The authenticator is an encrypted package designed to demonstrate to the TGS knowledge of the secret session key $K_{u,tgs}$:

$$encrypt(K_{u,tgs}, \langle\langle \text{ursa}, add_u, timestamp \rangle\rangle).$$

The idea here is that only principals knowing the session key $K_{u,tgs}$ could create the authenticator. The timestamp indicates freshness and provides protection against replay attacks, while the user name and address must match those that appear in the TGT.

Upon receiving this request, the TGS first verifies that it is intact and well-formed. The TGS must then use the TGT and authenticator to determine whether or not to grant the request.

Recall that the TGT has been created as follows:

$$encrypt(K_{tgs}, \langle\langle K_{u,tgs}, \text{ursa}, add_u, ticket\text{-}validity\ period \rangle\rangle).$$

The TGS uses its secret key K_{tgs} to decrypt the TGT, from which it then extracts the session key $K_{u,tgs}$. In doing so, the TGS also verifies that the ticket is within its validity period and that the network address in the ticket (add_u) matches the network address of the request itself. If the TGS deems the ticket to be valid, then it has in effect interpreted the TGT as follows:

$$K_{tgs} \text{ says } (K_{u,tgs} \text{ controls } \langle \textit{get ticket, } \text{FS, } \texttt{ursa}@add_u \rangle)$$

That is, the TGT indicates which session key should be trusted with regards to requests for tickets for user $\texttt{ursa}$ at the network address add_u. Furthermore, the TGS must associate the secret key K_{tgs} with AS and trust in AS's jurisdiction regarding ticket requests:

$$K_{tgs} \Rightarrow AS,$$
$$AS \text{ controls } (K_{u,tgs} \text{ controls } \langle \textit{get ticket, } \text{FS, } \texttt{ursa}@add_u \rangle).$$

Having verified the validity of the TGT, the TGS then uses the extracted session key $K_{u,tgs}$ to decrypt the authenticator. For integrity checking, the TGS must verify that the authenticator timestamp is sufficiently recent (typically, within 5 minutes), that the user name is the same in both the ticket and authenticator, and that the network address given in the authenticator is the same as that given in the TGT. If everything checks out, then the TGS effectively interprets the authenticator as the following statement:

$$K_{u,tgs} \text{ says } \langle \textit{get ticket, } \text{FS, } \texttt{ursa}@add_u \rangle.$$

That is, the session key is certifying a request to create a ticket for $\texttt{ursa}$ for the file server.

At this point, it should be straightforward to see why the TGS determines it appropriate to grant the ticket request. In fact, the TGS decision to grant the request corresponds to an instance of the following derivable operating rule:

Grant Service
Ticket

$$\frac{\begin{array}{c} K \text{ says } (K_{session} \text{ controls } \langle \textit{get ticket, service, } P@add \rangle) \\ K \Rightarrow AS \\ AS \text{ controls } (K_{session} \text{ controls } \langle \textit{get ticket, service, } P@add \rangle) \\ K_{session} \text{ says } \langle \textit{get ticket, service, } P@add \rangle \end{array}}{\langle \textit{get ticket, service, } P@add \rangle}.$$

It is important to note that the TGS never directly associates the session key with the apparent requesting user, because its decision is not identity-based. Instead, the analysis depends on trust in the secrecy of the keys K (K_{tgs}) and $K_{session}$ ($K_{u,tgs}$). At this stage of the protocol, the user's name and network address exist only so that the correct service ticket can be created.

To grant the request, TGS creates a random session key $K_{u,fs}$ to be used between Ursula's Kerberos client and FS. The TGS sends the following two items back to the Kerberos client, in much the same way that the AS responded to the initial request for authentication:

$$encrypt(K_{u,tgs}, \langle\langle K_{u,fs}, n_w \rangle\rangle),$$
$$encrypt(K_{fs}, \langle\langle K_{u,fs}, \texttt{ursa}, add_u, \textit{ticket-validity period} \rangle\rangle).$$

As before, the Kerberos client can decrypt the first item to obtain the session key and to associate this response with the appropriate request; this decision again corresponds to an application of the *Session Key Receipt* rule. The second item is the file-service ticket, where K_{fs} is the secret key that the KDC's authentication database associates with FS.

8.2.3 Requests for Services

The Kerberos client now sends to the file server FS a request with the following components: the user name `ursa`, the file-service ticket previously received from the TGS, an authenticator $encrypt(K_{u,fs}, \langle\langle \text{ursa}, add_u, timestamp \rangle\rangle)$ for the file-service ticket, and any necessary application-specific information (in this case, the actual request to read the file `book.tex`). This request corresponds to arrow 5 in Figure 8.4.

The FS proceeds in much the same fashion as the TGS did earlier. Specifically, the FS uses its secret key K_{fs} to decrypt the ticket and extract the session key $K_{u,fs}$. However, the interpretation of this ticket is different, because—unlike the TGS—the file server must make an identity-based access decision. The file-service ticket must therefore provide an association between the secret session key $K_{u,fs}$ and the user `ursa`:

$$K_{fs} \text{ says } (K_{u,fs} \Rightarrow \text{ursa}).$$

The file server must also associate the secret key K_{fs} with the TGS and trust in the TGS's jurisdiction:

$$K_{fs} \Rightarrow TGS,$$
$$TGS \text{ controls } (K_{u,fs} \Rightarrow \text{ursa}).$$

As before, the FS uses the session key to decrypt the authenticator and performs the basic integrity check: the authenticator timestamp must be sufficiently recent, the user name must be the same in both the ticket and authenticator, and the network address given in the authenticator is the same as that in the ticket. If the authenticator checks out, then FS interprets the authenticator in the following way:

$$K_{u,fs} \text{ says } \langle read, \text{book.tex} \rangle.$$

It is straightforward for the FS to conclude that

$$\text{ursa says } \langle read, \text{book.tex} \rangle.$$

Such a conclusion corresponds to an instance of the following derivable operating rule:

$$\text{Service} \atop \text{Request} \qquad \frac{\begin{array}{c} TGS \text{ controls } (K_{session} \Rightarrow P) \\ K \text{ says } (K_{session} \Rightarrow P) \\ K \Rightarrow TGS \\ K_{session} \text{ says } servicerequest \end{array}}{P \text{ says } servicerequest}.$$

At this point, the file server can perform its usual process—such as checking the appropriate access-control list—to determine whether or not to grant the request.

8.2.4   Proxiable Tickets

Having described the basic Kerberos interactions, we return to an issue mentioned briefly earlier: Kerberos also supports *proxiable* and *forwardable* tickets. We describe the use of proxiable tickets in this section, and leave discussion of forwardable tickets to Exercise 8.2.5.

In many situations, a network service must make a request of another service on behalf of its client. For example, suppose our user Ursula decides that she wants to print out the file story.pdf. In such a scenario, the print service will need to contact the file server on Ursula's behalf to obtain the file. Kerberos has a mechanism for the creation and use of *proxiable tickets*, which can be used for proxy requests.

The initial authentication (i.e., Steps 1 and 2) for Ursula is very similar to that described in Subsection 8.2.1. However, the first step must also include a request for a *proxiable TGT*. Likewise, the TGT that the AS transmits back must have the *proxiable* flag set, so that the TGT has the following form:

$$encrypt(K_{tgs}, \langle\langle K_{u,tgs}, \text{ursa}, add_u, proxiable, ticket\text{-}validity\ period \rangle\rangle).$$

When Ursula decides to print her file, her Kerberos client requests (and obtains) a print-service ticket and session key, exactly as described in Subsection 8.2.2. However, the client must also request a *proxy ticket* that allows the print service to make requests on Ursula's behalf from the file service.. Therefore, the Kerberos client sends to the TGS a request containing the following components, most of which we have seen before: the user name ursa, the name of the requested service (in this case, the file server FS), a specific request for a proxy ticket, the network addresses of the allowable proxies (in this case, the address add_{ps} of the print server), a random nonce n_v, the proxiable TGT previously received and stored, and an authenticator $encrypt(K_{u,tgs}, \langle\langle \text{ursa}, add_u, timestamp \rangle\rangle)$ for the TGT. The request may also include service-specific information: in this scenario, the client might include the specific request(s) that the file service should honor (e.g., "read story.pdf").

Upon receiving this request, TGS uses its secret key K_{tgs} to decrypt the TGT, from which it then extracts the session key $K_{u,tgs}$. In doing so, TGS also verifies that the ticket is within its validity period and that the network address in the ticket (add_u) matches the network address of the request itself. If the TGS deems the ticket to be valid, then it has in effect interpreted the TGT as follows:

K_{tgs} says ($K_{u,tgs}$ controls

  (ursa@add_u controls

    $\langle get\ proxy\ ticket,\ FS, \text{ursa}@add_u, add_{ps}, \text{"read story.pdf"} \rangle$))).

That is, the TGT indicates which session key should be trusted with regards to requests for tickets for user ursa at network address add_u.

TGS must also associate the secret key K_{tgs} with AS and trust in AS's jurisdiction regarding ticket requests:

$K_{tgs} \Rightarrow AS$

AS controls $(K_{u,tgs}$ controls

      $(\mathtt{ursa}@add_u$ controls

           $\langle get\ proxy\ ticket,\ FS, \mathtt{ursa}@add_u, add_{ps}, "read\ \mathtt{story.pdf}"\rangle))$.

The TGS then uses the extracted session key $K_{u,tgs}$ to decrypt the authenticator. For integrity checking, the TGS must verify that the authenticator timestamp is sufficiently recent (typically, within 5 minutes), that the user name is the same in both the ticket and authenticator, and that the network address given in the authenticator is the same as that given in the TGT. If everything checks out, then the TGS effectively interprets the authenticator as the following statement:

$K_{u,tgs}$ says $(\mathtt{ursa}@add_u$ controls

           $\langle get\ proxy\ ticket,\ FS, \mathtt{ursa}@add_u, add_{ps}, "read\ \mathtt{story.pdf}"\rangle))$.

That is, the session key is certifying that user $\mathtt{ursa}$ is authorized to receive the requested ticket.

This analysis is identical to that performed for a regular (i.e., nonproxy) ticket, and it is straightforward to see why TGS determines it appropriate to grant the ticket request (the *Grant Service Ticket* rule still applies). To grant the request, as before, TGS creates a random session key $K_{u,fs}$ to be used with FS. The TGS sends the following two items back to W:

$$encrypt(K_{u,tgs}, \langle\langle K_{u,fs}, n_w\rangle\rangle),$$

$encrypt(K_{fs}, \langle\langle K_{u,fs}, \mathtt{ursa}, add_u, add_{ps}, proxy, tkt\text{-}validity\ pd, "read\ \mathtt{story.pdf}"\rangle\rangle)$.

As before, the Kerberos client can decrypt the first portion to obtain the session key and to associate this response with the appropriate request. The second portion is the file-service proxy ticket—in particular, the ticket contains all addresses that may be used with this ticket, namely $\mathtt{ursa}$'s workstation and the print server's address.

The Kerberos client sends the previously obtained print-service ticket and authenticator to PS as described in the previous subsection; the ticket includes a session key $K_{u,ps}$. The Kerberos client also forwards the newly obtained proxy ticket, along with the session key $K_{u,fs}$ (encrypted with the key $K_{u,ps}$) to the print service PS. The printer service PS is then able to make its proxy request to the file server FS, using this new session key. In particular, the printing service sends a request with the following components: the user's name ($\mathtt{ursa}$), the file-service ticket that the TGS sent in step 4, an authenticator $encrypt(K_{u,fs}, \langle\langle \mathtt{ursa}, add_{ps}, timestamp\rangle\rangle)$ for the ticket, and necessary application-specific information (in this case, the actual request to read the file $\mathtt{story.pdf}$).

The FS proceeds in much the same fashion as before: it uses its secret key K_{fs} to decrypt the ticket and extract the session key $K_{u,fs}$. Because this ticket is a proxy ticket, however, its interpretation is slightly different:

$$K_{fs} \text{ says } ((K_{u,fs} \Rightarrow add_{ps} \mid \texttt{ursa}) \land (add_{ps} \text{ reps } \texttt{ursa} \text{ on } \langle read, \texttt{story.pdf}\rangle)).$$

That is, the file-service ticket associates the secret session key $K_{u,fs}$ with the principal $add_{ps} \mid \texttt{ursa}$; it also specifies that add_{ps} is a valid proxy for $\texttt{ursa}$. To make use of this credential, FS must also associate the secret key K_{fs} with TGS and trust in TGS's jurisdiction:

$$K_{fs} \Rightarrow TGS$$
$$TGS \text{ controls } K_{u,fs} \Rightarrow add_{ps} \mid \texttt{ursa}$$
$$TGS \text{ controls } (add_{ps} \text{ reps } \texttt{ursa} \text{ on } \langle read, \texttt{story.pdf}\rangle).$$

As before, FS uses the session key to decrypt the authenticator and performs the basic integrity checking: the authenticator timestamp must be sufficiently recent, the user name must be the same in both the ticket and authenticator, and the network address given in the authenticator must also appear in the ticket. If the authenticator checks out, then FS interprets the authenticator in the following way:

$$K_{u,fs} \text{ says } \langle read, \texttt{story.pdf}\rangle.$$

It's straightforward for FS to conclude that

$$add_{ps} \mid \texttt{ursa} \text{ says } \langle read, \texttt{story.pdf}\rangle,$$

and therefore that

$$\texttt{ursa} \text{ says } \langle read, \texttt{story.pdf}\rangle.$$

This analysis corresponds to the following operating rule for the file service:

$$
\begin{array}{c}
\text{\textit{Proxied}} \\
\text{\textit{Service}} \\
\text{\textit{Request}}
\end{array}
\quad
\cfrac{
\begin{array}{c}
\textit{Authority} \text{ controls } (K_{session} \Rightarrow Q \mid P) \\
\textit{Authority} \text{ controls } (Q \text{ reps } P \text{ on } \textit{servicerequest}) \\
K \text{ says } ((K_{session} \Rightarrow Q \mid P) \land Q \text{ reps } P \text{ on } \textit{servicerequest}) \\
K \Rightarrow \textit{Authority} \\
K_{session} \text{ says } \textit{servicerequest}
\end{array}
}{
P \text{ says } \textit{servicerequest}
} \, .
$$

Exercise 8.2.1   *Give a formal proof of the* Session Key Receipt *rule.*

Exercise 8.2.2   *Give a formal proof of the* Grant Service Ticket *rule.*

Exercise 8.2.3   *Give a formal proof of the* Service Request *rule.*

Exercise 8.2.4   *Give a formal proof of the* Proxied Service Request *rule.*

Exercise 8.2.5 *A disadvantage of proxy tickets in Kerberos is that the Kerberos client must obtain the proxy tickets and then pass them on to the proxy service. Doing so requires the client to know the names of all of the services that the proxy will need to fulfill a specific request, which is not always possible on a distributed system. For this reason, Kerberos also supports* forwardable *(and* forwarded*) tickets, which the client can pass on (or* forward*) to the services that work on its behalf. The responsibility for obtaining subsequent tickets falls to the given service.*

The Kerberos client must request a forwardable TGT when initially authenticating a user to Kerberos; the request must indicate the addresses that will be able to act on the user's behalf. Likewise, the TGT that the AS sends back must have the forwardable *flag set. Thus, a forwardable TGT for user name* ursa *that allows the addresses addₐ and addₚₛ to make service requests has the following form:*

$$encrypt(K_{tgs}, \langle\langle K_{u,tgs}, \texttt{ursa}, add_u, add_{ps}, forwardable, ticket\text{-}validity\ period\rangle\rangle)$$

When Ursula decides she wants to print the file story.pdf*, her Kerberos client sends the forwardable TGT to the print service, along with the session key $K_{u,tgs}$. (As in the case of proxiable tickets, the client must also obtain and pass along a print-service ticket and authenticator; these together provide the necessary key by which the session key $K_{u,tgs}$ can be encrypted.)*

The print service PS then has the responsibility for obtaining the necessary ticket for the file service, or any other necessary tickets. The request that the print service sends to the TGS to obtain a file-service ticket contains the standard information (user name, requested service, forwardable TGT, and authenticator) plus a request for a forwarded *ticket. The TGS performs an analysis very similar to the previous cases, while also ensuring that the print service's address is one of the addresses included in the forwardable TGT. If everything checks out, the TGS sends both an encrypted session key and a forwarded file-service ticket to the print service:*

$$encrypt(K_{u,tgs}, \langle\langle K_{u,fs}, n'_w\rangle\rangle),$$
$$encrypt(K_{fs}, \langle\langle K_{u,fs}, U, add_u, add_{ps}, forwarded, ticket\text{-}validity\ period\rangle\rangle).$$

The print service can now send a request to the file service, containing the following information: the user name, the forwarded file-service ticket, an authenticator for the ticket, and any necessary application-specific information. The file service proceeds in much the same fashion as for other file-service tickets: it uses its secret key K_{fs} to decrypt the ticket and extract the session key $K_{u,fs}$.

    a. Give interpretations in the access-control logic of the forwarded file-service ticket and its authenticator. Note that the interpretation of forwarded tickets will differ from those for standard or proxy tickets.

    b. What additional assumptions—expressed as statements in the logic—must the file service make in order to process this request?

    c. Formalize and prove a derivable rule that captures the operating rules of the file service in this context.

8.3   Financial Networks

The previous two sections explored common protocols that are used to support authentication and delegation across distributed computer systems, including the web. In this section, we focus on financial networks, looking at how *electronic clearinghouses* use electronic records and images to eliminate the passing of paper checks. Specifically, we describe a banking network that uses electronic credits and debits and the Automated Clearing House (ACH) network, a trusted third-party settlement service. Detailed descriptions of retail payment systems and the ACH network can be found in the Federal Financial Institutions Examination Council's (FFIEC) handbook on Retail Payment Systems (FFIEC, 2004) and the National Automated Clearing House Association's guide to rules and regulations governing the ACH network (National Automated Clearing House Association, 2006). This section builds on the simple-checking example of Section 7.3.

8.3.1   Electronic Clearinghouses

The banking system uses *clearinghouses* (or *clearing corporations*) to collect and settle individual transactions while minimizing the number of actual payments made between banks. The FFIEC defines a *clearing corporation* as follows (FFIEC, 2004, page B-4):

> A central processing mechanism whereby members agree to net, clear, and settle transactions involving financial instruments. Clearing corporations fulfill one or all of the following functions:
>
> - nets many trades so that the number and the amount of payments that have to be made are minimized,
>
> - determines money obligations among traders, and
>
> - guarantees that trades will go through by legally assuming the risk of payments not made or securities not delivered. This latter function is what is implied when it is stated that the clearing corporation becomes the "counter-party" to all trades entered into its system. Also known as a clearinghouse or clearinghouse association.

To understand how a clearinghouse works, suppose that the depositors of $Bank_P$ and $Bank_Q$ exchange a total of two checks as follows during the day:

1. Bob (a $Bank_Q$ depositor) deposits a \$100 check from Alice, a $Bank_P$ depositor.

2. Dan (a $Bank_P$ depositor) deposits a \$250 check from Carol, a $Bank_Q$ depositor.

$Bank_P$ and $Bank_Q$ send the deposited checks to a clearinghouse to total up the transactions between them. The clearinghouse will let each bank know how much it owes to (or is owed from) other banks to settle their accounts each banking day. In this example, $Bank_P$ and $Bank_Q$ settle by having $Bank_Q$ transfer \$150 to $Bank_P$. $Bank_P$ will credit \$250 to Dan's account and debit Alice's account by \$100. $Bank_Q$ will credit \$100 to Bob's account and debit \$250 from Carol's account. In the (one hopes unlikely) event that $Bank_Q$ is unable to cover its debts, the clearinghouse will pay $Bank_P$ what it is owed.

To allow faster check processing, banks typically employ *check truncation*, which the FFIEC defines as follows (FFIEC, 2004, page B-3): "The practice of holding a check at the institution at which it was deposited (or at an intermediary institution) and electronically forwarding the essential information on the check to the institution on which it was written. A truncated check is not returned to the writer."

To support check truncation, banks and other financial institutions use *electronic check conversion* (ECC) to convert endorsed physical checks into legally equivalent check images. During electronic check conversion, magnetic-ink character recognition (MICR) captures information from a check's MICR line, including: the bank's routing number, account number, check number, check amount, and other information printed near the bottom of the check in magnetic ink in accordance with generally applicable industry standards. We represent $Bank_Q$'s ECC of an endorsed check as follows:

$$ECC_{Bank_Q} \text{ says } (Q \mid Signature_P) \text{ says } (\langle Pay \text{ amt}, Q\rangle \wedge \langle debit \text{ amt}, acct_P\rangle).$$

That is, the result of $Bank_Q$'s ECC process is an electronic claim that Q presented an integrity-checked signed check for the specified amount.

The use of electronically converted checks in the context of check truncation is known as *electronic check presentment (ECP)*. The FFIEC defines ECP as follows (FFIEC, 2004, page B-6): "Check truncation methodology in which the paper check's MICR line information is captured and stored electronically for presentment. The physical checks may or may not be presented after the electronic files are delivered, depending on the type of ECP service that is used."

$Bank_Q$'s presentation of the electronic check image can be represented as:

$$Bank_Q \text{ says } (ECC_{Bank_Q} \text{ says }$$
$$(Q \mid Signature_P) \text{ says } (\langle Pay \text{ amt}, Q\rangle \wedge \langle debit \text{ amt}, acct_P\rangle)).$$

That is, $Bank_Q$ is relaying the output of its ECC process. Presumably, $Bank_Q$ makes this statement (i.e., vouches for its electronic check conversion process) only when it believes the process is working correctly.

Figure 8.5 illustrates the use of a clearinghouse and check images. Bob, the payee, deposits Alice's check at his bank (arrow 2). Bob's bank does not present the check endorsed by Bob to Alice's bank directly. Rather, Bob's bank *truncates* the check, credits Bob's account (arrow 3), and sends an electronic version of the check—usually in a batch with other orders—to an Automated Clearing House (ACH) operator (arrow 4), who sends the image and information to Alice's bank (arrow 5) to debit Alice's account (arrow 6). The ACH operator settles the accounts between Alice's and Bob's respective banks each day (arrows 7 and 8).

FIGURE 8.5 Interbank checking using the ACH electronic clearinghouse

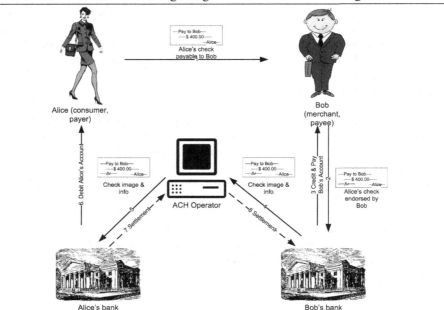

Clearing corporations such as the Federal Reserve Banks guarantee payments for depository financial institutions using services such as FedACH. Consequently, the Federal Reserve Banks take on the financial risk if a depository financial institution (DFI) defaults and has insufficient funds to settle. Hence, both the ACH and the DFIs are signatories to transactions. Thus, the ACH is not merely relaying information but also assuming liability.

We represent the presentation of a check image created by $Bank_Q \mid ECC_{Bank_Q}$ by an ACH operator ACH as follows:

$$((ACH \ \& \ Bank_Q) \mid ECC_{Bank_Q}) \mid Q \text{ says}$$
$$(Signature_P \text{ says } (\langle Pay \text{ amt}, Q \rangle \wedge \langle debit \text{ amt}, acct_P \rangle)).$$

The operator is functioning as a clearing corporation and *countersigns* the check image. By so doing, the ACH operator assumes the risk of the transaction if $Bank_P$ defaults at settlement time.

In this system, checks are cleared immediately without first checking payers' account balances. If there is an insufficient balance to cover the amount of the check, the check in question is returned to the depositor, and the amount is ultimately charged back to his or her account as a separate transaction. In Figure 8.5, if Alice's check bounces, then Alice's check (or a truncated version of her check) is returned by her bank to the ACH operator to debit Bob's bank the amount of the returned check.

8.3.2 Bank Authorities, Jurisdiction, and Policies

The controlling authorities in this case include the bank owners as well as the Automated Clearing House (ACH) association, whose rules all members agree to follow as a condition of membership. We begin by formalizing the necessary policies for each of these authorities, starting with the paying bank $Bank_P$. In the next subsection, we show how these policies are instrumental to the operating rules these institutions use for making access-control decisions related to interbank checking.

8.3.2.1 Policies of the Paying Bank

At the individual account level, depositors are allowed to write checks. If there are insufficient funds in the account, another transaction will reverse the debit. Therefore, the policy allowing depositor P to write checks to payee Q can be expressed by the following two statements:

$$Bank_P \; Owner \; \text{controls} \; (P \; \text{controls} \; (\langle Pay \; \text{amt}, Q \rangle \wedge \langle debit \; \text{amt}, acct_P \rangle)),$$

$$Bank_P \; Owner \; \text{says} \; (P \; \text{controls} \; (\langle Pay \; \text{amt}, Q \rangle \wedge \langle debit \; \text{amt}, acct_P \rangle)).$$

That is, the owner of $Bank_P$ not only has the authority to set this policy but also—as a condition of ACH membership—indeed does set it. Furthermore, $Bank_P$ must have a policy that allows payees to be the delegates of the payers indicated on checks:

$$Bank_P \; Owner \; \text{controls} \; (Q \; \text{reps} \; P \; \text{on} \; (\langle Pay \; \text{amt}, Q \rangle \wedge \langle debit \; \text{amt}, acct_P \rangle)),$$

$$Bank_P \; Owner \; \text{says} \; (Q \; \text{reps} \; P \; \text{on} \; (\langle Pay \; \text{amt}, Q \rangle \wedge \langle debit \; \text{amt}, acct_P \rangle)).$$

Applying the *Controls* inference rules to the above statements produces the following policy statements for $Bank_P$:

$$P \; \text{controls} \; (\langle Pay \; \text{amt}, Q \rangle \wedge \langle debit \; \text{amt}, acct_P \rangle)$$

$$Q \; \text{reps} \; P \; \text{on} \; (\langle Pay \; \text{amt}, Q \rangle \wedge \langle debit \; \text{amt}, acct_P \rangle).$$

Because $Bank_P$ is part of the ACH network, it must recognize *ACH* as a countersigner with any ACH network bank that uses ECP:

$Bank_P \; Owner \; \text{controls}$

$$((ACH \; \& \; Bank_Q) \; | \; ECC_{Bank_Q}) \; \text{reps} \; (Q \; | \; Signature_P) \; \text{on}$$
$$(\langle Pay \; \text{amt}, Q \rangle \wedge \langle debit \; \text{amt}, acct_P \rangle),$$

$Bank_P \; Owner \; \text{says}$

$$((ACH \; \& \; Bank_Q) \; | \; ECC_{Bank_Q}) \; \text{reps} \; (Q \; | \; Signature_P) \; \text{on}$$
$$(\langle Pay \; \text{amt}, Q \rangle \wedge \langle debit \; \text{amt}, acct_P \rangle).$$

Again, the *Controls* inference rule lets us derive $Bank_P$'s policy regarding check images and information forwarded to it by *ACH*:

$$((ACH \; \& \; Bank_Q) \; | \; ECC_{Bank_Q}) \; \text{reps} \; (Q \; | \; Signature_P) \; \text{on}$$
$$(\langle Pay \; \text{amt}, Q \rangle \wedge \langle debit \; \text{amt}, acct_P \rangle).$$

8.3.2.2   Policies of the ACH Operator

The ACH operator accepts transactions only from ACH members. In this example, the policies for the ACH operator regarding $Bank_P$ and $Bank_Q$ are as follows:

$$Bank_P \text{ controls } \langle Pay \text{ amt}, Q \rangle.$$

That is, the ACH operator will accept a payment from $Bank_P$ as part of the settlement process. Furthermore, $Bank_Q$ is allowed to present electronically converted checks to the operator:

$$Bank_Q \text{ reps } ECC_{Bank_Q} \text{ on}$$
$$(Q \mid Signature_P) \text{ says } ((\langle Pay \text{ amt}, Q \rangle \wedge \langle debit \text{ amt}, acct_P \rangle)).$$

8.3.2.3   Policies of the Receiving Bank

The controlling authority for $Bank_Q$ is $Bank_Q$'s owner. The following policies result from recognizing $Bank_P$ as a banking partner as part of the ACH network (which can be determined from the MICR line). The first policy states that checks drawn upon accounts in $Bank_P$ may be deposited in $Bank_Q$'s accounts:

$Bank_Q$ *Owner* controls
$$((Q \mid Signature_P \text{ says } (\langle Pay \text{ amt}, Q \rangle \wedge \langle debit \text{ amt}, acct_P \rangle)) \supset$$
$$(\langle Pay \text{ amt}, Q \rangle \wedge (Q \text{ controls } \langle credit \text{ amt}, acct_Q \rangle)))),$$
$Bank_Q$ *Owner* says
$$((Q \mid Signature_P \text{ says } (\langle Pay \text{ amt}, Q \rangle \wedge \langle debit \text{ amt}, acct_P \rangle)) \supset$$
$$(\langle Pay \text{ amt}, Q \rangle \wedge (Q \text{ controls } \langle credit \text{ amt}, acct_Q \rangle)))).$$

We are assuming here that funds are immediately available (i.e., there is no float time). The second policy states that $Bank_Q$ recognizes ACH's settlement statement:

$$Bank_Q \text{ } Owner \text{ controls } (ACH \text{ controls } \langle Pay \text{ amt}, Q \rangle),$$
$$Bank_Q \text{ } Owner \text{ says } (ACH \text{ controls } \langle Pay \text{ amt}, Q \rangle).$$

As before, $Bank_Q$'s policies can be obtained by applying the *Controls* inference rule to the previous statements:

$$(Q \mid Signature_P \text{ says } (\langle Pay \text{ amt}, Q \rangle \wedge \langle debit \text{ amt}, acct_P \rangle)) \supset$$
$$(\langle Pay \text{ amt}, Q \rangle \wedge Q \text{ controls } \langle credit \text{ amt}, acct_Q \rangle),$$
ACH controls $\langle Pay \text{ amt}, Q \rangle.$

8.3.3   Bank Operating Rules

There are five access-control decisions to be made during the course of check processing, corresponding to the arrows labeled 3–8 in Figure 8.5. The first decision (arrow 3) is made by the receiving bank $Bank_Q$ in response to Bob's request to deposit Alice's check, credit his account by the same amount, and have the funds made available to him. This decision is made by the *ACH Check Deposit* rule, whose proof (like those for all other inference rules in this section) is left as an exercise:

$$
\text{ACH Check Deposit} \quad
\frac{
\begin{array}{c}
Signature_Q \mid Signature_P \text{ says } (\langle Pay \text{ amt}, Q \rangle \wedge \langle debit \text{ amt}, acct_P \rangle) \\
Signature_Q \text{ says } \langle credit \text{ amt}, acct_Q \rangle \\
Signature_Q \Rightarrow Q \\
(Q \mid Signature_P \text{ says } (\langle Pay \text{ amt}, Q \rangle \wedge \langle debit \text{ amt}, acct_P \rangle)) \supset \\
\langle Pay \text{ amt}, Q \rangle \wedge (Q \text{ controls } \langle credit \text{ amt}, acct_Q \rangle)
\end{array}
}{
\langle Pay \text{ amt}, Q \rangle \wedge \langle credit \text{ amt}, acct_Q \rangle
}.
$$

The first two premises correspond to Q's presentation of both the endorsed check and a signed deposit slip, respectively. The third premise corresponds to a signature check for Q, while the fourth premise reflects $Bank_Q$'s policy to accept checks drawn on $Bank_P$ accounts.

The second decision (arrow 4) is also made by $Bank_Q$, which must decide whether or not to electronically present the check endorsed by Q to the ACH operator. If the check is endorsed by a depositor Q of $Bank_Q$, $Signature_Q$ is Q's signature, and the check itself passes whatever integrity check the bank uses, then the check is converted to its electronic version and passed on to the ACH operator. This decision is made by the *ACH Check Presentation* rule:

$$
\text{ACH Check Presentation} \quad
\frac{
\begin{array}{c}
Signature_Q \mid Signature_P \text{ says } (\langle Pay \text{ amt}, Q \rangle \wedge \langle debit \text{ amt}, acct_P \rangle) \\
Signature_Q \Rightarrow Q
\end{array}
}{
Bank_Q \text{ says } (ECC_{Bank_Q} \text{ says } (Q \mid Signature_P) \text{ says } (\langle Pay \text{ amt}, Q \rangle \wedge \langle debit \text{ amt}, acct_P \rangle))
}.
$$

The third decision (arrow 5) is made by the ACH operator to countersign the electronically converted check and present it to $Bank_P$. This decision uses the *ACH Countersign* rule:

$$
\text{ACH Countersign} \quad
\frac{
\begin{array}{c}
Bank_Q \text{ says } (ECC_{Bank_Q} \text{ says } (Q \mid Signature_P) \text{ says } (\langle Pay \text{ amt}, Q \rangle \wedge \langle debit \text{ amt}, acct_P \rangle)) \\
Bank_Q \text{ controls } (ECC_{Bank_Q} \text{ says } (Q \mid Signature_P) \text{ says } (\langle Pay \text{ amt}, Q \rangle \wedge \langle debit \text{ amt}, acct_P \rangle))
\end{array}
}{
(ACH \,\&\, Bank_Q) \text{ says } (ECC_{Bank_Q} \text{ says } ((Q \mid Signature_P) \text{ says } (\langle Pay \text{ amt}, Q \rangle \wedge \langle debit \text{ amt}, acct_P \rangle)))
}.
$$

Here, the first premise corresponds to $Bank_Q$'s presentation of the electronic check image. The second premise indicates that the ACH operator must trust that $Bank_Q$ is correctly reporting the result of its ECC process.

The fourth decision (arrows 6 and 7) is made by the paying bank $Bank_P$, which must determine whether to debit the appropriate account and pay toward settlement. The *ACH Check Funding* rule reflects this decision:

$$
\text{ACH Check Funding} \quad
\frac{
\begin{array}{c}
(ACH \,\&\, Bank_Q) \text{ says } (ECC_{Bank_Q} \text{ says } ((Q \mid Signature_P) \text{ says } (\langle Pay \text{ amt}, Q \rangle \wedge \langle debit \text{ amt}, acct_P \rangle))) \\
((ACH \,\&\, Bank_Q) \mid ECC_{Bank_Q}) \text{ reps } Q \text{ on } (Signature_P \text{ says } (\langle Pay \text{ amt}, Q \rangle \wedge \langle debit \text{ amt}, acct_P \rangle)) \\
Signature_P \Rightarrow P \\
P \text{ controls } (\langle Pay \text{ amt}, Q \rangle \wedge \langle debit \text{ amt}, acct_P \rangle) \\
Q \text{ reps } P \text{ on } (\langle Pay \text{ amt}, Q \rangle \wedge \langle debit \text{ amt}, acct_P \rangle)
\end{array}
}{
(Bank_P \text{ says } \langle Pay \text{ amt}, Q \rangle) \wedge \langle debit \text{ amt}, acct_P \rangle
}.
$$

The premises of this rule capture many necessary conditions: $Bank_P$'s must receive the electronic check image countersigned by the ACH (premise 1), recognize the countersigned check image as being relayed on behalf of the payee Q (premise 2), verify the signature of the payer P (premise 3), recognize the payer P's authority to write checks on the account $acct_P$ (premise 4), and recognize that the payee Q is the check writer P's delegate in this context (premise 5).

The final decision (arrow 8) is made by the ACH operator using the *ACH Check Settlement* rule:

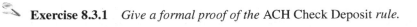

$$\text{ACH Check Settlement} \quad \frac{Bank_P \text{ says } \langle Pay \text{ amt}, Q \rangle \quad Bank_P \text{ controls } \langle Pay \text{ amt}, Q \rangle}{ACH \text{ says } \langle Pay \text{ amt}, Q \rangle}.$$

Exercise 8.3.1   *Give a formal proof of the* ACH Check Deposit *rule.*

Exercise 8.3.2   *Give a formal proof of the* ACH Check Presentation *rule.*

Exercise 8.3.3   *Give a formal proof of the* ACH Countersign *rule.*

Exercise 8.3.4   *Give a formal proof of the* ACH Check Funding *rule.*

Exercise 8.3.5   *Give a formal proof of the* ACH Check Settlement *rule.*

Exercise 8.3.6   *Consider the concept of operations of ACH checking as presented in Figure 8.5. What are the risks?*

8.4   Summary

Taken together, the SSL/TLS protocols, Kerberos, and the ACH network all illustrate the complexity of providing authentication, authorization, and accountability in both public and private networks. These industry-standard protocols all employ a series of requests and responses carefully designed to provide specific assurances to their different participants.

In this chapter, we showed how to use the access-control logic to help explicate the policies, underlying trust assumptions, and concepts of operations employed by the various protocol principals. These case studies demonstrate that it is possible to take real industry standards and describe them concisely in our access-control logic.

The learning outcomes associated with this chapter appear in Figure 8.6.

FIGURE 8.6 Learning outcomes for Chapter 8

After completing this chapter, you should be able to achieve the following learning outcomes at several levels of knowledge:

Application

- Given a derivable inference rule related to a network protocol, you should be able to give a formal proof of the rule.

Synthesis

- Given an informal but clear description of a network protocol, you should be able to construct the derivable inference rules that capture the protocol's concept of operations.

Evaluation

- Given a formalization of a protocol in the access-control logic, you should be able to evaluate the potential risks associated with the protocol's concept of operations.

8.5 Further Reading

The IETF Internet Draft for SSL 3.0 (Freier et al., 1996) and the *Requests for Comments (RFC)* for TLS version 1.1 (Dierks and Rescorla, 2006) and Kerberos version 5 (Neuman et al., 2005) provide detailed descriptions of the messages and data structures that comprise these protocols. For an informative but less technical description of Kerberos, we refer interested readers to Bryant and Ts'o's fictional dialogue describing the design of a Kerberos-like system (Bryant, 1988).

Part III

Isolation and Sharing

Chapter 9

A Primer on Computer Hardware

At the core of cybersecurity lies the need for hardware security. The bits and bytes that support cyberspace ultimately exist in physical memory and in the registers inside processors. These bits move from place to place via data paths guided by timing and control logic. Deficiencies or discrepancies at the hardware level may significantly compromise system security: even the most secure cryptographic protocol is useless if someone can alter the keys stored in physical memory. As a consequence, systems engineers must have at least an elementary knowledge of computer hardware as it relates to security.

In this chapter, we provide a hardware primer for readers who may be unfamiliar with the concepts and terminology of synchronous hardware design and microcode. We introduce combinational logic circuits and registers, as well as their descriptions using truth tables, block diagrams, and timing diagrams. We start with basic definitions of components and then show how more complicated functions such as arithmetic logic units (ALUs) are created.

This primer provides the necessary background for the rest of Part III, whose topics include virtual machines, memory protection, process isolation and sharing, descriptors, and capabilities.

9.1 Ones and Zeros

In hardware design, it is customary to blur the distinction between truth values and binary values and therefore to use 0 (respectively, 1) to represent both the truth value *false* (respectively, *true*) and the binary value *0* (respectively, *1*). The particular interpretation is determined by the context in which 0 or 1 is used.

Electrically, 0 and 1 are implemented as electrical voltages within a particular range. For example, some designs consider 0 to be any voltage between 0 and 0.5 volts and 1 to be any voltage between 4.0 and 5.0 volts. Because the only allowed values are 0 and 1, voltages between 0.5 and 4.0 volts would have no meaning.

All numerical values have a binary representation in hardware. How many different values a given processor can represent ultimately depends upon its *word length*. A processor's word length is the number of *bits* (i.e., *binary digits*) in a *word*, which is the smallest addressable unit of data in memory. For example, a data memory that

FIGURE 9.1 Timing diagram for synchronous registers and memory

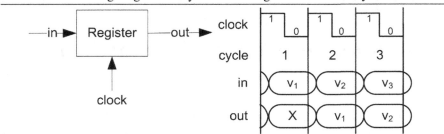

consists of eight 4-bit words has a word length of four bits, and each 4-bit word has 16 possible values (0000 through 1111). Furthermore, each of the eight 4-bit words in memory is addressable by a 3-bit address (000 through 111).

The number of bits in data registers is usually the same as the word length of data. Typical microprocessors have word lengths of 16, 32, or 64 bits. Thus, data registers and memory would be 16-, 32-, or 64-bits wide. Data buses—a collection of two or more related signal lines—are typically 16-, 32-, or 64-bits wide. In our descriptions, we are not concerned about the details of word length, so we omit from our diagrams any mention of word lengths. We assume that words are wide enough to represent all values of interest.

9.2   Synchronous Design

Most computer hardware is designed using *synchronous* design principles. That is, the registers and memory that are used to store values are updated relative to a central system *clock*. In this section, we describe the behavior of various kinds of registers, including synchronous registers, registers with load control, and registers with tri-state outputs. We also provide a description of combinational-logic design that includes the development of a simple arithmetic logic unit (ALU). Registers combined with ALUs are the core of synchronous central processing units (CPUs).

9.2.1   Synchronous Registers

Figure 9.1 contains two diagrams of a synchronous register. On the left of the figure, we see a register with two inputs (*in* and *clock*) and a single output (*out*). On the right is a timing diagram that shows the values of *clock, in,* and *out* at different cycles. At the top of the timing diagram is the *clock* signal—a square wave whose value alternates from 1 to 0 and back again. In synchronous design, *clock cycles* are bounded by what are called *active clock edges*. Figure 9.1 illustrates the case where the active clock edges are the 0-to-1 clock transitions.

A single clock cycle corresponds to one cycle of the system clock signal that is bounded by two active clock edges. The simplest approach to synchronous design is *single-phase* clocking, in which there is only one system clock and one active clock edge (i.e., either 0-to-1 or 1-to-0). Our descriptions assume that the active edges are the 0-to-1 clock edges, and thus the 1-to-0 clock transitions are of no consequence. Figure 9.1 displays three clock cycles, labeled 1, 2, and 3. In practice, multiple clocks and phases may be used (e.g., two- and four-phased clocks). However, for our purposes, single-phase clocking is sufficient.

The third row in the timing diagram shows the values that appear on the input line *in* during cycles 1, 2, and 3: the values v_1, v_2, and v_3, respectively. At the beginning of each clock cycle, the values may change as a result of an active clock edge. These delays correspond to the time necessary for circuits to charge or discharge. For correct design behavior, all input signals to registers and memory must be stable prior to the next active clock edge. The maximum time to charge or discharge determines the maximum clock frequency.

The fourth row of the timing diagram shows the values that appear on the output line *out* during cycles 1, 2, and 3. In cycle 1, the value of *out* is labeled X: that is, the value is either unknown or a *don't-care* value. The values of *out* in cycles 2 and 3 are v_1 and v_2, respectively.

The behavior of the register in Figure 9.1 is best described as a delayed repetition: its output value at cycle $n+1$ is the same as its input value at cycle n. The relationship between *out* and *in* is described by

$$out(n+1) = in(n),$$

where, for any given cycle number i, $out(i)$ and $in(i)$ respectively denote the output value and input value at cycle i.

9.2.2 Registers with Load Control

The simple register shown in Figure 9.1 stores a potentially different value each clock cycle. In contrast, Figure 9.2 shows a register with an additional control signal *LD*, which controls whether or not values on *in* are loaded into the register. In this register, input values are loaded precisely when the value of *LD* is *active* (i.e., when *LD's* value is 1). When *LD's* value is 1 during cycle n, the value of *out* during cycle $n+1$ will be $in(n)$; when *LD's* value is 0 during cycle n, the value of *out* in cycle $n+1$ remains unchanged. This relationship is shown below:

$$out(n+1) = \begin{cases} out(n), & \text{if } LD(n) \text{ is } 0, \\ in(n), & \text{if } LD(n) \text{ is } 1. \end{cases}$$

9.2.3 Registers with Tri-State Outputs

All digital circuits in computer hardware have electrical values corresponding to 0 and 1. Some digital circuits also have the additional capability to have a third value

FIGURE 9.2 Timing diagram for synchronous registers with load control

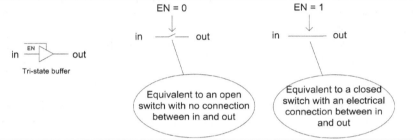

FIGURE 9.3 Tri-state buffer

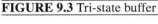

called a *high-impedance* state, which is denoted by Hi-Z. Circuits that have three values—0, 1, and Hi-Z—are known as tri-state circuits. Electrically, Hi-Z corresponds to an open switch—that is, a path of infinite resistance (hence the term "high impedance").

One of the simplest digital circuits with a tri-state capability is a *tri-state buffer*. Figure 9.3 shows the standard symbol for a tri-state buffer with two inputs (*in* and *EN*) and a single output (*out*). Logically, buffers are analogous to switches, and Figure 9.3 also shows the analogous switch states associated with the output-enable signal *EN*. When *EN* is 0, the tri-state buffer output behaves like an open switch, where *out* is electrically isolated from *in*. When *EN* is 1, the tri-state buffer output behaves like a closed switch, where *out* is electrically connected to *in* and *out* = *in*.

We can express the relationship between inputs and outputs for a tri-state buffer in clock cycle *n* as follows:

$$out(n) = \begin{cases} in(n), & \text{if } EN = 1, \\ \text{Hi-Z}, & \text{if } EN = 0. \end{cases}$$

Notice that tri-state buffers are effectively instantaneous: the value on the output line *out* depends upon the values of *in* and *EN* for the very same cycle.

Circuits with tri-state outputs are useful when inputs and outputs come from multiple sources, as in the following example.

FIGURE 9.4 Tri-state bus example

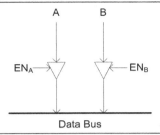

Data Bus

EN_A	EN_B	A	B	Data Bus
1	1	X	X	Not permitted: electrical conflict
1	0	val_A	X	val_A
0	1	X	val_B	val_B
0	0	X	X	Hi-Z

Table 9.1: Tri-state data-bus values

Example 9.1

Consider a data bus in a processor with two input sources, *A* and *B*. These sources are electrically connected to the data bus using tri-state buffers with the enable controls EN_A and EN_B, as shown in Figure 9.4.

Table 9.1 shows the values that appear on the data bus for all combinations of values for the tri-state buffer controls EN_A and EN_B. As before, X denotes an unknown or a *don't-care* value. Note that enabling both tri-state buffer outputs simultaneously results in an electrical conflict—for example, *A* might be at 0 volts at the same time that *B* is at 5 volts—and must therefore be avoided. When both control signals are 0, then both A and B inputs are electrically isolated from the data bus; if they are the only inputs, the data bus itself is in a Hi-Z state. The other two cases correspond to exactly one of *A* and *B* being enabled, and the data bus takes on the value of the enabled input. ◊

Registers are frequently equipped with tri-state buffers so that their outputs can be enabled in sequence onto a data- or memory-address bus. Figure 9.5 shows an implementation of a register with load control and tri-state outputs. Specifically, the figure contains a register with load control whose output is fed into a tri-state buffer. Note that we have left out the clock line: for synchronous designs, the clock is assumed to go to all registers and is omitted from high-level descriptions.

Table 9.2 fully describes a register with load control and tri-state outputs under control of a control input *EN*. When *EN* is active (i.e., has the value 1), then the register behaves exactly like the register with load control from Figure 9.2: either 0 or 1 appears on the output, as appropriate. When *EN* is *inactive*, however, the corresponding value of *out* is Hi-Z, regardless of any other input.

FIGURE 9.5 Register with tri-state output

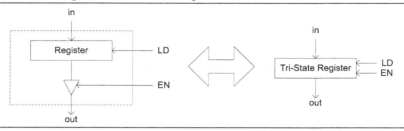

EN(n+1)	LD(n)	in(n)	out(n)	out(n+1)
1	1	1	X	1
1	1	0	X	0
1	0	X	1	1
1	0	X	0	0
0	X	X	X	Hi-Z

Table 9.2: Register with high-impedance output

9.2.4   Combinational Logic and Functions

In addition to registers and memory components, computer hardware consists of combinational logic and arithmetic functions. Table 9.3 gives the truth-table definitions of *inverters* (i.e., *not* gates), *and* gates, *nand* gates, *or* gates, *nor* gates, and *exclusive-or* gates, while Figure 9.6 shows their symbolic representation. These gates are the basic components for all digital computer hardware. Like the tri-state buffers, pure combinational-logic circuits are effectively instantaneous: their output values for a given cycle depend on the input values of the very same cycle.

The following example illustrates how the combinational-logic gates are used to implement a *full adder*, which serves as a basic building block for developing more complex hardware components. Specifically, a full adder is a circuit that adds three single bits to compute a 2-bit result.

Example 9.2
A full adder has three inputs: x, y, and the *carry input* c_{in}. It also has two outputs: the *carry output* c_{out} and the *sum s*. Table 9.4 provides an arithmetic interpretation for a

x	y	$not(x)$	$and(x,y)$	$nand(x,y)$	$or(x,y)$	$nor(x,y)$	$xor(x,y)$
1	1	0	1	0	1	0	0
1	0	0	0	1	1	0	1
0	1	1	0	1	1	0	1
0	0	1	0	1	0	1	0

Table 9.3: Simple combinational-logic functions

FIGURE 9.6 Basic combinational-logic gates

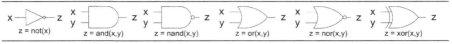

Inputs			Outputs		Arithmetic Interpretation
x	y	c_{in}	c_{out}	s	$2 \times c_{out} + s = x + y + c_{in}$
1	1	1	1	1	$2 \times 1 + 1 = 1 + 1 + 1$
1	1	0	1	0	$2 \times 1 + 0 = 1 + 1 + 0$
1	0	1	1	0	$2 \times 1 + 0 = 1 + 0 + 1$
1	0	0	0	1	$2 \times 0 + 1 = 1 + 0 + 0$
0	1	1	1	0	$2 \times 1 + 0 = 0 + 1 + 1$
0	1	0	0	1	$2 \times 0 + 1 = 0 + 1 + 0$
0	0	1	0	1	$2 \times 0 + 1 = 0 + 0 + 1$
0	0	0	0	0	$2 \times 0 + 0 = 0 + 0 + 0$

Table 9.4: An arithmetic interpretation of a full adder

full adder, showing all eight combination of inputs, the corresponding carry and sum outputs, and the arithmetic relationship that holds between the inputs and outputs.

For example, the first line of the table corresponds to the case where x, y, and c_{in} all have the value 1. Their base-10 sum $x + y + c_{in} = 1 + 1 + 1$ is 3_{10}, which can be expressed in base-2 as 11_2; this result is identical to that obtained by looking at the bit sequence $c_{out}s = 11$.[1] Similarly, the fifth line of the table covers the case where x has the value 0, while both y and c_{in} have the value 1. Their base-10 sum $x + y + c_{in} = 0 + 1 + 1$ is 2_{10}, which can be expressed in base-2 as 10_2; again, this result is identical to that obtained by looking at the bit sequence $c_{out}s = 10$.

Using this table, one can verify that the carry and sum output functions are correctly defined using combinational logic as follows:[2]

$$c_{out} = or(and(x, y), and(x, c_{in}), and(y, c_{in})),$$
$$s = xor(xor(x, y), c_{in}).$$

Figure 9.7(a) contains a block-diagram representation of a full adder with inputs X_i, Y_i, and C_i, and outputs C_{i+1} and S_i. Figure 9.7(b) contains a gate-level implementation of the full adder, which comes directly from the sum and carry output functions defined above. ◊

---

[1] Following standard conventions, we use the notation $b_{n-1}b_{n-2} \cdots b_0$ to indicate a sequence of bits that starts with b_{n-1} and terminates with b_0.

[2] In our diagrams and notations, we often make use of n-ary operators and gates—such as $or(x, y, z)$—rather than expanding them to a series of binary operators or gates, such as $or(x, (or(y, z)))$. Such presentations are more concise, and are common among hardware designers.

FIGURE 9.7 Full-adder implementation

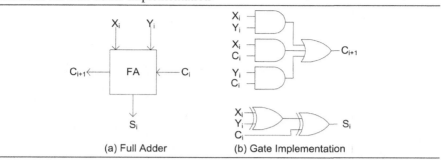

(a) Full Adder (b) Gate Implementation

Basic combinational-logic gates and full adders are used to create more complex arithmetic and logic units, as we show in the next subsection.

9.2.5 Arithmetic Logic Units

In the previous example, we showed how combinational-logic gates are combined to form basic arithmetic building blocks such as full adders. These basic arithmetic building blocks are combined with combinational-logic functions to create arithmetic logic units (ALUs), which are the computational core of central processing units (CPUs).

A simple example is an n-bit adder, which adds two n-bit words (X and Y) and a carry-input bit C_0 to produce an $(n+1)$-bit result that consists of a carry-output bit C_n and an n-bit sum S. Figure 9.8(a) contains a block diagram of an n-bit adder. The n-bit adder is easily implemented by a linear array of full adders called a *ripple* adder (so called because the carry bits "ripple" from the least significant bit to the most significant bit). Figure 9.8(b) shows an implementation of an n-bit adder by an n-bit ripple adder.

The arithmetic relationship between the inputs ($X = X_{n-1}\ldots X_o$, $Y = Y_{n-1}\ldots Y_0$, and C_0) and the outputs (C_n and $S = S_{n-1}\ldots S_0$) is as follows:

$$2^n \times C_n + 2^{n-1} \times S_{n-1} + \cdots + 2^0 \times S_0 =$$
$$2^{n-1} \times X_{n-1} + 2^{n-2} \times X_{n-2} + \cdots + 2^0 \times X_0 +$$
$$2^{n-1} \times Y_{n-1} + 2^{n-2} \times Y_{n-2} + \cdots + 2^0 \times Y_0 + 2^0 \times C_0.$$

That is, the binary value of the $(n+1)$-bit sequence $C_n S_{n-1} \cdots S_0$ is equal to the sum of the inputs' binary values.

The following example illustrates this relationship between inputs and outputs.

FIGURE 9.8 An *n*-bit adder and ripple adder

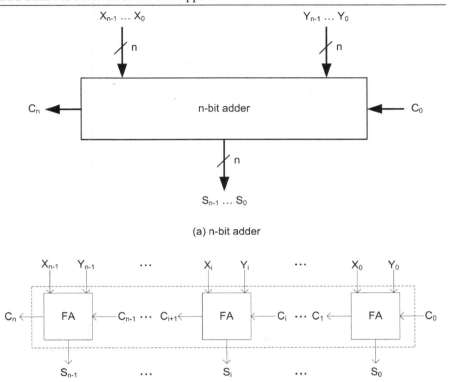

(a) n-bit adder

(b) n-bit ripple adder

Example 9.3

Suppose we have a 4-bit adder with the following inputs:

$$X = X_3X_2X_1X_0 = 1000_2 = 8_{10},$$
$$Y = Y_3Y_2Y_1Y_0 = 1001_2 = 9_{10},$$
$$C_0 = 1_2 = 1_{10}.$$

The result of adding X, Y, and C_0 together is 18_{10}, which in binary is given by the carry output and sum bits as follows:

$$C_4S_3S_2S_1S_0 = 10010_2 = 18_{10}.$$

One can also verify that the ripple-adder implementation computes this sum cor-

FIGURE 9.9 ALU implementation

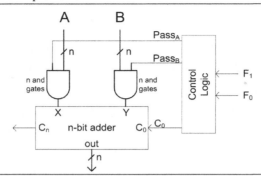

rectly, as follows:

$$C_1 S_0 = X_0 + Y_0 + C_0 = 0 + 1 + 1 = 10_2,$$
$$C_2 S_1 = X_1 + Y_1 + C_1 = 0 + 0 + 1 = 01_2,$$
$$C_3 S_2 = X_2 + Y_2 + C_2 = 0 + 0 + 0 = 00_2,$$
$$C_4 S_3 = X_3 + Y_3 + C_3 = 1 + 1 + 0 = 10_2. \qquad \Diamond$$

Finally, we show how to construct a simple ALU with four operations from an n-bit adder and combinational-logic gates that control the inputs to the adder.

Example 9.4
Figure 9.9 shows a high-level block diagram of a four-function ALU. The ALU has two n-bit data inputs (A and B), an n-bit data output (*out*), and two one-bit ALU-function inputs (F_1 and F_0). Taken together, the function inputs F_1 and F_0 specify which one of four operations the ALU is to perform: *Inc B* (i.e., pass the value of $B + 1$ to *out*), *Pass A* (i.e., pass A to *out*), *Pass B* (i.e., pass B to *out*), and *ADD A B* (i.e., pass the value of $A + B$ to *out*). The ALU output at clock cycle i is described as follows:

$$out(i) = \begin{cases} B(i) + 1, & \text{if } F_1(i) F_0(i) = 00, \\ A(i), & \text{if } F_1(i) F_0(i) = 01, \\ B(i), & \text{if } F_1(i) F_0(i) = 10, \\ A(i) + B(i) & \text{if } F_1(i) F_0(i) = 11. \end{cases}$$

Recall that the inputs and outputs of the n-bit adder obey the following relation:

$$C_n S_{n-1} \cdots S_0 = (X_{n-1} \cdots X_0) + (Y_{n-1} \cdots Y_0) + C_0.$$

The four ALU operations are implemented by an n-bit adder by appropriately controlling the ALU inputs, as shown in Figure 9.9. Note that the X and Y inputs to

ALU Operation & Code			Internal Control Signals			
Function	F_1	F_0	$Pass_B$	$Pass_A$	C_0	*out*
Inc B	0	0	1	0	1	B + 1
Pass A	0	1	0	1	0	A
Pass B	1	0	1	0	0	B
ADD A B	1	1	1	1	0	A+B

Table 9.5: ALU functions

the adder both come from *and* gates: each one of the n input lines to the n-bit X (respectively, Y) adder input comes from an *and* gate that combines an individual bit of A (respectively, B) with $Pass_A$ (respectively, $Pass_B$). That is, the following relationships hold:

$$X_i = and(A_i, Pass_A),$$
$$Y_i = and(B_i, Pass_B).$$

The net result is that X is 0 whenever $Pass_A$ is set to 0, and otherwise X is A (and similarly for Y, $Pass_B$, and B). For simplicity, we write $and(A, Pass_A)$ to mean the bit-wise *"and"ing* of $Pass_A$ with the individual bits of A, and similarly for $and(B, Pass_B)$:

$$and(A, Pass_A) = and(A_{n-1}, Pass_A) \cdots and(A_0, Pass_A),$$
$$and(B, Pass_B) = and(B_{n-1}, Pass_A) \cdots and(B_0, Pass_A).$$

Thus, provided that $Pass_A, Pass_B$, and C_0 are appropriately controlled, the n-bit adder produces each of the four ALU functions, as follows:

$$C_n S_{n-1} \cdots S_0 = (X_{n-1} \cdots X_0) + (Y_{n-1} \cdots Y_0) + C_0 =$$
$$\begin{cases} and(A,0) + and(B,1) + 1 = B+1, & \text{if } Pass_A = 0, Pass_B = 1, C_0 = 1, \\ and(A,1) + and(B,0) + 0 = A, & \text{if } Pass_A = 1, Pass_B = 0, C_0 = 0, \\ and(A,0) + and(B,1) + 0 = B, & \text{if } Pass_A = 0, Pass_B = 1, C_0 = 0, \\ and(A,1) + and(B,1) + 0 = A+B, & \text{if } Pass_A = 1, Pass_B = 1, C_0 = 0. \end{cases}$$

The task of controlling $Pass_A$, $Pass_B$, and C_0 falls to the control-logic component on the righthand side of Figure 9.9. Using both this figure and Table 9.5, it is straightforward to verify that the following logic will properly control each signal:

$$Pass_A = F_0,$$
$$Pass_B = nand(not(F_1), F_0),$$
$$C_0 = and(not(F_1), not(F_0)). \qquad \Diamond$$

✎ **Exercise 9.2.1**   *Consider the following logical expression:*

$$out = and(or(A,B),C)$$

    a. *Devise a truth table showing the value of out for all possible input combinations.*

    b. *Draw a schematic diagram of gates showing a hardware implementation of out.*

🔨 **Exercise 9.2.2**   *Consider the following truth table:*

x	y	z	out
0	0	0	0
0	0	1	0
0	1	0	0
0	1	1	1
1	0	0	0
1	0	1	0
1	1	0	1
1	1	1	1

    a. *Give a logical formula that expresses out as a function of x, y, and z.*

    b. *Implement out as defined above using only* inverters, and *gates, and* or *gates. Try to use as few gates as possible.*

    c. *Implement out as defined above using only* nand *gates. As a hint, the following relationship (known as DeMorgan's Law) is helpful:*

$$not(and(A,B)) = or(not(A), not(B)).$$

Exercise 9.2.3   *Positive and negative numbers are typically represented using a two's-complement representation. In a two's-complement representation, the most significant bit x_{n-1} has a weight of -2^{n-1}; in contrast, an unsigned-binary representation gives the most significant bit a weight of 2^{n-1}. Thus, the following relationships hold, depending upon whether the representation is two's complement or unsigned binary:*

$$(x_{n-1}x_{n-2}\cdots x_0)_2$$
$$= \begin{cases} 2^{n-1} \times x_{n-1} + 2^{n-2} \times x_{n-2} + \cdots + 2^0 \times x_0, & \text{in unsigned binary,} \\ (-2^{n-1} \times x_{n-1}) + 2^{n-2} \times x_{n-2} + \cdots + 2^0 \times x_0, & \text{in two's complement.} \end{cases}$$

    a. *Fill in the following table, giving both the unsigned binary and the two's-complement interpretations of all 4-bit binary numbers.*

x_3	x_2	x_1	x_0	unsigned binary	two's-complement
0	0	0	0		
0	0	0	1		
0	0	1	0		
0	0	1	1		
0	1	0	0		
0	1	0	1		
0	1	1	0		
0	1	1	1		
1	0	0	0		
1	0	0	1		
1	0	1	0		
1	0	1	1		
1	1	0	0		
1	1	0	1		
1	1	1	0		
1	1	1	1		

b. *Using the table from part (a), devise a method that uses only logical negation and addition to negate any two's-complement number. That is, devise a method that, when given a two's-complement bit sequence*

$$x_{n-1}x_{n-2}\cdots x_0$$

whose base-10 value is X_{10}, produces a two's-complement bit sequence

$$y_{n-1}y_{n-2}\cdots y_0$$

whose base-10 value is $-X_{10}$.

c. *What is the maximum positive number that can be represented in n bits, using two's-complement representation? What is the most negative number that can be represented in n bits, using two's-complement representation?*

d. *Using only full adders and basic combinational-logic gates as components, devise a 4-function ALU with the following specifications:*

F_1	F_0	Function
0	0	$A + B$
0	1	$A - B$
1	0	$-A + B$
1	1	$-A - B$

You should assume a two's-complement interpretation.

9.3   Microcode

In the previous section, we described several forms of synchronous registers, introduced basic combinational logic gates, showed how n-bit adders are built, and designed a simple ALU. Taken together, these components are sufficient for describing the operation of processors in terms of their *data paths* and *control paths*. A *central processing unit's (CPU)* data and control paths determine which computations are performed and in what order. In this section, we discuss how a CPU's data and control paths are controlled using instructions called *microcode* or *microinstructions*.

9.3.1   Data Paths and Control Paths

Data paths consist of registers and memory that store data, the paths that data can follow, and the arithmetic and logic functions on those paths. Control paths consist of the control lines that direct the timing and flow of data, the control lines that direct which functions are performed by arithmetic and logic units, and the sequence in time that values appear on the control lines.

Figure 9.10 shows a simple data path and control path. The data path consists of the following seven components:

- The ALU

- Three registers (Reg_1, Reg_2, and ACC, which is known as the *accumulator*)

- A bus (*Data Bus*) used to supply inputs to the a input of the ALU from the outputs of Reg_1 and Reg_2

- A data line connecting the output of ACC to the b input of the ALU.

The control path consists of the seven control signals ($LD_1, LD_2, LD_{ACC}, EN_1, EN_2,$ F_0, and F_1) and the *timing and control unit (TCU)*.

The TCU accepts a machine-language instruction and converts it to a sequence of *microinstructions*, which are very fine-grained instructions that correspond to the CPU's data path. Microinstructions typically take only a single clock cycle to execute, whereas machine-language instructions usually take two or more clock cycles.

For example, the data and control paths in Figure 9.10 might have the following microinstructions, all of which are executable in a single clock cycle:

- $ACC \leftarrow Reg_1$: load ACC with the contents of Reg_1

- $ACC \leftarrow Reg_2$: load ACC with the contents of Reg_2

- $ACC \leftarrow Reg_1 + ACC$: add the contents of Reg_1 to the contents of ACC and store the result in the ACC

- $ACC \leftarrow Reg_2 + ACC$: add the contents of Reg_2 to the contents of ACC and store the result in the ACC

FIGURE 9.10 Simple data- and control-path example

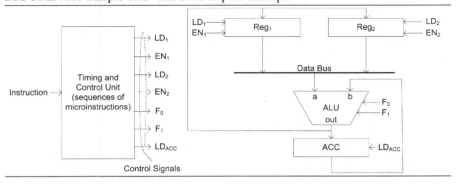

- $Reg_1 \leftarrow ACC$: store the contents of ACC into Reg_1

- $Reg_2 \leftarrow ACC$: store the contents of ACC into Reg_2

- $Reg_1 \leftarrow Reg_2$: store the contents of Reg_2 into Reg_1

- $Reg_2 \leftarrow Reg_1$: store the contents of Reg_1 into Reg_2

The TCU implements each microinstruction by appropriately setting the values of the control-path signals to perform the specified operation, as illustrated in the following example.

Example 9.5

Suppose that the ALU of Figure 9.10 is the 4-function ALU described by Table 9.5, and further suppose that we wish to implement the microinstruction

$$ACC \leftarrow Reg_1,$$

which should load ACC with the contents of Reg_1.

The following table shows the control-path settings necessary to implement this microinstruction:

Microinstruction	LD_1	EN_1	LD_2	EN_2	F_1	F_0	LD_{ACC}
$ACC \leftarrow Reg_1$	0	1	0	0	0	1	1

The control-path settings have the following effects upon the data-path operations:

- $LD_1 = 0$: The contents of Reg_1 are unchanged by the microinstruction.

- $EN_1 = 1$: The contents of Reg_1 are enabled onto the *Data Bus*.

- $LD_2 = 0$: The contents of Reg_2 are unchanged by the microinstruction.

- $EN_2 = 0$: The contents of Reg_2 are isolated from the *Data Bus*.

- $F_1 F_0 = 01$: The ALU operation is PASS A, which in this case passes the contents of Reg_1 to the ALU output.

- $LD_{ACC} = 1$: The contents of the accumulator ACC are updated with the ALU output, namely the contents of Reg_1.   ◊

9.3.2   Microprogramming

Microprograms are sequences of microcode instructions. Although microprograms can be implemented directly in hardware, they are typically implemented in *firmware*: that is, the microinstructions are stored in read-only memory and are accessed by hardware known as a *microprogram sequencer*. The advantage of firmware over hardware is that firmware is changeable (although not by users), which allows a machine's behavior to be altered without modifying the hardware. In particular, altering the contents of the read-only memory containing microinstructions permits the same hardware to emulate different machine instruction sets. A disadvantage of firmware, however, is that it is slower than instructions implemented by hardware alone.

Microprograms are the interface between hardware and software. In our descriptions, we will frequently describe operations at the microprogram level using example data and control paths.

Example 9.6
Suppose we wish to implement a machine instruction that swaps the contents of registers Reg_1 and Reg_2, using the data and control path shown in Figure 9.10. The following microprogram implements the swap instruction:

$$1.\ ACC \leftarrow Reg_1$$
$$2.\ Reg_1 \leftarrow Reg_2$$
$$3.\ Reg_2 \leftarrow ACC$$

◊

✎ **Exercise 9.3.1**   *Using Figure 9.9 as a starting point, design the control logic for the internal control signals shown in Table 9.5.*

That is, determine the logical formulas for each control signal, and then draw the schematic of a 4-bit ALU using full adders and the basic combinational logic gates shown in Figure 9.6.

✗ **Exercise 9.3.2**   *For each of the following machine instructions, draw a timing diagram and a sequence of microinstructions that show the sequence of control signals for the data path in Figure 9.10 that implements the given instruction:*

a. $ACC \leftarrow Reg_2$: load ACC with the contents of Reg_2

b. $ACC \leftarrow Reg_1 + ACC$: add the contents of Reg_1 to the contents of ACC and store the result in the ACC

c. $ACC \leftarrow Reg_2 + ACC$: add the contents of Reg_2 to the contents of ACC and store the result in the ACC

d. $Reg_1 \leftarrow ACC$: store the contents of ACC into Reg_1

e. $Reg_2 \leftarrow ACC$: store the contents of ACC into Reg_2

f. $Reg_1 \leftarrow Reg_2$: store the contents of Reg_2 into Reg_1

g. $Reg_2 \leftarrow Reg_1$: store the contents of Reg_1 into Reg_2

Exercise 9.3.3 *Devise a sequence of microinstructions that implements the assembly language instruction* ADD Reg_1 Reg_2 *(i.e.,* ACC *is updated with the sum of the contents of Reg_1 and Reg_2).*

Exercise 9.3.4 *Draw the timing diagram for the operation* ADD Reg_1 Reg_2 *(see the previous exercise), using the following template:*

clock cycle	1	2	3	4	
LD_1					
EN_1					
Reg_1					
LD_2					
EN_2					
Reg_2					
F_1					
F_0					
out					
LD_{ACC}					
ACC					

9.4 Summary

In this chapter, we introduced the fundamentals of synchronous hardware design and microprogramming: understanding these fundamentals is essential to understanding hardware security, which we will be exploring in the next few chapters. Common to all synchronous hardware is a central clock that synchronizes all state changes: registers can change their values only on active clock edges.

FIGURE 9.11 Learning outcomes for Chapter 9

After completing this chapter, you should be able to achieve the following learning outcomes at several levels of knowledge:

Comprehension

- When given a block diagram of combinational-logic gates, you are able to write the output of any logic gate as a function of the inputs to the block diagram.

- When given a data-path diagram and a microinstruction, you are able to describe the computation performed and the next state of the system.

Application

- When given a logical function, you are able to translate that function into a block diagram of combinational-logic gates.

Analysis

- When given a data path and control path description, a microprogram, and the values in all relevant registers and memory, you are able to determine what computation or operation is performed and the values in all relevant registers and memory.

Synthesis

- When given a description of a machine-level instruction and a block diagram of a processor with its control lines, devise microprograms that implement the machine-level instruction.

Synchronous hardware designs are described by a combination of data and control paths. Data paths are the paths along which data travel and on which data operations are performed. Control paths comprise the control signals that direct both data and the operations on data. During any clock cycle, the values of the control signals are viewed as a microinstruction. Sequences of microinstructions form microprograms, which are used to implement the instruction set of a processor.

In this chapter, we described the operation of real processor hardware. In the next chapter, we show how simulations of processors—virtual machines—are created. Virtual machines provide the illusion to users of controlling an entire processor when in fact the same processor and memory are safely and securely shared among many users.

The learning outcomes associated with this chapter appear in Figure 9.11.

9.5 Further Reading

There are numerous books on digital hardware design, microprogramming, and computer architecture. Wakerly's book—*Digital Design: Principles and Practices* (Wakerly, 2006)—covers combinational-logic design and sequential logic design. Comer's book—*Essentials of Computer Architecture* (Comer, 2005)—covers CPUs, instruction sets, microcode, and memory management.

Chapter 10

Virtual Machines and Memory Protection

Controlling access to memory is critical for sharing one machine among many users and processes. Security is impossible without the capabilities to isolate one process from another and to control how data are shared. For example, if Alice and Bob are running their programs on the same machine, their programs should be protected from one another. Such protection requires that Alice's calculations should not spill over into the memory used by Bob. Furthermore, unless Alice has authorization from Bob or other appropriate controlling authorities, Alice should not be able to read from or write to Bob's data stored in memory.

Many of the basic concepts of memory protection—including virtual memory and access control—were worked out in the era of time-shared mainframe computers. These mainframes were viewed as centralized resources to be shared among many users simultaneously. With the introduction of minicomputers and microprocessors— which later evolved into personal computers—many memory-protection mechanisms were discarded for efficiency reasons, under the assumption that personal computers were ultimately controlled by single users and not shared. Widespread networking has since falsified this assumption, making memory-protection mechanisms and virtual-machine technologies relevant once again.

A *virtual machine* (VM) is a simulation of a physical machine. This simulation provides the illusion to operating systems and programs that they are running directly on the hardware. Protecting the real machine, processes, and one user from another is the task of the *virtual machine monitor* (VMM), which is a layer (often implemented in microcode or software) separating virtual machines and hardware. Figure 10.1 illustrates this idea, showing three operating systems supported by a VMM that operates on a single hardware platform. Each operating system executes within an environment created by the VMM; each of these environments is a VM.

The VMM manages the hardware (memory, processor, and input/output) with three objectives in mind:

1. Creation of an identical execution environment to that of the hardware being emulated

2. Efficient execution of instructions to maintain acceptable program execution speeds

3. Intervention by the VMM in any attempt to alter the allocation of resources

FIGURE 10.1 Virtual machine monitor protecting memory

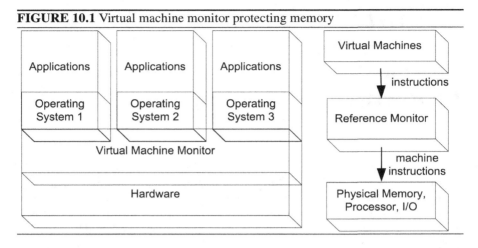

As Figure 10.1 shows, VMMs are reference monitors that check the instructions issued by VMs in order to guard the integrity of the physical system. Virtual machine monitors are also called *hypervisors* or *security kernels*: we use the *virtual machine monitor* nomenclature in this text to emphasize the VMM's role as a reference monitor. In this chapter, we analyze the details of memory protection and the basic structure and operation of VMMs. Because VMs operate at the boundary between hardware and software, we start with a description of a simple processor that provides a concrete context for the movement and control of data. We then look at memory protection based on memory *segmentation*. After that, we develop the mandatory access control policies for accessing memory. Finally, we look at the structure and function of VMMs.

10.1   A Simple Processor

In this section, we introduce a concrete example of a simple processor, shown in Figure 10.2. By specifying a specific processor, we can give concrete examples for the underlying mechanisms that implement memory protection and the structure and function of virtual machine monitors. The ideas we present, however, are applicable to any standard processor. We start by describing the processor's components, its data path, and its control path. We follow with a description of the processor's machine-language instructions.

FIGURE 10.2 A simple processor

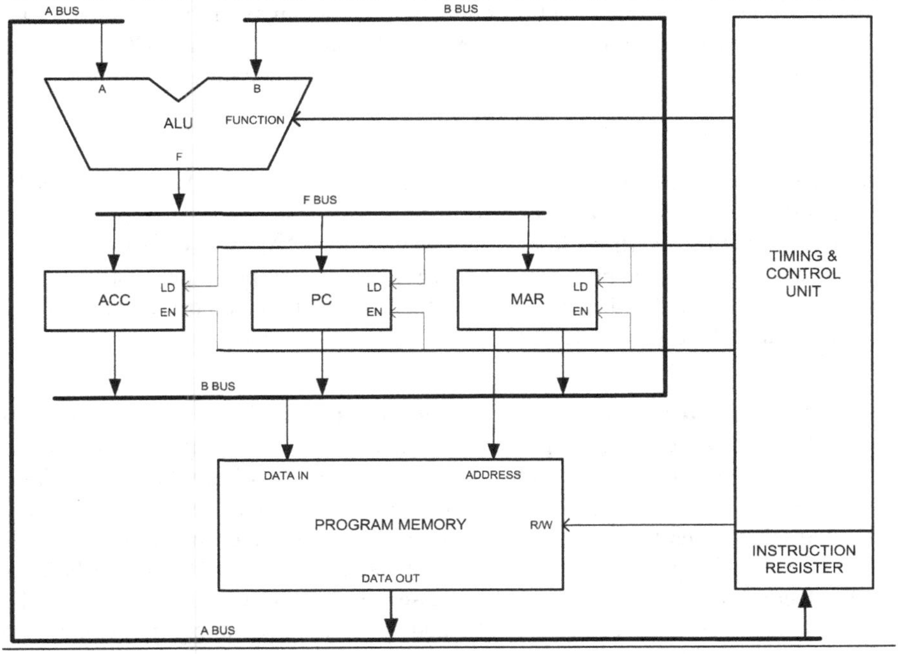

10.1.1   Processor Components

Our simple processor has the following major components, which we describe in turn.

Data Buses: There are three data buses: the A BUS, the B BUS, and the F BUS, all of which are used to convey data to the components of the processor.

Arithmetic Logic Unit: The *arithmetic logic unit* (ALU) has data input ports A and B, control input FUNCTION, and output port F. The ALU performs operations on inputs A and B as specified by FUNCTION, and the output appears on F. Typical operations of the ALU include: PASS A, PASS B, and ADD A B, which correspond respectively to "F = A," "F = B," and "F = A+B."

Accumulator: The *accumulator* (ACC) register is used to store intermediate values produced by the ALU during calculations that extend over multiple instructions. When LD is asserted, the ACC updates its contents from the F BUS at the beginning of the next cycle. When EN is asserted, the output of ACC is immediately put onto the B BUS.

Program Counter: The *program counter* (PC) register is used to point to the address of the next machine instruction stored in the program memory. The PC register updates its contents from the F BUS in exactly the same way as the ACC. Likewise, the output of the PC is immediately put onto the B BUS when the EN input to the PC is asserted.

Memory Address Register: The *memory address register* (MAR) is used to point to the address of instructions and data to be fetched or stored in program memory. The control line LD functions in the same way for the MAR as it does for the ACC and PC registers. In our processor, the MAR has two outputs: the first is always enabled and connected to the ADDRESS input of the program memory, and the second is connected to the B BUS under the control of EN.

Instruction Register: The *instruction register* (IR) holds the machine instruction currently being executed by the processor. The input to the IR is the A BUS.

We assume that all instructions have two fields: an *op-code* field and an *address* field. The op-code is a numerical encoding of the instruction to be performed, while the address specifies the memory address. For example, the operation that loads the accumulator register with the contents of memory address 100 would be LDA 100. Operations for which memory addresses are irrelevant (e.g., CLA: clear the accumulator) ignore the contents of the address field. Operations for which two memory addresses are needed (e.g., LD 100 200: load the contents of location 100 with the contents of 200) actually take up two locations in memory: LD 100 followed by 200, where the op-code field of the instruction containing address 200 is ignored.

Program Memory: The *program memory* (PM) holds machine instructions and data for user programs. PM has DATA IN and DATA OUT ports. The DATA IN port gets its value from the B BUS, while the DATA OUT port is the sole input to the A BUS. PM behaves like a linearly addressable array of q registers, starting at location 0 and ending at location q-1. At the start of each cycle, the contents of location ADDRESS of PM, which we denote by PM[ADDRESS], appear on the DATA OUT port, where the value of ADDRESS comes from the MAR during the *previous* cycle. If a memory-read operation is specified by the R/W control, then value PM[ADDRESS] is unchanged. However, if a memory-write operation is specified by R/W, then the value on the B BUS from the prior cycle is placed into PM at location ADDRESS and that value also appears on DATA OUT.

Timing and Control Unit: The *timing and control unit* (TCU) is responsible for fetching instructions from the PM, sequencing the flow of data in the processor, and sequencing the operations performed by the ALU. The TCU controls the processor operations and data flow by the following control lines:

- FUNCTION: this line controls the function performed by the ALU.

- LD: this bus controls which registers (ACC, PC, or MAR) are loaded from the F BUS at the start of the next cycle. Any combination of these registers (i.e., ranging from none to all of them) is possible.

- EN: this bus controls which register's output (ACC, PC, or MAR) is placed on the B BUS. At most one register's output should be placed on the bus.

- R/W: this line specifies whether the contents of PM is a read or write.

Having described the processor's data and control paths, we turn our attention to the processor's instructions at the machine level and microcode level.

10.1.2 Machine Instructions

All the registers (ACC, PC, IR, and MAR) and state-holding devices (such as PM) are *synchronous*—that is, they change state on active clock edges.

We now consider a concrete example. Suppose we wish to execute the program-level operation PM[B] ← PM[A] + PM[B], which should add the contents of program memory at addresses A and B and store the result back into address B. To execute this program-level operation requires three machine-level instructions to be executed in the following order:

1. LDA @A: load the ACC with the contents of PM at address A, $ACC \leftarrow PM[A]$.

2. ADD @B: load the ACC with the results of adding the contents of the ACC with the contents of PM at address B, $ACC \leftarrow ACC + PM[B]$.

3. STO @B: store the contents of the ACC into the PM at address B, $PM[B] \leftarrow ACC$.

To execute each of the machine-level instructions requires a third and final level of programming at the *microprogram* level. The TCU executes microprograms that set and sequence the appropriate values on the various control lines (e.g., FUNCTION, LD, and EN).

All three levels of programming—program level, machine level, and microcode— are shown in Table 10.1. The left column corresponds to a high-level operation that is compiled into the machine-level instructions in the middle column. Each machine-level instruction is realized by a series of micro-coded operations as shown in the rightmost column. We use the notation $MAR \leftarrow PM[MAR].addr$ to denote that MAR is loaded with the address portion of the instruction found in PM[MAR].

The remainder of this section is targeted towards hardware designers, who typically must account for all of the calculations that occur during each and every clock cycle. Readers who are not interested in such low-level details may safely skip to Section 10.2.

Table 10.2 details the values for each control line for each microprogram operation listed in Table 10.1. Because microprograms are intricate, we examine in detail what happens with the instruction LDA @A. To help us keep track of all the details, we use a timing diagram, as shown in Figure 10.3.

Program Level Operation	Instructions Stored in Program Memory	Microcode Operations Sequenced by Timing and Control Unit
$@B \leftarrow @A + @B$	i. LDA @A	1. $MAR \leftarrow PC$
		2. $PC \leftarrow PC + 1$
		3. $IR \leftarrow PM[MAR], MAR \leftarrow PM[MAR].addr$
		4. $ACC \leftarrow PM[MAR]$
	i+1. ADD @B	5. $MAR \leftarrow PC$
		6. $PC \leftarrow PC + 1$
		7. $IR \leftarrow PM[MAR], MAR \leftarrow PM[MAR].addr$
		8. $ACC \leftarrow PM[MAR] + ACC$
	i+2. STO @B	9. $MAR \leftarrow PC$
		10. $PC \leftarrow PC + 1$
		11. $IR \leftarrow PM[MAR], MAR \leftarrow PM[MAR].addr$
		12. $PM[MAR] \leftarrow ACC$

Table 10.1: Operations for $@B \leftarrow @A + @B$

	Microcode Operations	LD	EN	ALU	R/W	A Bus	B Bus	F Bus
1.	$MAR \leftarrow PC$	MAR	PC	Pass B	R	X	PC	PC
2.	$PC \leftarrow PC + 1$	PC	PC	Inc B	R	X	PC	PC+1
3.	$IR \leftarrow PM[MAR]$ $MAR \leftarrow PM[MAR].addr$	IR, MAR	X	Pass A	R	PM[MAR]	X	PM[MAR]
4.	$ACC \leftarrow PM[MAR]$	ACC	X	Pass A	R	PM[MAR]	X	PM[MAR]
5.	$MAR \leftarrow PC$	MAR	PC	Pass B	R	X	PC	PC
6.	$PC \leftarrow PC + 1$	PC	PC	Inc B	R	X	PC	PC+1
7.	$IR \leftarrow PM[MAR]$ $MAR \leftarrow PM[MAR].addr$	IR, MAR	X	Pass A	R	PM[MAR]	X	PM[MAR]
8.	$ACC \leftarrow$ $PM[MAR] + ACC$	ACC	ACC	Add	R	PM[MAR]	X	PM[MAR] + ACC
9.	$MAR \leftarrow PC$	MAR	PC	Pass B	R	X	PC	PC
10.	$PC \leftarrow PC + 1$	PC	PC	Inc B	R	X	PC	PC+1
11.	$IR \leftarrow PM[MAR]$ $MAR \leftarrow PM[MAR].addr$	IR, MAR	X	Pass A	R	PM[MAR]	X	PM[MAR]
12.	$PM[MAR] \leftarrow ACC$	X	ACC	X	W	PM[MAR]	ACC	X

Table 10.2: Timing and control unit operations

Conceptually, the first machine operation—i.e., loading ACC with the contents of PM at location A—requires the following three steps:

1. Fetch the LDA @A instruction from location i in PM and store it the instruction register IR. We assume that the program counter PC has the address i of the machine instruction to be executed.

2. Fetch the contents of PM at address A.

3. Store the contents of PM at address A into the accumulator ACC.

Completing these three conceptual steps requires a total of four micro-operations (i.e., four clock cycles), as follows:

Cycle 1 objective: Copy the contents of the PC into the MAR.

> **Initial state:** PC = i. The values of the MAR, ACC, IR, and PM[MAR] depend on previous operations and are unimportant at this point.

> **Control lines:** EN = PC, LD = MAR, FUNCTION = PASS B.

FIGURE 10.3 Timing of CPU operations

Cycle	1	2	3	4	5	6	7	8	9	10	11	12
PC	i	i	i+1	i+1	i+1	i+1	i+2	i+2	i+2	i+2	i+3	i+3
IR	XXXXXXX	XXXXXXX	XXXXXXX	LDA @A	LDA @A	LDA @A	LDA @A	ADD @B	ADD @B	ADD @B	ADD @B	STO @B
MAR	XXXXXXX	i	i	A	A	i+1	i+1	B	B	i+2	i+2	B
ACC	XXXXXXX	XXXXXXX	XXXXXXX	XXXXXXX	Mem[A]	Mem[A]	Mem[A]	Mem[A]	Mem[B] + Mem[A]	Mem[B] + Mem[A]	Mem[B] + Mem[A]	Mem[B] + Mem[A]
LD	MAR	PC	IR, MAR	ACC	MAR	PC	IR, MAR	ACC	MAR	PC	IR, MAR	XXXXXXX
EN	PC	PC	XXXXXXX	XXXXXXX	PC	PC	XXXXXXX	ACC	PC	PC	XXXXXXX	ACC
FUNCTION	Pass B	Inc B	Pass A	Pass A	Pass B	Inc B	Pass A	A+B	Pass B	Inc B	Pass A	XXXXXXX
R/W	R	R	R	R	R	R	R	R	R	R	R	W
A BUS	XXXXXXX	XXXXXXX	LDA @A	LDA @A	Mem[A]	Mem[A]	ADD @B	ADD @B	Mem[B]	Mem[B]	STO @B	STO @B
B BUS	i	i	XXXXXXX	XXXXXXX	i+1	i+1	XXXXXXX	Mem[A]	i+2	i+2	XXXXXXX	Mem[B] + Mem[A]
F BUS	i	i+1	LDA @A	LDA @A	i+1	i+2	ADD @B	Mem[B] + Mem[A]	i+2	i+2	i+3	STO @B

Setting EN to PC puts the output of the PC onto the B BUS. Setting FUNCTION to PASS B passes the values on the B BUS through the ALU to the F BUS. Setting LD to MAR causes the F BUS values to be loaded into the MAR at the start of the next clock cycle.

Cycle 2 objective: Increment the PC to point to the next instruction.

Initial state: PC = i, MAR = i. The values of ACC, IR, and PM[MAR] are due to previous operations.

Control lines: EN = PC, LD = PC, FUNCTION = INC B.

Setting EN to PC puts the output of the PC onto the B BUS. Setting FUNCTION to INC B increments the current value stored in the PC, which is i, to $i+1$. This is the ALU output and is put on to the B BUS. Setting LD to PC loads $i+1$ into the PC at the start of the next cycle.

Cycle 3 objective: Fetch the instruction at location i—LDA @A—and store the instruction in the instruction register IR and memory address A in the MAR.

State: PC = $i+1$, MAR = i, PM[MAR] = PM[i] = LDA @A. The values of ACC and IR are due to previous operations.

Control lines: EN = X, LD = IR, MAR, FUNCTION = PASS A.

The MAR contains i from the previous cycle. So, the output of PM is PM[i], namely the ith instruction LDA @A. We enable the instruction register IR and the MAR to load LDA @A and address A respectively in the next cycle by arranging the ALU function to pass the output of PM on the A BUS through to the ALU output by setting FUNCTION to PASS A.

Cycle 4 objective: Load the contents of address A in PM into the ACC.

State: PC = $i+1$, MAR = A, IR = LDA @A, and PM[MAR] = A. The contents of the ACC are due to previous operations.

Control lines: EN = X, LD = ACC, FUNCTION = PASS A.

The values of IR and MAR are set to the value LDA @ A. Setting LD to ACC puts the value of the ALU output (PM[A]) into the ACC at the beginning of the next cycle. As the ALU is passing through the output of PM, it is unimportant which register (ACC, PC, or MAR) output is enabled onto the B BUS.

Cycles 5 through 12 can be described in a similar fashion and their descriptions are left as an exercise for the reader.

Next, we turn our attention to the virtual machine monitor, which protects physical memory and user processes.

✎ **Exercise 10.1.1** *In a similar fashion to the description of the four microcode cycles implementing* LDA @ A *in the text based on Tables 10.1, 10.2, and Figure 10.3, describe the micro-cycle objectives, state, and control line values for cycles 5 through 8 implementing* ADD @ B.

✎ **Exercise 10.1.2** *In a fashion similar to Table 10.1, work out the details of a* CLA *(i.e., clear accumulator ACC) instruction. Assume that the ALU has a function* ZERO, *which outputs 0 regardless of the inputs on* A *and* B. *Work out the microcode cycles and draw the timing diagram.*

✎ **Exercise 10.1.3** *In a similar fashion to the description of the four microcode cycles implementing* LDA @ A *in the text based on Tables 10.1, 10.2, and Figure 10.3, describe the micro-cycle objectives, state, and control line values for cycles 8 through 12 implementing* STO @ B.

10.2   Processors with Memory Segmentation

The simple processor developed thus far gives user programs access to all locations in program memory PM. When multiple user programs are stored in program memory, the simple processor is unable to protect one program from reading or writing over the programs or data of other users. In this section, we examine how processors can provide this protection through *memory segmentation*.

10.2.1   Segmentation Using a Relocation Register

To protect the programs and data of each user, physical memory is *segmented*: that is, memory is partitioned to simultaneously isolate one user from another while giving each user the illusion that he or she controls the entire processor memory. Segmentation is accomplished by the addition of a *relocation register* (RR) that specifies the starting address of each memory segment (i.e., the *base address*) and the size of the memory segment (i.e., its *bound*).

FIGURE 10.4 Memory segmentation

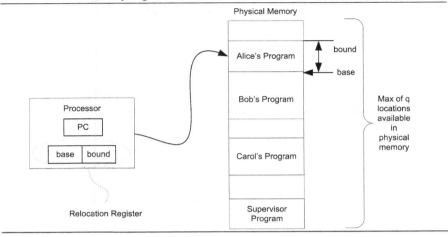

Figure 10.4 shows a physical memory with q locations partitioned into four segments: one segment each for Alice, Bob, Carol, and the Supervisor. The *base* and *bound* values stored in the relocation register uniquely locate each memory segment. The idea is that, within each segment, users access *virtual* memory locations 0 through *bound - 1*, when in fact they are really accessing *physical* memory locations *base* through *base + bound - 1*. Thus, the physical-memory location that corresponds to the virtual address in the program counter PC is determined by adding the base-address value to the virtual-address value in the PC. If the virtual address a is less than *bound* and $a + base < q$, then the address being read from or written to is within the user's memory segment in physical memory. Otherwise, the operation is *trapped*—that is, control is passed on to the Supervisor.

This policy for controlling access to physical memory is enforced for all programs and users. Thus, it is a *mandatory access-control* policy.

The following example illustrates the use of the base and bound values in the relocation register.

Example 10.1
Suppose that the value in the program counter is 57, the base-bound value in the relocation register is $(128, 256)$, and the size of physical memory is 1024: thus, the virtual address is defined relative to a base value of 128 and a bound of 256. The location of the next instruction is found in absolute address $128 + 57 = 185$. The absolute address falls within the bounds of physical memory (i.e., $185 \leq 1023$) and within the bound set by the relocation bound register (i.e., $57 \leq 255$). Therefore, the address falls within the user's allotted memory segment, and the operation should be allowed to proceed. $\Diamond$

FIGURE 10.5 Processor model for virtual machines

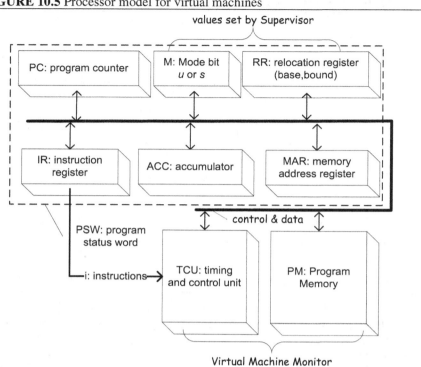

To accommodate memory segmentation, we must add a relocation register RR and a mode bit M to our simple processor. Figure 10.5 contains a diagram of our enhanced processor that supports virtual machines.

The mode bit M is used to indicate whether the processor is operating in *user* mode or *supervisor* mode (denoted by *u* and *s*, respectively). In user mode, access to security-sensitive instructions (such as writing values into RR) is trapped, which means that the processor is limited to the segment identified by RR. In supervisor mode, all instructions are available, including the security-sensitive instructions that alter the values in RR. This capability to alter the values in RR gives the processor access to all segments in PM.

Normally, the processor operates in user mode. When a program operating in user mode either wishes to transfer control to the Supervisor or has an instruction trapped, the mode bit is changed from *u* to *s* and control is passed to the Supervisor program.

The next three subsections develop the details of traps and how control is transferred to the Supervisor program.

10.2.2 Processor State and Instructions

The state S of a processor is given by the values stored in its state-holding elements: program memory PM, accumulator ACC, program counter PC, memory address register MAR, instruction register IR, mode bit M, and relocation register RR. We denote these values in lower case by *pm, acc, pc, mar, ir, m,* and *(base,bound)*, and we represent the state S by a seven-tuple:

$$S = (pm, acc, pc, mar, ir, m, (base, bound))$$

Note that *pm* is an array of values $pm[0]$ through $pm[q-1]$, where $q-1$ is the largest available address in physical program memory PM.

Because each component of S is finite, there are a finite number of processor states S; we call this set of states *PStates*. Each machine instruction i can therefore be viewed as a total function from *PStates* to *PStates*.

Example 10.2

Suppose the machine instruction LDA @ 15 is stored in address 0 of program memory PM and $S = (pm, acc, pc, mar, ir, u, (256, 128))$ is the current state of the processor. Because the mode bit is u and the relocation register RR is $(256, 128)$, the virtual machine is in *user* mode and the memory segment starts at location 256 in PM and ends at location $256 + 127 = 383$. Consulting Table 10.1, we can check the result of the first four micro-cycles to calculate the state that results from applying LDA @ 15. If we assume that $PM[256 + 15]$ contains the value 12 and that the values of ACC, MAR, and IR are *acc, mar,* and *ir* respectively, then the state that results from applying the instruction LDA @ 15 is as follows:

$$(\text{LDA } @ 15)(pm, acc, 0, mar, ir, u, (256, 128)) =$$
$$(pm, 12, 1, 15, \text{LDA } @ 15, u, (256, 128)). \qquad \Diamond$$

10.2.3 Program Status Word

The context of a program is given by the *program status word* (PSW). As Figure 10.5 shows, the PSW consists of the accumulator (ACC), memory address register (MAR), mode bit (M), program counter (PC), relocation register (RR), and instruction register (IR). The PSW value *psw* is a 6-tuple consisting of the contents of the respective registers:

$$psw = (acc, pc, mar, ir, m, (base, bound)).$$

Thus, the PSW specifies the current state of the processor, modulo the contents of program memory.

Example 10.3

Suppose the value of the PSW is $(25, 42, 56, \text{CLA}, s, (0, 65536))$, where the underlying executable memory size is $2^{16} = 65536$ locations. From the PSW, we see that the current program is operating in supervisor mode, the accumulator value is 25, the MAR is pointing to relative address 56, the program counter is pointing to relative address 42 in executable memory (which is also the absolute address as the base value of R is 0), the current program is able to access the entire executable memory, and the instruction in IR is *clear accumulator*.   ◇

The PSW is a mechanism by which the program in control of the processor can by changed. Changing programs or execution threads is essential for supporting multiprocessing. By loading the PSW registers with values corresponding to the Supervisor or other programs, the processor's execution context is changed or switched.

For simplicity, we assume that the value of the PSW fits entirely into one storage location in PM. We also assume that PM[1] (i.e., the second location in memory) has a fixed value that never changes and that corresponds to the default state in which the Supervisor program always starts.[1] This state corresponds to a PSW value of form

$$psw_{super} = (acc_{super}, addr_{super}, mar_{super}, ir_{super}, s, (0, q)),$$

where $addr_{super}$ is the starting address of the Supervisor program, and acc_{super}, mar_{super}, and ir_{super} are the default starting values for the ACC, MAR, and IR registers. Note that the mode bit is set to s (for supervisor), and the relocation register specifies that the full address range of memory is accessible.

When it is necessary to transfer control to the Supervisor program, the content of the currently executing program (i.e., the current PSW value) is stored in memory location PM[0]. The fixed value psw_{super} stored in location PM[1] is then copied to the PSW, which allows the Supervisor program to take control of the processor. When the Supervisor has completed its execution, control can be returned to the original program by copying the value temporarily stored in PM[0] back to the PSW.

Now that we have explained the concept and use of the PSW, we can introduce some of the details of traps.

10.2.4 Traps

Trapping an instruction transfers control to the Supervisor program. If all security-sensitive instructions are trapped (i.e., inspected or executed under the supervision of the Supervisor control program), then the privacy and integrity of program memory can be maintained, provided that the Supervisor is itself correct and trustworthy.

---

[1]Correct implementation of memory segmentation will ensure that user programs can never change the value of location PM[1]. The Supervisor program must also be implemented in a way that prevents alterations to this location.

An instruction *i* is said to *trap* if the contents of program memory are unchanged except for the contents of PM[0]; the program status word prior to trapping instruction *i* is stored in PM[0]; and the new program status word takes its value from PM[1].

Presumably, the updated value of PSW is the starting address and values of the Supervisor program. During its execution, the Supervisor program can look at the contents of PM[0] to find the previous value of *psw* and to see the virtual machine state just before instruction *i* trapped.

For now, we defer the description of the structure and contents of the Supervisor program until later. In the next section we look at the access-control policy for accessing program memory.

✎ **Exercise 10.2.1** *Consider Table 10.1. To which states are* ADD @B *and* STO @B *applied? Which states are the result of these function applications?*

✎ **Exercise 10.2.2** *Consider the application of machine instruction* LDA @200 *stored in address 300 of program memory PM. Let* $S = (pm, acc, pc, mar, ir, u, (256, 128))$ *be the state of the processor to which* LDA @200 *is applied. What is the next state?*

10.3 Controlling Access to Memory and Segmentation Registers

Having introduced the idea and mechanisms behind memory segmentation, we now turn to describing the mandatory access control policy for program memory. We treat the processor registers IR, M, and RR as principals who make statements about their values. For example, suppose that the instruction register IR has the value LDA @A. We can model this situation as

$$IR \text{ says } \langle \text{LDA @A} \rangle,$$

where we interpret $\langle \text{LDA @A} \rangle$ as the proposition "it would be a good idea to execute the instruction LDA @A." Likewise, we can express the situation where RR contains the value (*base, bound*) as

$$RR \text{ says } \langle (base, bound) \rangle,$$

where we interpret $\langle (base, bound) \rangle$ as the proposition "the base value is *base*, and the bound value is *bound*." We can similarly model the situation where M has the value *u* by

$$M \text{ says } \langle u \rangle,$$

where $\langle u \rangle$ is interpreted as "the virtual machine is in user mode."

As Figure 10.5 illustrates, the virtual machine monitor comprises the timing and control unit (TCU) and the program memory. Virtual machines provide privacy and integrity protection for users so long as all resource allocation is controlled by the Supervisor (i.e., by the virtual machine monitor). Thus, only the Supervisor should be able to alter the relocation register RR; user programs should not have that capability.

Throughout the remainder of this chapter, we assume that all supervisory functions are implemented by the TCU. In other words, the TCU is designed to reflect the wishes of the Supervisor,

$$TCU \Rightarrow Supervisor.$$

10.3.1   Access to Program Memory

Access to program memory PM is governed by the value of RR and the size of PM, which we represent by q. For each instruction that involves accessing PM, such as LDA @ A, we have an access-control policy.

In general, for an instruction OP @ A that involves an operation OP on relative address A, we have the following considerations:

- The absolute address must fall within the addressable locations of PM. That is, we must have $A + base < q$, where q is the size of PM. If this condition is violated, then a memory trap occurs.

- The relative address must fall within the bound of the memory segment assigned to the virtual machine (i.e., $A + base < bound$). If this condition is violated, then a memory trap occurs.

- If the above two conditions are satisfied, then the memory operation is performed.

To be explicit, there are certain classes of instructions—*privileged* and *sensitive* instructions, which we will define more formally in Section 10.4—for which additional conditions may force traps. For now, we consider only *innocuous* instructions, whose only traps are memory traps.

For an innocuous instruction OP @ A, the behavior of the VMM when executing OP @ A is specified by the three derived inference rules in Figure 10.6: Memory Trap 1, Memory Trap 2, and OP @ A. Memory Trap 1 states that, if the address $A + base$ exceeds the physical limits of memory, then OP @ A should be trapped. Similarly, Memory Trap 2 states that an operation involving relative address A should be trapped if A exceeds the segment boundary *bound*. The OP @ A rule states that, if the operation OP @ A does not require a memory trap, then it should be performed.

In the simple processor model we have introduced (Figures 10.2 and 10.5), the instruction register IR is under control of the virtual machine. Hence, for our processor model, we have

$$IR \Rightarrow VM.$$

FIGURE 10.6 Derived inference rules for an operation OP @ A

Memory
Trap 1

$$\frac{\begin{array}{l} TCU \text{ controls } (VM \text{ says } \langle \text{OP} @ \text{A} \rangle \\ \qquad \supset RR \text{ says } \langle (base, bound) \rangle \supset \text{A} + base \geq q \supset \langle trap \rangle) \\ TCU \text{ says } (VM \text{ says } \langle \text{OP} @ \text{A} \rangle \\ \qquad \supset RR \text{ says } \langle (base, bound) \rangle \supset \text{A} + base \geq q \supset \langle trap \rangle) \\ VM \text{ says } \langle \text{OP} @ \text{A} \rangle \qquad RR \text{ says } \langle (base, bound) \rangle \qquad \text{A} + base \geq q \end{array}}{\langle trap \rangle}$$

Memory
Trap 2

$$\frac{\begin{array}{l} TCU \text{ controls } (VM \text{ says } \langle \text{OP} @ \text{A} \rangle \\ \qquad \supset RR \text{ says } \langle (base, bound) \rangle \supset \text{A} \geq bound \supset \langle trap \rangle) \\ TCU \text{ says } (VM \text{ says } \langle \text{OP} @ \text{A} \rangle \\ \qquad \supset RR \text{ says } \langle (base, bound) \rangle \supset \text{A} \geq bound \supset \langle trap \rangle) \\ VM \text{ says } \langle \text{OP} @ \text{A} \rangle \qquad RR \text{ says } \langle (base, bound) \rangle \qquad \text{A} \geq bound \end{array}}{\langle trap \rangle}$$

OP @ A

$$\frac{\begin{array}{l} TCU \text{ controls } (RR \text{ says } \langle (base, bound) \rangle \\ \qquad \supset \text{A} + base < q \supset \text{A} < bound \supset VM \text{ controls } \langle \text{OP} @ \text{A} \rangle) \\ TCU \text{ says } (RR \text{ says } \langle (base, bound) \rangle \\ \qquad \supset \text{A} + base < q \supset \text{A} < bound \supset VM \text{ controls } \langle \text{OP} @ \text{A} \rangle) \\ VM \text{ says } \langle \text{OP} @ \text{A} \rangle \qquad RR \text{ says } \langle (base, bound) \rangle \\ \qquad \text{A} + base < q \qquad \text{A} < bound \end{array}}{\langle \text{OP} @ \text{A} \rangle}$$

Thus, whenever *IR* says $\langle$OP @ A$\rangle$, we can deduce that *VM* says $\langle$OP @ A$\rangle$ as well.

Example 10.4

Consider the case where the machine instruction is LDA @ A (load ACC with the contents of PM[*base* +A]), where A is a relative address within a segment in PM given by $(base, bound)$ in RR, and the maximum address in PM is $q - 1$. The relevant access-control rules for LDA @ A are as follows:

LDA *memory trap 1*

$$\frac{\begin{array}{c} TCU \text{ controls} \\ (VM \text{ says } \langle \text{LDA} @ \text{A} \rangle \supset RR \text{ says } \langle (base, bound) \rangle \supset \text{A} + base \geq q \supset \langle trap \rangle) \\ TCU \text{ says} \\ (VM \text{ says } \langle \text{LDA} @ \text{A} \rangle \supset RR \text{ says } \langle (base, bound) \rangle \supset \text{A} + base \geq q \supset \langle trap \rangle) \\ VM \text{ says } \langle \text{LDA} @ \text{A} \rangle \qquad RR \text{ says } \langle (base, bound) \rangle \qquad \text{A} + base \geq q \end{array}}{\langle trap \rangle}$$

LDA *memory trap 2*

$$\frac{\begin{array}{c} TCU \text{ controls} \\ (VM \text{ says } \langle \text{LDA} @ \text{A} \rangle \supset RR \text{ says } \langle (base, bound) \rangle \supset \text{A} \geq bound \supset \langle trap \rangle) \\ TCU \text{ says} \\ (VM \text{ says } \langle \text{LDA} @ \text{A} \rangle \supset RR \text{ says } \langle (base, bound) \rangle \supset \text{A} \geq bound \supset \langle trap \rangle) \\ VM \text{ says } \langle \text{LDA} @ \text{A} \rangle \qquad RR \text{ says } \langle (base, bound) \rangle \qquad \text{A} \geq bound \end{array}}{\langle trap \rangle}$$

$$
\text{LDA }@\text{A} \quad \frac{
\begin{array}{c}
TCU \text{ controls } (RR \text{ says } \langle(base, bound)\rangle) \supset \\
\text{A} + base < q \supset \text{A} < bound \supset VM \text{ controls } \langle\text{LDA }@\text{A}\rangle) \\
TCU \text{ says } (RR \text{ says } \langle(base, bound)\rangle) \supset \\
\text{A} + base < q \supset \text{A} < bound \supset VM \text{ controls } \langle\text{LDA }@\text{A}\rangle) \\
VM \text{ says } \langle\text{LDA }@\text{A}\rangle \quad RR \text{ says } \langle(base, bound)\rangle \\
\text{A} + base < q \quad \text{A} < bound
\end{array}
}{\langle\text{LDA }@\text{A}\rangle}
$$

These three rules follow directly from the general template presented for OP @ A in Figure 10.6. The first two rules check for a memory trap caused by either attempting to access an address beyond the maximum size of program memory or beyond the segment boundary. If a memory trap does not occur, then the virtual machine can load the accumulator with the contents of program memory at address A.   ◊

The preceding approach suffices as a simple memory access-control policy. In Section 10.3.3, we refine this policy to cover what are known as *privileged* and *sensitive* instructions, some of which include memory operations. In the remainder of this section, however, we describe the hardware-level details of implementing this simple memory-access policy. Readers uninterested in these details may safely skip ahead to Section 10.3.3.

10.3.2   Implementation Details

We now turn to some implementation details for protecting physical memory based on the processor model for virtual machines given in Figure 10.5. That model extends the simple processor shown in Figure 10.2 by adding a relocation register and a mode bit. In this model, all memory accesses make use of the memory address register (MAR).

We can enforce the mandatory access control policy for memory addresses by checking all addresses prior to loading them into the MAR. If the memory address exceeds the boundary of either physical memory or the assigned segment, then a trap occurs. Otherwise, the MAR is loaded with the address.

Based on Table 10.1, we can modify the Timing and Control Unit (TCU) microcode that generates the timing and control signals for the processor. The modifications are straightforward, in that the MAR is loaded with a new value only if the new value does not cause a memory trap. We can specify this using a conditional "if-then-else" expression:

$$
condition \rightarrow a \mid b = \begin{cases} a, & \text{if } condition \text{ is } true \\ b, & \text{if } condition \text{ is } false \end{cases} .
$$

For the LDA @ A, ADD @ B, and STO @ B instructions shown in Table 10.1, the following changes are made:

Instructions Stored in Program Memory		Microcode Operations Sequenced by Timing and Control Unit	
i.	LDA @A	1.	$(((base + PC) \geq q)$ or $(PC \geq bound)) \rightarrow trap \mid (MAR \leftarrow base + PC)$
		2.	$PC \leftarrow PC + 1$
		3.	$IR \leftarrow PM[MAR]$, $(((base + PM[MAR].addr) \geq q)$ or $(PM[MAR].addr \geq bound)) \rightarrow trap \mid (MAR \leftarrow base + PM[MAR].addr)$
		4.	$ACC \leftarrow PM[MAR]$
i+1.	ADD @B	5.	$(((base + PC) \geq q)$ or $(PC \geq bound)) \rightarrow trap \mid (MAR \leftarrow base + PC)$
		6.	$PC \leftarrow PC + 1$
		7.	$IR \leftarrow PM[MAR]$, $(((base + PM[MAR].addr) \geq q)$ or $(PM[MAR].addr \geq bound)) \rightarrow trap \mid (MAR \leftarrow base + PM[MAR].addr)$
		8.	$ACC \leftarrow PM[MAR] + ACC$
i+2.	STO @B	9.	$(((base + PC) \geq q)$ or $(PC \geq bound)) \rightarrow trap \mid (MAR \leftarrow base + PC)$
		10.	$PC \leftarrow PC + 1$
		11.	$IR \leftarrow PM[MAR]$, $(((base + PM[MAR].addr) \geq q)$ or $(PM[MAR].addr \geq bound)) \rightarrow trap \mid (MAR \leftarrow base + PM[MAR].addr)$
		12.	$PM[MAR] \leftarrow ACC$

Table 10.3: Memory-protected operations for LDA @A, ADD @A, and STO @B

- The simple assignment $MAR \leftarrow PC$ is changed to the conditional expression

$$(((base + PC) \geq q) \text{ or } (PC \geq bound)) \rightarrow trap \mid (MAR \leftarrow base + PC).$$

- The simple assignment $MAR \leftarrow PM[MAR].addr$ is changed to the conditional expression

$$(((base + PM[MAR].addr) \geq q) \text{ or } (PM[MAR].addr \geq bound))$$
$$\rightarrow trap \mid (MAR \leftarrow base + PM[MAR].addr).$$

Notice that the addresses are treated as *relative addresses* in the virtual processor and must be converted to *real* addresses by adding the value *base*. The resulting changes to Table 10.1 are shown in Table 10.3.

10.3.3 Access to the Relocation Register

Memory segmentation depends directly on the values stored in the relocation register RR, because the integrity of physical memory depends on the integrity of RR. Therefore, only the Supervisor should be able to read from (or write to) RR: users should never have read or write access to RR.

Access to RR is protected by the mode bit M: the VM is able read or write RR only when M is set to s (i.e., supervisor mode). Otherwise, any attempt to access RR is trapped.

FIGURE 10.7 Simple processor with relocation register

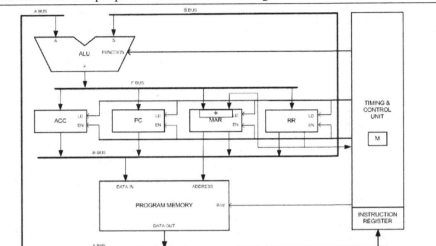

As a concrete illustration, consider the instruction LDARR (i.e., load the accumulator ACC with the contents of RR). Assume that the simple processor is extended in the following ways, as shown in Figure 10.7:

- The relocation register RR uses the same data path as the ACC, PC, and MAR registers with similar timing and control for LD and EN. The timing and control unit has the mode bit M added to it.

- The contents of RR are always available both to the timing and control unit and to the MAR.

- The MAR is enhanced so that the address it stores is the *summation* of the inputs from the F BUS and the *base* value stored in RR.

For a LDARR instruction stored at relative address *i*, the following four steps must be taken:

1. Convert the address *i* in PC to its read address *base* + *i* and check for a memory trap. If the address is not trapped, then pass *i* through the ALU and set up the LD control on MAR to load *i* off the F BUS at the beginning of the next cycle.

2. Increment *i* in PC. The control lines on PC are set to enable its output on to the B BUS and load the contents of the F BUS at the start of the next cycle. ALU FUNCTION is set to INC B.

3. The instruction LDARR at address *i* of PM is fetched and stored in IR. The output of RR is enabled onto the B BUS, ALU FUNCTION is set to PASS B, and the ACC input is set to load the ALU output at the beginning of the next cycle, which is the contents of RR.

Instructions Stored in Program Memory	Microcode Operations Sequenced by Timing and Control Unit
i. LDARR	1. $(((base + PC) \geq q)$ or $(PC \geq bound)) \to trap \mid (MAR \leftarrow base + PC)$
	2. $PC \leftarrow PC + 1$
	3. $IR \leftarrow PM[MAR]$
	4. $M = u \to trap \mid ACC \leftarrow RR$

Table 10.4: LDARR: Reading the contents of relocation register

	Microcode Operations	LD	EN	ALU
1.	$(((base + PC) \geq q)$ or $(PC \geq bound)) \to trap \mid$ $(MAR \leftarrow base + PC)$	MAR	PC	Pass B
2.	$PC \leftarrow PC + 1$	PC	PC	Inc B
3.	$IR \leftarrow PM[MAR]$	IR	X	Pass A
4.	$M = s \to ACC \leftarrow RR \mid trap$	ACC	RR	Pass B

Table 10.5: Timing and control unit operations for LDARR

4. If the mode bit M is set to u, then the instruction is trapped. Otherwise, the contents of RR are loaded into ACC.

The details of the above operations are illustrated in Tables 10.4 and 10.5, as well as in the timing diagram found in Figure 10.8.

There are two derived inference rules that specify the operation of LDARR:

LDARR *trap*
$$\frac{\begin{array}{c} TCU \text{ controls } (M \text{ says } \langle u \rangle \supset VM \text{ says } \langle \text{LDARR} \rangle \supset \langle trap \rangle) \\ TCU \text{ says } (M \text{ says } \langle u \rangle \supset VM \text{ says } \langle \text{LDARR} \rangle \supset \langle trap \rangle) \\ M \text{ says } \langle u \rangle \quad VM \text{ says } \langle \text{LDARR} \rangle \end{array}}{\langle trap \rangle},$$

LDARR
$$\frac{\begin{array}{c} TCU \text{ controls } (M \text{ says } \langle s \rangle \supset VM \text{ controls } \langle \text{LDARR} \rangle) \\ TCU \text{ says } (M \text{ says } \langle s \rangle \supset VM \text{ controls } \langle \text{LDARR} \rangle) \\ M \text{ says } \langle s \rangle \quad VM \text{ says } \langle \text{LDARR} \rangle \end{array}}{\langle \text{LDARR} \rangle}.$$

The first rule indicates that the instruction LDARR is trapped if the processor is in user mode. The second rule indicates that LDARR is allowed to execute if the processor is in supervisor mode.

A similar set of derived inference rules and implementation details exist for LDRR @ A (i.e., store the memory contents found in relative address A into RR). The details are left as an exercise for the reader.

10.3.4   Setting the Mode Bit

The final area to consider in the simple memory-segmentation design is the control of the mode bit M. Improper control of the privileged state bit M could cause a user program to be incorrectly labeled as the Supervisor. It is therefore essential to trap any introduction by a user program that attempts to set M to supervisor mode.

FIGURE 10.8 Timing diagram for loading RR into ACC

Cycle	1	2	3	4	5
PC	i	i	i+1	i+1	i+1
IR	XXXXXXX	XXXXXXX	XXXXXXX	LDARR	LDARR
MAR	XXXXXXX	i	i	i	i
ACC	XXXXXXX	XXXXXXX	XXXXXXX	XXXXXXX	RR
LD	MAR	PC	IR	ACC	MAR
EN	PC	PC	XXXXXXX	RR	PC
FUNCTION	Pass B	Inc B	Pass A	Pass A	Pass B
R/W	R	R	R	R	R
A BUS	XXXXXXX	XXXXXXX	LDARR	LDARR	LDARR
B BUS	i	i	XXXXXXX	XXXXXXX	i+1
F BUS	i	i+1	LDARR	LDARR	i+1

As a concrete illustration, suppose we have an instruction SSM (set supervisor mode), which is trapped if the processor is in *user* mode and otherwise executed. The resulting rules are as follows:

SSM *trap*
$$\frac{TCU \text{ controls } (M \text{ says } \langle u \rangle \supset VM \text{ says } \langle \text{SSM} \rangle \supset \langle trap \rangle) \quad TCU \text{ says } (M \text{ says } \langle u \rangle \supset VM \text{ says } \langle \text{SSM} \rangle \supset \langle trap \rangle) \quad M \text{ says } \langle u \rangle \quad VM \text{ says } \langle \text{SSM} \rangle}{\langle trap \rangle},$$

SSM
$$\frac{TCU \text{ controls } (M \text{ says } \langle s \rangle \supset VM \text{ controls } \langle \text{SSM} \rangle) \quad TCU \text{ says } (M \text{ says } \langle s \rangle \supset VM \text{ controls } \langle \text{SSM} \rangle) \quad M \text{ says } \langle s \rangle \quad VM \text{ says } \langle \text{SSM} \rangle}{\langle \text{SSM} \rangle}.$$

It turns out that the ability to set a processor's operating mode to user mode should also be limited to the Supervisor. In particular, user programs are restricted from any knowledge of supervisory functions. Put another way, only the Supervisor should be able to transfer control of a processor to a user program. This policy prevents a user program from downgrading the Supervisor program to user mode and thereby denying it access to supervisory functions.

For example, suppose we have an instruction SUM (set user mode). Letting $\langle \text{SUM} \rangle$ denote "it is a good idea to set the mode bit M to u (i.e., enter user mode)," we can identify the derived inference rules corresponding to SUM as follows:

$$
\text{SUM } trap \quad \frac{
\begin{array}{c}
TCU \text{ controls } (M \text{ says } \langle u \rangle \supset VM \text{ says } \langle \text{SUM} \rangle \supset \langle trap \rangle) \\
TCU \text{ says } (M \text{ says } \langle u \rangle \supset VM \text{ says } \langle \text{SUM} \rangle \supset \langle trap \rangle) \\
M \text{ says } \langle u \rangle \quad VM \text{ says } \langle \text{SUM} \rangle
\end{array}
}{\langle trap \rangle} ,
$$

$$
\text{SUM} \quad \frac{
\begin{array}{c}
TCU \text{ controls } (M \text{ says } \langle s \rangle \supset VM \text{ controls } \langle \text{SUM} \rangle) \\
TCU \text{ says } (M \text{ says } \langle s \rangle \supset VM \text{ controls } \langle \text{SUM} \rangle) \\
M \text{ says } \langle s \rangle \quad VM \text{ says } \langle \text{SUM} \rangle
\end{array}
}{\langle \text{SUM} \rangle} .
$$

The implementation details in terms of microcode operations and timing diagrams can be devised in a similar fashion as for previous machine instructions. These tasks are left as exercises for the reader.

Exercise 10.3.1 *Work out the inference rules for the operation* LDRR @A *(i.e., loading RR with the values found in relative address* A *in PM). Prove the validity of the inference rules.*

Exercise 10.3.2 *Work out the table of timing and control unit operations for the operation* LDRR @A *(similar to Tables 10.4 and 10.5). Draw the corresponding timing diagram for* LDRR @A.

Exercise 10.3.3 *Work out the table of timing and control unit operations for the operation* SSM. *Draw the corresponding timing diagram for* SSM.

Exercise 10.3.4 *Work out the table of timing and control unit operations for the operation* SUM. *Draw the corresponding timing diagram for* SUM.

Exercise 10.3.5 *Suppose a new machine instruction is required of the simple processor with relocation register RR, as shown in Figure 10.7. The new instruction is* LD @A @B *(i.e., load the contents of virtual address* B *into virtual address* A).

a. *Show the microcode implementation of* LD @A @B *as a sequence of microcode instructions, similar to what is found in Table 10.4.*

b. *Devise and prove valid the access-control rules for* LD @A @B.

10.4 Design of the Virtual Machine Monitor

We now take a more detailed look at the design of virtual machine monitors. An instruction-set architecture is said to be *virtualizable* if it is possible to build a virtual machine monitor that satisfies the following three objectives:

1. The VMM creates an execution environment that is essentially identical to the execution environment of the hardware being emulated.

2. The VMM efficiently executes instructions, so that program execution times are not seriously degraded.

3. The VMM maintains control over all system resources, so that any attempt by users to change the resources allocated to them will cause the VMM to intervene.

The virtualization techniques we present in this section were originally developed in the context of mainframe computers (such as the IBM 360) and continued into the design of minicomputers (such as the Digital Equipment Corporation's VAX architecture). These machines had to support multiple users executing programs on the same hardware. Today's systems face the same problem, whereby (due to widespread networking) multiple processes and potentially multiple users use the same hardware.

It turns out that not all instruction-set architectures are virtualizable. Because virtualization is a key security capability, it is important to understand the conditions under which virtualization is possible and how a VMM is constructed under such conditions. These details were worked out by Popek and Goldberg (Popek and Goldberg, 1974).

Virtualization depends on identifying three types of instructions:

1. *Privileged* instructions: instructions that are trapped in user mode but not trapped in supervisor mode.

2. *Sensitive* instructions: instructions whose behavior depends on the value of relocation register RR or mode bit M (i.e., behavior that is location or mode sensitive, or instructions that attempt to alter the allocation of resources, such as memory).

3. *Innocuous* instructions: instructions that are neither privileged nor sensitive.

The key property for an instruction-set architecture to be virtualizable is that *all sensitive instructions must be privileged instructions*. If this property holds, then all sensitive instructions are automatically trapped by the VMM's control program, which is deliberately constructed to control any change in allocated resources and to faithfully simulate the execution of privileged instructions. This construction addresses the first and third objectives of VMMs: creation of an identical execution environment to the hardware being emulated, and control over all resources allocated to VMs. Innocuous instructions, which are neither privileged nor sensitive, are passed on for direct execution by hardware. This approach satisfies the second objective of VMMs, namely the efficient execution of instructions.

In the discussion that follows, we assume that the specific instruction-set architecture is virtualizable (i.e., all sensitive instructions are also privileged instructions).

FIGURE 10.9 Top-level operation of virtual machine monitor

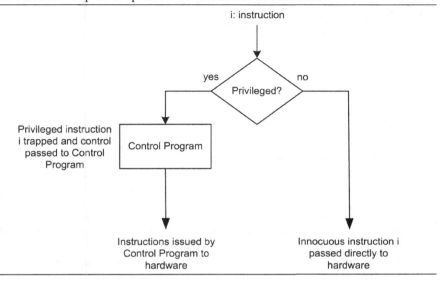

The VMM's operation at the conceptual level is illustrated by Figure 10.9. Instructions that are not privileged (i.e., innocuous instructions) are passed unchanged directly to the hardware for execution. Instructions that are privileged are trapped and handled by the control program CP. The three objectives for VMMs are met as follows:

1. *Identical execution environment*: The execution environment for innocuous instructions is identical, because innocuous instructions are passed unchanged to the hardware. Privileged instructions are trapped by the control program CP. If CP accurately simulates the execution of instructions, then the VMM will provide an identical execution environment.

2. *Efficient execution of instructions*: Passing on innocuous instructions (instead of simulating them) provides the same execution speed as executing them on hardware.

3. *Control over all system resources*: Because all sensitive instructions that attempt to change the allocation of system resources are trapped, the VMM is in control.

We now focus on how trapped instructions are handled by the VMM. Conceptually, the control program CP has three main components:

1. A dispatcher D, which is the top-level module called when a trap occurs. The value of the program status word PSW—in particular, the instruction register IR and the program counter PC—enables D to decide which module to call, based on the instruction that was trapped.

FIGURE 10.10 Graphic representation of control program for handling trapped instructions

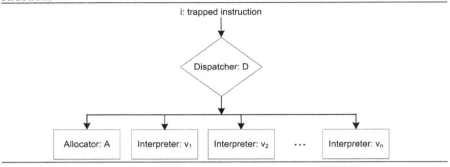

2. An allocator A, which is called every time a privileged instruction attempts to change resources associated with the computing environment, such as the value of the relocation register *RR*. The main task of the allocator is to decide what system resources are provided to the various programs running on the machine.

3. A set *V* of interpreters, which contains a distinct interpreter routine v_i for each privileged instruction *i*. These interpreters simulate the effect of running the instruction that was trapped. In practice, each interpreter might be nothing more than a table that looks up the state of the machine when the instruction *i* was called and returns the state the machine should be in after executing *i*.

Figure 10.10 illustrates the function of the control program CP. Each trapped instruction *i* is examined by the dispatcher D, which determines whether to invoke the allocator A or a specific interpreter $v_i \in V$.

We now examine more closely how privileged, sensitive, and innocuous instructions are classified.

10.4.1 Privileged Instructions

Privileged instructions are those that are intended to be executed only in supervisor mode: they always trap when executed in user mode, but never when executed in supervisor mode (unless, of course, there is a memory trap due to out-of-bounds addressing). An instruction *i* is said to be *privileged* if (in the absence of memory traps) it exhibits the following behavior, for all states:

$$i(pm, acc, pc, mar, ir, m, (base, bound)) \begin{cases} \text{traps, if } m = u \\ \text{doesn't trap, if } m = s. \end{cases}$$

Example 10.5

Loading the contents $(base, bound)$ of the relocation register RR into the accumulator ACC is a privileged instruction, which only the Supervisor program can execute. Recall the definition of LDARR, which is expressed as the following two derived inference rules:

$$
\text{LDARR } trap \quad \frac{\begin{array}{c} TCU \text{ controls } (M \text{ says } \langle u \rangle \supset VM \text{ says } \langle \text{LDARR} \rangle \supset \langle trap \rangle) \\ TCU \text{ says } (M \text{ says } \langle u \rangle \supset VM \text{ says } \langle \text{LDARR} \rangle \supset \langle trap \rangle) \\ M \text{ says } \langle u \rangle \quad VM \text{ says } \langle \text{LDARR} \rangle \end{array}}{\langle trap \rangle},
$$

$$
\text{LDARR} \quad \frac{\begin{array}{c} TCU \text{ controls } (M \text{ says } \langle s \rangle \supset VM \text{ controls } \langle \text{LDARR} \rangle) \\ TCU \text{ says } (M \text{ says } \langle s \rangle \supset VM \text{ controls } \langle \text{LDARR} \rangle) \\ M \text{ says } \langle s \rangle \quad VM \text{ says } \langle \text{LDARR} \rangle \end{array}}{\langle \text{LDARR} \rangle}.
$$

From these rules we can see that, if M says $\langle u \rangle$, then LDARR is trapped. If M says $\langle s \rangle$, then LDARR is executed. Thus, LDARR is a privileged instruction. ◊

10.4.2 Sensitive Instructions

Informally, there are two types of sensitive instructions:

1. *Control-sensitive instructions*, which attempt to *change* either the processor mode (i.e., user or supervisor) or the memory resources allocated to the processor (via the relocation register)

2. *Behavior-sensitive instructions*, whose behavior is *affected by* either the processor mode or the physical location in real memory specified by the relocation register

To define these notions more precisely, we must first introduce two simple definitions.

Definition 10.1 *Let* $S = (pm, acc, pc, mar, ir, m, (base, bound))$ *be a processor state.*

- *An instruction* i *is* mode preserving *on* S *if* $i(S)$ *either address traps or has the same mode bit as* S *(i.e., the value m).*

- *An instruction* i *is* resource preserving *on* S *if* $i(S)$ *either address traps or has the same* $(base, bound)$ *value as* S. ∎

Intuitively, control-sensitive instructions are instructions that attempt to change either the contents of the relocation register RR, the mode bit M, or both. That is, an instruction i is control sensitive if there exists at least one state S such that i is not mode preserving on S, not resource preserving on S, or both.

Example 10.6

Consider the SUM (i.e., set user mode) instruction. Its behavior is defined by the following two derived inference rules:

SUM *trap*
$$\frac{\begin{array}{c} TCU \text{ controls } (M \text{ says } \langle u \rangle \supset VM \text{ says } \langle \text{SUM} \rangle \supset \langle trap \rangle) \\ TCU \text{ says } (M \text{ says } \langle u \rangle \supset VM \text{ says } \langle \text{SUM} \rangle \supset \langle trap \rangle) \\ M \text{ says } \langle u \rangle \quad VM \text{ says } \langle \text{SUM} \rangle \end{array}}{\langle trap \rangle},$$

SUM
$$\frac{\begin{array}{c} TCU \text{ controls } (M \text{ says } \langle s \rangle \supset VM \text{ controls } \langle \text{SUM} \rangle) \\ TCU \text{ says } (M \text{ says } \langle s \rangle \supset VM \text{ controls } \langle \text{SUM} \rangle) \\ M \text{ says } \langle s \rangle \quad VM \text{ says } \langle \text{SUM} \rangle \end{array}}{\langle \text{SUM} \rangle}.$$

From these rules, we can see that SUM is a privileged instruction that is trapped in user mode but not in supervisor mode. However, the second rule states that an attempt to execute SUM in supervisor mode should be granted: the result of the instruction would be to change the mode bit from s to u. As a result, the instruction SUM is also control sensitive. ◊

In contrast, behavior-sensitive instructions are either *location sensitive* (i.e., depend on the value of the relocation register) or *mode sensitive* (i.e., depend on the value of the mode bit). Recall that a virtual-machine program accesses memory through the use of *virtual* addresses. In theory, a program's behavior should be independent of the physical locations in which its segment resides. Specifically, its behavior should be governed by what is stored within the memory segment it can access (whose boundaries are defined by RR), what is stored in location PM[1] because of the way we defined traps, and the value stored in the program status word PSW, namely the values stored in ACC, PC, MAR, IR, M, and RR. What is stored in other segments should not affect the behavior of the processor under the control of the segment referenced by *(base, bound)* in RR.

We therefore introduce the following notion of equivalence, which equates states whose contents of accessible memory segments are identical (independent of their physical locations in memory).

Definition 10.2 *Let x be an integer. Two states S_1 and S_2 are equivalent modulo x (written $S_1 \approx_x S_2$) if and only if there exist values $pm_1, pm_2, acc, pc, mar, ir, m, base,$ and bound such that the following conditions all hold:*

- $S_1 = (pm_1, acc, pc, mar, ir, m, (base, bound))$,

- $S_2 = (pm_2, acc, pc, mar, ir, m, (base + x, bound))$,

- $pm_1[1] = pm_2[1]$,

- *For all j such that $base \le j < base + bound$, $pm_1[j] = pm_2[j + x]$.* ∎

Intuitively, when $S_1 \approx_x S_2$ (for whatever value of x), S_1 and S_2 differ only in the physical locations of their segments and in the contents of memory *outside* of their respective segments. In particular, they share the same values for the ACC, PC, MAR, IR, and M registers; in the contents of memory location PM[1]; and in the logical locations associated with their segments.

With this definition in hand, we can define behavior sensitivity precisely. An instruction i is behavior sensitive if there exists states S_1 and S_2 such that the following conditions all hold:

- $S_1 \approx_x S_2$,

- i is mode preserving and resource preserving on both S_1 and S_2,

- i does not address trap on S_1 or S_2,

- $i(S_1) \not\approx_x i(S_2)$.

Intuitively, i is behavior sensitive when it fails to behave similarly on two equivalent states.

Example 10.7

Consider the instruction LDARR, which loads the value of RR into ACC if the processor is in supervisor mode and traps if the processor is in user mode. (Notice that this behavior makes LDARR a privileged instruction.)

Consider the following two states, where $S_1 \approx_x S_2$ for some $x \neq 0$:

$$S_1 = (pm_1, acc, pc, mar, ir, s, (base, bound)),$$
$$S_2 = (pm_2, acc, pc, mar, ir, s, (base + x, bound)).$$

Because the values of the mode bits are both s, executing LDARR from either state will load the relevant RR value into the accumulator. Thus, the accumulator value for $i(S_1)$ will be $(base, bound)$, whereas the accumulator value for $i(S_2)$ will be $(base + x, bound)$. It follows that $i(S_1) \not\approx_x i(S_2)$, and hence LDARR is behavior sensitive. $\Diamond$

10.4.3 Virtualizable Processor Architectures

A key result of Popek and Goldberg's work (Popek and Goldberg, 1974) is that a virtual machine monitor can be constructed for processors that have relocation mechanisms, user and supervisor modes, and traps, *if the set of sensitive instructions is a subset of the set of privileged instructions.* In other words, an instruction-set architecture is virtualizable if every sensitive instruction is also a privileged instruction. The proof of this property can be found in the original paper.

Exercise 10.4.1 *Consider the machine instructions of the simple processor described in Chapter 9—A Primer on Computer Hardware.*

a. *Classify each of the following instructions as privileged, control sensitive, behavior sensitive, or innocuous:*

> LDA @ A
> LDA @ A @ B
> ADD @ B
> STO @ B
> LDARR
> SSM
> SUM
> LDRR @ A

b. *Assume that the above list of machine instructions fully enumerates the instruction set of the processor. Is the processor virtualizable? Justify your answer.*

Exercise 10.4.2 *Suppose the processor state for a program in a segment described by* $(base, bound) = (256, 1024)$ *is given by*

$$S = (pm, acc, 0, mar, ir, m, (256, 1024)).$$

Answer the following questions.

a. *What locations in physical memory does the active memory segment occupy?*

b. *Suppose the active segment is to be relocated to base address = 128 in physical memory and executed. This new state is* S':

$$S' = (pm, acc, 0, mar, ir, m, (128, 1024)).$$

What must be true for the program in the relocated segment to behave exactly like the program in the original segment, where "behave exactly" means all PSW values in the relocated segment will match for each execution state with the exception of $base = 256$ *and* $base' = 128$? *Justify your answer.*

10.5   Summary

The goal of this chapter was to introduce the fundamentals of memory protection, virtual machines, and virtual machine monitors. Central to protecting memory is segmentation as supported by a relocation register and a mode bit to protect the relocation register.

Central to virtual machine monitors is the control program that consists of a dispatcher, resource allocator, and interpreters of privileged instructions. The equivalence of machines with and without a virtual machine monitor was demonstrated using a mapping function that mapped states of one machine to equivalent states in the other. A key result is that those instruction-set architectures where all sensitive instructions are also privileged instructions are virtualizable.

The learning outcomes associated with this chapter appear in Figure 10.11.

10.6   Further Reading

Saltzer and Schroeder's paper, *The Protection of Information in Computer Systems* (Saltzer and Schroeder, 1975), is a classic paper on memory protection mechanisms. The protection methods described in this chapter and following chapters are developed based on this paper. Popek and Goldberg's paper *Formal Requirements for Virtualizable Third Generation Architectures* (Popek and Goldberg, 1974) is a classic paper on virtual machine monitors. Its findings are still relevant in current virtual machines.

FIGURE 10.11 Learning outcomes for Chapter 10

After completing this chapter, you should be able to achieve the following learning outcomes at several levels of knowledge:

Comprehension

- When given a block diagram of a processor using memory segmentation, describe how virtual memory addresses are related to physical memory addresses.

Application

- When given a block diagram of a processor and control lines to registers and arithmetic logic units, interpret timing diagrams describing processor behavior.

Analysis

- When given the value of the program status word and an instruction, determine if the instruction will be address trapped or passed on for execution.

- When given the definition of an instruction, be able to determine if it is innocuous, privileged, behavior sensitive, or control sensitive.

- When given a request to access a virtual (logical) address, determine if accessing the address is permitted.

Synthesis

- When given a description of a machine-level instruction and a block diagram of a processor with its control lines, devise microprograms that implement the machine-level instruction.

- When given a description of a machine-level instruction, be able to describe when the operation is performed or trapped through the use of derived inference rules.

Chapter 11

Access Control Using Descriptors and Capabilities

In Chapter 10, we introduced a simple memory-segmentation scheme based on a single relocation register guarded by a mode bit. Under this scheme, each virtual machine has access to precisely one memory segment, whose location is determined by the base-address value *base* stored in the relocation register RR. The relocation register thus serves as a single mechanism to support both *segment addressing* and *memory protection*.

In this chapter, we introduce a more sophisticated and flexible scheme, known as a *capability system*. This scheme separates the notions of addressing and protection by distinguishing *address descriptors* (which serve as pointers to memory segments in physical memory) from *capabilities* (unforgeable tickets that specify permitted operations on a given memory segment). In this scheme, each machine is given a *catalog* (i.e., collection) of capabilities that together define its privileges to access various memory segments. As a consequence, a single virtual machine may be granted a variety of access privileges (e.g., read, write, or execute) to multiple memory segments.

11.1 Address Descriptors and Capabilities

When writing programs, programmers typically do not know the precise location of memory segments. Thus, it is convenient to refer to memory segments by *name* or by a *unique identifier*, as opposed to a specific $(base, bound)$ value. *Address descriptors* provide the means to associate segment names (or unique identifiers) with physical locations in memory. In turn, capabilities bind access rights (such as *read* or *write*) to object identifiers or names. In the case of segments, this binding is made possible by appending read and write permissions to segment names and storing the results in capability registers.

Figure 11.1 shows how address descriptors and capabilities fit together. Each address descriptor has the form $(N_s, (base_{N_s}, bound_{N_s}))$, where N_s is a segment name (i.e., a unique identifier) and $(base_{N_s}, bound_{N_s})$ point to the physical location of that segment in memory. Taken together, these descriptors form a memory map that is stored in the *address descriptor segment* (ADS). To provide protection, the ADS must be under supervisory control, inaccessible to users, and trustworthy.

FIGURE 11.1 Memory protection with address descriptors and capabilities

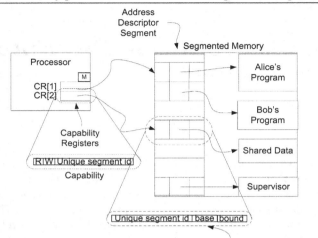

Figure 11.1 also includes a processor with two capability registers (CR[1] and CR[2]), which are both protected by mode bit M. Each capability register holds a capability, which comprises a read bit (R), a write bit (W), and a unique segment id. The value of the read (respectively, write) bit indicates whether or not read (respectively, write) access to the given segment is permitted.[1] In this figure, CR[1] contains a capability that points to the address descriptor for Alice's program segment; in contrast, CR[2] contains a capability that points to the address descriptor for a shared-data segment.

We can express in the logic the contents of the ADS and of the capability registers in the same way that we previously expressed the contents of other registers: that is, we can treat ADS, CR[1], and CR[2] as principals who make statements about their values. For example, the formula

$$ADS \text{ says } (\langle (N_1, (base_{N_1}, bound_{N_1})) \rangle \ \land \ \cdots \ \land \ \langle (N_n, (base_{N_n}, bound_{N_n})) \rangle)$$

expresses that there are n address descriptors stored in the ADS, with the jth descriptor associating the segment name N_j with the physical locations given by the pair $(base_{N_j}, bound_{N_j})$. In a similar vein, Table 11.1 provides the possible interpretations for a given capability stored in capability register CR[i].

---

[1] In many systems, there will also be an execute bit (X), which governs the ability to execute a segment. To keep our discussion and diagrams simpler, we adopt the convention that read access also provides execute access. Alternatively, one could incorporate the additional bit into capabilities and the capability registers.

Contents of CR[i]	Interpretation
$(read, write, N_s)$	$CR[i]$ says $(\langle read, N_s \rangle \wedge \langle write, N_s \rangle)$
$(read, not\ write, N_s)$	$CR[i]$ says $(\langle read, N_s \rangle \wedge \neg \langle write, N_s \rangle)$
$(not\ read, write, N_s)$	$CR[i]$ says $(\neg \langle read, N_s \rangle \wedge \langle write, N_s \rangle)$
$(not\ read, not\ write, N_s)$	$CR[i]$ says $(\neg \langle read, N_s \rangle \wedge \neg \langle write, N_s \rangle)$

Table 11.1: Interpretation of capability-register values

Example 11.1

Suppose capability register CR[1] has the value $(read, not\ write, Math\ Program)$. The contents of CR[1] can be expressed in the logic as follows:

$$CR[1] \text{ says } (\langle read, Math\ Program \rangle \wedge \neg \langle write, Math\ Program \rangle).$$

The process possessing the capability in CR[1] is able to read (and therefore also execute) the shared math program, but the process is not allowed to modify it. ◇

Instructions previously defined using the simple memory protection scheme of Chapter 10 must be redefined to incorporate the use of capabilities and address descriptors. At a minimum, the new definitions must accommodate the use of capability registers and the introduction of segment names N_s into virtual addresses. The following example shows how the instruction STO (which stores the contents of the ACC into a particular memory address) is altered to accommodate the new protection scheme.

Example 11.2

Consider the instruction STO $@(N_s, A)$, which stores the contents of the accumulator ACC into address A of segment N_s. This instruction should be allowed to execute *only* when the following conditions are all satisfied (otherwise, a trap should occur):

- One of the capability registers $CR[i]$ possesses a write capability for the segment N_s:

$$CR[i] \text{ says } \langle write, N_s \rangle.$$

- The ADS contains an address descriptor for N_s that associates it with some particular physical segment $(base_{N_s}, bound_{N_s})$:

$$ADS \text{ says } (N_s, (base_{N_s}, bound_{N_s})).$$

- The virtual address A is within bounds of the segment N_s and thus will not trigger an address trap:

$$(A + base_{N_s}) < q, \qquad A < bound_{N_s}.$$

These conditions are collectively summarized by the following derived inference rule:

$$
\begin{array}{c}
\textit{Supervisor } \mathsf{controls}\ (CR[i]\ \mathsf{says}\ \langle(\textit{write}_{N_s},N_s)\rangle \supset ADS\ \mathsf{says}\ \langle(N_s,(\textit{base}_{N_s},\textit{bound}_{N_s}))\rangle) \supset \\
(\text{A} + \textit{base}_{N_s} < q) \supset (\text{A} < \textit{bound}_{N_s}) \supset VM\ \mathsf{controls}\ \langle\textsc{sto}\ @(N_s,\text{A})\rangle) \\
\textit{Supervisor } \mathsf{says}\ (CR[i]\ \mathsf{says}\ \langle(\textit{write}_{N_s},N_s)\rangle \supset ADS\ \mathsf{says}\ \langle(N_s,(\textit{base}_{N_s},\textit{bound}_{N_s}))\rangle) \supset \\
(\text{A} + \textit{base}_{N_s} < q) \supset (\text{A} < \textit{bound}_{N_s}) \supset VM\ \mathsf{controls}\ \langle\textsc{sto}\ @(N_s,\text{A})\rangle) \\
VM\ \mathsf{says}\ \langle\textsc{sto}\ @(N_s,\text{A})\rangle \quad CR[i]\ \mathsf{says}\ \langle(\textit{write}_{N_s},N_s)\rangle
\end{array}
$$

$$
\textsc{sto}\ \dfrac{ADS\ \mathsf{says}\ \langle(N_s,(\textit{base}_{N_s},\textit{bound}_{N_s}))\rangle \quad \text{A} + \textit{base}_{N_s} < q \quad \text{A} < \textit{bound}_{N_s}}{\langle\textsc{sto}\ @(N_s,\text{A})\rangle}
$$
$@(N_s,\text{A})$

$\diamond$

The memory protection scheme shown in Figure 11.1 protects the contents of the two capability registers CR[1] and CR[2] using the mode bit M. In particular, the capability registers CR[i] are only accessible if the processor is in *supervisor* mode. The following example illustrates how this protection works.

Example 11.3

Consider the instruction LDACR[i], which loads the ACC with the contents of CR[i], provided that the virtual machine is in supervisor mode; when the virtual machine is in user mode, the instruction is trapped. (This instruction is the capability-register analogue of the LDARR instruction introduced in Chapter 10.)

The following derived inference rules define the behavior of LDACR[i]:

$$
\text{LDACR}[i]\ \dfrac{\begin{array}{c}\textit{Supervisor } \mathsf{controls}\ (M\ \mathsf{says}\ \langle s\rangle \supset VM\ \mathsf{controls}\ \langle\textsc{ldacr}[i]\rangle) \\ \textit{Supervisor } \mathsf{says}\ (M\ \mathsf{says}\ \langle s\rangle \supset VM\ \mathsf{controls}\ \langle\textsc{ldacr}[i]\rangle) \\ M\ \mathsf{says}\ \langle s\rangle \quad VM\ \mathsf{says}\ \langle\textsc{ldacr}[i]\rangle\end{array}}{\langle\textsc{ldacr}[i]\rangle}\ ,
$$

$$
\text{LDACR}[i]\ \textit{trap}\ \dfrac{\begin{array}{c}\textit{Supervisor } \mathsf{controls}\ (M\ \mathsf{says}\ \langle u\rangle \supset VM\ \mathsf{says}\ \langle\textsc{ldacr}[i]\rangle \supset \langle\textit{trap}\rangle) \\ \textit{Supervisor } \mathsf{says}\ (M\ \mathsf{says}\ \langle u\rangle \supset VM\ \mathsf{says}\ \langle\textsc{ldacr}[i]\rangle \supset \langle\textit{trap}\rangle) \\ M\ \mathsf{says}\ \langle u\rangle \quad VM\ \mathsf{says}\ \langle\textsc{ldacr}[i]\rangle\end{array}}{\langle\textit{trap}\rangle}\ .
$$

In particular, LDACR[i] is executed only when the mode bit M indicates that the VM is in supervisor mode. If M indicates that the VM is in user mode, then a trap occurs instead. $\diamond$

In the next section, we look at an alternative way to protect the capability registers, without using a mode bit. This alternative—known as a *tagged architecture*—permits user programs to load the capability registers, but only with values that are known to be authorized descriptor values.

Exercise 11.1.1 *Recall the* LDA @A *instruction in Chapter 10, which loads the accumulator ACC with the contents of PM[base + A]]. Revise the inference rules defining the behavior of* LDA @A (LDA *memory trap 1,* LDA *memory trap 1, and* LDA @A), *using address descriptors and capabilities.*

Exercise 11.1.2 *Consider the instruction* STOCR*[i], which loads the contents of the accumulator ACC into capability register CR[i] provided the virtual machine is in supervisor mode. Letting* ⟨STOCR[i]⟩ *denote that the ACC contents should be loaded into CR[i], propose and formally prove a derived inference rule for* STOCR*[i].*

11.2   Tagged Architectures

The security of segmented memory depends on the integrity of relocation registers and capability registers: if users are able to load these registers with arbitrary or unauthorized permissions, then the security and integrity of physical and program memory are lost. There are at least two ways to achieve integrity of these registers.

The first approach is to grant access to capability registers only to those principals trusted to create legitimate capabilities (e.g., the Supervisor). This approach can be accommodated through the use of mode bits that indicate when the processor is under supervisory control. To maintain the integrity of the capability registers, user processes are denied access to the registers; only the Supervisor is granted access to the capability registers. While secure, this approach is inflexible. For example, suppose that there are two capability registers, but more than two memory segments that a particular user's program is allowed to access. If users lack the ability to load capability values into capability registers, then they can access only the two memory segments that the Supervisor loaded into the capability registers. Such a situation is both limiting and inconvenient.

The second (and more flexible) approach is to limit the *values that can be loaded* into capability registers, rather than to limit the *principals who can alter* the capability registers. This approach can be accommodated through the use of *tagged architectures*. Essentially, the contents of memory are classified into one of two types: capabilities (i.e., permissions) and non-capabilities (i.e., data). The type of information stored at any memory location is indicated by a tag bit, which is part of the word stored at any memory location.

To be explicit, tagged architectures do not necessarily eliminate the need for mode bits. Although the mode bits are not used for determining whether to grant access to capability registers, they are still useful for determining whether or not the Supervisor is in control of the processor.

In tagged architectures, each memory location has an associated *tag bit* that is either *on* or *off*. Thus, each memory location $PM[(N_s, \text{A})]$ stores a pair comprising both a value and a tag. When the tag bit is *on*, the value in address A of segment N_s is interpreted as a capability. When the tag bit is *off*, the value of address A in segment N_s is interpreted as ordinary data and cannot be used as a capability. Table 11.2 shows how the values of these pairs can be interpreted in the logic.

The mandatory access control policy for reading from and writing to memory and capability registers CR[i] is as follows:

Contents of $PM[(N_s, \text{A})]$	Interpretation
$(value, off)$	$PM[(N_s, \text{A})]$ says $(\langle value \rangle \wedge \langle data \rangle)$
$(value, on)$	$PM[(N_s, \text{A})]$ says $(\langle value \rangle \wedge \langle capability \rangle)$

Table 11.2: Interpretation of tag bit

1. Instructions that load a capability register with the value stored in a particular memory location are executed only if the tag bit in that location is *on*. Otherwise, the instruction is trapped.

2. Instructions that store values from capability registers into memory are permitted provided that there are no address traps and the virtual machine possesses write permission on the relevant memory segment. The corresponding *tag bit* is turned *on* as a result of storing a capability value.

3. All other memory store instructions turn the tag bit *off*.

The following example illustrates the mandatory access control policy for an instruction that attempts to update a capability register.

Example 11.4

Consider the instruction $\text{LDCR}(i, @(N_s, \text{A}))$ that attempts to load CR[i] with the value in address A in segment N_s. The operation is successful provided that address A does not address trap, the associated tag bit indicates the value is a capability value, and the virtual machine has *read* permission on N_s.

Let $\langle \text{LDCR}\ (i, @(N_s, a)) \rangle$ denote that the operation should be permitted. The following inference rule describes the conditions under which the operation is allowed:

$$\textit{Supervisor } \textsf{controls } (CR[j] \textsf{ says } \langle read_{N_s} \rangle \supset PM[(N_s, \text{A})] \textsf{ says } \langle capability \rangle \supset$$
$$ADS \textsf{ says } \langle (N_s, (base_{N_s}, bound_{N_s})) \rangle \supset \text{A} + base_{N_s} < q \supset \text{A} < bound_{N_s} \supset$$
$$VM \textsf{ controls } \langle \text{LDCR}\ (i, @(N_s, a)) \rangle)$$

$$\textit{Supervisor } \textsf{says } (CR[j] \textsf{ says } \langle read_{N_s} \rangle \supset PM[(N_s, \text{A})] \textsf{ says } \langle capability \rangle \supset$$
$$ADS \textsf{ says } \langle (N_s, (base_{N_s}, bound_{N_s})) \rangle \supset \text{A} + base_{N_s} < q \supset \text{A} < bound_{N_s} \supset$$
$$VM \textsf{ controls } \langle \text{LDCR}\ (i, @(N_s, a)) \rangle)$$

$$VM \textsf{ says } \langle \text{LDCR}\ (i, @(N_s, a)) \rangle \quad CR[i] \textsf{ says } \langle read_{N_s} \rangle$$

$$PM[(N_s, \text{A})] \textsf{ says } \langle capability \rangle$$

$$\text{LDCR} \quad \frac{ADS \textsf{ says } \langle (N_s, (base_{N_s}, bound_{N_s})) \rangle \quad \text{A} + base_{N_s} < q \quad \text{A} < bound_{N_s}}{\langle \text{LDCR}\ (i, @(N_s, a)) \rangle}$$
$$(i, @(N_s, \text{A}))$$

$\Diamond$

In the next section, we show how tagged architectures are used to support capability systems, which provide secure and flexible sharing of data and programs among users.

Exercise 11.2.1 *Propose derived inference rules for* LDCR $(i, @(N_s, a))$ *that indicate the conditions under which the* LDCR *instruction will trap. Provide an informal argument justifying your inference rules and formally derive them.*

Exercise 11.2.2 *Consider the instruction* STOCR $(i, @(N_s, A))$, *which attempts to store the contents of capability register CR[i] into address* A *of segment* N_s. *This operation should be allowed, provided address* A *does not cause an address trap and the virtual machine has* write *permission on* N_s; *otherwise, the instruction is trapped.*

Let $\langle$STOCR $(i, @(N_s, A))\rangle$ *denote that the operation should be permitted. Propose and formally prove a derived inference rule called* STOCR $(i, @(N_s, A))$ *that formally defines the behavior of* STOCR *when there is no address trap and the user has write permission on* N_s.

Exercise 11.2.3 *As we have seen, tagged architectures depend on the trustworthy segregation of capability values from ordinary data. Identify the crucial elements of micro-coded timing and control operations necessary for any implementation of a tagged architecture to be trustworthy.*

11.3   Capability Systems

The concepts of descriptors, capabilities, and tagged architectures combine to support *capability systems*. Capability systems are organized around the principle that access to protected objects and services is granted using capabilities, which incorporate descriptors that refer to the protected objects and services. Because they incorporate tags, capability systems can grant user programs the ability to load and store capabilities to and from the capability registers.

11.3.1   Catalogs

Capability systems are more flexible than the simple segmented memory system described in Chapter 10, which used a mode bit for protecting descriptors. The ability of user programs to read and store valid capabilities allows the use of *catalogs of capabilities*, which simplifies the task of securely sharing memory.

To see how catalogs work in capability systems, consider the processor and physical memory shown in Figure 11.2, which shows a processor with four capability registers (CR[1] through CR[4]). The contents of these registers are as follows:

- CR[1] contains a capability (*read, write,* Alice's Program), which gives read and write access to the segment in physical memory that is Alice's program.

- CR[2] contains a capability (*read, write,* Alice's Catalog), which gives both read and write access to Alice's catalog of capabilities.

FIGURE 11.2 Catalogs and capabilities

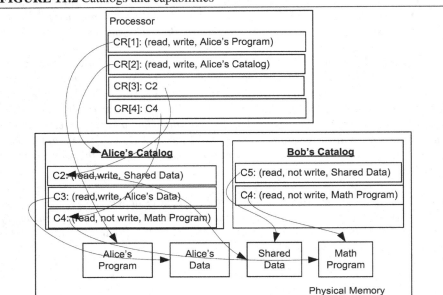

- CR[3] contains capability C2, which is a capability in Alice's catalog that allows Alice to read to or write from the *Shared Data* segment she shares with Bob.

- CR[4] contains capability C4, which is a capability in Alice's catalog that gives her read access to the *Math Program* segment, which she also shares with Bob.

The capabilities in Figure 11.2 serve as both pointers and privileges to memory segments that contain data and/or programs. Because the capabilities exist within the context of a tagged architecture, they can be read from memory into capability registers and written from capability registers into memory. For each user's virtual machine, the Supervisor provides a memory segment (i.e., the user's catalog) that contains the capabilities that the user is authorized to use.

The following example illustrates the use of catalogs to provide flexible storage and use of user capabilities.

Example 11.5
Consider the situation shown in Figure 11.2. Suppose we wish to have the contents of CR[1] point to the math program, while still preserving the processor's access to Alice's program. We can see that the math-program capability C4 is in Alice's capability catalog; the capability for Alice's program is not. For simplicity, let us refer to the capability for Alice's program as C6 and the virtual address of any capability Ci as $addr_{Ci}$.

The contents of Alice's catalog are as follows:

$$PM[(\text{Alice's Catalog}, addr_{C2})] = (read, write, \text{Shared Data}),$$
$$PM[(\text{Alice's Catalog}, addr_{C3})] = (read, write, \text{Alice's Data}),$$
$$PM[(\text{Alice's Catalog}, addr_{C4})] = (read, not\ write, \text{Math Program}).$$

If C4 is loaded immediately into the register CR[1], then the processor will lose the capability to access Alice's program. Hence, two steps are necessary: the first stores C6 into $addr_{C6}$ of Alice's Catalog, and the second loads C4 into CR[1]. In this way, access to Alice's program can be maintained through Alice's catalog. ◇

11.3.2 Creating New Segments

Recall from Chapter 10 that one of the requirements for virtualizability is that all security-sensitive instructions are trapped and executed under supervisory control. In particular, any attempt to alter the allocation of memory must be done under control of the Supervisor. Therefore, user requests for additional memory resources in the form of new memory segments must be handled by the Supervisor control program, because they reflect requests to change the resources allocated to users.

To illustrate how new memory segments could be created in ways that support virtualization, suppose that the instruction CREATESEG N_s is employed by users to create a memory segment N_s. When invoked by a user, CREATESEG N_s is trapped, and control is turned over to the control program's resource allocation module.

When CREATESEG N_s is trapped, the program status word PSW—which includes the contents of the instruction register IR containing CREATESEG N_s—is stored in PM[0]. In this way, the control program's dispatcher module can detect that the user is attempting to create a new memory segment with the name N_s and then pass control to the allocation module.

The allocation module then decides whether or not to honor the request CREATE-SEG N_s. If the allocation module decides to honor the request and N_s is not already being used as a segment name in the ADS, then the allocation module assigns resources to the user by (1) allocating a memory segment $(base_{N_s}, bound_{N_s})$ for N_s, (2) placing the address descriptor $(N_s, (base_{N_s}, bound_{N_s}))$ into the ADS at some location $addr_{N_s}$, and (3) writing the capability $(read, write, N_s)$ into one of the capability registers.

The above process can be performed with either hardware or microcode support by another instruction MKSEG $(i, N_s, addr_{N_s}, read, write, (base_{N_s}, bound_{N_s}))$. MKSEG should only be executed by a processor in supervisor mode, and only when the new segment is within the bounds of physical memory.

Figure 11.3 contains three inference rules, which collectively define the operation of MKSEG. The first rule (MKSEG *user trap*) states that MKSEG traps when called from a virtual machine in user mode. The second rule (MKSEG *address trap*) states that MKSEG also traps when the base and bound address parameters of segment N_s

FIGURE 11.3 Inference rules for MKSEG instruction

MKSEG
user
trap
$$\frac{\begin{array}{c}Supervisor \text{ controls } (M \text{ says } \langle u \rangle \supset \\ VM \text{ says } \langle \text{MKSEG}(i, N_s, addr_{N_s}, read, write, (base_{N_s}, bound_{N_s}))\rangle \supset \langle trap \rangle) \\ Supervisor \text{ says } (M \text{ says } \langle u \rangle \supset \\ VM \text{ says } \langle \text{MKSEG}(i, N_s, addr_{N_s}, read, write, (base_{N_s}, bound_{N_s}))\rangle \supset \langle trap \rangle) \\ M \text{ says } \langle u \rangle \quad VM \text{ says } \langle \text{MKSEG}(i, N_s, addr_{N_s}, read, write, (base_{N_s}, bound_{N_s}))\rangle \end{array}}{\langle trap \rangle}$$

MKSEG
address
trap
$$\frac{\begin{array}{c}Supervisor \text{ controls } (base_{N_s} + bound_{N_s} \geq q \supset \\ VM \text{ says } \langle \text{MKSEG}(i, N_s, addr_{N_s}, read, write, (base_{N_s}, bound_{N_s}))\rangle \supset \langle trap \rangle) \\ Supervisor \text{ says } (base_{N_s} + bound_{N_s} \geq q \supset \\ VM \text{ says } \langle \text{MKSEG}(i, N_s, addr_{N_s}, read, write, (base_{N_s}, bound_{N_s}))\rangle \supset \langle trap \rangle) \\ base_{N_s} + bound_{N_s} \geq q \\ VM \text{ says } \langle \text{MKSEG}(i, N_s, addr_{N_s}, read, write, (base_{N_s}, bound_{N_s}))\rangle \end{array}}{\langle trap \rangle}$$

MKSEG
$$\frac{\begin{array}{c}Supervisor \text{ controls } (M \text{ says } \langle s \rangle \supset base_{N_s} + bound_{N_s} < q \supset \\ VM \text{ says } \langle \text{MKSEG}(i, N_s, addr_{N_s}, read, write, (base_{N_s}, bound_{N_s}))\rangle \supset \\ \langle \text{MKSEG}(i, N_s, addr_{N_s}, read, write, (base_{N_s}, bound_{N_s}))\rangle) \\ Supervisor \text{ says } (M \text{ says } \langle s \rangle \supset base_{N_s} + bound_{N_s} < q \supset \\ VM \text{ says } \langle \text{MKSEG}(i, N_s, addr_{N_s}, read, write, (base_{N_s}, bound_{N_s}))\rangle \supset \\ \langle \text{MKSEG}(i, N_s, addr_{N_s}, read, write, (base_{N_s}, bound_{N_s}))\rangle) \\ M \text{ says } \langle s \rangle \quad base_{N_s} + bound_{N_s} < q \\ VM \text{ says } \langle \text{MKSEG}(i, N_s, addr_{N_s}, read, write, (base_{N_s}, bound_{N_s}))\rangle \end{array}}{\langle \text{MKSEG}(i, N_s, addr_{N_s}, read, write, (base_{N_s}, bound_{N_s}))\rangle}$$

exceed the size of physical memory q. The third rule (MKSEG) captures the non-trapping behavior of the instruction: a new memory segment is formed when the virtual machine is in supervisor mode and segment N_s falls within the bounds of physical memory (i.e., $base_{N_s} + bound_{N_s} < q$).

The following example illustrates how a user's request to create a new memory segment N_s is handled.

Example 11.6

Suppose Alice wishes to create a new memory segment N_s over which she will have *read* and *write* access. Let us assume that, in this particular capability system, the capability $(read, write, N_s)$ will always be placed in CR[3]—the thinking here is that CR[1] holds the capability for Alice's program and CR[2] holds the capability for Alice's capability catalog.

The following sequence of events creates Alice's new segment:

1. Alice requests creation of a new memory segment N_s via the instruction CRE-ATESEG N_s.

2. CREATESEG N_s is trapped, and control is passed to the Supervisor control program.

3. The resource allocation module of the control program decides whether or not to grant the request. If the request is granted, then memory is allocated for the new segment N_s: that is, $(base_{N_s}, bound_{N_s})$ is set, and the control program executes the instruction MKSEG $(i, N_s, addr_{N_s}, read, write, (base_{N_s}, bound_{N_s}))$.

4. The address descriptor $(N_s, (base_{N_s}, bound_{N_s}))$ is added to the address descriptor segment ADS, and the capability $(read, write, N_s)$ is placed into CR[3].

5. Control of the processor is returned to Alice by restoring the values of the PSW (except for CR[3]). ◇

11.3.3 Dynamic Sharing

The description of catalogs presented so far support only *static* sharing: the authorizations for memory segments are determined prior to program execution. In many cases, however, it is desirable to support *dynamic sharing*, whereby users may share segments that are created during a program's execution. As we shall see, dynamic sharing of memory segments requires trusted communication of capabilities among principals.

For example, recall Example 11.6, where Alice created a new memory segment (let us call it $Shared_{Alice}$). As a result of this action, she possesses the capability

$$(read, write, Shared_{Alice}).$$

Now, suppose that Alice wishes to make this newly created memory segment accessible to Bob as well. Because users can copy capabilities, granting access to $Shared_{Alice}$ is possible by creating a set of circumstances whereby Bob can both (1) copy the capability $(read, write, Shared_{Alice})$ and (2) know and trust that $Shared_{Alice}$ is the named segment intended for him to share with Alice. There are at least two approaches for accomplishing this task. Both are based on the idea of *communication segments*, which are memory segments set up to exchange capabilities among users.

The first approach, which is illustrated in Figure 11.4, uses two communication segments for each pair of users. When Alice wishes to share a capability with Bob, she writes the capability into the segment *Alice2Bob*, to which she has read and write access. Bob—who has read access to *Alice2Bob*—can then copy the capability into one of his capability registers or to a memory location to which he has write access.

Bob will believe that the capability came from Alice if he believes that Alice is the only user (other than the trusted Supervisor) who can write into the *Alice2Bob* segment. That is, Bob must believe the following:

$$Alice2Bob \Rightarrow Alice.$$

FIGURE 11.4 Pairwise shared communications segments

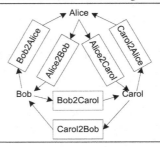

FIGURE 11.5 Formal analysis for pairwise shared communication segment

1. $Alice2Bob \Rightarrow Alice$	Trust assumption
2. $Alice$ controls $\varphi_{capability}$	Alice's jurisdiction over her capabilities
3. $Alice2Bob$ says $\varphi_{capability}$	Capability in $Alice2Bob$
4. $Alice$ says $\varphi_{capability}$	1, 3 Derived speaks for
5. $\varphi_{capability}$	2, 4 Controls

If Bob believes that the segment *Alice2Bob* is in fact under Alice's sole control, then the analysis of the situation from Bob's perspective can be summarized as in Figure 11.5, where $\varphi_{capability}$ is the expression that represents the capability Alice passed to Bob.

The downside to this approach is that it is relatively expensive in terms of communication segments: if there are N users, then each user requires $N - 1$ communication segments (i.e., one for each other user), resulting in a total of $N \times (N - 1)$ communication segments.

A more economical approach is illustrated in Figure 11.6. This approach uses a single communication segment for each user, resulting in a need for only N communication segments for N users. Each user's communication segment serves as a mailbox: when users wish to send capabilities to other users, they ask the Supervisor to place the capabilities in the recipient's mailbox on their behalf. When doing so, the Supervisor indicates the sender of each capability.

To understand the idea behind this approach, suppose that Alice sends a capability $(read, write, Shared_{Alice})$ to Bob via the Supervisor: the Supervisor places something like $(Alice, (read, write, Shared_{Alice}))$ into Bob's mailbox *ForBob*. From Bob's perspective, this state of affairs can be expressed in the logic as follows, where $\varphi_{capability}$ is the expression that represents the passed capability:

$$ForBob \mid Alice \text{ says } \varphi_{capability}.$$

That is, Bob's mailbox *ForBob* asserts that Alice sent the capability. Because the Supervisor is in control of Bob's mailbox, Bob believes that anything in his mailbox

FIGURE 11.6 Mailbox segments

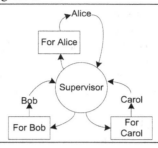

FIGURE 11.7 Formal analysis for mailbox communication segment

1. $Supervisor \mid Alice \Rightarrow Alice$	Trust assumption
2. $Alice$ controls $\varphi_{capability}$	Alice's jurisdiction over her capabilities
3. $ForBob \mid Alice$ says $\varphi_{capability}$	Capability in Bob's mailbox
4. $ForBob \Rightarrow Supervisor$	Trust assumption
5. $Alice \Rightarrow Alice$	Idempotency of $\Rightarrow$
6. $ForBob \mid Alice \Rightarrow Supervisor \mid Alice$	4, 5 Monotonicity of $\Rightarrow$
7. $Supervisor \mid Alice$ says $\varphi_{capability}$	6, 3 Derived Speaks For
8. $Alice$ says $\varphi_{capability}$	1, 7 Derived speaks for
9. $\varphi_{capability}$	2, 8 Controls

is placed there by the Supervisor:

$$ForBob \Rightarrow Supervisor.$$

From the idempotency and monotonicity of $\Rightarrow$, Bob can conclude that

$$ForBob \mid Alice \Rightarrow Supervisor \mid Alice.$$

Bob relies upon the trust assumption that the Supervisor correctly authenticates messages from each user (in this case, Alice). This assumption is expressed as

$$Supervisor \mid Alice \Rightarrow Alice.$$

The complete formal justification for Bob's interpretation of the situation appears in Figure 11.7. This justification depends upon two essential trust assumptions that Bob must make: (1) that only the Supervisor can place items in the mailbox segments, and (2) that the Supervisor is trustworthy.

11.3.4 Revocation of Capabilities

As we have seen, capability systems allow users to load, store, and share capabilities. However, it is sometimes necessary to *revoke* previously granted privileges. As we shall see, capability revocation can be difficult, unless restrictions are imposed on how capabilities are stored or shared.

For example, consider what happens when Alice sends Bob a capability to access one of her segments. After receiving the capability, Bob can load it into one of his capability registers and then freely store it in any location in memory that he can access. In particular, he can store it in an arbitrary number of arbitrary locations— even the Supervisor will not necessarily know how many copies exist and where they are located.

If Alice later decides to revoke Bob's access to her segment, then the system must be able to invalidate all of Bob's copies of the capability. To accomplish this task, either (1) the Supervisor must perform an exhaustive search of all memory accessible to Bob, or (2) Alice must move the contents of the segment she shared with Bob to a new segment, destroy the original segment, and issue capabilities to the new one. Both options are unattractive from an efficiency perspective.

To reduce the task of locating revoked capabilities, we can institute a mandatory access-control policy that restricts capability storing to a relatively small number of known locations. For example, each user might be restricted to having just one segment for storing capabilities. If the policy is enforced without exception, then searching for revoked capabilities is greatly simplified: only a small number of locations must be checked.

Another approach is to use indirect references to intermediate objects. For example, if Alice wishes to grant Bob access to segment A, she creates a new object B that points to A, and gives Bob a capability to access B. She follows a similar approach for each principal to whom she wishes to grant access to A; in each case, she creates a different intermediate object. If Alice wishes to revoke Bob's capability to access A, she simply removes B, thus destroying Bob's link to A. All other principals with capabilities to access A still retain their privileges.

A third approach is to limit which capabilities can be copied. The simplest way to accomplish this task is to include a *copy bit* with each capability. When a user program attempts to store a capability from the capability register into memory, the capability's copy bit is checked. If the copy bit is on, then the attempt succeeds and the capability is stored; if the copy bit is off, then the attempt is trapped and blocked. This type of use of a copy bit amounts to an all-or-nothing approach: more sophisticated schemes can be developed to permit a capability to be copied a specific number of times.

Exercise 11.3.1   *Figure 11.2 illustrated the use of descriptors as capabilities while omitting the use of address descriptors for simplicity. Redraw the figure explicitly showing the application of address descriptors.*

Exercise 11.3.2   *Consider the following specifications for a small system:*

- *Ali and Boris run separate programs to which only they as program owners have access.*

- *Ali trusts Boris to be careful about not overwriting her data. She wishes to share data with Boris that she creates, and she needs to access data that Boris creates for her.*

- *Ali has mistakenly overwritten Boris's data in the past, so he is more careful about granting write access to Ali. He needs to share data that he creates for her, and he needs to see data that Ali creates for him.*

- *Ali has private data that only she should see.*

- *Ali has data that she needs to share only with Clancy.*

- *Ali, Boris, and Clancy need to read a common database under the control of the Supervisor.*

Devise a collection of capabilities that satisfy the above, and distribute the capabilities into catalogs for Ali, Boris, and Clancy. Draw a diagram of physical memory (similar to Figure 11.2) illustrating the contents of the catalogs and referenced memory segments. You may omit address descriptors.

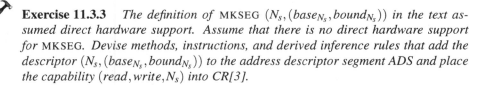

Exercise 11.3.3 *The definition of* MKSEG $(N_s, (base_{N_s}, bound_{N_s}))$ *in the text assumed direct hardware support. Assume that there is no direct hardware support for* MKSEG. *Devise methods, instructions, and derived inference rules that add the descriptor* $(N_s, (base_{N_s}, bound_{N_s}))$ *to the address descriptor segment ADS and place the capability* $(read, write, N_s)$ *into CR[3].*

11.4 Summary

In this chapter, we introduced capability systems, which provide a flexible scheme that supports both segment addressing and memory protection. In capability systems, descriptors (i.e., protected physical addresses) provide the means for segment addressing, while capabilities (i.e., unforgeable tickets that authorize access to memory) provide for memory protection. Capability systems employ tagged architectures to distinguish capabilities from other data, thereby safely allowing user programs the flexibility to load, store, and share authorized capability values.

Although capabilities are easy to issue and to distribute, they can be challenging to revoke. Typical revocation solutions impose some limitations on capabilities, either in terms of where they may be stored, whether they may be copied, or how they may be shared with other users.

Figure 11.8 summarizes the learning outcomes for this chapter.

11.5   Further Reading

In their classic paper (Saltzer and Schroeder, 1975), Saltzer and Schroeder provide a thorough overview of the underlying concepts of capabilities and descriptors. They also describe access-control list (ACL) systems as an alternative to capability systems: instead of distributing capabilities to principals, each protected object has its own access controller. Each access controller has the form of an address descriptor with an access-control list that enumerates principals and their access rights on that object.

The use of capabilities is not limited to granting access rights to memory segments. If address descriptors are used for other objects—such as communications channels, printers, I/O devices, and applications in general—then capabilities can be used for the relevant operations on those objects. This more extensive use of capabilities is discussed in Levy's book (Levy, 1984), which provides details of thirteen experimental and commercial computer systems that use descriptors and capabilities.

FIGURE 11.8 Learning outcomes for Chapter 11

After completing this chapter, you should be able to achieve the following learning
outcomes at several levels of knowledge:

Comprehension

- When given a diagram of address descriptors and capabilities, be able to interpret or describe how objects are identified and physically addressed, as well as how operations on objects are authorized.

Application

- When given the protection goals of a system, apply the concepts of capabilities and address descriptors to devise protection policies and mechanisms.

Analysis

- When given an access request, determine if the capabilities at hand are sufficient to grant access.

Synthesis

- When given the protections goals of a system, design appropriate policies, architectures, instructions, and mechanisms for implementing address descriptors and capabilities.
- When given descriptions of policies, architectures, instructions, and mechanisms, create formal descriptions of each.

Evaluation

- When given formal descriptions of policies, architectures, instructions, and mechanisms, express access-control decisions as formally derived theorems in the access-control logic.

Chapter 12

Access Control Using Lists and Rings

In Chapter 11, we introduced capability systems, which separate the notions of addressing and protection by distinguishing address descriptors from capabilities. Each virtual machine associated with a process was given a catalog of capabilities that identified the segments the virtual machine could access as well as the associated access rights on those segments. The alternative to capabilities is access-control lists (ACLs), which grant privileges to principals by name.

In this chapter, we describe how to use ACLs to provide discretionary access control for memory segments. When a principal requests access to a segment, the segment's ACL is checked to determine whether the principal's request is allowed. The advantage of using ACLs is that removing or changing access to a resource does not entail searching through each and every memory segment for a capability. As we will see, however, the price for adding access-control lists to segment protection is another layer of indirection.

We also introduce *protection rings*, which support mandatory access control for memory segments. Protection rings are a generalization of the *user* and *supervisor* modes, which provides a finer-grained approach to protecting system integrity. Ring-based access control is a *layered* approach to mandatory access control: processes operating in the innermost rings have the greatest access, and data stored in the innermost rings are afforded the greatest protection. This finer-grained approach to access control provides greater flexibility and specificity on how data and processes are accessed and by whom.

12.1   Generalized Addresses

Figure 12.1 illustrates a sample user's conceptual view of memory that contains four segments: each segment has a name, an associated access-control list, and data contents. From the user's point of view, the segments do not have specific addresses associated with them. Instead, the user refers to the given segments and their contents through the use of symbolic names, allowing her to write programs that are independent of the segments' physical locations in memory. For example, the program may have a data segment named *AliceInformation* from which it attempts to

FIGURE 12.1 User view of memory

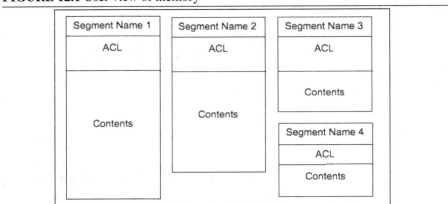

extract the contents of the symbolic location *phoneNumber*.

Of course, the actual layout of physical memory is quite different, and requests to access memory ultimately must be converted into physical addresses. The first step in the conversion process occurs when the program is linked. The linker translates the location-within-a-segment reference into a *generalized address* (s, i), where s and i are both natural numbers. The value s serves to identify the particular memory segment, while the value i identifies a particular location within that segment. Conceptually, the generalized address (s, i) refers to location i within the segment numbered s. The details of the linker's translation process are beyond the scope of this text. Instead, in this section and the next, we turn to the details of how the generalized address (s, i) is converted into a physical address in memory.

As we saw in Chapter 11, address descriptors—which give the starting location and the size of segments—are stored in a catalog called the *address descriptor segment* (ADS). Each virtual machine has a *descriptor base register* (DBR) that points to the *base* location of the ADS and contains the *bound* of the ADS.

The address descriptor for a segment numbered s is stored in the sth location of the ADS. Thus, for example, if the linker associates the natural number K with the symbolic segment name N_s, then the address descriptor for N_s is stored in location K of the ADS. Furthermore, the value K is stored in one of two registers, depending on the contents of the segment:[1] (1) the procedure base register, if the segment is a procedure segment (i.e., contains instructions only), or (2) the temporary base register, if the segment contains data.

Figure 12.2 illustrates how the relevant registers of a virtual machine are used to determine the location of segment N_s's address descriptor. The DBR contains the

---

[1]A common design discipline is to separate executable instructions from alterable data by keeping them in separate segments. This approach supports *pure procedures* (i.e., executable code kept separate from writable data), which reduce the likelihood of mistakenly executing data as instructions. The mechanisms we describe in this chapter support pure procedures.

FIGURE 12.2 Address formation for address descriptor

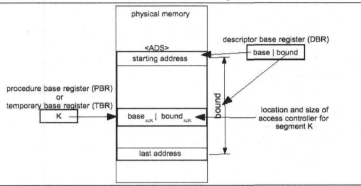

address descriptor for the ADS. Depending upon whether N_s is a procedure or data segment, either the procedure base register (PBR) or temporary base register (TBR) contains the location of N_s's address descriptor, *relative* to the base address of the ADS. This value is the natural number that the linker associated with N_s (i.e., K in our example). The physical address of N_s's address descriptor is therefore

$$DBR.base + K,$$

provided that $K < DBR.bound$ and $DBR.base + K < q$, where q is the size of physical memory. That is, the value K must be within bounds of both the ADS and physical memory.

Throughout the remainder of this chapter, we will refer to segments and their locations via their linker-associated numbers, rather than their symbolic names.

12.2   Segment Access Controllers

In the capability systems of Chapter 11, address descriptors to generic memory segments were $(base, bound)$ values that corresponded directly to that segment's starting address and its number of locations in physical memory. For systems that use access-control lists to protect memory segments, address descriptors instead point to the *access-controller segment* that guards the named memory segment.

Access controllers have two parts: (1) the $(base, bound)$ pair that points to the segment being guarded, and (2) a list of authorized principal identifiers paired with their access rights to the guarded memory segment. Whenever a processor running a process with a particular principal identifier wishes to access a specific memory segment, the access controller for that segment is consulted to determine whether the principal identifier is listed with the requested access right. If so, then the operation is permitted; otherwise, the request is trapped.

FIGURE 12.3 Segment access controller

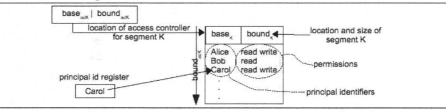

FIGURE 12.4 Data or instruction segment

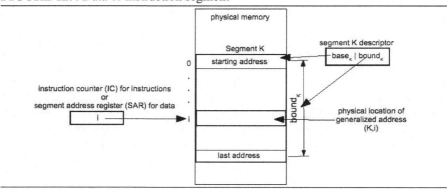

Figure 12.3 illustrates an access controller for a memory segment K. The first location of the access controller contains the address descriptor $(base_K, bound_K)$, which points to the block of addresses in physical memory that define the guarded memory segment K. The remaining locations contain the ACL entries, which consist of principal identifiers and their associated permissions. For example, if the principal identifier register contains the principal identifier Carol, then both *read* and *write* access to the protected memory segment is permitted.

Figure 12.4 shows the segment K itself. The contents of the instruction counter IC (if K is a procedure segment) or the segment address register SAR (if K is a data segment) indicates the specific location within K to be accessed. Thus, for example, an attempt to access generalized address (K, ℓ) would have ℓ as the value of the IC or SAR.

Figure 12.5 summarizes the four steps of converting a generalized address (s, i) into an actual location in physical memory:

1. The address descriptor for the ADS assigned to the processor is located in the descriptor base register (DBR); its value is $(base_1, bound_1)$.

2. The address descriptor for s's access controller is located in address s of the ADS (i.e., in physical address $base_1 + s$). Its value is $(base_2, bound_2)$, which points to the access controller that guards segment s.

FIGURE 12.5 Generalized address formation and access control

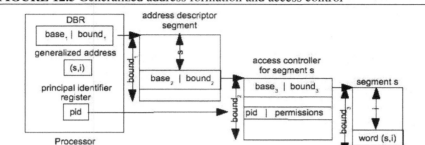

3. Location 0 of the access controller for segment s (i.e., physical location $base_2$) contains the address-descriptor value ($base_3, bound_3$), which points to the actual segment s. The remaining locations of the access controller contain the ACL entries for principals who have access rights to segment s.

4. Location i within the segment s can be found at physical address $base_3 + i$.

Exercise 12.2.1 *Suppose George creates a data segment that he wishes to share with Karen. George as the creator of the segment has read and write permission; he wishes Karen to have read permission only.*

Draw a diagram similar to Figure 12.5 that contains the explicit values for the registers in Karen's processor, the address descriptors, and the access-control list entries to describe the following situation:

- *The generalized address for the relevant location within the shared segment is* (5, 12).

- *Karen's address descriptor segment is located in physical addresses 100 through 199.*

- *The access controller for the shared segment is located in physical addresses 200 through 250.*

- *The shared segment is located in physical addresses 300 through 400.*

12.3 ACL-Based Access Policy for Memory Accesses

In the previous section, we fully described the process for calculating a physical address from a generalized one. We now introduce a simple virtual machine (VM) and virtual machine monitor (VMM) that supports generalized addresses and uses ACLs to control memory accesses.

FIGURE 12.6 Virtual machine and virtual machine monitor for ACL system

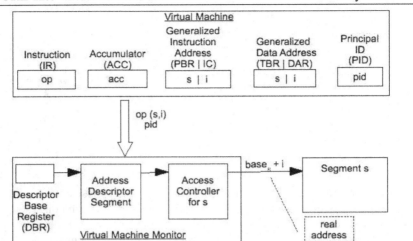

Figure 12.6 shows a partitioning of registers and segments that support VM and VMM functions. The VM has the following five registers: (1) the instruction register (IR); (2) the accumulator (ACC); (3) the generalized instruction address, which comprises the procedure base register (PBR) and instruction counter (IC); (4) the generalized data address, which comprises the temporary base register (TBR) and data address register (DAR); and (5) the principal ID register (PID).

The VMM has one register: the descriptor base register (DBR), which points to the catalog of address descriptors in the ADS available to the VM. The ADS and access controller segment for segment s are also used by the VMM to evaluate instruction requests made by the VM.

Based on this structure, we develop the access-control policy for a generic instruction OP $[s:i]$, which involves the operation OP on the generalized address (s,i). As we will see, three memory fetches are required. For each memory fetch, we identify both the relevant address descriptor and the required mandatory access-control (MAC) condition:

1. *Look up the location of the ADS*

   As we saw in the previous section, the segment parameters for the ADS are found in the *base* and *bound* fields of the DBR:

   $$base_1 = DBR.base,$$
   $$bound_1 = DBR.bound.$$

   The necessary MAC conditions are that the address value $base_1 + s$ must be within the limits of physical memory and that s is within the segment boundary of the ADS:

   $$(base_1 + s < q) \wedge (s < bound_1).$$

2. *Look up the location of the access-controller segment*

The parameters for the access-controller segment are found in the *base* and *bound* fields of the sth location of the ADS segment:

$$base_2 = PM[base_1 + s].base,$$
$$bound_2 = PM[base_1 + s].bound.$$

We assume that, within the access-controller segment for s, $index_{id}$ gives the location of the permissions associated with id. The MAC address conditions therefore check to determine whether $base_2 + index_{id}$ and $index_{id}$ are within the bounds of physical memory and of the access-controller segment, respectively:

$$(base_2 + index_{id} < q) \land (index_{id} < bound_2).$$

In addition to the MAC conditions are the discretionary access control conditions. In this case, the permission field corresponding to OP is checked to determine whether the principal requesting to perform OP has permission to do so:

$$PM[base_2 + index_{id}].op \text{ says } \langle OP \rangle.$$

For example, when OP corresponds to a memory-write operation, the write permission field of $PM[base_2 + index_{id}]$ (i.e., $PM[base_2 + index_{id}].write$) must be checked.

3. *Look up the generalized address* (s, i)

The parameters for segment s are given by the following descriptor values:

$$base_3 = PM[base_2].base,$$
$$bound_3 = PM[base_2].bound.$$

The MAC conditions are as expected, namely that $base_3 + i$ must be within the limits of physical memory and i must be within segment boundaries:

$$(base_3 + i < q) \land (i < bound_3).$$

We can combine these three sets of requirements to form the access-control policy for approving execution of the operation OP $[s : i]$. The access-control policy consists of the typical three parts:

1. The state of the machine, as given by the contents of IR, DBR, PID, and the contents of physical memory PM

2. Discretionary access permission, as indicated by the statement

$$PM[base_2 + index_{id}].op \text{ says } \langle OP \rangle.$$

3. The absence of any addressing problems, as indicated by the following three conditions:

$$(base_1 + s < q) \wedge (s < bound_1),$$
$$(base_2 + index_{id} < q) \wedge (index_{id} < bound_2),$$
$$(base_3 + i < q) \wedge (i < bound_3).$$

The entire policy can be expressed in the logic as follows:

$$IR \text{ says } \langle \text{OP}[s:i] \rangle \supset (DBR \text{ says } \langle (base_1, bound_1) \rangle) \supset (PID \text{ says } \langle index_{id} \rangle) \supset$$
$$(PM[base_2 + index_{id}].op \text{ says } \langle \text{OP} \rangle) \supset ((base_1 + s < q) \wedge (s < bound_1)) \supset$$
$$((base_2 + index_{id} < q) \wedge (index_{id} < bound_2)) \supset ((base_3 + i < q) \wedge (i < bound_3)) \supset$$
$$(IR \text{ controls } \langle \text{OP}[s:i] \rangle)$$

$$\frac{
\begin{array}{c}
IR \text{ says } \langle \text{OP}[s:i] \rangle \qquad DBR \text{ says } \langle (base_1, bound_1) \rangle \qquad PID \text{ says } \langle index_{id} \rangle \\[4pt]
PM[base_2 + index_{id}].op \text{ says } \langle \text{OP} \rangle \qquad (base_1 + s < q) \wedge (s < bound_1) \\[4pt]
(base_2 + index_{id} < q) \wedge (index_{id} < bound_2) \qquad (base_3 + i < q) \wedge (i < bound_3)
\end{array}
}{\langle \text{OP}[s:i] \rangle}$$

The following example shows how this general access-control policy can be instantiated for a specific operation on a given generalized address.

Example 12.1

Consider a request to execute the operation $\text{LDA}[s:i]$, which loads the accumulator ACC with the contents of generalized address (s,i). The derivable inference rule that captures the conditions under which the request should be granted is as follows:

$$IR \text{ says } \langle \text{LDA}[s:i] \rangle \supset (DBR \text{ says } \langle (base_1, bound_1) \rangle) \supset (PID \text{ says } \langle index_{id} \rangle) \supset$$
$$(PM[base_2 + index_{id}].read \text{ says } \langle \text{LDA} \rangle) \supset ((base_1 + s < q) \wedge (s < bound_1)) \supset$$
$$((base_2 + index_{id} < q) \wedge (index_{id} < bound_2)) \supset ((base_3 + i < q) \wedge (i < bound_3)) \supset$$
$$(IR \text{ controls } \langle \text{LDA}[s:i] \rangle)$$

$$\frac{
\begin{array}{c}
IR \text{ says } \langle \text{LDA}[s:i] \rangle \qquad DBR \text{ says } \langle (base_1, bound_1) \rangle \qquad PID \text{ says } \langle index_{id} \rangle \\[4pt]
PM[base_2 + index_{id}].read \text{ says } \langle \text{LDA} \rangle \qquad (base_1 + s < q) \wedge (s < bound_1) \\[4pt]
(base_2 + index_{id} < q) \wedge (index_{id} < bound_2) \qquad (base_3 + i < q) \wedge (i < bound_3)
\end{array}
}{\langle \text{LDA}[s:i] \rangle} \qquad \diamond$$

Exercise 12.3.1 *Prove the soundness of the behavioral theorem of Example 12.1.*

Exercise 12.3.2 *Devise and prove sound the access-control policy for* STO $[s:i]$ *(i.e., storing the contents of generalized address (s,i) into the accumulator ACC).*

FIGURE 12.7 Protection rings

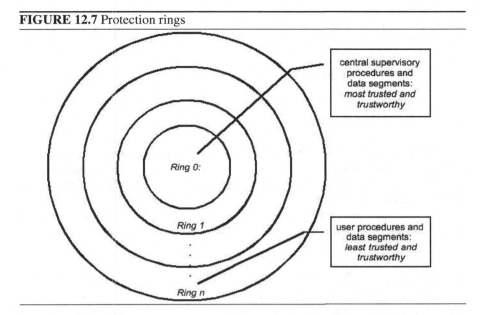

12.4   Ring-Based Access Control

Protection rings are a means to provide *layered protection*: the most trusted and trustworthy procedures and data segments are in the innermost rings, while less trusted and trustworthy processes and data are in the outermost rings.

Figure 12.7 illustrates the notions behind protection rings. The innermost ring is *ring 0*: it lies at the center of concentric rings of *privilege*. The most trusted (and, one hopes, most trustworthy) supervisory procedures and data segments are in ring 0: ring-0 procedures have the greatest access privileges, and ring-0 data have the most protection. Subsequent rings are labeled 1 through *n*, with each successive ring having fewer access rights than the ring that precedes it. User processes and data, located in the outermost rings, have relatively few access privileges and are accessible by more privileged processes.

Protection rings were introduced in the Multics operating system (Schroeder and Saltzer, 1972). Although Multics segments were guarded by both rings and ACLs, neither ACLs or capabilities are necessary for ring-based protection. Instead, associated with each segment are the following permission-related components: privilege bits to indicate which types of access (i.e., *read*, *write*, or *execute*) are permitted on the segment;[2] a *ring bracket*, specified by three *ring numbers* (r_1, r_2, r_3); and (for

---

[2]Note that, if the system does use ACLs or capabilities, then these privilege bits are unnecessary. In such cases, read/write/execute access for a given segment is determined on a principal-by-principal basis. In

procedure segments) an integer field *gate* that indicates its number of call gates. We describe the purpose of the ring-bracket and *gate* fields in the following subsections.

12.4.1 Access Brackets

Each segment's ring bracket (r_1, r_2, r_3) must satisfy the following condition:

$$r_1 \leq r_2 \leq r_3.$$

Collectively, the three ring numbers define two additional brackets: an *access bracket* (which we describe here) and a *call bracket* (which we defer to Subsection 12.4.2). Intuitively, a segment's access and call brackets constrain the ring levels from which processes can access that segment.

Consider a segment with ring bracket (r_1, r_2, r_3). We say that ring r is within the target segment's *access bracket* if the following condition holds:

$$r_1 \leq r \leq r_2.$$

That is, ring r must be within the inclusive bounds set by r_1 and r_2. We say that ring r is *below* the segment's access bracket if $r < r_1$.

Being within or below a segment's access bracket is a necessary but insufficient condition for being granted read, write, or execute access to that segment. The following mandatory access-control policy applies to any process in ring r that attempts to access a segment s having ring bracket (r_1, r_2, r_3):

- **Read access** is granted if and only if s has read access turned on and $r \leq r_2$.

- **Execute access** is granted if and only if s has execute access turned on and $r \leq r_2$.

- **Write access** is granted if and only if s has write access turned on and one of the following conditions holds: (1) s is a procedure segment and $r \leq r_2$, or (2) s is a data segment and $r \leq r_1$.

Thus, read and execute access are granted to any processes within or below a target segment's access bracket, provided that the segment has the corresponding access turned on. The policy for write access to procedure segments is the same. However, only processes at more privileged ring levels are allowed to alter a data segment's contents: write access to data segments is limited to processes operating at the lower bound of (or below) the segment's access bracket, and only when the segment has write access turned on.

The following example illustrates how the ring-based access-control policy applies to both procedure and data segments.

---

the rest of this chapter, we use the terminology "access turned on" to indicate either that the appropriate privilege bit is set (for systems without ACLs and capabilities) or that the particular principal making the request possesses the appropriate permission for that segment.

Example 12.2

Consider three processes Q_1, Q_4, Q_6, which are executing in rings 1, 4, and 6, respectively. Furthermore, let *PS* and *DS* both be segments with ring bracket $(2, 5, 8)$ and with read, write, and execute access turned on. Assume that *PS* is a procedure segment and that *DS* is a data segment.

The following table shows the results of attempts by the processes to access the two segments under the ring-based access policy:

Access type	Access to PS			Access to DS		
	Q_1	Q_4	Q_6	Q_1	Q_4	Q_6
Read	Granted	Granted	Denied	Granted	Granted	Denied
Execute	Granted	Granted	Denied	Granted	Granted	Denied
Write	Granted	Granted	Denied	Granted	Denied	Denied

This table highlights two important points. First, the ring requirements prevent Q_6 from accessing either segment, despite that read, write, and execute access are turned on for both segments: Q_6 is neither within nor below the segments' access bracket. Second, Q_4 is granted write access to the procedure segment *PS* but not to the data segment *DS*: despite being within the appropriate access bracket, Q_4's ring level is too high to write to the data segment. ◊

12.4.2 Call Brackets

In addition to an access bracket, segments may also have a call bracket. The purpose of a call bracket is to allow procedure segments to be called under controlled conditions by processes at ring levels above the segment's access bracket. This mechanism allows less trusted user processes to call more trusted (i.e., at a lower ring level) system processes.

Let s be a segment with ring bracket (r_1, r_2, r_3). We say that a ring r is within s's *call bracket* if the following condition holds:

$$r_2 + 1 \leq r \leq r_3.$$

That is, r must be strictly greater than r_2 and less than or equal to r_3. Thus, in the case where $r_2 = r_3$, the segment has no call bracket, because there is no r such that $r_2 + 1 \leq r \leq r_2$.

Conceptually, a procedure segment s has a list of n entry points—known as *call gates*—associated with it. As illustrated in Figure 12.8, these call gates appear at the beginning of s and are pointers to locations within the segment s. The purpose of call gates is to limit the available entry points for processes that might be within s's call bracket but outside of s's access bracket. The pointers ensure that s cannot be executed at some incorrect, inappropriate, or arbitrary location.

Recall that each procedure segment has a permission field named *gate*, which contains the number of call gates for s. A process in the calling bracket that wishes

FIGURE 12.8 Call gates

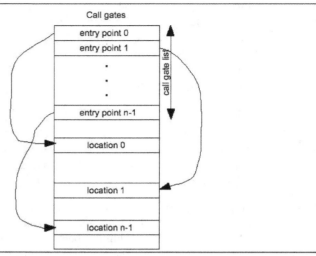

to call the ith location in s requests that the operation CALL $[s : i]$ be executed. If $i \geq gate$, then the calling process is attempting to enter s at an unauthorized point and execute permission is denied. Otherwise, if $i < gate$, then the procedure call is within the stated gate list, and permission to execute the CALL $[s : i]$ instruction is granted, provided other necessary conditions related to s's call bracket and execute permissions are met.

Suppose a process running in ring r requests that the operation CALL $[s : i]$ be executed on a segment s that has ring bracket (r_1, r_2, r_3). The following mandatory access-control policy applies:

- CALL $[s : i]$ **access** is granted if and only if s has execute access turned on and one of the following situations holds: (1) r is below or within s's access bracket, or (2) s is a procedure segment, r is within s's calling bracket, and $i < gate$.

Note that, for rings within or below a segment's access bracket, CALL access corresponds exactly to the standard execute access described in the previous section.

The following example illustrates how the ring-based access-control policy applies to CALL requests.

Example 12.3

Consider four processes Q_1, Q_4, Q_6, Q_{10}, which are executing in rings 1, 4, 6, and 10, respectively. Furthermore, let PS_3, PS_9, and DS all be segments with ring bracket $(2, 5, 8)$ and with read, write, and execute access turned on. Assume that DS is a data segment; PS_3 and PS_9 are procedure segments with gate values of 3 and 9, respectively.

The following table shows the results of attempts by the processes to execute the CALL $[s : 7]$ instruction on the various segments s:

Segment s	Q_1	Q_4	Q_6	Q_{10}
PS_3	Granted	Granted	Denied	Denied
PS_9	Granted	Granted	Granted	Denied
DS	Granted	Granted	Denied	Denied

This table highlights several important aspects of how ring protection works in the context of call brackets. First, CALL access reverts to standard execute access for processes operating within or below a segment's access bracket: for this reason, all of Q_1's and Q_4's attempts are granted. Second, a process operating in a ring level higher than a segment's call bracket is ineligible to use the CALL instruction: for this reason, all requests by Q_{10} are denied. Finally, a process operating within a specific call bracket can call only procedure segments, and only at locations i permitted by the segment's gate value: for this reason, Q_6's attempts to access the seventh location of data segment DS and of procedure segment PS_3 are denied.

Finally, all attempts to execute CALL $[PS_2 : 7]$ are denied, because the requested entry point 7 exceeds the gate value 2. ◇

The following series of exercises is inspired by exercises in (Organick, 1972).

Exercise 12.4.1 *For each of the following situations, give the 3-tuple* (r_1, r_2, r_3) *that defines the requested access and call brackets.*

a. *A single ring of access, r.*

b. *An access bracket* (k, l)*, but no call bracket.*

c. *An access bracket* (k, l) *and a call bracket* $(l + 1, m)$*.*

d. *A single ring of access r and a call bracket* $(r + 1, m)$*.*

Exercise 12.4.2 *For each of the following situations, give the set of rings r from which read, write, and execute access to the* data *segment s would be granted.*

a. *s has ring bracket* $(0, 63, 63)$*, with read and execute access turned on.*

b. *s has ring bracket* $(0, 1, 63)$*, with read and execute access turned on.*

c. *s has ring bracket* $(1, 1, 63)$*, with read and execute access turned on.*

d. *s has ring bracket* $(0, 0, 1)$*, with read and execute access turned on.*

e. *s has ring bracket* $(48, 48, 48)$*, with read and write access turned on.*

f. *s has ring bracket* $(5, 48, 48)$*, with read and write access turned on.*

Exercise 12.4.3   *For each of the following situations, give the set of rings r from which read, write, and execute access to the* procedure *segment s would be granted.*

  a. *s has ring bracket* $(0,1,63)$, *with read and execute access turned on.*

  b. *s has ring bracket* $(1,1,63)$, *with read and execute access turned on.*

  c. *s has ring bracket* $(48,48,48)$, *with read and write access turned on.*

  d. *s has ring bracket* $(5,48,48)$, *with read and write access turned on.*

Exercise 12.4.4   *For each of the following situations, give the set of rings r and set of values i for which* CALL $[s:i]$ *access to the segment s would be granted.*

  a. *s is a data segment with ring bracket* $(0,1,63)$ *and read and execute access turned on.*

  b. *s is a procedure segment with ring bracket* $(0,1,63)$, *gate value 5, and read and execute access turned on.*

  c. *s is a procedure segment with ring bracket* $(0,0,1)$, *gate value 5, and read and execute access turned on.*

  d. *s is a procedure segment with ring bracket* $(0,0,1)$, *gate value 5, and read and write access turned on.*

12.5   Summary

In this chapter, we introduced both access-control list (ACL) systems and ring-based access control, which extend the memory-protection mechanisms we saw in previous chapters. These schemes can be used together (as in the Multics operating system) or separately. In ACL systems, access-controller segments specify the location of specific memory segments, as well as the access capabilities for individual principals on that segment. ACL systems more easily support permission revocation than capability systems, but at the cost of an additional level of indirection. Protection rings provide a *layered* protection approach that offers both flexibility and specificity on how data and processes are accessed. Processes in the innermost rings are the most trusted processes and have the greatest access privileges. Processes in the outer rings are typically less trusted user processes with fewer privileges.

Both segmentation and protection rings were first developed for use in the 1960s for mainframe computing systems such as Multics. When mainframes and mini-computers gave way to personal computers, protection schemes such as rings and segmentation were dropped for economic reasons. At the time, personal computers were physically isolated machines with single users, which obviated the need to isolate one user's processes from those of other users. The additional cost of

---

FIGURE 12.9 Learning outcomes for Chapter 12

After completing this chapter, you should be able to achieve the following learning outcomes at several levels of knowledge:

Comprehension

- When given an address descriptor, access controller with ACL entries, and ring brackets for a segment, determine when access to a target segment is granted or denied.

Application

- When given the protection goals of a system, apply the concepts of access-control lists and ring brackets to devise protection policies and mechanisms.

Analysis

- When given an access request, determine if the permissions at hand are sufficient to grant access.

Synthesis

- When given descriptions of policies, architectures, instructions, and mechanisms, create formal descriptions of each.

Evaluation

- When given formal descriptions of policies, architectures, instructions, and mechanisms, express access-control decisions as formally derived theorems in the access-control logic.

---

having hardware dedicated to security and isolation seemed impractical. No one anticipated the global internetworking and unprecedented access and vulnerability the Internet would bring. Decades later, security and access control are now essential, and support for segmentation and protection rings is now routinely included in microprocessors.

Figure 12.9 summarizes the learning outcomes for this chapter.

12.6 Further Reading

The ideas behind the use of access-control lists and rings to control access to segments were developed in the 1960s and 1970s on mainframe computer systems such as Multics. Numerous papers chart the development of generalized addressing (Daley and Dennis, 1968), virtualized memory (Bensoussan et al., 1972), access-control lists (Saltzer and Schroeder, 1975), and rings (Schroeder and Saltzer, 1972; Organick, 1972).

Part IV

Access Policies

Chapter 13

Confidentiality and Integrity Policies

In Chapter 5, we introduced *military security policies*, which are primarily concerned with controlling the disclosure of classified information. We also introduced *commercial security policies*, which focus on preserving the integrity (e.g., quality or trustworthiness) of information. In both cases, the policies depend on assigning classification levels—either security levels or integrity levels, as appropriate—to both subjects and objects; access-control decisions are then based in part on the relationships among those levels.

In this chapter, we expand on those ideas to support more finely tuned confidentiality and integrity policies. The first step is to introduce a somewhat richer notion of confidentiality and integrity levels, which is based on *categories* of information in addition to the *classification* of information. As we will see, the underlying Kripke semantics introduced in Chapter 5 also work for these richer levels. We then recap both the Bell–La Padula model for confidentiality and Biba's strict-integrity model, highlighting how they apply to the more refined notions of confidentiality and integrity levels. We also address how Biba's notion of strict integrity applies to invocation access requests, a topic previously deferred. Finally, we introduce Lipner's integrity model, which applies a combination of the Bell–La Padula and Biba models to develop an integrity policy for production systems. His approach serves as a useful case study for designers and verifiers who must develop their own policies to meet specific design requirements.

13.1 Classifications and Categories

So far, we have considered only simple confidentiality and integrity levels. It is also possible to construct compound levels for both confidentiality and integrity by combining a *classification level* (as we saw in Chapter 5) with a set of *categories* to which it applies. Specifically, each compound level is a pair (L, C), where L is a classification level and $C \subseteq Cat$ is a (possibly empty) set of categories drawn from the set *Cat*.

As we saw in Chapter 5, the classification levels used for confidentiality or integrity are related to one another by a partial order $\leq$. Recall that partial orders are binary relations that are reflexive, transitive, and anti-symmetric. Therefore, the classification-level relation $\leq$ must satisfy the following properties:

- Reflexivity: For all classification levels L, $L \leq L$.

- Transitivity: For all classification levels L_1, L_2, and L_3, if $L_1 \leq L_2$ and $L_2 \leq L_3$, then $L_1 \leq L_3$.

- Anti-symmetry: For all classification levels L_1 and L_2, if $L_1 \leq L_2$ and $L_2 \leq L_1$, then $L_1 = L_2$ (i.e., no cycles exist in the relation $\leq$).

The sets of categories are also related to one another by a partial order, namely the subset relation $\subseteq$. It is therefore possible to define a partial order *dom* over compound levels (L, C) as follows:

$$(L_1, C_1) \; dom \; (L_2, C_2) \text{ if and only if } (L_2 \leq L_1) \; and \; C_2 \subseteq C_1.$$

That is, the compound level (L_1, C_1) dominates (L_2, C_2) if and only L_1 and C_1 are each at least as high as L_2 and C_2, respectively. The proof that *dom* is indeed a partial order is left as an exercise.

The following two examples provide concrete illustrations of compound levels and how the *dom* relation works.

Example 13.1

Consider the set of classification levels $L = \{\text{HI}, \text{LO}\}$, with the partial order $\leq$ defined over L as follows:

$$\text{LO} \leq \text{HI}.$$

Furthermore, suppose the set of categories is the set $Cat = \{\text{BIN}_1, \text{BIN}_2\}$.

This combination of sets L and Cat yields eight possible compound levels:

$$(\text{HI}, \{\text{BIN}_1, \text{BIN}_2\}) \quad (\text{HI}, \{\text{BIN}_1\}) \quad (\text{HI}, \{\text{BIN}_2\}) \quad (\text{HI}, \{\})$$
$$(\text{LO}, \{\text{BIN}_1, \text{BIN}_2\}) \quad (\text{LO}, \{\text{BIN}_1\}) \quad (\text{LO}, \{\text{BIN}_2\}) \quad (\text{LO}, \{\})$$

The $dom \subseteq L \times Cat$ relation is presented graphically by the *Hasse diagram* in Figure 13.1. Each compound level appears as a node in the Hasse diagram, but not every element of *dom* shows up as an explicit edge in the diagram. Each edge (i.e., downward line) from a compound level $\ell_1 = (L_1, C_1)$ to a level $\ell_2 = (L_2, C_2)$ corresponds to an element $(\ell_1, \ell_2) \in dom$ that cannot be deduced through reflexivity or transitivity. Thus, for example, no edge is necessary to indicate that $(\text{HI}, \{\text{BIN}_1\}) \; dom \; (\text{LO}, \{\})$: that relationship can be deduced by recognizing that $(\text{HI}, \{\text{BIN}_1\}) \; dom \; (\text{HI}, \{\})$ and $(\text{HI}, \{\}) \; dom \; (\text{LO}, \{\})$. $\qquad \Diamond$

FIGURE 13.1 Partial ordering on confidentiality levels

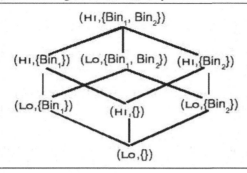

Example 13.2
Consider the compound levels and *dom* relation given in Example 13.1, and suppose
that Arthur has confidentiality level (HI, {BIN₁}). His confidentiality level *dominates*
documents with the following levels:

$$(\text{HI}, \{\text{BIN}_1\}),\ (\text{LO}, \{\text{BIN}_1\}),\ (\text{HI}, \{\}),\ (\text{LO}, \{\}). \qquad \diamond$$

As a final note, we point out that the compound levels introduced here still fit
within the syntax and semantics introduced for confidentiality and integrity policies
in Chapter 5. In particular, compound levels can be viewed as additional elements of
the syntactic sets **SecLabel** and **IntLabel**, and the *dom* relation can be represented
by the $\leq_s$ and $\leq_i$ operators of the logic. The following example reinforces this point.

Example 13.3
Suppose that Jane's confidentiality level is $(\text{LO}, \{\text{BIN}_1, \text{BIN}_2\})$ and that object O has
confidentiality level $(\text{LO}, \{\text{BIN}_2\})$. We can express these facts in the logic as follows:

$$\mathsf{slev}(\textit{Jane}) = (\text{LO}, \{\text{BIN}_1, \text{BIN}_2\})\ \wedge\ \mathsf{slev}(O) = (\text{LO}, \{\text{BIN}_2\}).$$

We can also express the following consequence, namely that Jane's confidentiality
level dominates O's level:

$$\mathsf{slev}(O) \leq_s \mathsf{slev}(\textit{Jane}). \qquad \diamond$$

Exercise 13.1.1 *Prove that the subset relation $\subseteq$ is a partial order.*

Exercise 13.1.2 *Prove that the dom relation is a partial order.*

13.2   Bell–La Padula Model, Revisited

We saw in Chapter 5 that the Bell–La Padula model for confidentiality mandates that the following two properties be satisfied:

1. **Simple security condition:** A principal P can read object O *if and only if* P's confidentiality level is at least as high as O's and P has discretionary read access to O.

2. ***-property:** A principal P can write to object O *if and only if* O's confidentiality level is at least as high as P's and P has discretionary write access to O.

As pointed out previously, the "if and only if" requirements in these properties mean that each property actually involves two implications. For example, the simple security condition contains the following two implications:

1. If P's confidentiality level is at least as high as O's and P has discretionary read access to O, then P can read O.

2. If P can read O, then P's confidentiality level is at least as high as O's and P has discretionary read access to O.

The first implication represents an *access-control condition*: it states the conditions under which a reference monitor should grant access to O (i.e., the access policy). Such conditions will often occur in the context of a formal justification for granting access to a specific object. In contrast, the second implication represents a *safety condition* for the entire system: this sort of property cannot be assumed, but instead must be verified by checking every potential consequence of the rules and mechanisms that govern access. Proving such a property—which relies on the completeness, isolation, and verifiability of *every* reference monitor in the system—is beyond the scope of the access-control logic. In the discussion that follows, we focus on the access-control conditions.

We can formulate the access-control policies that correspond to the simple security condition and the *-property as follows:

1. **Simple-security access-control policy:**

$$(\; \mathsf{slev}(O) \leq_s \mathsf{slev}(P)) \supset (P \; \mathsf{controls} \; \langle \mathit{read}, O \rangle)$$

2. ***-property access-control policy:**

$$(\; \mathsf{slev}(P) \leq_s \mathsf{slev}(O)) \supset (P \; \mathsf{controls} \; \langle \mathit{write}, O \rangle)$$

The following example illustrates the specification of access policies associated with the Bell–La Padula model.

Subject or Object	Confidentiality Level
Carol	$(\text{HI}, \{\text{BIN}_1, \text{BIN}_2\})$
Kate	$(\text{LO}, \{\text{BIN}_2\})$
O_1	$(\text{HI}, \{\text{BIN}_1, \text{BIN}_2\})$
O_2	$(\text{LO}, \{\text{BIN}_2\})$
O_3	$(\text{LO}, \{\text{BIN}_1\})$
O_4	$(\text{LO}, \{\})$

Table 13.1: Confidentiality levels

	Object			
Subject	O_1	O_2	O_3	O_4
Carol	read	-	read	-
Kate	write	-	-	read

Table 13.2: Discretionary access-control matrix

Example 13.4

Consider Tables 13.1 and 13.2: the former lists the confidentiality levels of two subjects (Carol and Kate) and four objects (O_1, O_2, O_3, O_4), while the latter specifies the discretionary access of subjects to objects.

Together, these two tables satisfy the Bell–La Padula model: read permission for object O_i is granted only to subjects whose confidentiality level is at least as high as O_i's, and write permission for object O_i is granted only to subjects whose confidentiality level is no higher than O_i's. Note that, although both Carol and Kate have confidentiality levels high enough to read object O_2, neither has been granted that discretionary access.

The access-control policy can be expressed in the access-control logic by the following statements:

$$(\text{ slev}(O_1) \leq_s \text{slev}(Carol)) \supset (Carol \text{ controls } \langle read, O_1 \rangle),$$
$$(\text{ slev}(O_1) \leq_s \text{slev}(Carol)) \supset (Carol \text{ controls } \langle read, O_3 \rangle),$$
$$(\text{ slev}(Kate) \leq_s \text{slev}(O_1)) \supset (Kate \text{ controls } \langle write, O_1 \rangle),$$
$$(\text{ slev}(O_4) \leq_s \text{slev}(Kate)) \supset (Kate \text{ controls } \langle read, O_4 \rangle). \qquad \Diamond$$

We conclude this section with an example that illustrates why the safety aspects of Bell–La Padula must be verified through system audit, rather than within the system itself.

Example 13.5

Dexter is a corrupt system administrator who has supervisory privileges in an organization's information system. Because Dexter is trusted (but not trustworthy), he is in a position to bypass the security of the system.

Prior to being fired, Dexter installs a back door so that he can rewrite personnel records. He alters the reference monitor that guards the personnel records so that it accepts a secret identifier:

$$secretID \text{ controls } \langle write, \text{personnel records} \rangle.$$

By doing so, Dexter has bypassed all the mandatory access-control checks. This back door can be detected only by auditing Dexter's actions and by inspecting the subsystems accessed by Dexter: no reference monitor can possibly detect that Dexter's change violates the access policy.   ◊

Exercise 13.2.1   *Consider the confidentiality-level assignments and discretionary access specified in Example 13.4. Provide formal proofs in the access-control logic that, when requested, Carol can read objects O_1 and O_3 and Kate can write O_1 and read O_4.*

Exercise 13.2.2   *Reformulate the extended example in Section 5.4.3 for the FX-1 and FX-2 fighter projects. In particular, reformulate all the level assignments to subjects and objects using both clearance levels and the categories FX-1 and FX-2. Make sure that you assign the clearance levels to preserve the privileges as described in Section 5.4.3.*

In addition, suppose General Jane in the Department of Defense heads the entire Next Generation Fighter project. Thus, both the FX-1 and FX-2 projects are in her jurisdiction. What should her confidentiality level be, and how are the FX-1 and FX-2 access matrices altered so that she has read access to all documents?

Exercise 13.2.3   *Correctional facilities (prisons) have several classifications of directives.[1] These classifications are as follows:*

- Level A*: accessible to anyone, including inmates. Level A documents are public information.*

- Level B*: not accessible by inmates but accessible to officers, sergeants, and management. Level B documents generally deal with* normal *facility operations.*

- Level C*: confidential (but not emergency-related) information. Level C documents generally deal with confidential personnel information. These documents are available to sergeants and above, but not to officers and inmates.*

- Level D*: emergency-response information. Level D documents are highly confidential that, if possessed by inmates, would threaten the security of the prison. These documents are available only to management.*

---

[1]This exercise was inspired by a conversation with Gary Tyler, Lieutenant (retired), New York State Department of Corrections.

a. *Fill in the following table with classification levels for each subject and object:*

Subject or Object	Classification Level
Inmate	
Officer	
Sergeant	
Chief of Security	
Prison Visiting Hours	
Vacation Policy for Officers	
Confidential Performance Reviews of Officers	
Emergency Response Plans for Riots	

b. *Fill in the following access-control matrix so that it meets the following conditions:*

- *It satisfies the Bell–La Padula confidentiality model.*
- *It follows the intent of the classification levels described in the scenario.*
- *Only the Chief of Security can write or read the Emergency Response Plan for Riots.*
- *Sergeants write the confidential performance review for officers, which is then readable by the Chief of Security.*

Subject	Visiting Hours (A)	Vacation Policy (B)	Performance Reviews (C)	Emergency Response Plans (D)
Inmate (A)				
Officer (B)				
Sergeant (C)				
Chief of Security (D)				

c. *Express in the access-control logic the policy that the Chief of Security (CS) has the capability to read and write Emergency Response Plans (ERPs).*

d. *Propose a derived inference rule that states that the Chief of Security (CS) can read emergency response plans (ERPs). Give a formal proof of the derived rule.*

13.3 Confidentiality Levels: Some Practical Considerations

Our discussion of confidentiality levels so far has ignored one pragmatic point: people, processes, and information are rarely fully isolated in wholly separate enclaves. Instead, people and information move across boundaries, be they physical or virtual. For example, within secure facilities, people with high security clearances communicate with people who have lower or no security clearances. Those who work in secure facilities head home and spend time with family and friends in unsecured environments. Similarly, sensitive government documents are routinely released to the public under freedom-of-information laws.

Several approaches are used to prevent sensitive information from being leaked as people and information move across boundaries. These approaches include *maximum and current confidentiality levels*, *sanitization* and *confinement*. We describe these approaches in turn, illustrating each with one or more examples.

The Bell–La Padula model imposes constraints on how subjects with high confidentiality levels may communicate with subjects at lower levels. For example, consider the case of Kamal, a Senior Scientist at a military research lab who has a confidentiality level of $(\text{TS}, \{\text{NUC}, \text{US}, \text{EUR}, \text{ASIA}\})$. Kamal needs to send a message (i.e., a file) to one of his staff engineers (Sarah), whose confidentiality level is $(\text{TS}, \{\text{NUC}, \text{US}\})$.

As presented so far, Bell–La Padula prohibits Sarah from reading any file that Kamal writes, because his confidentiality level is higher than Sarah's. However, in fact the Bell–La Padula model makes the following allowance: subjects have both a *maximum* confidentiality level and a *current* confidentiality level. For understandable reasons, the maximum level must always dominate the current level. When two subjects need to communicate with one another, the subject with the higher level reduces his or her current level appropriately, so that they can communicate as needed.

In practice, the adoption of different confidentiality levels often requires a subject to switch systems to effectively lower his or her level. For example, a person with top-secret clearance will log on to a secret system to communicate with people at the secret level. The following example illustrates how this approach lets Kamal send a message that Sarah can read.

Example 13.6
Kamal has a confidentiality level of $(\text{TS}, \{\text{NUC}, \text{US}, \text{EUR}, \text{ASIA}\})$, and his staff engineer Sarah has a confidentiality level of $(\text{TS}, \{\text{NUC}, \text{US}\})$. To communicate with Sarah, Kamal logs onto a TS system that has only NUC,US as allowable categories, and sends his message. Having reduced his current confidentiality level to Sarah's, any message he writes will be readable by Sarah. ◊

In many cases—such as the public release of documents through freedom-of-information requests—it is an object's confidentiality level that is problematic, rather than a subject's level. *Sanitization* is the process of removing classified or restricted information from a document or file, thereby allowing the remaining information to be released at a lower classification level. In essence, the document in question is edited or rewritten without the sensitive information. The following two examples illustrate the types of contexts in which sanitization is used.

Example 13.7
Court proceedings are typically considered public records. However, in cases that involve crimes against children, there are often requirements that prevent disclosure of the identities of child victims. In such situations, the court records released to the public have the names of children removed or hidden. ◊

Example 13.8
Before government reports are released to the public, classified information (e.g., the names of spies) is removed, hidden, or blocked out. The resulting document is then reclassified to a lower level before being released. ◊

A third pragmatic concern is the potential leaking of protected information from a protected environment to a less protected environment. *Confinement* is the means by which such leaks are prevented, be they in the virtual or physical environments. For example, a secure server may be placed on a secure network, to prevent insecure processes from accessing it and then transmitting information insecurely. The following example illustrates an approach to confinement in the physical world.

Example 13.9
A Sensitive Compartmented Information Facility (SCIF, pronounced "skiff") is a secure location with appropriate access controls to ensure that classified information can be accessed securely. Recently, Tom listened to a secret briefing in his laboratory's SCIF, which is contained within a larger office building that has a lower clearance level. Being a new and inexperienced employee, Tom took his engineering notebook with him into the SCIF without considering the consequences.

Before exiting the SCIF, Tom had to surrender his engineering notebook to the SCIF security office, who will inspect the notebook to verify that it does not contain any classified information. This inspection may take up to a week or more. ◊

Exercise 13.3.1 *Consider the situation described in Example 13.6. In whom and in what must we trust to prevent the leakage of information downwards to Sarah from Kamal? What are some things that can be done to mitigate some of the risks and vulnerabilities?*

Exercise 13.3.2 *Consider the situation described in Example 13.7. Suppose that Mary is in charge of court records, including the censoring of sensitive court documents for public release. Furthermore, suppose that the court employs two computer systems, one for sensitive **unsanitized** (U) documents and another for publicly releasable **sanitized** (S) documents.*

Devise a concept of operations that describes how Mary takes a file $Case_{Sensitive}$ (where $slev(Case_{Sensitive}) = U$), censors it, and produces a publicly releasable file $Case_{Releasable}$ (where $slev(Case_{Releasable}) = S$).

Your concept of operations should satisfy the Bell–La Padula model and include the following:

- *The partial order that relates* U *and* S

- *The discretionary access-control matrix that shows Mary's privileges*

- *The formulation in the access-control logic of the access-control policy for Mary's reading and writing of Case$_{Sensitive}$ and Case$_{Releasable}$*

- *The formulation in the access-control logic of the assignment of confidentiality levels to Mary and to the two case files*

- *Theorems in the access-control logic that justify letting Mary read and write the relevant case files*

Exercise 13.3.3   *Consider the situation in Example 13.9, and suppose that Tom's notebook can be released only if it contains only unclassified information. John, as the SCIF security officer, determines whether or not Tom's notebook can be released.*

    Describe in the access-control logic John's jurisdiction over whether or not the notebook is released or held. Using your formulation, formally justify in the access-control logic the release of Tom's notebook if John says so.

13.4   Biba's Strict Integrity, Revisited

Biba's strict-integrity model is the dual of the Bell–La Padula model: it uses the same structure as Bell–La Padula (i.e., partially order levels), but the direction of information flow is reversed. Whereas the catch phrase for Bell–La Padula is "no read up and no write down," the catch phrase for Biba is "no read down and no write up."

We introduced the underlying concepts and definitions for Biba's strict-integrity model in Chapter 5, where we focused on direct-access operations (i.e., observations and modifications). In this section, we briefly review the requirements for Biba's strict integrity, but we focus on filling in the details as they apply to indirect access (i.e., the *invocation* of one subject by another).

As we saw previously, strict integrity requires that the following three properties be met:

1. **Simple integrity condition:** A subject S can observe O *if and only if* $\mathsf{ilev}(S) \leq \mathsf{ilev}(O)$ and S has discretionary observe access to O.

2. **Integrity *-property:** A subject S can modify O *if and only if* $\mathsf{ilev}(O) \leq \mathsf{ilev}(S)$ and S has discretionary modify access to O.

3. **Invocation condition:** A subject S_1 and invoke subject S_2 *if and only if* $\mathsf{ilev}(S_2) \leq \mathsf{ilev}(S_1)$ and S_1 has discretionary invocation rights to S_2.

In effect, strict integrity requires that the integrity level of each object and subject in a transfer path must be at least as high as that of the subject or object that immediately follows it. Thus, for example, in a transfer path where (for each i such that $1 \leq i \leq n$) subject S_i can read from object O_i and write to object O_{i+1}, the following condition must hold:

$$\text{ilev}(O_{n+1}) \leq_i \text{ilev}(S_n) \leq_i \text{ilev}(O_n) \leq_i \cdots \leq_i \text{ilev}(O_2) \leq \text{ilev}(S_1) \leq_i \text{ilev}(O_1).$$

In the case of indirect operations, strict integrity requires that the integrity level of the invoking subject S_1 must be at least as high as that of the invoked subject S_2. Otherwise, less trustworthy subjects could direct the actions of more trustworthy subjects: for example, users could direct system administrators to disable system safeguards such as malware detectors and perimeter defenses.

As we saw with the Bell–La Padula properties, the three strict-integrity properties implicitly involve two implications: an access-control condition and a system-wide safety (or audit) property. The access-control conditions, which represent the access policies used by reference monitors, can be expressed in the logic as follows:

1. **Simple-integrity access-control condition:**

$$(\text{ilev}(S) \leq \text{ilev}(O)) \supset (S \text{ controls } \langle observe, O \rangle)$$

2. **Integrity *-property access-control condition:**

$$(\text{ilev}(O) \leq \text{ilev}(S)) \supset (S \text{ controls } \langle modify, O \rangle)$$

3. **Invocation access-control conditions:**

$$(\text{ilev}(S_2) \leq_i \text{ilev}(S_1)) \supset (S_1 \text{ controls } \langle i, S_2, o, O \rangle),$$
$$(\text{ilev}(S_2) \leq_i \text{ilev}(S_1)) \supset (S_1 \text{ controls } \langle i, S_2, m, O \rangle),$$

where $\langle i, S, o, O \rangle$ and $\langle i, S, m, O \rangle$ respectively denote the propositions *"invoke subject S to observe O"* and *"invoke subject S to modify O."*

The following example demonstrates how such conditions can be used to express strict-integrity policies.

Example 13.10

Consider Tables 13.3 and 13.4, which respectively (1) list the integrity levels for two subjects (Carol and Kate) and four objects (O_1, O_2, O_3, O_4) and (2) specify the subjects' discretionary observe, modify, and invocation rights. Together, these two tables satisfy Biba's strict-integrity properties.

The access-policy regarding Carol's discretionary modify access to O_3 can be expressed as follows:

$$(\text{ilev}(O_3) \leq_i \text{ilev}(Carol)) \supset (Carol \text{ controls } \langle modify, O_3 \rangle). \qquad \Diamond$$

Subject or Object	Integrity Level
Carol	$(\text{LEV}_1, \{\text{CAT}_1, \text{CAT}_2\})$
Kate	$(\text{LEV}_2, \{\text{CAT}_2\})$
O_1	$(\text{LEV}_1, \{\text{CAT}_1, \text{CAT}_2\})$
O_2	$(\text{LEV}_2, \{\text{CAT}_2\})$
O_3	$(\text{LEV}_2, \{\text{CAT}_1\})$
O_4	$(\text{LEV}_2, \{\})$

Table 13.3: Integrity levels

	Object				Subject	
Subject	O_1	O_2	O_3	O_4	Carol	Kate
Carol	observe	-	modify	-	-	invoke observe, invoke modify
Kate	observe	-	-	modify	-	-

Table 13.4: Discretionary access-control matrix

Table 13.4 includes indirect access rights for Carol: she has invocation rights on Kate for both observe and modify actions. Consequently, Kate must have a policy on how she will respond to Carol's requests. There are three possibilities when Carol invokes Kate:

1. Kate denies Carol's request.

   Because the request is denied, there is nothing further to analyze: strict integrity is preserved.

2. Kate honors Carol's request, and Kate has discretionary access to the object she must access on Carol's behalf.

   We explore this case in Example 13.11.

3. Kate honors Carol's request, and Kate does *not* have discretionary access to the object she must access on Carol's behalf.

   This case is left for Exercise 13.4.3.

Example 13.11
Consider the integrity levels given in Table 13.3 and the discretionary access-control matrix of Table 13.4. Furthermore, suppose that Carol requests that Kate modify object O_4 on her behalf.

Figure 13.2 illustrates the three steps that must occur for Carol's indirect request for the modification of O_4 to be granted:

1. Kate's reference monitor must conclude that Carol's invocation request should be honored by Kate.

FIGURE 13.2 Carol's request and Kate's response

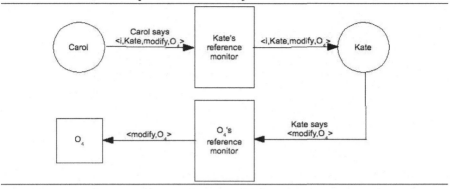

The reference monitor must ensure that Carol's integrity level is at least as high as Kate's integrity level *and* that Carol has discretionary invocation access on Kate.

Letting $\langle i, Kate, modify, O_4 \rangle$ denote the proposition "it is good to grant the invocation request for Kate to modify object O_4," the reference monitor's behavior can be represented by the following derived inference rule:

$$\frac{\begin{array}{c} \mathsf{ilev}(Carol) =_i (\mathrm{LEV}_1, \{\mathrm{CAT}_1, \mathrm{CAT}_2\}) \\ \mathsf{ilev}(Kate) =_i (\mathrm{LEV}_2, \{\mathrm{CAT}_2\}) \\ (\mathrm{LEV}_2, \{\mathrm{CAT}_2\}) \leq_i (\mathrm{LEV}_1, \{\mathrm{CAT}_1, \mathrm{CAT}_2\}) \\ \mathsf{ilev}(Kate) \leq_i \mathsf{ilev}(Carol) \supset (Carol \text{ controls } \langle i, Kate, modify, O_4 \rangle) \\ Carol \text{ says } \langle i, Kate, modify, O_4 \rangle \end{array}}{\langle i, Kate, modify, O_4 \rangle.}$$

2. Kate's behavior is governed by her policy regarding invocations that are passed on to her by her reference monitor.

   If her policy is to make any direct-access request that the reference monitor passes on to her, then her behavior upon receiving Carol's request can be expressed by the following derived inference rule:

$$\frac{\langle i, Kate, modify, O_4 \rangle \supset \langle modify, O_4 \rangle}{Kate \text{ says } \langle modify, O_4 \rangle.}$$

3. Ultimately, Kate's request on Carol's behalf must be approved by the reference monitor for object O_4.

   The reference monitor must ensure that Kate's integrity level is at least as high as O_4's integrity level. The reference monitor's eventual decision can be expressed by the following derived inference rule:

$$\mathsf{ilev}(O_4) =_i (\text{LEV}_2, \{\})$$
$$\mathsf{ilev}(Kate) =_i (\text{LEV}_2, \{\text{CAT}_2\})$$
$$(\text{LEV}_2, \{\}) \leq_i (\text{LEV}_2, \{\text{CAT}_2\})$$
$$\mathsf{ilev}(O_4) \leq_i \mathsf{ilev}(Kate) \supset (Kate \text{ controls } \langle modify, O_4 \rangle)$$

$$\frac{Kate \text{ says } \langle modify, O_4 \rangle}{\langle modify, O_4 \rangle.} \qquad \Diamond$$

Exercise 13.4.1   *Consider the discretionary-access control matrix in Table 13.4. For each object O_1 through O_4, write the strict-integrity access-control policy for the reference monitor that guards the object. Given the integrity levels in Table 13.3, formally prove that (1) Carol can observe and modify objects O_1 and O_3, respectively, and (2) that Kate can observe and modify objects O_1 and O_4, respectively.*

Exercise 13.4.2   *Formally derive the inference rules from Example 13.11 that describe the behavior of Kate's reference monitor, Kate, and O_4's reference monitor.*

Exercise 13.4.3   *Suppose everything is the same as described in Example 13.11 with the following exception: Carol invokes Kate to modify O_3 instead of O_4. Show how the direct access policies work to prevent Kate from accessing O_3. Be as precise, detailed, and formal as possible.*

13.5   Lipner's Integrity Model

In the previous sections, we reviewed the Bell–La Padula and Biba models for confidentiality and integrity. In this section, we introduce Lipner's integrity model (Lipner, 1982), which builds upon both models. Lipner developed his model for so-called *production systems*, which depend on software to deliver commercial services (e.g., banking, data processing, or inventory control). In such systems, data integrity is paramount: imagine the chaos that would ensue if a bank's account data became corrupted or if an inventory-control program had incorrect information on what was on store shelves and in warehouses.

Lipner's model serves as an interesting case study for designers and verifiers who must develop their own policies to meet design requirements. To be explicit, Lipner does not provide an abstract model such as Bell–La Padula or Biba. Rather, he specifies a collection of requirements for commercial integrity and then employs a combination of the Bell–La Padula and Biba models to identify specific confidentiality and integrity levels suitable for meeting those requirements.

13.5.1 Commercial Integrity Requirements

To understand the type of commercial scenario that Lipner's work addresses, consider a financial-services company that offers online banking and credit services. Bank customers use programs supplied by the bank to access and manipulate their accounts online: they can view account information, pay bills, transfer funds between accounts, and so on. Thus, customers are *users* of bank services, and the data and programs they use comprise the *production domain.* Unseen by customers are the *application developers* and *system programmers*, who develop (respectively) the applications software and the underlying IT infrastructure used by customers. These people work in the *development domain.*

Experience shows that it is essential to isolate the production domain from the development domain. Otherwise, programs under development could destroy or corrupt customer account information, thereby destroying the bank's reputation and business. Before programs can be moved from the development domain into the production domain, they must be thoroughly reviewed and tested. The decisions and processes used to move a program out of development and into production are managed by *system controllers*, *managers*, and *auditors.*

Lipner proposed the following commercial-integrity requirements for such production systems:

1. Users can use production programs and data, but they cannot write their own programs to operate on the production databases.

2. Application developers and system programmers perform their development and testing in a special test environment; they have no access to the production programs or databases. Should they require such access, a special process will provide them with copies of the information they need.

3. Only system controllers may change the status of a program from *development* to *production.*

4. The act of changing a program's status from *development* to *production* is audited.

5. Managers and auditors have access to the system state and audit logs.

In the next two subsections, we examine Lipner's two approaches to meeting these five requirements: the first approach uses only the Bell–La Padula model, while the second uses a combination of both Bell–La Padula and Biba's strict integrity.

13.5.2 Commercial Integrity via Bell–La Padula

Lipner's requirements for commercial integrity explicitly identify five classes of subjects: (1) production-environment users (e.g., customers); (2) application programmers; (3) system programmers; (4) system controllers; and (5) system managers or auditors. The requirements also implicitly identify seven classes of objects:

(1) production data (e.g., customer account information); (2) production code (i.e., application software available to users); (3) system programs in the production environment (e.g., database query engines or key-distribution software invoked by production code); (4) application programs in development; (5) system programs and data in development; (6) software tools used by development personnel (i.e., programmer support software, such as compilers); and (7) audit logs.

Table 13.5 gives the desired discretionary access-control matrix for this situation. It is straightforward to verify that the matrix meets the imposed commercial-integrity requirements:

1. Users may use production code and system programs, and they may modify production data. However, they are unable to create or modify production code, system programs, or anything in the development environment.

2. Application programmers and system programmers have no access to production data and code; however, they may use (but not modify) system programs in the application environment, as well as software tools. Application programmers can read and modify application programs within the development environment, and system programmers can read and modify system programs within the development environment.

3. System controllers—who need to be able to install programs within both the production and development environments—have read and write permissions for all programs and data in both environments.

4. All subjects' actions are written to the audit logs, including system controllers' installations of programs.

5. System managers and auditors—who must monitor the entire system's state—have read access to all aspects of the system, including the audit logs.

Lipner's goal was to identify confidentiality levels for the subjects and objects in such a way that (1) the desired access-control matrix is consistent with Bell–La Padula and (2) subjects have as many permissions as possible. Towards this end, he used compound levels built from the set of classification levels $L = \{\text{AM}, \text{SL}\}$ and the set of categories $Cat = \{\text{PD}, \text{PC}, \text{D}, \text{SD}, \text{T}\}$.

Intuitively, the classification level AM (short for "audit manager") is for system managers and auditors; the classification level SL ("system low") is for all other subjects in the system. Because system managers and auditors have greater privileges than the other subjects, the partial order $\leq$ on L is defined such that $\text{SL} \leq \text{AM}$.

The categories reflect the types of data and programs that can be used or modified by users, application programmers, and system programmers: production data (PD), production code (PC), development code and test data (D), system programs in development (SD), and software tools (T). Categories are assigned to *subjects* based on the types of data and code that they can modify, as well as the programs that they can use. For example, ordinary users should be able to modify production data and to use production code; therefore, they are assigned the set of categories $\{\text{PD}, \text{PC}\}$.

Subject	Object						
	Prod Data	Prod Code	System Prog	Dev App Prog	Dev Sys Prog	SW Tools	Audit Logs
Production Users	read, write	read	read	-	-	-	write
Application Prgmers	-	-	read	read, write	-	read	write
System Prgmers	-	-	read	-	read, write	read	write
System Controllers	read, write	read, write	read, write	read, write	read, write	read, write	write
Managers & Auditors	read	read	read	read	read	read	read, write

Table 13.5: Access-control matrix for commercial integrity via Bell–La Padula

Subject Class	Confidentiality Level
Ordinary user	$(\mathrm{SL},\{\mathrm{PD},\mathrm{PC}\})$
Application programmer	$(\mathrm{SL},\{\mathrm{D},\mathrm{T}\})$
System programmer	$(\mathrm{SL},\{\mathrm{SD},\mathrm{T}\})$
System controller	$(\mathrm{SL},\{\mathrm{PD},\mathrm{PC},\mathrm{D},\mathrm{SD},\mathrm{T}\})$ and downgrade privilege
System management or auditor	$(\mathrm{AM},\{\mathrm{PD},\mathrm{PC},\mathrm{D},\mathrm{SD},\mathrm{T}\})$

Table 13.6: Confidentiality levels for subjects

Similarly, system managers and auditors should be able to read every sort of data and code; they are therefore assigned the full set of categories $\{\mathrm{PD},\mathrm{PC},\mathrm{D},\mathrm{SD},\mathrm{T}\}$.

Table 13.6 shows the confidentiality levels assigned to each kind of subject. Note that subjects with classification level SL—such as ordinary users and application programmers—have the lowest possible classification level. Therefore, under Bell–La Padula's *-property (i.e., "no write down"), their ability to modify a given object is limited only by the set of categories associated with that object. For example, application programmers are assigned the set of categories $\{\mathrm{D},\mathrm{T}\}$: they can modify any object whose associated categories include both D and T. System managers and auditors are further limited by their classification level AM: they cannot write to objects whose classification level is SL.

In contrast, confidentiality levels are assigned to *objects* based on the levels of those subjects who must be able to read them. In particular, objects are assigned confidentiality levels as high as possible, subject to the constraint imposed by the simple security condition of Bell–La Padula (i.e., "no read up"): no object's confidentiality level can be higher than that of a subject who must be able to read

Object Class	Confidentiality Level
Production data	$(\text{SL},\{\text{PD},\text{PC}\})$
Production code	$(\text{SL},\{\text{PC}\})$
Systems programs	$(\text{SL},\{\})$
Development code & test data	$(\text{SL},\{\text{D},\text{T}\})$
System programs in modification	$(\text{SL},\{\text{SD},\text{T}\})$
Software tools	$(\text{SL},\{\text{T}\})$
System and application audit logs	$(\text{AM},\{\text{PD},\text{PC},\text{D},\text{SD},\text{T}\})$

Table 13.7: Confidentiality levels for objects

it. For example, software tools must be readable by both application programmers (who have confidentiality level $(\text{SL},\{\text{D},\text{T}\})$) and system programmers (who have confidentiality level $(\text{SL},\{\text{SD},\text{T}\})$). Consequently, the highest confidentiality level that can be assigned to software tools is $(\text{SL},\{\text{T}\})$. Similarly, audit logs must be readable by system managers and auditors, and hence they are assigned the level $(\text{AM},\{\text{PD},\text{PC},\text{D},\text{SD},\text{T}\})$. Table 13.7 shows the confidentiality levels for each class of object.

One class of subjects requires special mention: system controllers have the special role of moving programs out of development and into production. Consequently, they need full read and write access to all files except audit logs. Satisfying both the simple security condition and the *-property, however, means that a subject can have both read and write access to a given object only if the subject's level exactly matches the object's level. We have already seen that production data, production code, development code, software tools, and system programs in modification all have different confidentiality levels. How, then, do we assign an appropriate level to system controllers? The answer is that system controllers—and *only* system controllers—must be allowed to *downgrade* their classification level. Therefore, system controllers are assigned the confidentiality level $(\text{SL},\{\text{PD},\text{PC},\text{D},\text{SD},\text{T}\})$, along with the privilege to downgrade their levels as necessary.

It is straightforward to translate the contents of the Table 13.5 access-control matrix into the access-control logic. For example, the ability of users to read and write production data is given by the following two statements:

$$\text{slev}(\textit{Production Data}) \leq_s \text{slev}(\textit{User}) \supset (\textit{User} \text{ controls } \langle \textit{read}, \textit{Production Data} \rangle),$$

$$\text{slev}(\textit{User}) \leq_s \text{slev}(\textit{Production Data}) \supset (\textit{User} \text{ controls } \langle \textit{write}, \textit{Production Data} \rangle).$$

Although this scheme satisfies the five commercial-integrity requirements initially proposed, Lipner points out a potential drawback: it is unclear how special-purpose software (such as a database-repair program) fits into this scheme. Such programs must be able to operate on production data but cannot be under the control of users. He addresses this shortcoming via a combination of Bell–La Padula confidentiality and Biba strict integrity, which we explore in the next subsection.

Subjects	Objects							
	Prod Data	Prod Code	System Prog	Dev App Prog	Dev Sys Prog	SW Tools	Audit Logs	Repair Code
Production Users	read, write	read	read	-	-	-	write	-
Application Prgmrs	-	-	read	read, write	-	read	write	-
System Prgmrs	-	-	read	-	read, write	read	write	-
System Controllers	read, write	read, write	read, write	read, write	read, write	read, write	write	read, write
Managers & Auditors	read	read	read	read	read	read	read, write	read
Repair	read, write	read	read	-	-	-	write	read

Table 13.8: Access-control matrix for both confidentiality and strict integrity

13.5.3　Commercial Integrity via Bell–La Padula and Strict Integrity

A major objective for combining the Bell–La Padula model with Biba's strict integrity is to allow the use of special-purpose software to repair errors or inconsistencies in production databases. Lipner states this additional requirement as follows (Lipner, 1982, page 7):

> Special-purpose application software shall be provided to effect "data base repair" on the production data base. This software may be used by members of the application programmer or system control population under special circumstances.

The desired discretionary access-control matrix for this new situation appears in Table 13.8. Note that this table is identical to Table 13.5, except for the addition of a new class of subjects (Repair) and a new class of objects (Repair Code). Lipner identified a combination of confidentiality and integrity levels that, when suitably assigned to subjects and objects, permits this access-control matrix to be consistent with *both* Biba's strict integrity and the Bell–La Padula confidentiality policies.

For example, Table 13.8 shows that system managers have both read and write access to the audit logs. Granting read access to system managers requires that the following two properties hold:

$$\mathsf{slev}(Audit\ Log) \leq_s \mathsf{slev}(System\ Manager),$$
$$\mathsf{ilev}(System\ Manager) \leq_i \mathsf{ilev}(Audit\ Log).$$

The first property is the mandatory access-control condition for read operations in Bell–La Padula (i.e., "no read up"), while the second condition is the "no read down" condition for strict integrity. The combination of these two requirements can be expressed in the logic as follows:

$$\text{slev}(Audit\ Log) \leq_s \text{slev}(System\ Manager) \supset$$
$$\text{ilev}(System\ Manager) \leq_i \text{ilev}(Audit\ Log) \supset$$
$$(System\ Manager\ \text{controls}\ \langle read, Audit\ Log \rangle).$$

Similarly, for write operations, we have a combination of Bell–La Padula's "no write down" and Biba's "no write up" requirements:

$$\text{slev}(System\ Manager) \leq_s \text{slev}(Audit\ Log) \supset$$
$$\text{ilev}(Audit\ Log) \leq_i \text{ilev}(System\ Manager) \supset$$
$$(System\ Manager\ \text{controls}\ \langle write, Audit\ Log \rangle).$$

Lipner's revised model handles confidentiality levels in a very similar manner to the original model. In particular, the confidentiality classifications from the first model are retained: $\mathcal{L}_{conf} = \{\text{AM}, \text{SL}\}$, with $\text{SL} \leq_s \text{AM}$. However, only three confidentiality categories are required: $Cat_{conf} = \{\text{P}_c, \text{D}_c, \text{SD}_c\}$. These categories loosely correspond to the types of code and the domains in which they may reside: production data and code (P_c), application code under development (D_c), and system programs under development (SD_c).

As in the initial model, the higher level AM ("audit manager") is assigned to managers and auditors, while the lower level SL ("system low") is assigned to all other subjects. Likewise, categories are assigned to subjects based on the types of data and programs that they can modify and use. Thus, for example, application programmers are assigned the category D_c, because they can modify application code under development. In contrast, system managers and auditors are assigned the set of categories $\{\text{P}_c, \text{D}_c, \text{SD}_c\}$, because they require read access to production data and code, application code under development, and system programs under development.

Confidentiality levels are then assigned to objects based on the confidentiality levels of the subjects who can read them. In particular, objects are assigned as high a level as possible, subject to the "no read up" constraint imposed by Bell–La Padula. For example, software tools should be readable by everyone, regardless of their confidentiality level: thus software tools must be assigned the lowest possible confidentiality level (i.e., $(\text{SL}, \{\})$). In contrast, audit logs should be read only by system managers and auditors, and hence audit logs are assigned the confidentiality level $(\text{AM}, \{\text{P}_c, \text{D}_c, \text{SD}_c\})$.

The new aspect of this model is the assignment of integrity levels that prevent users and programs from corrupting data and programs at higher integrity levels. The set of integrity classifications is $\mathcal{L}_{int} = \{\text{SP}_i, \text{OI}, \text{SL}_i\}$, where

$$\text{SL}_i \leq_i \text{OI} \leq_i \text{SP}_i.$$

System programs and repair programs are given the highest integrity classification (SP_i), and thus can be modified only by subjects with sufficiently high levels. Production code and software tools—which can be modified by a certain segment of users—are given the intermediate OI ("operational infrastructure") classification. Audit logs

Object	Level Confidentiality	Integrity
Production Data	$(\mathrm{SL},\{P_c\})$	$(\mathrm{SL}_i,\{P_i\})$
Production Code	$(\mathrm{SL},\{P_c\})$	$(\mathrm{OI},\{P_i\})$
System Programs	$(\mathrm{SL},\{\})$	$(\mathrm{SP}_i,\{P_i,D_i\})$
Development Code & Test Data	$(\mathrm{SL},\{D_c\})$	$(\mathrm{SL}_i,\{D_i\})$
System Programs in Modification	$(\mathrm{SL},\{SD_c\})$	$(\mathrm{SL}_i,\{D_i\})$
Software Tools	$(\mathrm{SL},\{\})$	$(\mathrm{OI},\{D_i\})$
Audit Logs	$(\mathrm{AM},\{P_c,D_c,SD_c\})$	$(\mathrm{SL}_i,\{\})$
Repair	$(\mathrm{SL},\{P_c\})$	$(\mathrm{SP}_i,\{P_i\})$

Table 13.9: Confidentiality and integrity levels for objects

are given the lowest integrity classification (SL_i), because they must be writable by everyone. Similarly, production data is classified at the SL_i level, because data can be written by users at the lowest level.

The set of integrity categories is $Cat_{int} = \{P_i, D_i\}$, where the categories are used to distinguish between the production and development domains. The assignment of objects to these integrity categories is intuitive. Production code, production data, and repair programs are assigned the P_i ("production integrity") category, while application code, system programs in modification, and software tools are assigned the D_i category ("development integrity"). The result is that programs in development are effectively isolated from production code and production data. System programs—which are used by both users and developers—are assigned both categories. In contrast, audit logs (which must be writable by everyone) are assigned the lowest integrity level ($\mathrm{SL}_i, \{\}$). Table 13.9 summarizes both the confidentiality and integrity levels for objects.

Integrity levels are then granted to subjects based on the objects that they must be able to modify: subjects are granted as low an integrity level as possible, subject to the "no write up" constraint imposed by Biba's strict-integrity policy. For example, application programmers must be able to write to both development code (integrity level $(\mathrm{SL}_i, \{D_i\})$) and the audit logs (integrity level $(\mathrm{SL}_i, \{\})$): the lowest integrity level that allows write access to both items is $(\mathrm{SL}_i, \{D_i\})$.

Table 13.10 shows the assignment of confidentiality and integrity levels to subjects. Given this assignment and that of Table 13.9, it is straightforward to check that all operations in Table 13.8 are permitted by the Bell–La Padula model. However, two aspects of this assignment deserve special mention.

First, system controllers alone have the ability to downgrade their integrity or confidentiality level by altering their categories, which enables them to match integrity and confidentiality levels with any objects other than audit logs. Consequently, system controllers are able to read and write to objects as necessary to move them from development to production.

Second, people operating in the repair function have exactly the same integrity and confidentiality levels as production users. However, the discretionary access

	Level	
Subject	**Confidentiality**	**Integrity**
Production Users	$(\text{SL}, \{P_c\})$	$(\text{SL}_i, \{P_i\})$
Application Programmers	$(\text{SL}, \{D_c\})$	$(\text{SL}_i, \{D_i\})$
System Programmers	$(\text{SL}, \{\text{SD}_c\})$	$(\text{SL}_i, \{D_i\})$
Sys Controllers (incl. downgrade privilege)	$(\text{SL}, \{P_c, D_c, \text{SD}_c\})$	$(\text{SP}_i, \{P_i, D_i\})$
Managers & Auditors	$(\text{AM}, \{P_c, D_c, \text{SD}_c\})$	$(\text{SL}_i, \{\})$
Repair	$(\text{SL}, \{P_c\})$	$(\text{SL}_i, \{P_i\})$

Table 13.10: Confidentiality and integrity levels for subjects

matrix in Table 13.8 shows that production users and repair people do not have the same privileges: repair people have the additional privilege of reading repair code. Although the mandatory access-control policies would permit production users to read repair code, doing so is not a requirement for the system: users have no need to have that privilege. Thus, in accordance with the principle of least privilege, users are denied discretionary read access to repair code.

Exercise 13.5.1   *Consider the access-control matrix in Table 13.5.*

    a. Using the access-control logic, formulate access-control policy statements for production users that reflect both the mandatory access-control requirements of Bell–La Padula and the discretionary access-control matrix.

    b. Using the access-control logic, devise a theorem that shows under what conditions access is granted for production users. Give a formal proof for each theorem.

Exercise 13.5.2   *Consider the access rights of system controllers, as given by the access-control matrix in Table 13.5.*

    a. Describe precisely how system controllers are able to read and write to all objects (with the exception of audit logs).

    b. Downgrading clearance levels is limited to system controllers only. Describe what undesirable effects would occur if other subjects could downgrade their clearance level.

Exercise 13.5.3

    a. Consider the assignment of confidentiality levels to subjects and objects given in Tables 13.10 and 13.9. Using the access-control matrix in Table 13.8 as a guide, devise an access-control matrix that shows the maximum privileges allowable to subjects when only the confidentiality levels of subjects and objects are considered.

b. Consider the assignment of integrity levels to subjects and objects given in Tables 13.10 and 13.9. Using the access-control matrix in Table 13.8 as a guide, devise an access-control matrix that shows the maximum privileges allowable to subjects when only the integrity levels of subjects and objects are considered

c. Consider the privileges of subjects obtained by intersecting the above two tables. How and why does this table differ from the access-control matrix in Table 13.8?

Exercise 13.5.4 *Extend the access-control logic to accommodate the use of both confidentiality and integrity levels. Devise the extensions to both the syntax and semantics.*

13.6 Summary

In this chapter, we introduced compound levels for both confidentiality and integrity, based on the combined notions of classification levels and categories. We also introduced the related notions of level downgrading, sanitization, and containment.

We reviewed both the Bell–La Padula model for confidentiality and Biba's strict-integrity model. We also described in detail Lipner's approach to commercial integrity: this approach relies on a combination of Bell–La Padula's confidentiality model and Biba's strict-integrity model. Lipner's work provides a good illustration of how levels can be assigned to subjects and objects to satisfy a model's policy constraints.

The learning outcomes for this chapter appear in Figure 13.3.

13.7 Further Reading

Bell and La Padula's work on confidentiality is contained in two reports (Bell and La Padula, 1975) and (Bell and La Padula, 1973). An alternate approach for confidentiality in commercial contexts is given by the *Chinese Wall* model (Brewer and Nash, 1989), which is used to handle conflicts of interests in situations where staff members in the same business (e.g., a law firm or accounting firm) work for clients who are competitors. The Chinese Wall policy places competitors in the same conflict-of-interest class. Employees are then restricted to accessing at most one member in the same conflict-of-interest class: once an employee has accessed one member of a conflict-of-interest class, all other members of the class are off limits. In this way, access restrictions in the Chinese Wall become more restrictive over time, whereas restrictions in Bell–La Padula do not.

In addition to strict integrity, Biba's original report (Biba, 1975) proposed two related and alternative policies: the low-watermark policy and the ring policy. Both policies impose the same restrictions on modifications and invocations that strict integrity does, but they impose different restrictions upon observations. The low-water-mark policy allows a subject to observe objects below its integrity level, provides that the subject's integrity level is reduced to that of the observed object. The ring policy imposes no mandatory access controls on subjects' observations of objects; as a result, there are fewer built-in integrity protections if a subject unwisely chooses to read an untrustworthy source.

FIGURE 13.3 Learning outcomes for Chapter 13

After completing this chapter, you should be able to achieve the following learning outcomes at several levels of knowledge:

Application

- When given the confidentiality- or integrity-level assignments and the discretionary access-control matrix of a system, you should be able to calculate whether or not a read or write access request should be permitted.

- Express confidentiality policies consistent with the Bell–La Padula model in the access-control logic.

- Express integrity policies consistent with the Biba strict-integrity model in the access-control logic.

Synthesis

- When given an access-control scenario involving confidentiality and/or integrity, you should be able to define confidentiality and/or integrity levels for subjects and objects, and devise a discretionary access-control matrix that accurately reflects the scenario.

- When given an access-control scenario that involves the Bell–La Padula model, you should be able to formalize the scenario, identify all necessary trust assumptions, and formally justify the granting of a request.

- When given an access-control scenario that involves the Biba strict-integrity model, you should be able to formalize the scenario, identify all necessary trust assumptions, and formally justify the granting of a request.

Evaluation

- When given a set of policy definitions alleged to be consistent with the Bell–La Padula or strict-integrity models, you should be able to judge whether they are consistent and (if not) identify the inconsistencies.

Chapter 14

Role-Based Access Control

In the previous chapter, we examined confidentiality and integrity policies, which permit access based in part on principals' and objects' classification levels. In many organizations, however, access-control policies are based instead upon employees' job functions: for example, programmers must have both read and write access to relevant source code, while salespeople may require access to internal marketing reports. *Role-based access control (RBAC)* was designed to simplify the task of managing such policies by explicitly introducing a notion of *roles*, which serve as intermediate links between users (i.e., employees) and permissions (i.e., their required access rights).

In this chapter, we introduce the basic components of RBAC, which are based on the related but independent notions of *users*, *roles*, and *permissions*. We also discuss notions of *separation of duty*, which provide constraints that can limit the potential for fraud or conflicts of interest. Finally, we show how the access-control logic can be used to reason about access-control decisions within RBAC systems.

14.1 RBAC Fundamentals

The key idea behind RBAC is that an organization comprises many people (i.e., *users*), each of whom perform several job functions (i.e., *roles*). In turn, a person performing a certain job function requires a collection of *permissions* to successfully complete their tasks (e.g., an accountant must have the ability to read and modify the accounting ledger). Therefore, at its core, an RBAC system can be described by the following five sets:

- *Users*, the set of *users*

- *Roles*, the set of *roles*

- *Perms*, the set of *permissions*

- $UA \subseteq Perms \times Roles$, the *user-to-role assignment* (or simply *user assignment*)

- $PA \subseteq Perms \times Roles$, the *permission-to-role assignment* (or simply *permission assignment*)

The user-to-role assignment catalogs the associations between users and the roles they perform: a pair $(u, r) \in UA$ indicates that user u has been explicitly assigned to role r. Similarly, the permission-to-role assignment indicates which permissions are associated with which roles: a pair $(p, r) \in UA$ indicates that permission p has been explicitly assigned to role r.

The following example provides a simple RBAC description of a small restaurant.

Example 14.1
Consider a local restaurant with five employees (Pat, Mel, Lee, Sam, and Kim) and four identified job functions (host, server, chef, and manager). At present, the restaurant management has assigned responsibilities as follows: hosts may seat customers and take reservations; servers may take orders, serve food to customers, clear tables, and accept payment from customers; chefs may cook food; and managers may offer customers a free meal, in addition to anything that a host or server can do.

The restaurant's operations can be described by the following RBAC components:

$Users = \{Pat, Mel, Lee, Sam, Kim\}$,

$Roles = \{Host, Server, Chef, Manager\}$,

$Perms = \{\langle seat, customer \rangle, \langle take, reservation \rangle, \langle take, order \rangle, \langle cook, food \rangle,$
$\qquad \langle serve, food \rangle, \langle clear, table \rangle, \langle accept, payment \rangle, \langle offer, free\ meal \rangle\}$,

$UA = \{(Pat, Host), (Pat, Server), (Lee, Server), (Mel, Chef), (Mel, Server),$
$\qquad (Kim, Manager), (Sam, Manager), (Sam, Chef)\}$,

$PA = \{(\langle seat, customer \rangle, Host), (\langle take, reservation \rangle, Host), (\langle cook, food \rangle, Chef),$
$\qquad (\langle take, order \rangle, Server), (\langle serve, food \rangle, Server), (\langle clear, table \rangle, Server),$
$\qquad (\langle accept, payment \rangle, Server), (\langle offer, free\ meal \rangle, Manager),$
$\qquad (\langle seat, customer \rangle, Manager), (\langle take, reservation \rangle, Manager),$
$\qquad (\langle take, order \rangle, Manager), (\langle serve, food \rangle, Manager),$
$\qquad (\langle clear, table \rangle, Manager), (\langle accept, payment \rangle, Manager) \}. \qquad \Diamond$

As the previous example illustrates, the same user (e.g., Pat) may be assigned to multiple roles. Similarly, the same permission (e.g., $\langle seat, customer \rangle$) may be assigned to multiple roles.

14.1.1   Role Inheritance

RBAC also introduces a notion of *role inheritance*, which reflects the fact that some job functions subsume others. For example, an accounting supervisor may need to perform the standard accountant duties, in addition to her supervisory duties.

To express such situations more concisely, RBAC incorporates a *role-inheritance* (also known as a *role-hierarchy* or *role-dominance*) relation

$$\succeq\ \subseteq Roles \times Roles,$$

FIGURE 14.1 Sample Hasse diagram

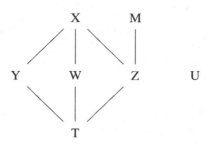

which is a partial order on roles. Thus, the role-inheritance relation $\succeq$ necessarily satisfies the following properties:

- Reflexivity: For all roles r, $r \succeq r$ (i.e., every role inherits itself).

- Transitivity: For all roles r_1, r_2, r_3, if $r_1 \succeq r_2$ and $r_2 \succeq r_3$, then $r_1 \succeq r_3$.

- Anti-symmetry: For all roles r_1, r_2, if $r_1 \succeq r_2$ and $r_2 \succeq r_1$, then $r_1 = r_2$ (i.e., no cycles exist in the inheritance relation).

As with other partial orders, it is often convenient to present the role-inheritance relation graphically as a Hasse diagram. As an example, Figure 14.1 presents a Hasse diagram for the relation

$$\succeq \; = \{(r,r) \mid r \in \{M,T,U,X,Y,W,Z\}\}$$
$$\cup \; \{(X,Y),(X,W),(X,T),(X,Z),(M,Z),(M,T)\}.$$

The primary purpose of the role-inheritance relation is to allow more succinct descriptions of user and permission assignments. Towards this end, we introduce two functions

$$auth\_users : Roles \rightarrow \mathcal{P}(Users), \qquad auth\_perms : Roles \rightarrow \mathcal{P}(Perms),$$

which, when given a specific role, respectively return the sets of authorized users and authorized permissions for that role:

$$auth\_users(r) = \{u \mid \exists r' \in Roles.(r' \succeq r \text{ and } (u,r') \in UA)\},$$
$$auth\_perms(r) = \{p \mid \exists r' \in Roles.(r \succeq r' \text{ and } (p,r') \in PA)\}.$$

Thus, the authorized users of a role r are all those users explicitly assigned (through the user-to-role assignment) to a role that inherits r. In contrast, the authorized permissions of a role r are all those permissions explicitly assigned (through the permission-to-role assignment) to a role that r inherits.

It is straightforward to show that the following properties hold:

- If $r_1 \succeq r_2$, then $auth\_users(r_1) \subseteq auth\_users(r_2)$.

- If $r_1 \succeq r_2$, then $auth\_perms(r_2) \subseteq auth\_perms(r_1)$.

In this sense, users "flow down" the role hierarchy while permissions "flow up."

The following example shows how the judicious choice of a role-inheritance relation simplifies the permission assignment for the restaurant of Example 14.1.

Example 14.2
Recall the restaurant from Example 14.1, and suppose the role-inheritance relation $\succeq$ is given by the following Hasse diagram:

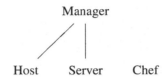

The restaurant's operations can be described by the following RBAC components (the sets *Users*, *Roles*, *Perms*, and *UA* remain unchanged from Example 14.1):

$Users = \{Pat, Mel, Lee, Sam, Kim\},$

$Roles = \{Host, Server, Chef, Manager\},$

$Perms = \{\langle seat, customer\rangle, \langle take, reservation\rangle, \langle take, order\rangle, \langle cook, food\rangle,$
$\qquad\qquad \langle serve, food\rangle, \langle clear, table\rangle, \langle accept, payment\rangle, \langle offer, free\ meal\rangle\},$

$UA = \{(Pat, Host), (Pat, Server), (Lee, Server), (Mel, Chef), (Mel, Server),$
$\qquad\qquad (Kim, Manager), (Sam, Manager), (Sam, Chef)\},$

$PA = \{(\langle seat, customer\rangle, Host), (\langle take, reservation\rangle, Host), (\langle cook, food\rangle, Chef),$
$\qquad\qquad (\langle take, order\rangle, Server), (\langle serve, food\rangle, Server), (\langle clear, table\rangle, Server),$
$\qquad\qquad (\langle accept, payment\rangle, Server), (\langle offer, free\ meal\rangle, Manager)\}.$

Given these base sets, we can calculate the authorized users for the roles *Host* and *Manager* as follows:

$$
\begin{aligned}
auth\_users(Host) &= \{u \mid \exists r' \in Roles.(r' \succeq Host\ \text{and}\ (u, r') \in UA)\} \\
&= \{u \mid (u, Host) \in UA\} \cup \{u \mid (u, Manager) \in UA\} \\
&= \{Pat, Kim, Sam\}, \\
auth\_users(Manager) &= \{u \mid \exists r' \in Roles.(r' \succeq Manager\ \text{and}\ (u, r') \in UA)\} \\
&= \{u \mid (u, Manager) \in UA\} \\
&= \{Kim, Sam\}.
\end{aligned}
$$

Both Kim and Sam are authorized users of the role *Host* by virtue of role inheritance. Similarly, we can calculate the authorized permissions for the same two roles:

$$auth\_perms(Host) = \{p \mid \exists r' \in Roles.(Host \succeq r' \text{ and } (p,r') \in PA)\}$$
$$= \{p \mid (p,Host) \in PA\}$$
$$= \{\langle seat, customer\rangle, \langle take, reservation\rangle\}$$
$$auth\_perms(Manager) = \{p \mid \exists r' \in Roles.(Manager \succeq r' \text{ and } (p,r') \in PA)\}$$
$$= \{p \mid (p,Host) \in PA\} \cup \{p \mid (p,Server) \in PA\}$$
$$\cup \{p \mid (p,Manager) \in PA\}$$
$$= \{\langle seat, customer\rangle, \langle take, reservation\rangle, \langle take, order\rangle,$$
$$\langle serve, food\rangle, \langle clear,\ table\rangle,$$
$$\langle accept, payment\rangle, \langle offer, free\ meal\rangle\}.$$

In particular, the *Manager* role inherits all of the permissions associated with the *Host* and *Server* roles. ◇

✎ **Exercise 14.1.1** *Consider the following collection of RBAC definitions:*

$$Users = \{Ian, Moe, Sal, Pam, Rob\}$$
$$Perms = \{a,b,c,d,e,g,h,k,w,y\}$$
$$Roles = \{A,B,C,D,E,G,H,K,W,Y\}$$
$$UA = \{(Ian,A),(Moe,C),(Moe,E),(Pam,Y),$$
$$(Pam,H),(Rob,B),(Sal,K)\}$$
$$PA = \{(a,A),(b,B),(c,C),(d,D),(e,E),(f,F),$$
$$(g,G),(h,H),(k,K),(w,W),(y,Y)\}$$

The relation $\succeq$ *is given by the following Hasse diagram:*

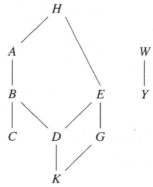

Calculate the following:

   a. auth_users(A).

   b. auth_users(E).

   c. auth_users(W).

   d. auth_perms(A).

   e. auth_perms(E).

   f. auth_perms(W).

Exercise 14.1.2 *A small construction firm has the following staff:*

- *Alex, a carpenter who sometimes also fills in as supervisor*

- *Blake, an electrician*

- *Cal, a plumber's apprentice who sometimes also fills in as office manager*

- *Dana, a plumber*

- *Eddy, a carpenter's apprentice and sometimes electrician's apprentice*

- *Fran, a supervisor and sometimes electrician*

Due to a combination of factors (city licensing statutes, ongoing labor negotiations, and the like), the firm has developed a collection of guidelines to govern the permissible work-related activities of its employees. No permissions other than those explicitly stated in the following rules are granted:

- *Carpenters may lay flooring (**floor**), hang drywall (**drywall**), and install cabinets (**cabs**).*

- *Electricians may install or reconfigure wiring (**wire**), **test** wiring, and install **outlets**.*

- *Plumbers may lay **pipes** and install **fixtures**.*

- *Apprentices are there to **assist**, plus they have specific duties related to their basic trades: a carpenter's apprentice may lay flooring (**floor**), an electrician's apprentice may **test** wiring, and a plumber's apprentice may lay **pipes**.*

- *Electricians and plumbers are also able to help **design** their respective systems.*

- *The supervisor can naturally **supervise** work, and **assist** when needed.*

- *The office manager may **schedule** jobs, **order** supplies, and **bill** customers.*

- *All employees can **review** the current work plan.*

Thus, for example, a carpenter may neither schedule jobs nor assist, but she can always review the current work plan.

For the purposes of this question, let Users and Perms be defined as follows, with the obvious correspondence with the firm's staff and work-related activities:

$$Users = \{A, B, C, D, E, F\}$$

$$Perms = \{floor, drywall, cabs, wire, test, outlets, pipes, fixtures, assist,$$
$$design, supervise, schedule, order, bill, review\}$$

a. *Define a set Roles of roles, along with a permission-to-role assignment PA, a user-role assignment UA, and a role-dominance relation $\succeq$ to accurately capture the above guidelines.*

   To fully appreciate the implications of the role hierarchy, specify PA in such a way that it maps each permission to exactly one role (i.e., PA should contain exactly 15 pairs). Therefore, you will need to include roles that do not directly correspond to particular job titles.

b. *Using your definitions from Part a, calculate the following:*

   (a) *The set of authorized permissions (i.e., auth_perms(r)) for each role $r \in R$*

   (b) *The set of authorized users (i.e., auth_users(r)) for each role $r \in R$*

14.1.2 Sessions

Although a specific user might be authorized for many roles, there are times that she may wish to *activate* only a subset of roles, perhaps to avoid a conflict of interest or simply to minimize unnecessary privileges. For example, suppose that Annie is authorized for both the User and Superuser roles on her department's computer system. She may purposely elect to activate only the User role when she plans to edit her personal files, to avoid the possibility of accidentally altering system files that can be accessed only through the Superuser role.

RBAC provides the ability to activate only a subset of authorized roles through the abstract notion of *sessions*. Intuitively, a session represents a period of time during which a certain subset of a user's authorized roles is activated. In the digital world, a session might correspond to a user's login session or to a specific open window or shell. In the physical world—such as the restaurant described in Example 14.2—a session might correspond to a specific work shift for an employee.

More formally, an RBAC system includes a set *Sessions* of sessions, in the same way that it includes sets of users, roles, and permissions. Each session has precisely one user associated with it, but zero or more roles associated with it.

When given a session s, the functions

$$user : Sessions \rightarrow Users, \qquad roles : Sessions \rightarrow \mathcal{P}(Roles)$$

respectively return the user and the roles associated with s. As an important note, these two functions must be consistent with one another: for any specific session s, $user(s)$ must be an authorized user for each of the roles in $roles(s)$. That is, for all sessions s, the following constraint must hold:

$$roles(s) \subseteq \{r \in Roles \mid user(s) \in auth\_users(r)\}.$$

The following example extends the earlier restaurant example by introducing some sessions that correspond to work shifts for particular employees.

Example 14.3
Recall the restaurant from Example 14.2, and consider the following work schedule:

- On Monday night, Pat works as a server, and Kim works as manager.

- On Tuesday afternoon, Kim works as both host and server; Pat has the day off, and does not work at all.

This situation allows for the four sessions $\{s_1, s_2, s_3, s_4\}$, where s_1 is Pat's Monday-night shift, s_2 is Kim's Monday-night shift, s_3 is Pat's Tuesday-afternoon shift, and s_4 is Kim's Tuesday-afternoon shift.
The users and roles associated with each shift are as follows:

$$
\begin{aligned}
user(s_1) &= Pat, & roles(s_1) &= \{Server\}, \\
user(s_2) &= Kim, & roles(s_2) &= \{Manager\}, \\
user(s_3) &= Pat, & roles(s_3) &= \emptyset, \\
user(s_4) &= Kim, & roles(s_4) &= \{Host, Server\}.
\end{aligned}
$$

One can easily verify that, for each shift s_i,

$$roles(s_i) \subseteq \{r \in Roles \mid user(s_i) \in auth\_users(r)\}. \qquad \Diamond$$

Exercise 14.1.3 *Which of the following proposed sessions would be permitted under the RBAC descriptions from Example 14.2? Explain your answers.*

a. *Session s_a, where $user(s_a) = Mel$ and $roles(s_a) = \{Chef, Server\}$*

b. *Session s_b, where $user(s_b) = Lee$ and $roles(s_b) = \{Server, Manager\}$*

c. *Session s_c, where $user(s_c) = Sam$ and $roles(s_c) = \{Chef, Server\}$*

14.2 Separation of Duty

When developing security policies, a common approach is to divide critical operations among two or more principals, so that no single principal can compromise security. For example, banks often require two people to be present when ATM deposits are opened and processed. Likewise, health-insurance companies may require multiple doctors to assert that a medical procedure is necessary before the company will pay for the procedure.

RBAC provides a means for enforcing such divisions by introducing *separation-of-duty* constraints. RBAC recognizes the following two forms of separation of duty:

1. *Static* separation of duty enforces constraints on the user assignment, so that users are prevented from ever becoming authorized for conflicting roles.

2. *Dynamic* separation of duty enforces constraints on the roles that may be activated concurrently (i.e., within a single session): a user may be authorized for conflicting roles, but he will be unable to activate them simultaneously.

We look at these two types of constraints in sequence.

14.2.1 Static Separation of Duty

To support static separation of duty, RBAC introduces a relation

$$SSD \subseteq \mathcal{P}(Roles) \times (\mathbb{N} - \{0,1\}),$$

whose purpose is to constrain how the user assignment UA is constructed.

Note that each element of SSD has the form (rs,n), where rs is a set of roles and n is an integer greater than 1. Each such element reflects a particular separation-of-duty constraint. In particular, for each $(rs,n) \in SSD$, the following condition must hold: for every subset rs' of rs that contains at least n elements,

$$\bigcap_{r \in rs'} auth\_users(r) = \emptyset.$$

That is, each constraint $(rs,n) \in SSD$ mandates that no user may be authorized for n or more roles from the set rs.

The following example illustrates how the SSD relation can be used to impose static separation of duty.

Example 14.4
A small business is concerned about the possibility of embezzlement, so they have split up the financial duties among three separate job functions: only a manager can approve expenses, only an account clerk can record expenses, and only a cashier can

actually release funds. Thus, they have adopted the following roles, permissions, and permission assignment:

$$Roles = \{Manager, AccountClerk, Cashier\},$$
$$Perms = \{\langle approve, expense\rangle, \langle record, expense\rangle, \langle release, funds\rangle\},$$
$$PA = \{(\langle approve, expense\rangle, Manager), (\langle record, expense\rangle, AccountClerk),$$
$$(\langle release, funds\rangle, Cashier)\}.$$

A significant danger of embezzlement exists if a single person becomes authorized for all three roles (*Manager*, *AccountClerk*, and *Cashier*). The following *SSD* relation imposes a constraint to prevent such an occurrence:

$$SSD = \{(\{AccountClerk, Cashier\}, 2)\}.$$

This relation prevents anyone from being an authorized user for more than one of the roles *AccountClerk* and *Cashier*. Thus, for example, any user authorized for the *Cashier* role could not also be authorized for the *AccountClerk* role.   ◇

It is important to realize that a *SSD* constraint constrains the number of roles for which a given user may be *authorized*. As a result, to verify that static separation-of-duty constraints are met, it is important to consider not only the user-to-role assignment but also the role hierarchy. The following example illustrates how the combination of role hierarchy and *SSD* constraints may introduce unintended effects.

Example 14.5
Recall the RBAC descriptions for the small business in Example 14.4, and suppose that the role-inheritance relation $\succeq$ has been defined such that

$$Manager \succeq AccountClerk, \quad Manager \succeq Cashier.$$

It therefore follows that

$$auth\_users(Manager) \subseteq auth\_users(AccountClerk),$$
$$auth\_users(Manager) \subseteq auth\_users(Cashier),$$

and thus anyone authorized for the *Manager* role is also authorized for both the *AccountClerk* and *Cashier* roles. Because the *SSD* constraint requires that

$$auth\_users(AccountClerk) \cap auth\_users(Cashier) = \emptyset,$$

it must also be the case that $auth\_users(Manager) = \emptyset$, even though *Manager* does not explicitly show up in the *SSD* relation.   ◇

The next example elaborates on the possible interactions between role inheritance and static separation of duty.

FIGURE 14.2 Role hierarchy for a CS/CE department

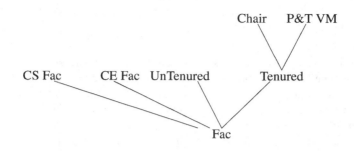

Example 14.6

Consider a hypothetical academic department that houses both Computer Science (CS) and Computer Engineering (CE) programs. The department includes both tenured and untenured faculty, and every faculty member is associated with at least one of the two academic programs. In addition, the department has a chairperson and a collection of voting members for a Promotion & Tenure (P& T) committee. Thus, there are seven relevant roles for this example:

$$Roles = \{Fac, Tenured, UnTenured, CS\ Fac, CE\ Fac, Chair, P\&T\ VM\}.$$

The role hierarchy appears in Figure 14.2: note that the roles *Chair* and *P&T VM* both inherit the tenured-faculty role *Tenured*.

The standard academic situation is that no one can be both tenured and untenured, and hence the roles *Tenured* and *UnTenured* should be mutually exclusive. Furthermore, the department's bylaws mandate that the department chair cannot be a P&T voting member. These constraints can be represented by the following static separation-of-duty relation:

$$SSD = \{(\{Tenured, UnTenured\}, 2), (\{P\&T\ VM, Chair\}, 2)\}.$$

Note that these two constraints also prevent untenured faculty from being department chair and from being voting members of the P&T committee, because the roles *Chair* and *P&T VM* both inherit the *Tenured* role.   ◊

14.2.2   Dynamic Separation of Duty

Although static separation of duty is easy to administer, in many cases it is not flexible enough. There are many situations in which a person may need to be authorized for different roles (e.g., parent and doctor) that nevertheless should never be activated at the same time due to conflict-of-interest concerns. Dynamic separation of duty provides a way to manage such constraints.

As with static separation of duty, RBAC supports dynamic separation of duty through a relation

$$DSD \subseteq \mathcal{P}(Roles) \times (\mathbb{N} - \{0, 1\}).$$

This relation imposes constraints on sessions and the roles activated therein. In particular, each element $(rs, n) \in DSD$ requires that no session can have n or more roles from the set rs simultaneously activated. That is, for each $(rs, n) \in DSD$, the following condition must hold: for any session s, every subset rs' of $rs \cap roles(s)$ contains fewer than n elements.

The following example illustrates how the DSD relation can be used to impose dynamic separation of duty.

Example 14.7
Recall the academic department from Example 14.6. As it turns out, the department's bylaws also require the P&T Committee to contain a fixed number of representatives from each of the CS and CE programs. Thus, for the purposes of P&T deliberations, no faculty member can simultaneously represent both the CS and CE programs, although she may be associated with both programs. This constraint can be represented by the following dynamic separation-of-duty relation:

$$DSD = \{(\{CS\ Fac, CE\ Fac, P\&T\ VM\}, 3)\}.$$

Thus, no one may simultaneously act as CS faculty, CE faculty, and a P&T voting member, although they may authorized for all three roles and may act in any two of those roles simultaneously.   ◇

Because the definition of dynamic separation constrains *activated* roles instead of *authorized* roles, it does not implicitly incorporate the role hierarchy in the same way that static separation of duty does. The difference is that the RBAC notion of sessions permits a role to be activated without the roles that it inherits being activated, whereas the same does not hold of role authorization. As a result, a DSD relation may allow a role to be activated, even if it inherits two roles that cannot be simultaneously activated. The following example illustrates this important difference.

Example 14.8
Recall the RBAC descriptions for the small business in Example 14.4, along with the role-inheritance relation $\succeq$ introduced in Example 14.5:

$$Manager \succeq AccountClerk, \quad Manager \succeq Cashier.$$

Suppose the SSD relation from Example 14.4 is instead replaced by the corresponding DSD relation:

$$DSD = \{(\{AccountClerk, Cashier\}, 2)\}.$$

In this case, it is permissible for a session s to be defined such that

$$roles(s) = \{Manager\},$$

because every subset of $roles(s) \cap \{AccountClerk, Cashier\}$ has fewer than 2 elements (in fact, the only such subset is the empty set).

Note, however, that the role *Manager* still possesses all of the permissions of *AccountClerk* and *Cashier*. As a result, there is still a potential conflict on permissions, even though there is no conflict on roles. ◇

As the previous example illustrates, both static and dynamic separation of duty are defined in terms of *roles*. When avoiding potential conflicts of interests, however, the real concern lies in the sets of permissions that a given user possesses. Therefore, when designing an RBAC system, it is important to verify that permissions assigned to non-considered roles do not create loopholes.

Exercise 14.2.1 *A small accounting firm has recently fired their security administrator for gross incompetence. They're now looking to you to help them identify some fundamental flaws—such as session or separation-of-duty violations—in the access-control system he set up.*

Identify all of the various RBAC violations and inconsistencies inherent in the following set of RBAC definitions:

$$Users = \{Lyn, Mike, Nell, Opal, Per\}$$
$$Perms = \{p_0, p_1, p_2, p_3, p_4, p_5, p_6, p_7, p_8, p_9\}$$
$$Roles = \{A, B, C, D, E, F, G, H, J\}$$
$$UA = \{(Lyn, D), (Lyn, B), (Mike, F), (Nell, D), (Nell, F), (Mike, J),$$
$$(Per, H), (Per, J), (Opal, A), (Opal, H)\}$$
$$PA = \{(p_1, E), (p_2, E), (p_3, D), (p_4, C), (p_5, G), (p_6, J),$$
$$(p_7, A), (p_8, B), (p_9, F), (p_0, H)\}$$
$$SSD = \{ (\{B, C\}, 2), (\{G, A, F\}, 3), (\{B, J\}, 2) \}$$
$$DSD = \{ (\{H, C, J\}, 3), (\{F, C, J\}, 2) \}$$
$$\succeq \quad \text{given by :}$$

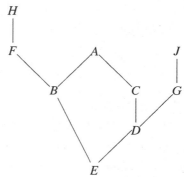

The system's current implementation also allows the sessions s_1, s_2, and s_3 as follows:

$$\text{user}(s_1) = Opal, \quad \text{roles}(s_1) = \{B, D\}$$
$$\text{user}(s_2) = Nell, \quad \text{roles}(s_2) = \{G, F\}$$
$$\text{user}(s_3) = Per, \quad \text{roles}(s_3) = \{J, H\}$$

Exercise 14.2.2 *A small engineering firm has decided to purchase a system to help manage their R&D projects. Here are the key features the company wants the system to handle (do not assume any permissions or restrictions other than those explicitly mentioned):*

- *Every project has some number of design engineers (DEs), test engineers (TEs), and project managers (PMs) assigned to it.*

- *A project's DEs can **build prototypes**, and the TEs can **write tests** for the project.*

- *Project managers (PMs) can **revise requirements** at any time during the course of their project.*

- *No engineer (i.e., DE or TE) may be assigned to more than two projects.*

- *No one can be both a DE and a TE on the same project. However, it is perfectly acceptable for someone to be a DE for one project and a TE for a different project.*

- *Because of the need for focus, PMs are prohibited from working on other projects; however, a PM is allowed to work as an engineer on the same project for which (s)he is PM.*

- *When project members log into the system, they should be prompted to indicate which project they'll be working on during that session; they are not allowed to work on more than one project during a single session.*

As part of the system's initial test run, the firm is going to focus on its three major projects: Alpha, Bravo, *and* Charlie. *Thus, they've identified the following roles and permissions for this system:*

$$Roles = \{PM_A, PM_B, PM_C, DE_A, DE_B, DE_C, TE_A, TE_B, TE_C\}$$
$$Perms = \{build_A, build_B, build_C, test_A, test_B, test_C, rev_A, rev_B, rev_C\}$$

For example, $build_A$, $test_A$, and rev_A are the permissions to (respectively) build a prototype, write tests, and revise requirements for project Alpha.

Your task: *Provide the following RBAC components to accurately meet and fulfill all of the company's desired features/criteria:*

- *a. A role-hierarchy relation $\succeq$ and a permission-assignment relation PA*

    You may add additional roles if you like.

  b. A static separation-of-duty relation to capture static constraints

  c. A dynamic separation-of-duty relation to capture dynamic constraints

Exercise 14.2.3   *A local law firm wants to buy a system to help them keep track of their legal cases. Listed below are the key features the practice wants the system to handle (do not assume any permissions or restrictions other than those explicitly mentioned):*

- *The legal staff includes* lawyers *(both **partners** and **associates**) and **paralegals**. The three groups are mutually disjoint.*

- *All members of the legal staff can **research** cases.*

- *Associates can **depose** witnesses.*

- *All lawyers can **present** cases in court.*

- *Partners can **reject** prospective clients.*

- *The law firm handles both **criminal defense** and **civil** cases.*

- *The law firm occasionally handles **pro bono** cases (i.e., cases taken on for the public good for which no payment is required). Pro bono cases may be either criminal defense or civil cases.*

- *No partner may be assigned to more than one pro bono case.*

- *No paralegal may be assigned to more than three cases.*

- *Lawyers cannot double-bill their time to multiple cases: that is, at any moment in time (i.e., session), lawyers can work on at most one case.*

  As part of the system's initial test run, the firm is going to focus on its four major cases:

- *The **A**nderson case is a pro bono, civil case.*

- *The **B**rady case is a pro bono, criminal defense case.*

- *The **C**ortland case is a civil case (but not pro bono).*

- *The **D**erby case is a criminal defense case (but not pro bono).*

  To date, the following roles and permissions have been identified:

  Roles = {Partner, Assoc, ParaLegal, ProBono, Civil, CrimDef, A, B, C, D}
  Perms = {research, depose, present, reject }

Your task: *Provide the following RBAC components to accurately meet and fulfill all of the company's desired features/criteria:*

   a. *A role-hierarchy relation $\succeq$ and a permission-assignment relation PA. You may add additional roles if you like.*

   b. *A static separation-of-duty relation to capture static constraints*

   c. *A dynamic separation-of-duty relation to capture dynamic constraints*

14.3   Representing RBAC Systems in the Logic

Given an RBAC description of a system, it is useful to be able to justify formally the resulting access-control decisions that occur. Fortunately, it is straightforward to translate the relevant aspects of an RBAC description into our access-control logic. In this section, we introduce small extensions to the logic—along with a procedure for translating RBAC descriptions into the logic—that support reasoning about RBAC systems.

14.3.1   RBAC Extensions to the Logic

We start by extending the syntax of the logic to accommodate statements that express equality among principals:

$$\textbf{Form} ::= (\textbf{Princ} = \textbf{Princ}).$$

As with controls and reps, this new syntax is syntactic sugar for a construction that already exists in the logic:

$$P = Q \stackrel{\text{def}}{=} P \Rightarrow Q \wedge Q \Rightarrow P.$$

Consequently, its Kripke semantics is given as follows, for any Kripke structure $\mathcal{M}$:

$$
\begin{aligned}
\mathcal{E}_{\mathcal{M}}[\![P = Q]\!] &= \mathcal{E}_{\mathcal{M}}[\![P \Rightarrow Q \wedge Q \Rightarrow P]\!] \\
&= \mathcal{E}_{\mathcal{M}}[\![P \Rightarrow Q]\!] \cap \mathcal{E}_{\mathcal{M}}[\![Q \Rightarrow P]\!] \\
&= \begin{cases} W, & \text{if } J(P) = J(Q) \\ \emptyset, & \text{otherwise.} \end{cases}
\end{aligned}
$$

Figure 14.3 presents three rules that are particularly useful for reasoning about principal equality in the context of RBAC. The first rule (*Principal Equality*) states that, if $P = Q$, then any occurrences of P in a formula φ can safely be replaced by Q. This rule is the principal-specific analogue to the *Equivalence* rule that allows one to safely replace one formula in a larger expression by an equivalent one.

FIGURE 14.3 Logical rules regarding principal equality

$$\textit{Principal Equality} \quad \frac{P = Q \qquad \varphi[P/A]}{\varphi[Q/A]}$$

$$\textit{Distributivity of } | \quad \frac{}{P \mid (R_1 \And \cdots \And R_k) = (P \mid R_1) \And \cdots \And (P \mid R_k)} \ (k \geq 1)$$

$$\textit{Quoting Simplification} \quad \frac{P \mid (Q \And R) \text{ says } \varphi}{P \mid Q \text{ says } \varphi}$$

The second rule (*Distributivity of* $|$) states that quoting ($|$) distributes over principal conjunction ($\And$). All three rules are sound, the proofs of which are left as exercises; in fact, the third rule is derivable from existing rules. There are additional rules related to principal equality that can be useful in general; because they are less directly applicable to the discussion of RBAC, however, we leave them for exercises.

Exercise 14.3.1 *Prove the soundness of the Principal Equality inference rule.*

Exercise 14.3.2 *Prove the soundness of the Distributivity of $|$ inference rule.*

Exercise 14.3.3 *Give a formal proof for the derived inference rule Quoting Simplification.*

Exercise 14.3.4 *Prove the soundness of the following inference rule:*

$$\textit{Commutativity of } \And \quad \frac{}{P \And Q = Q \And P}$$

Exercise 14.3.5 *Prove the soundness of the following inference rule:*

$$\textit{Associativity of } \And \quad \frac{}{P \And (Q \And R) = (P \And Q) \And R}$$

Exercise 14.3.6 *Prove the soundness of the following inference rule:*

$$\textit{Associativity of } | \quad \frac{}{P \mid (Q \mid R) = (P \mid Q) \mid R}$$

14.3.2 Translating RBAC into the Logic

We are now ready to consider the procedure for translating RBAC descriptions into the logic. In particular, we are interested in those aspects of RBAC that provide the basis for determining whether or not an access-control decision should be granted: roles and role inheritance, the permission and user assignments, and sessions. We consider each of these items in turn.

Roles   In the logic, roles are simply principals, and role inheritance is represented by the speaks-for ($\Rightarrow$) relation. Specifically, we translate $R_2 \succeq R_1$ into the logical statement $R_2 \Rightarrow R_1$.

Recall that an important aspect of role inheritance is that it is a partial order; the logic must support reasoning about consequences of this property. Fortunately, the speaks-for relation is well suited for this purpose: the *Idempotency* and *Transitivity of* $\Rightarrow$ inference rules account for role-inheritance reflexivity and transitivity, and the definition of principal equality accurately accounts for the anti-symmetry of role inheritance.

Permission and user assignments   Each element (p, R) in the permission assignment reflects a statement that the permission p is associated with role R (i.e., that R is authorized to perform p). Consequently, each such $(p, R) \in PA$ can be translated into the logical statement

$$R \text{ controls } p.$$

Furthermore, every authorized user of R (as determined by the combination of the user assignment and role inheritance) is authorized to use role R to request to perform p (i.e., an authorized user can be viewed as an official representative of the role R). Consequently, the single element (p, R) also induces, for each user X in the set $auth\_users(R)$, the following statement:

$$X \text{ reps } R \text{ on } p.$$

Sessions   Every access request in an RBAC system occurs in the context of a particular session, which in turn has an associated set of roles activated. For example, consider a particular session s, in which

$$user(s) = P, \quad roles(s) = \{R_1, \cdots, R_k\}.$$

Any request φ made during session s can be expressed as follows:

$$P \mid (R_1 \ \& \ \cdots \ \& \ R_k) \text{ says } \varphi.$$

That is, P asserts the activated roles $R_1, \ldots, R_k$ when making the request φ.

The following small example illustrates the translation procedure, along with the resulting formal justification to grant an RBAC request.

Example 14.9

A small academic department has set up the following RBAC definitions for an electronic system to support two users (Dora and Liu), two roles (department chair and faculty member), and two permissions (the abilities to read student grades and to assign a course instructor):

$$UA = \{(Dora, Chair), (Liu, Faculty)\},$$
$$PA = \{(readGrades, Faculty), (assignInstructor, Chair)\},$$
$$\succeq \ = \{(Chair, Chair), (Chair, Faculty), (Faculty, Faculty)\}.$$

Furthermore, let s_D be a login session in which Dora activates the single role *Chair*. This RBAC system can be expressed in the logic as follows:

1. Role hierarchy

   The role *Chair* inherits the role *Faculty*, which results in the following logical expression:

   $$Chair \Rightarrow Faculty.$$

   Note that, technically speaking, one should also specify the following two statements:

   $$Chair \Rightarrow Chair, \quad Faculty \Rightarrow Faculty.$$

   However, these statements are both instances of the *Idempotency of* $\Rightarrow$ rule. Hence, neither statement would ever have to appear as an assumption in any formal analysis.

2. Permission and user assignments

   The pair $(readGrades, Faculty) \in PA$ gives rise to the following collection of statements:

   $$Faculty \text{ controls } readGrades,$$
   $$Liu \text{ reps } Faculty \text{ on } readGrades,$$
   $$Dora \text{ reps } Faculty \text{ on } readGrades.$$

   Note that $Dora \in auth\_users(Faculty)$, even though the pair $(Dora, Faculty)$ does not explicitly appear in the user assignment *UA*.

   Likewise, the pair $(assignInstructor, Faculty) \in PA$ gives rise to the following collection of statements:

   $$Chair \text{ controls } assignInstructor,$$
   $$Dora \text{ reps } Chair \text{ on } assignInstructor.$$

3. Sessions

   Suppose Dora requests to read student grades as part of her session s_D. This request can be represented as follows:

   $$Dora \mid Chair \text{ says } readGrades.$$

   Because the session s_D has only one activated role (i.e., *Chair*), only one role is quoted in the access request.

The proof in Figure 14.4 then provides a formal justification for granting Dora's request to read student grades. Similar justifications are possible if one changes the set of activated roles for session s_D to either $\{Faculty\}$ (resulting in a shorter proof) or $\{Faculty, Chair\}$ (resulting in a slightly longer proof). $\Diamond$

FIGURE 14.4 Formal justification to allow Dora to read student grades

1. $Chair \Rightarrow Faculty$	$Chair \succeq Faculty$
2. $Faculty$ controls $readGrades$	$(readGrades, Faculty) \in PA$
3. $Dora$ reps $Faculty$ on $readGrades$	$(readGrades, Faculty) \in PA,$
	$Dora \in auth\_users(Faculty)$
4. $Dora \mid Chair$ says $readGrades$	Request in session s_D
5. $Dora \Rightarrow Dora$	Idempotency of $\Rightarrow$
6. $Dora \mid Chair \Rightarrow Dora \mid Faculty$	5,1 Monotonicity of $\mid$
7. $Dora \mid Faculty$ says $readGrades$	6,4 Derived speaks for
8. $readGrades$	2,3,7 Reps

As a final note, we point out that the separation-of-duty relations *SSD* and *DSD* do not enter explicitly into the translation from RBAC to the access-control logic. Both relations impose constraints on an RBAC policy, limiting either the user assignment (via *SSD*) or allowable sessions (via *DSD*). Those constraints must be checked when the user assignment is created or modified, or when a new session is activated. In contrast, the logic is used to formally justify an access-control decision that occurs due to a specific request in the context of a particular session: such requests necessarily occur after the point in time when separation-of-duty constraints are relevant.

Exercise 14.3.7 *Consider the following collection of RBAC definitions:*

$Users = \{Del, Earl, Fred, Guy, Hal\}$

$Perms = \{write\_loan, read\_balance, approve\_loan, sell\_loan, accept\_deposit,$
$\qquad\qquad cash\_check, close\_acct, open\_acct, void\_transaction, fire\_staff\}$

$Roles = \{Emp, Teller, AcctOfficer, LoanOfficer, MortgageOfficer,$
$\qquad\qquad LoanSupervisor, TellerSupervisor, BranchManager\}$

$UA = \{(Del, Teller), (Earl, MortgageOfficer), (Fred, TellerSupervisor),$
$\qquad\quad (Fred, AcctOfficer), (Guy, LoanSupervisor), (Hal, BranchManager)\}$

$PA = \{(read\_balance, Emp), (open\_acct, AcctOfficer), (close\_acct, AcctOfficer),$
$\qquad\quad (cash\_check, Teller), (accept\_deposit, Teller), (write\_loan, LoanOfficer),$
$\qquad\quad (void\_transaction, TellerSupervisor), (sell\_loan, MortgageOfficer),$
$\qquad\quad (approve\_loan, LoanSupervisor), (fire\_staff, BranchManager)\}$

$\succeq = \{(r, r), (BranchManager, r), (r, Emp) \mid r \in R\}$
$\quad \cup \{(LoanSupervisor, MortgageOfficer), (LoanSupervisor, LoanOfficer)\}$
$\quad \cup \{(MortgageOfficer, LoanOfficer), (TellerSupervisor, Teller)\}$

Furthermore, let s_H be a session such that

$$user(s_H) = Hal, \quad roles(s_H) = \{Teller, MortgageOfficer\}.$$

a. *Suppose you were to translate the* entire *RBAC description into the access-control logic. List* all *of the translations that have the form*

$$Fred\ reps\ X\ on\ p,$$

for some role X and some permission p.

b. *Suppose that, during session s_H, Hal requests to write_loan.*

Enumerate as formulas in the access-control logic precisely *the portions of the RBAC description necessary for determining that Hal's request should be granted; do not include anything that is unnecessary for the formal justification. (These formulas will serve as the only assumptions for your justification in part (c).)*

c. *Give a formal proof that justifies granting Hal's request.*

Exercise 14.3.8 *The company Industria has recently updated their entire computing infrastructure. These updates include the following:*

- *A public-key infrastructure*

  Industria assigned public/private keypairs to all employees and servers. These public keys are certified by Industria itself. In addition, Industria's own public key (K_I) is installed directly on all company machines.

- *An RBAC-based project-reporting system*

  *This system currently involves three projects (A, B, and C). Members of each project are authorized to **read** and **write** that project's report; only a project's manager(s) can officially **submit** that project's report. In addition, the company's research director(s) can read the reports from any project. Thus, the following RBAC components have been identified:*

$$Roles = \{Member_A, Member_B, Member_C, PM_A, PM_B, PM_C, Director\}$$
$$\succeq\ = \{(r,r) \mid r \in R\} \cup \{(PM_X, Member_X) \mid X \in \{A,B,C\}\}$$
$$Perms = \{read_X,\ write_X,\ submit_X \mid X \in \{A,B,C\}\}$$
$$PA = \{(read_X, Member_X),\ (write_X, Member_X) \mid X \in \{A,B,C\}\}$$
$$\cup\ \{(submit_X, PM_X),\ (read_X, Director) \mid X \in \{A,B,C\}\}$$

In the context of this new infrastructure, Cam has been assigned the public/private keypair (K_c, K_c^{-1}). Cam has also been assigned (in the UA) as both a project manager for project B and as a research director for Industria.

Over the weekend, Cam decides to log in from home to catch up on work. There are two phases that happen:

Phase 1 (Initiate Session) *Cam sends a digitally signed message to the RBAC server, requesting to initiate a session in which the roles PM_B and Director are both activated.*

For the purpose of this phase, let

$$\langle session, Cam, \{PM_B, Director\}\rangle$$

denote the proposition "it is good to start a session with user Cam and activated roles $\{PM_B, Director\}$."

If this phase is successful, then the RBAC server will start up the requested session, with Cam as the identified user and the requested roles active. Cam can then proceed to the next phase.

Phase 2 (Do Work) *In the context of the newly created session, Cam can now make various requests of the system, including reading, writing, and submitting project reports. These requests are interpreted as coming directly from Cam's session (as opposed to some cryptographic key).*

Answer the following questions regarding the relevant certifications, credentials, trust assumptions, and so on needed to analyze this situation. **All answers should be expressions in the access-control logic.**

a. *Give the collection of statements that capture the permission assignment PA with respect to which roles are authorized to* **read** *the reports of project B.*

b. *Give the (minimal) collection of statements that capture the permission assignment and the implicit user assignment with respect to all of Cam's various role-based authorizations.*

c. *Suppose that, in Phase 1, the RBAC server recognizes Cam's right to initiate the requested session. Express this recognition of authority as an expression in the access-control logic.*

d. *Express Cam's Phase 1 request as an expression in the access-control logic.*

e. *What additional* **certificates, recognition of authority, and trust assumptions regarding keys** *are necessary for the RBAC server to determine that the* **session-initiation request** *of Phase 1 should be granted?*

f. *As part of Phase 2, Cam makes a request to write to project B's report. Express this request as an expression in the access-control logic.*

g. *What additional assumptions regarding* **policies, recognition of authority, and the role hierarchy** *are necessary for the system to determine that Cam's* **write request** *in Phase 2 should be permitted?*

14.4 Summary

In this chapter, we introduced role-based access control (RBAC), in which a user's access rights (i.e., permissions) are determined based on the roles for which that user

FIGURE 14.5 Learning outcomes for Chapter 14

After completing this chapter, you should be able to achieve the following learning outcomes at several levels of knowledge:

Application

- When given an RBAC description of a system, you should be able to calculate the authorized users or authorized permissions of any role in that system.

- Express RBAC permission assignments, user authorizations, and role hierarchies in the access-control logic.

Synthesis

- When given an access-control scenario, you should be able to define a set of roles, role hierarchy, user and permission assignments, and separation-of-duty relations to accurately reflect the scenario.

- When given an access-control scenario that involves RBAC, you should be able to formalize the scenario, identify all necessary trust assumptions, and formally justify the granting of a request.

Evaluation

- When given a set of RBAC definitions, you should be able to judge whether they are consistent and (if not) identify the inconsistencies.

---

is authorized. RBAC was designed to reduce the administrative complexity associated with large organizations' access-control needs: the roles for which a user is authorized can be adjusted as that user acquires or sheds different job responsibilities, and permissions associated with a particular role can also be adjusted as necessary.

The essential RBAC components include user assignments, permission assignments, and the role-inheritance relation. RBAC also supports static and dynamic separation-of-duty constraints, which can be used to limit potential sources of collusion or conflicts of interest.

We also showed how the access-control logic can be used to reason about access requests in RBAC systems. We introduced a notion of principal equality and then defined a procedure for translating RBAC descriptions into the logic. The resulting translation specifies access-control policies in terms of roles and specifies users' role authorizations in terms of delegation. The speaks-for relation is used to capture role inheritance.

The learning outcomes associated with this chapter appear in Figure 14.5.

14.5   Further Reading

RBAC was first introduced by Ferraiolo and Kuhn (Ferraiolo and Kuhn, 1992), and then expanded upon by Sandhu and colleagues (Sandhu et al., 1996). These two frameworks were integrated and proposed as a NIST standard in 2001 (Ferraiolo et al., 2001); the standard was adopted in 2004.

The access-control logic introduced by Lampson and colleagues (Lampson et al., 1992; Abadi et al., 1993) included a notion of roles that differs significantly from the RBAC notion of roles. In the Lampson setting, roles are used to *limit* a principal's privileges, whereas RBAC roles provide a mechanism for users to *gain* privileges. Thumrongsak Kosiyatrakul was the first to use a notion of delegation to capture RBAC role authorization in an access-control logic (Kosiyatrakul et al., 2005; Kosiyatrakul, 2010). Due to his interpretation of delegation, his semantics is more complicated than the version presented here.

Appendix A

Summary of the Access-Control Logic

This appendix provides a summary of the syntax and inference rules of the access-control logic. It is intended as a canonical reference for the syntax and rules (both core and derived) introduced throughout the book.

A.1   Syntax

We define **PName** to be the collection of all simple principal names. The set **Princ** of all principal expressions is given by the following BNF specification:

$$\textbf{Princ} ::= \textbf{PName} \mathbin{/} \textbf{Princ \& Princ} \mathbin{/} \textbf{Princ} \mid \textbf{Princ}$$

The convention for compound principals is that & binds more tightly than $|$.

We let **PropVar** be the collection of all propositional variables. The set **Form** of all well-formed expressions is given by the following BNF specification:

$$
\begin{aligned}
\textbf{Form} ::=\ & \textbf{PropVar} \mathbin{/} \neg\, \textbf{Form} \mathbin{/} (\textbf{Form} \vee \textbf{Form}) \mathbin{/} \\
& (\textbf{Form} \wedge \textbf{Form}) \mathbin{/} (\textbf{Form} \supset \textbf{Form}) \mathbin{/} (\textbf{Form} \equiv \textbf{Form}) \mathbin{/} \\
& (\textbf{Princ} \Rightarrow \textbf{Princ}) \mathbin{/} (\textbf{Princ}\ \textsf{says}\ \textbf{Form}) \mathbin{/} (\textbf{Princ}\ \textsf{controls}\ \textbf{Form}) \\
& (\textbf{Princ}\ \textsf{reps}\ \textbf{Princ}\ \textsf{on}\ \varphi)
\end{aligned}
$$

Parentheses can be omitted according to the following conventions for operator precedence, in decreasing tightness of bindings:

$$\neg$$

$$\textsf{says} \qquad \textsf{controls} \qquad \textsf{reps}$$

$$\wedge$$

$$\vee$$

$$\supset$$

$$\equiv$$

The definition of **Form** defines the core syntax of the logic. Three extensions are made to describe confidentiality, integrity, and role-based access control policies.

Confidentiality   We define **SecLabel** to be the collection of *simple security labels*, which are used as names for the various levels associated with confidentiality. In addition to these specific security labels, we will often want to refer abstractly to the security level assigned to a particular principal P. For this reason, we define the larger set **SecLevel** of *all* possible security-level expressions:

$$\textbf{SecLevel} ::= \textbf{SecLabel} \; / \; \mathsf{slev}(\textbf{PName})$$

That is, a security-level expression is either a simple security label or an expression of the form $\mathsf{slev}(A)$, where A is a simple principal name.[1] Informally, $\mathsf{slev}(A)$ refers to the security level of principal A.

Finally, we extend our definition of well-formed formulas to support comparisons of security levels:

$$\textbf{Form} ::= \textbf{SecLevel} \leq_s \textbf{SecLevel} \; / \; \textbf{SecLevel} =_s \textbf{SecLevel}$$

Integrity   We define **IntLabel** to be the collection of *simple integrity labels*, and we define **IntLevel** to be the set of *all* possible integrity-level expressions:

$$\textbf{IntLevel} ::= \textbf{IntLabel} \; / \; \mathsf{ilev}(\textbf{PName})$$

Informally, $\mathsf{ilev}(A)$ refers to the integrity—i.e., quality or trustworthiness—level of principal A.

We then extend our definition of well-formed formulas to support comparisons of security levels:

$$\textbf{Form} ::= \textbf{IntLevel} \leq_i \textbf{IntLevel} \; / \; \textbf{IntLevel} =_i \textbf{IntLevel}$$

The symbol $\leq_i$ denotes a partial ordering on integrity levels, in the same way that $\leq_s$ denotes a partial ordering on security levels. In particular, $\leq_i$ is reflexive, transitive, and antisymmetric.

Role-based access control   We extend the syntax of the logic to accommodate statements that express equality among principals:

$$\textbf{Form} ::= (\textbf{Princ} = \textbf{Princ})$$

---

[1]This syntax precludes security-level expressions such as $\mathsf{slev}(P \;\&\; Q)$ or $\mathsf{slev}(P \mid Q)$, because there is no standard technique for associating security classification labels with compound principals.

A.2 Core Rules, Derived Rules, and Extensions

The following figures summarize the core rules, derived rules, and extensions for the access-control logic:

- Figure A.1 is a summary of the core inference rules.

- Figure A.2 is a summary of frequently used derived inference rules.

- Figure A.3 is a summary of inference rules for delegation.

- Figure A.4 is a summary of inference rules for relating security levels.

- Figure A.5 is a summary of inference rules for relating integrity levels.

- Figure A.6 is a summary of inference rules regarding principal equality.

FIGURE A.1 Summary of core rules for the access-control logic

---

Taut $\dfrac{}{\varphi}$ if φ is an instance of a prop-logic tautology

Modus Ponens $\dfrac{\varphi \quad \varphi \supset \varphi'}{\varphi'}$ *Says* $\dfrac{\varphi}{P \text{ says } \varphi}$

MP Says $\dfrac{}{(P \text{ says } (\varphi \supset \varphi')) \supset (P \text{ says } \varphi \supset P \text{ says } \varphi')}$

Speaks For $\dfrac{}{P \Rightarrow Q \supset (P \text{ says } \varphi \supset Q \text{ says } \varphi)}$

& Says $\dfrac{}{(P \& Q \text{ says } \varphi) \equiv ((P \text{ says } \varphi) \wedge (Q \text{ says } \varphi))}$

Quoting $\dfrac{}{(P \mid Q \text{ says } \varphi) \equiv (P \text{ says } Q \text{ says } \varphi)}$

Idempotency of $\Rightarrow$ $\dfrac{}{P \Rightarrow P}$

Transitivity of $\Rightarrow$ $\dfrac{P \Rightarrow Q \quad Q \Rightarrow R}{P \Rightarrow R}$ *Monotonicity of* $\Rightarrow$ $\dfrac{P \Rightarrow P' \quad Q \Rightarrow Q'}{P \mid Q \Rightarrow P' \mid Q'}$

Equivalence $\dfrac{\varphi_1 \equiv \varphi_2 \quad \psi[\varphi_1/q]}{\psi[\varphi_2/q]}$

$P \text{ controls } \varphi \overset{\text{def}}{=} (P \text{ says } \varphi) \supset \varphi$

FIGURE A.2 Summary of useful derived rules

$$\textit{Conjunction} \quad \frac{\varphi_1 \quad \varphi_2}{\varphi_1 \wedge \varphi_2}$$

$$\textit{Simplification (1)} \quad \frac{\varphi_1 \wedge \varphi_2}{\varphi_1} \qquad \textit{Simplification (2)} \quad \frac{\varphi_1 \wedge \varphi_2}{\varphi_2}$$

$$\textit{Disjunction (1)} \quad \frac{\varphi_1}{\varphi_1 \vee \varphi_2} \qquad \textit{Disjunction (2)} \quad \frac{\varphi_2}{\varphi_1 \vee \varphi_2}$$

$$\textit{Modus Tollens} \quad \frac{\varphi_1 \supset \varphi_2 \quad \neg\varphi_2}{\neg\varphi_1} \quad \textit{Double negation} \quad \frac{\neg\neg\varphi}{\varphi}$$

$$\begin{array}{c}\textit{Disjunctive}\\\textit{Syllogism}\end{array} \quad \frac{\varphi_1 \vee \varphi_2 \quad \neg\varphi_1}{\varphi_2} \qquad \begin{array}{c}\textit{Hypothetical}\\\textit{Syllogism}\end{array} \quad \frac{\varphi_1 \supset \varphi_2 \quad \varphi_2 \supset \varphi_3}{\varphi_1 \supset \varphi_3}$$

$$\textit{Controls} \quad \frac{P \text{ controls } \varphi \quad P \text{ says } \varphi}{\varphi}$$

$$\begin{array}{c}\textit{Derived}\\\textit{Speaks For}\end{array} \quad \frac{P \Rightarrow Q \quad P \text{ says } \varphi}{Q \text{ says } \varphi} \qquad \begin{array}{c}\textit{Derived}\\\textit{Controls}\end{array} \quad \frac{P \Rightarrow Q \quad Q \text{ controls } \varphi}{P \text{ controls } \varphi}$$

$$\begin{array}{c}\textit{Says}\\\textit{Simplification (1)}\end{array} \quad \frac{P \text{ says } (\varphi_1 \wedge \varphi_2)}{P \text{ says } \varphi_1} \qquad \begin{array}{c}\textit{Says}\\\textit{Simplification (2)}\end{array} \quad \frac{P \text{ says } (\varphi_1 \wedge \varphi_2)}{P \text{ says } \varphi_2}$$

FIGURE A.3 Summary of rules for delegation

$$P \text{ reps } Q \text{ on } \varphi \overset{\text{def}}{=} P \mid Q \text{ says } \varphi \supset Q \text{ says } \varphi$$

Reps
$$\frac{Q \text{ controls } \varphi \quad P \text{ reps } Q \text{ on } \varphi \quad P \mid Q \text{ says } \varphi}{\varphi}$$

Rep Controls
$$\overline{A \text{ reps } B \text{ on } \varphi \equiv (A \text{ controls } (B \text{ says } \varphi))}$$

Rep Says
$$\frac{A \text{ reps } B \text{ on } \varphi \quad A \mid B \text{ says } \varphi}{B \text{ says } \varphi}$$

FIGURE A.4 Inference rules for relating security levels

$$\ell_1 =_s \ell_2 \overset{\text{def}}{=} (\ell_1 \leq_s \ell_2) \wedge (\ell_2 \leq_s \ell_1)$$

Reflexivity of $\leq_s$
$$\overline{\ell \leq_s \ell}$$

Transitivity of $\leq_s$
$$\frac{\ell_1 \leq_s \ell_2 \quad \ell_2 \leq_s \ell_3}{\ell_1 \leq_s \ell_3}$$

FIGURE A.5 Inference rules for relating integrity levels

$$\ell_1 =_i \ell_2 \overset{\text{def}}{=} (\ell_1 \leq_i \ell_2) \wedge (\ell_2 \leq_i \ell_1)$$

Reflexivity of $\leq_i$
$$\overline{\ell \leq_i \ell}$$

Transitivity of $\leq_i$
$$\frac{\ell_1 \leq_i \ell_2 \quad \ell_2 \leq_i \ell_3}{\ell_1 \leq_i \ell_3}$$

FIGURE A.6 Logical rules regarding principal equality

$$P = Q \overset{\text{def}}{=} P \Rightarrow Q \land Q \Rightarrow P$$

$$\textit{Principal Equality} \quad \frac{P = Q \quad \varphi[P/A]}{\varphi[Q/A]}$$

$$\textit{Distributivity of } | \quad \frac{}{P \mid (R_1 \& \cdots \& R_k) = (P \mid R_1) \& \cdots \& (P \mid R_k)} \; (k \geq 1)$$

$$\textit{Quoting Simplification} \quad \frac{P \mid (Q \& R) \text{ says } \varphi}{P \mid Q \text{ says } \varphi}$$

Bibliography

Abadi, M., Burrows, M., Lampson, B., and Plotkin, G. (1993). A calculus for access control in distributed systems. *ACM Transactions on Programming Languages and Systems*, 15(4):706–734.

Bell, D. E. and La Padula, L. J. (1973). Secure computer systems: Mathematical foundations. Technical Report Technical Report MTR-2547, Vol. I, MITRE Corporation, Bedford, MA.

Bell, D. E. and La Padula, L. J. (1975). Secure computer system: Unified exposition and Multics interpretation. Technical Report MTR-2997 Rev. 1, MITRE Corporation, Bedford, MA.

Bensoussan, A., Clingen, C. T., and Daley, R. C. (1972). The Multics virtual memory: Concepts and design. *Communications of the ACM*, 15(5):308–318.

Biba, K. (1975). Integrity considerations for secure computer systems. Technical Report MTR-3153, MITRE Corporation, Bedford, MA.

Bishop, M. (2003). *Computer Security: Art and Science*. Addison-Wesley Professional.

Brewer, D. F. and Nash, M. J. (1989). The Chinese wall security policy. In *Proceedings of the 1989 IEEE Symposium on Security and Privacy*, pages pp. 206–214.

Bryant, B. (1988). Designing an authentication system: a dialogue in four scenes. (Afterword by Theodore Ts'o, 1997).

Comer, D. E. (2005). *Essentials of Computer Architecture*. Prentice Hall, New York.

Daley, R. C. and Dennis, J. B. (1968). Virtual memory, processes, and sharing in MULTICS. *Communications of the ACM*, 11(5):306–312.

Dierks, T. and Rescorla, E. (2006). The transport layer security (TLS) protocol version 1.1. RFC 4346 (Proposed Standard).

Ferraiolo, D. and Kuhn, R. (1992). Role-Based Access Control. In *15th NIST-NCSC National Computer Security Conference*, pages 554–563, Gaithersburg, MD.

Ferraiolo, D. F., Sandhu, R. S., Gavrila, S. I., Kuhn, D. R., and Chandramouli, R. (2001). Proposed NIST Standard for Role-Based Access Control. *ACM Transaction on Information and System Security*, 4(3):224–274.

FFIEC (2004). Retail payment systems booklet: IT examination handbook. Available at http://www.ffiec.gov/ under IT Booklets on the FFIEC IT Handbook InfoBase web page.

Freier, A., Karlton, P., and Kocher, P. C. (1996). The SSL protocol version 3.0. IETF Internet Draft, Transport Layer Security Working Group.

Hughes, G. and Cresswell, M. (1996). *A New Introduction to Modal Logic.* Routledge, New York.

Kosiyatrakul, T. (2010). *A Modal Logic for Role-Based Access Control within the Higher-Order Logic (HOL) Theorem Prover.* PhD thesis, Syracuse University.

Kosiyatrakul, T., Older, S., and Chin, S.-K. (2005). A modal logic for role-based access control. In Gorodetsky, V., Kotenko, I. V., and Skormin, V. A., editors, *MMM-ACNS*, volume 3685 of *Lecture Notes in Computer Science*, pages 179–193. Springer.

Lampson, B. (1971). Protection. In *Proceedings of the 5th Princeton Conference on Information Sciences and Systems.*

Lampson, B., Abadi, M., Burrows, M., and Wobber, E. (1992). Authentication in distributed systems: Theory and practice. *ACM Transactions on Computer Systems*, 10(4):265–310.

Levy, H. M. (1984). *Capability-Based Computer Systems.* Digital Press Inc., Daytona Beach, FL.

Lipner, S. B. (1982). Non-discretionary controls for commercial applications. In *Proceedings of the 1982 IEEE Symposium on Privacy and Security*, pages pp. 2–10.

Menezes, A. J., van Oorschot, P. C., and Vanstone, S. A. (1997). *Handbook of Applied Cryptography.* CRC Press, Boca Raton, FL.

National Automated Clearing House Association (2006). *2006 ACH Rules: A Complete Guide to Rules and Regulations Governing the ACH Network.* 13665 Dulles Technology Drive, Suite 300, Herndon, VA 20171.

National Institute of Standards and Technology (2001). Advanced encryption standard. FIPS Publication 197.

Neuman, C., Yu, T., Hartman, S., and Raeburn, K. (2005). The Kerberos Network Authentication Service (V5). RFC 4120 (Proposed Standard). Updated by RFCs 4537, 5021.

Organick, E. (1972). *The Multics System: An Examination of Its Structure.* MIT Press, Cambridge, MA.

Popek, G. J. and Goldberg, R. P. (1974). Formal requirements for virtualizable third generation architectures. *Communications of the ACM*, 17(7):412–421.

Rivest, R. L., Shamir, A., and Adelman, L. (1978). A method for obtaining digital signatures and public-key cryptosystems. *Communications of the ACM*, 21:120–126.

Rosen, K. H. (2003). *Discrete Mathematics and its Applications*, 5th edition. McGraw-Hill, New York.

Ross, K. A. and Wright, C. R. (2002). *Discrete Mathematics*, 5th edition. Prentice Hall, New York.

Saltzer, J. and Schroeder, M. (1975). The Protection of Information in Computer Systems. *Proceedings IEEE*.

Sandhu, R. S., Coyne, E. J., Feinstein, H. L., and Youman, C. E. (1996). Role-based access control models. *IEEE Computer*, 29(2):38–47.

Schroeder, M. D. and Saltzer, J. H. (1972). A hardware architecture for implementing protection rings. *Communications of the ACM*, 15(3):157–170.

Stallings, W. (2003). *Cryptography and Network Security Principles and Practices*, 3rd edition. Prentice Hall, New York.

Wakerly, J. F. (2006). *Digital Design: Principles and Practices*. Prentice Hall, New York.

Notation Index

General Index

Printed in the United States
by Baker & Taylor Publisher Services